DIGITAL
DESIGN
MEDIA

Second Edition

William J. Mitchell and Malcolm McCullough

 VAN NOSTRAND REINHOLD
I(T)P ™ A Division of International Thomson Publishing Inc.

New York • Albany • Bonn • Boston • Detroit • London • Madrid • Melbourne
Mexico City • Paris • San Francisco • Singapore • Tokyo • Toronto

Printed in the United States of America
For more information, contact:

Van Nostrand Reinhold
GmbH
115 Fifth Avenue
New York, NY 10003

International Thomson Publishing

Königswinterer Strasse 418
53227 Bonn
Germany

International Thomson Publishing Europe
Berkshire House 168-173
High Holborn
London WCIV 7AA
England

International Thomson Publishing Asia
221 Henderson Road #05-10
Henderson Building
Singapore 0315

Thomas Nelson Australia
102 Dodds Street
South Melbourne, 3205
Victoria, Australia

International Thomson Publishing Japan
Hirakawacho Kyowa Building, 3F
2-2-1 Hirakawacho
Chiyoda-ku, 102 Tokyo
Japan

Nelson Canada
1120 Birchmount Road
Scarborough, Ontario
Canada M1K 5G4

International Thomson Editores
Campos Eliseos 385, Piso 7
Col. Polanco
11560 Mexico D.F. Mexico

1 2 3 4 5 6 7 8 9 10 EDW-AA 01 00 99 98 97 96 95 94

Library of Congress Cataloging-in-Publication Data
Mitchell, William J. (William John), 1944–
    Digital design media / William J. Mitchell and Malcolm McCullough. 2nd ed.
        p.   cm.
    Includes bibliographical references and index.
    ISBN 0-442-01934-3 (acid-free paper)
    1. Computer-aided design. I. McCullough, Malcolm. II. Title.
TA174.M58   1994
620′.0042′0285—dc20

94-38689
CIP

Contents

COMPUTATION

ONE-DIMENSIONAL MEDIA

Char.	Code	Binary code
A	65	01000001
B	66	01000010
C	67	01000011
a	97	01100001
b	98	01100010
c	99	01100011
,	44	00101100
/	47	00101111
0	48	00110000
1	49	00110001

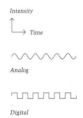

Intensity

Time

Analog

Digital

TWO-DIMENSIONAL MEDIA

6. Images

Scanning and storage. Low-resolution images. High-resolution images. Image compression. Tone-scale adjustment. Filtering. Selection, cutting, and transforming. Image transformation. Retouching and painting. The generalization to color. Display and printing. Image archives. Grid mapping and spatial analysis. Shape and character recognition. Uses and limitations of bitmapped images.

7. Drafted Lines

Coordinate systems. Point specification. Repertoires of line types. Chains of lines. Basic operations on lines. Geometric constructions. Selecting, transforming, and duplicating subshapes. Repeatable standard shapes. Parametric variation. Constraint solving. Syntax-directed editing. Interface dynamics. Structuring drawings. Formatting drawings. Printing and plotting. Automated measurement and analysis. Uses and limitations of two-dimensional drawings.

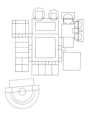

8. Polygons, Plans, and Maps

Representing and manipulating polygons. Union, intersection, and subtraction. Displaying and printing polygons. Compositions. Maps and tessellations. Map and plan topology. Space planning. Polygon grammars. Geographic information systems. Area analysis. Uses and limitations of polygon-modeling systems.

THREE-DIMENSIONAL MEDIA

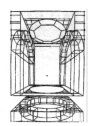

MULTIDIMENSIONAL MEDIA

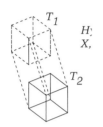

12. Motion Models

Keyframes. Translational motion paths. Rates of change. Motion vocabularies and compositions. Hierarchies of motions. Articulated motion of the human body. Mechanical joints and kinematic chains. Simulation of physical behavior. Uses and limitations of motion models.

13. Animation

Projection and animation. The virtual video camera. Frames of reference. Correlating object and camera motion. The time dimension. Design vectors. Computational strategies. Real-time, stored, and recorded animation. Video postproduction. Blending computer animation with live video. Virtual reality systems. Animation and holography. Conclusion: unfreezing images.

14. Hypermedia

Access structures. Indexing from one-dimensional structures. Branching sequences. Indexing from two-dimensional structures. Indexing from three-dimensional structures. Cyberspace. Implementation tools. Benefits and costs of access structures.

PRACTICE

15. Integrated Design Environments 327

Hardware integration. File transfer and translation. Databases. Coordinated software tool kits. Modifying and customizing the tool kit. Task controllers. Future directions.

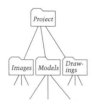

16. Design Database Management 353

Database-management software. The relational data model. Linking graphics and relational databases. Project databases and horizontal integration. Library databases. Version control. Consistency maintenance. The progression of representations and vertical integration. Document production by report generation. Access control and security. Backing up and archiving. New design products and roles.

17. Investing in Design Tools 383

Automating tasks. Reducing communication overhead. Eliminating errors and omissions. Reducing uncertainty. Increasing client and user understanding. Providing better construction documentation. Gaining access to design skills and knowledge. Replacing and multiplying experts. Expanding design boundaries. Acquiring or building a system. Costs and cost recovery. Measurement. Conclusion.

THE STUDIO OF THE 21ST CENTURY

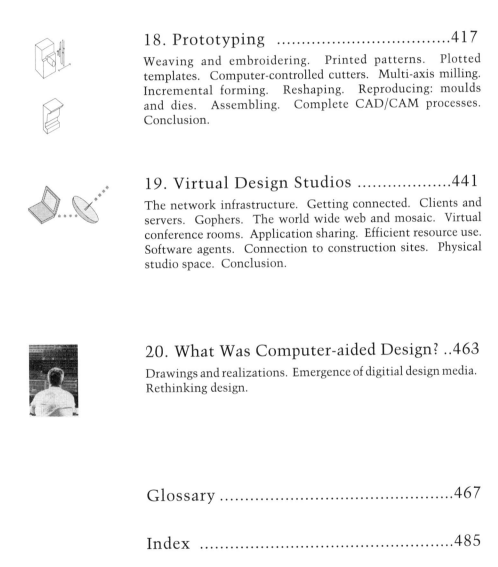

Preface

In the three years since we completed the first edition of *Digital Design Media* there have been some dramatic developments in the field; this revised and expanded edition reflects them. There is a new chapter on rapid prototyping and CAD/CAM, responding to the growing practical importance of these techniques in architecture and in product design. And another entirely new chapter introduces the topic of virtual design studios—use of digital telecommunications, networked multimedia, and videoconferencing to support the work of geographically distributed design teams. Chapter 8, "Polygons, Plans, and Maps," has been extensively revised and updated to provide a more complete coverage of geographic information systems. In response to numerous requests, a glossary of technical terms has been added. Further minor additions, corrections, and updates have been made throughout—particularly in the lists of suggested readings.

In shaping this new edition, we have drawn extensively on our experience of using the first edition as a primary text for introductory courses (at both undergraduate and graduate levels) at the Harvard University Graduate School of Design and at the MIT School of Architecture and Planning. We are grateful to our students and colleagues for the many insights and constructive suggestions that they have provided.

William J. Mitchell
Malcolm McCullough
Cambridge, 1994

Preface to the First Edition

Future historians will remember 2000 as the year by which the computer had become the standard means for accomplishing practical architectural, urban, and landscape design work. The challenge facing a creative designer in the 1990s is to develop a critical understanding of this decisive change in conditions of production, to take a position in relation to it, and to formulate an approach to practice based on this position.

This book aims to stimulate the necessary exploration and reflection by providing a concise, practical introduction to computer-aided design media. It does so not by enumerating the technical details of current computer-aided design systems and recounting the folklore of their use (since much of this information would be obsolete before the book was through the press), but by introducing some fundamental principles and illustrating these with examples of work.

A designer's viewpoint is taken throughout: devices and techniques are introduced as means of pursuing serious design intentions rather than as illustrations of the principles of computer science and technology. (Where necessary, however, concise explanations of key technical concepts are provided.) Each major type of computer-aided system is discussed in terms of the elements and operators that it provides for constructing and manipulating designs, the forms of immediate feedback that it supplies to the designer, the kinds of reporting and analysis that it can support, the opportunities that exist for connection to other types of systems, and the design roles for which its characteristics particularly suit it.

William J. Mitchell
Malcolm McCullough

Cambridge, 1991

Acknowledgments

This book was produced using the resources of the Harvard University Graduate School of Design's Daedalus network. It was laid out using Aldus Pagemaker. Illustrations were prepared with Aldus Freehand, Adobe Photoshop, Artisan, Alias, AutoCAD, Autosolid, and Computervision. The typeface is Adobe Trump Medieval.

Wade Hokoda produced illustrations, solved problems, and provided essential technical consultation. Mark Rosen supplied technical and logistical support. Stephen Ervin was a source of material and suggestions. C. Hax McCullough shared his knowledge of book design. Betty Bollinger and Robin Liggett read early drafts of the manuscript. Debra Edelstein provided editorial suggestions and corrected errors.

For the second edition, we are grateful to James Glymph of Frank O. Gehry Associates for new images. We also thank Takehiko Nagakura and Daniel Schodek for comments and material, and Stephen Ervin and Wade Hokoda for their ongoing support.

Many of the illustrations were provided by students, technical staff, and academic and professional colleagues, both at Harvard and at MIT School of Architecture and Planning. Some have been in our files for so long that the original authorship can no longer be traced, and some have been touched by so many hands that they can only be described as communal intellectual property. The following list represents our best effort to list the sources of images that we did not produce specially for this book. We apologize for the inevitable omissions.

Illustration credits

Illustration credits (continued)

Illustration credits (continued)

1

THE SECOND INDUSTRIAL REVOLUTION

How will architects, landscape architects and urban designers work in the emerging postindustrial era, and what will they produce? This book sketches some answers. Before going on to these, though, it will be useful to place the question in broad historical context.

Three Revolutions

At several points in the development of human society sweeping technological revolutions transformed economic, social, and cultural life. Each of them profoundly affected architecture and the making of towns and cities.

The first to occur was the Agricultural Revolution of the Neolithic Era. It was precipitated by the invention of the wheel and the plough and by the domestication of crops and animals. Its basic result was transformation of life based upon hunting and food gathering to life based upon the systematic production of food. A finer-grained division of labor within society was able to emerge, skilled artisan classes developed, and people began to live in towns and cities: architecture was born. This was a very slow revolution. It must have started, in Western Asia, somewhere around 8000 BC. Then it spread through Europe—taking about five thousand years to reach the British Isles.

The next great revolution, the Industrial Revolution of the nineteenth century, was very much faster. It began

1.1
A traditional setting for design work. A studio in the first American school of architecture at MIT ca. 1870

in Britain around 1780 and spread through most of the world in less than two hundred years. The precipitating factor was discovery of ways to replace human and animal muscle power by the power of machines that consume energy—first the coal-fired steam engine and later the electric motor, the internal combustion engine, and the nuclear reactor. A power economy developed. Machine-powered vehicles annihilated distance, and machine-powered factories produced manufactured goods in vast quantities. The pattern of work changed. In Britain, for example, the proportion of the labor force engaged in agriculture fell from about fifty percent in 1780 to less than five percent in 1980. Over the same period the number of industrial workers (in factories, transportation, and commercial agriculture) steadily grew. Division of labor intensified, and largely unskilled process workers or machine tenders replaced many skilled craftspersons and tradespersons.

We all know the story of how the Industrial Revolution altered architecture forever, so we need not rehearse it in detail here. Cities became larger and more complex. Mechanical and electrical systems were introduced into buildings and became increasingly important. New materials (particularly steel, reinforced concrete, and glass) and industrially produced construction components opened up unprecedented structural and organizational possibilities. It became necessary to document buildings more completely and precisely in drawings and specifications and to apply formalized methods for predicting cost and performance. The technical complexity of the architect's task increased, and the architect's role became more sharply differentiated from that of the builder on the one hand and the engineering consultant on the other. A framework of professional licensing, contractual relationships between members of the building team, and assignment of professional responsibility and liability developed and acquired legal status.

The third major revolution, the Computer Revolution, began to emerge in Britain and the United States in the years immediately following the Second World War. It was ignited by some great theoreticians (Alan Turing and

John Von Neumann in particular), fueled by wartime advances that had taken place in electronics, then accelerated explosively by the appearance of new technologies— first the transistor, next the integrated circuit, and finally the silicon chip. This revolution has spread throughout the world in just a few decades. It has been an order of magnitude faster than the Industrial Revolution, and two orders faster than the Agricultural Revolution.

Just as the Industrial Revolution replaced human muscle power by energy-consuming machines, the Computer Revolution is replacing human brain power by information-processing machines. We no longer have just an agricultural economy and a power economy, but also an increasingly important information economy. We are entering the postindustrial era, in which the collection, processing, and dissemination of information increasingly dominates economic life. Postindustrial society has, in fact, begun to develop upon a three-legged economic foundation: the systematic production of food and extraction of natural resources, the industrial production of goods and the rapid mechanical transportation of people and goods, and the electronic production, storage, and transmission of information. By the 1990s the computer industry and computing activities were accounting for ten percent of the gross national product of the United States— more than the automobile industry.

The Role of Inexpensive Intelligence

The discovery of ways to make powerful computers very small and very inexpensive has been the driving force of the computer revolution. This technological achievement, which has mostly resulted from advances in VLSI (Very Large Scale Integrated) chip technology, can be put in perspective by a few key facts. The price of each unit of computer performance (storage or processing of information) has, over the last couple of decades, decreased by a factor of approximately a million. The first computers of the 1940s and 1950s filled large rooms, were fragile and unreliable, consumed enormous amounts of power, and were confined to advanced research laboratories. Now some high-performance computer workstations (exclud-

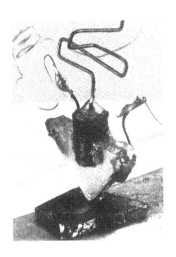

1.2
The first transistor, 1947

ing the monitor) are smaller than a telephone directory, work reliably in an everyday office environment, draw less power than a drafting lamp, and cost less than a compact automobile. Before the end of the century we can expect to see very inexpensive, robust, portable computers with more speed and capacity than recent multimillion dollar supercomputers.

The fundamental economic consequence of all this is simple, and perhaps shocking. Intelligence, which has traditionally been a very precious commodity, has suddenly become so cheap that, for all practical purposes, we will soon regard it as free. And it is not just inside heads, now: it is everywhere. Your car has VLSI chips in it, and so does your VCR. Even your toaster may have one.

Four decades ago, when the earliest portents of the coming Computer Revolution were appearing, Norbert Wiener anticipated with great clarity the profound social effects of the availability of very cheap intelligence. In the preface to his pioneering book *Cybernetics* (1948) he wrote:

> Perhaps I may clarify the historical background of the present situation if I say that the first industrial revolution, the revolution of the "dark satanic mills," was the devaluation of the human arm by the competition of machinery. There is no rate of pay at which a United States pick-and-shovel laborer can live which is low enough to compete with the work of a steam shovel as an excavator. The modern industrial revolution is similarly to devalue the human brain, at least in its simpler and more routine decisions. Of course, just as the skilled carpenter, the skilled mechanic, the skilled dressmaker have in some degree survived the first industrial revolution, so the skilled scientist and the skilled administrator may survive the second. However, taking the second revolution as accomplished, the average human being of mediocre attainments or less has nothing to sell that is worth anyone's money to buy.

He turned out to be right. Bank clerks have already been replaced by automated tellers and file clerks by database management systems. Information workers of perhaps less mediocre attainments are next, as the cost of computation continues to drop and as the sophistication of computer software continues to grow. This includes designers. We are very close to the point at which the average designer may have nothing to sell that is worth anyone's money to buy.

Software and Culture

The modern alchemist's stone, the agent that turns the base-grade intelligence of a silicon chip into the higher-grade intelligence of a sophisticated computer-aided design system, is software—programs and databases that encode architectural knowledge in machine-processable form. In the information economy such intellectual machinery plays much the same role as physical machinery in the manufacturing economy. It is the very means of production. You invest in it to become more competitive. And you must understand its properties and limitations in order to use it effectively.

Software has not only an economic role, but also a cultural one. A piece of software can be a work of imagination and scholarship. Mechanisms for software publication, dissemination, and collection in libraries are becoming increasingly important. Software has become a means for accumulating knowledge and transmitting culture—like its predecessors the oral epic, the handwritten manuscript, the printed book, and the phonograph record.

It takes very sophisticated software to equip a computer with the capacity to perform nontrivial design tasks effectively and efficiently. Such software is difficult and expensive to implement, and architects usually cannot afford to produce it solely for their own use. The cost of writing and maintaining it must be spread over as many users as possible. The result of this is an increasingly clear division of intellectual labor between the producers of software (collectors and encoders of architectural knowledge) and the users of software in execution of specific architectural projects.

Neither the role of software producer nor the role of software user corresponds to traditional professional definitions. Producers of software do not work directly for building clients. And users of software to solve architectural problems may not require anything like the level of skill and experience that we traditionally expect of a professional architect. (By the beginning of the 1990s, for example, hardware stores in the United States were providing computer-aided design systems that enabled customers to design their own timber decks in a few minutes, then produce a complete, priced bill of materials.) It seems very likely that there will be a de-skilling of designers—a development closely analogous to the de-skilling of craftsmen that took place in the Industrial Revolution of the nineteenth century.

New Crafts and Roles

But technological change brings opportunities and exciting intellectual challenges as well as threats. Just as some artisans went on to become leading inventors and industrialists as the machine era dawned, so skilled and thoughtful designers have the chance—if they will grasp it—to shape the emergence and development of digital design media and to apply the powerful new computational tools to social and cultural tasks that really matter. There are ways to make a difference.

1.3
Artisanry?

One cause for optimism is that the Computer Revolution partially reverses a troublesome consequence of the Industrial Revolution—its introduction of means of production that were far too large and costly for most individuals to own and operate. The resulting chronic tensions between labor and capital have largely been responsible for the widespread view that working with advanced technology is inescapably complicitous with oppressive power structures and authoritarian agendas. But this familiar condition is fundamentally redefined by the presence of over a hundred million computers in the world, by the availability of good personal computer systems at much lower cost than that of an ordinary automobile, and by the proliferation and wide distribution of inexpensive software products. Now, individuals and small groups with very limited resources at their disposal can often produce innovative and powerful new software, and they can certainly use existing design software to carry out major tasks that would have been far beyond their capacities in the past.

The emergence of new, computer-based, popular crafts has been a second encouraging development. Before the introduction of the first Macintosh computers in 1984, for example, the crafts of typography and page layout were practiced and seriously thought about by only a very few graphic design professionals and critics; but now, with the help of widely available software, millions of people who would never think of themselves as designers routinely choose fonts, make layout decisions, and even talk about these issues at cocktail parties. Digital imaging (the successor to photography), digital video, and digital music are all in the process of becoming popular crafts as well.

Much of the work that these digitally-empowered craftspeople produce is naive and imperfect, of course, and the old professionals who once totally controlled much graphic and musical production may deride it. But there is surely great cultural value in wide and vigorous practice of a craft, and the level of engagement and critical appreciation that this practice ultimately yields, especially by comparison with the alternative of passive mass consumption.

Finally, though the hand-eye skills that were so crucial in most traditional crafts become relatively unimportant in many computer-supported settings, the craftsperson's capacities for insight and trained, critically-informed discrimination become more vital than ever. Drawing, for example, is not just an athletic skill when it is done by hand and it is not just mechanical when a computer inscribes the lines; whether you mark a line directly with graphite on paper, or whether you indirectly cause it to be traced by an electron beam on the face of a cathode ray tube, the really important things are to know why you are putting it there and what qualities will make it serve its purpose most effectively. Good computer systems—like a calligrapher's brushes or a fine piano—are beautiful, precise instruments that richly reward the user's care and skill. Though we may well regret the passing of some familiar crafts, we will find that new crafts arise to take their place.

Taking Positions

We can assert traditional design skills and values against the more frightening aspects of today's developments of course, much as John Ruskin and William Morris asserted traditional craft skills and values against the Industrial

Revolution. That can be defended as a principled and honorable position—but it probably represents a losing bet with history.

The alternative, if we care about architecture, cities, and the landscape, is to seek critical insight into the conditions that now structure a designer's intellectual work and to find within them ways to extend the creative imagination. In particular, we must try to discover where various different kinds of software can take us. The historical parallel is obvious. The great pioneers of the modern movement sought to understand the means and conditions of architectural production that were inherent in the industrial era. They succeeded (at least in a certain way), and they made something new.

Suggested Readings

Giedion, Sigfried. 1969. *Mechanization Takes Command: A Contribution to Anonymous History.* New York: W. W. Norton.

Kranzberg, Melvin. 1989. "The Information Age." In Tom Forester (ed.), *Computers in the Human Context.* Cambridge: The MIT Press, 19–32.

Lyotard, Jean-François. 1984. *The Postmodern Condition: A Report on Knowledge.* Minneapolis: University of Minnesota Press.

Mitchell, William J. 1977. *Computer-Aided Architectural Design.* New York: Van Nostrand Reinhold.

Mumford, Lewis. 1963 [1934]. *Technics and Civilization.* Orlando: Harcourt Brace Jovanovich.

Porat, Marc Uri. 1977. *The Information Economy.* Washington, DC: US Department of Commerce.

Roszak, Theodore. 1986. *The Cult of Information: The Folklore of Computers and the True Art of Thinking.* New York: Pantheon.

Wiener, Norbert. 1961. *Cybernetics: Control and Communication in the Animal and the Machine.* Second edition. Cambridge: The MIT Press.

Zuboff, Shoshana. 1988. *In the Age of the Smart Machine: The Future of Work and Power.* New York: Basic Books.

2

PRACTICAL COMPUTATION

Consider an electric toaster: it takes bread as input, executes a process, and produces toast as output. Its function is to transform bread into toast. Similarly, a computer takes information as input, executes a process, and produces new information as output: its function is to transform information that we have into information that we want.

Computer Hardware

The analogy can be extended further. The toaster can accept a range of different inputs (muffins, bagels, etc.), and variations in the process can be specified by adjusting the controls, to produce correspondingly different results. A computer can accept a wide variety of information as input, and variations in the process can be specified by writing programs that describe what is to be done.

The simplest functional diagram of a computer, then, depicts it as a device for processing available information inputs to produce required information outputs (figure 2.1). To accomplish this it must have some internal memory for storing the program and the information that is being processed, plus a processor to perform the required operations. Usually, as well, there is some external memory for inexpensive, semi-permanent storage of information that is less immediately needed. The relationship of these parts is illustrated in figure 2.2. The packaging of many

Available information

↓

↓

Required information

2.1
An information-processing device

desktop computers directly reflects this functional organization: typically there is a box containing processor, internal memory, and a disk drive for external memory, plus a keyboard for entering input and a monitor for displaying output.

Variations in the capabilities and performances of computers are produced by substituting different types of input devices, output devices, processors, internal memories, and external memories within this functional organization. The input device might be not only a keyboard for characters, but also a digitizing tablet for coordinates, a scanner for images, or a microphone for spoken words. The output device might be a CRT display, a printer, a plotter, a film recorder, a speech synthesizer, or a robot arm. Magnetic disk, laser-read compact disk (CD) disk, or tape might be used for external memory (figure 2.3). An inexpensive system usually has a relatively slow processor and relatively little memory, but for a price you can get more speed and more storage capacity.

Hardware technology has progressed mostly through the substitution of smaller, cheaper, faster types of devices for larger and more costly ones within essentially the same functional organization. Charles Babbage's famous nineteenth-century calculating engines used elaborate mechanical contrivances to store and process numbers. Some early modern computers employed electromechanical telephone relays. The earliest electronic computers of the 1940s and 1950s were constructed from huge arrays of vacuum tubes. These were successively replaced by transistors, integrated circuits, and silicon chips. The process continues through development of techniques for fabrication of smaller, denser, more complex chips.

In more recent years progress has also been made through introduction of new concepts of functional organization—in particular, organizations that make use of multiple processors operating in parallel. Some of these organizations represent a departure from the very essence of computing as we have known it. For example, parallel architectures sometimes known as connectionist machines or neural networks achieve states never explicitly determined by machine code but "learned" through itera-

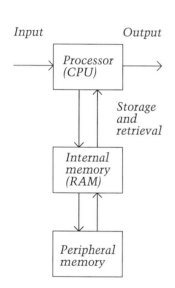

2.2
A single-processor, dual-memory computer

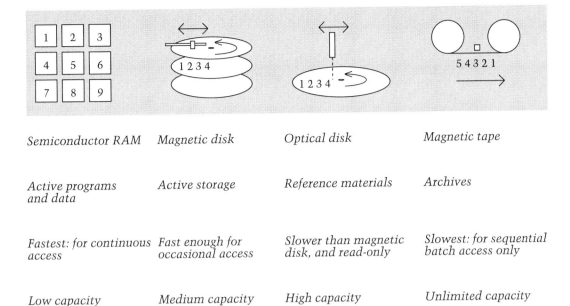

Semiconductor RAM	Magnetic disk	Optical disk	Magnetic tape
Active programs and data	Active storage	Reference materials	Archives
Fastest: for continuous access	Fast enough for occasional access	Slower than magnetic disk, and read-only	Slowest: for sequential batch access only
Low capacity	Medium capacity	High capacity	Unlimited capacity

2.3
A classification of memory

tive comparison of input and output conditions. However, consideration of the traditional single-processor, dual-memory style of computer still provides the best starting point for development of a practical understanding of computer technology.

Networks

Just as two people can talk on the telephone, two computers can exchange information via a telecommunications link. By combining computer and telecommunications technology we have been able to build increasingly extensive and sophisticated computer networks (figure 2.4).

Computer networking yields many benefits. Most obviously, it allows convenient exchange of data between distant machines, and remote access to important online resources such as library catalogs. It also facilitates remote collaboration; using sophisticated communications techniques, for example, designers at different locations can work on the same text, spreadsheet, or CAD database while videoconferencing.

Networking facilitates sharing hardware resources, as well. Thus a single printer might efficiently serve a cluster of computers linked to it via a network, eliminating the

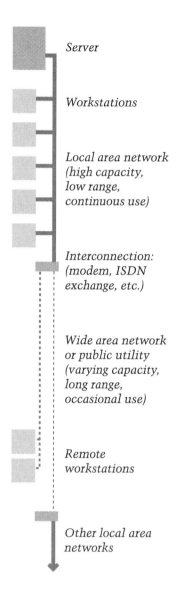

Server

Workstations

Local area network
(high capacity,
low range,
continuous use)

Interconnection:
(modem, ISDN
exchange, etc.)

Wide area network
or public utility
(varying capacity,
long range,
occasional use)

Remote
workstations

Other local area
networks

2.4
Combination of computing
and telecommunications
technology

need to provide individual printers at each machine location. Since this aggregates printing demand, and distributes printer costs over a larger number of computer users, a network printer can usually be a more expensive, higher-quality model than a printer that serves just one machine.

By extending this principle we can develop sophisticated computer networks in which (as in human organizations) there is division of labor, specialization of roles, and some sort of hierarchy of control. In a typical "client/server" network there is one large, powerful computer known as a file server; this acts as a central repository of information, and smaller machines connect to it to accomplish their work. There may also be a very fast machine—a compute server—which efficiently performs large computational tasks. Alternatively, a network may be organized so that any machine can play both "client" and "server" roles as required. Usually there are many workstations on desks, in offices, on factory floors, in design studios, in laboratories and classrooms, or wherever the work of a particular organization is done: users of the network interact directly with these, and they may be configured for particular tasks—word processing, graphics, musical composition, and so on. And there may be specialized input/output stations for production of printed text, plotting large drawings, recording sound, or scanning images.

Communication patterns among computers have changed as computer technology has evolved (figure 2.5). In the early days, processors and memory were extremely expensive, so processing and memory were centralized in large machines serving communications terminals which had little or no local intelligence. This was the era of the time-sharing system (up until about 1980). Then, when inexpensive silicon chips became available in large quantities, the era of the personal computer emerged (the later 1970s and the early 1980s). With personal computing, intelligence is fully distributed to the workstations of individual users, but there is no intercommunication or sharing of resources. Next, as the technology for interconnecting computers advanced, we entered the era of the network. In a network, computing resources can be

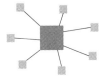

Time-sharing system

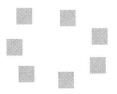

Personal computers

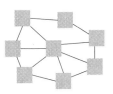

Network of workstations

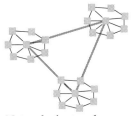

Network of networks

2.5
Evolving communications patterns

centralized or distributed as needed. And as networks have proliferated and connected to each other, huge networks of networks have emerged; such is the Internet, which grew explosively in the 1990s. Eventually, hitherto separate computing and telecommunications technologies will fuse to produce one, unified digital media environment. Your television will be a computer and your computer will be a teleconferencing station. You may still have one kind of computer on your desk, but you will probably also have smaller, wireless computing and telecommunications devices that you carry about with you or even wear like pieces of clothing. We are seeing the evolution of a global network of networks to which very mobile people may plug in—any time, any place.

Operating Systems

A computer system, like a human organization, has resources at its disposal and tasks to accomplish. The manager of a human organization accepts instructions specifying the tasks that need to be performed and appropriately allocates resources to accomplish them. In a computer, that same role is played by a piece of software known as the operating system. The computer user instructs the operating system (usually by typing commands or by pointing with a mouse). In response, the operating system governs the machine.

Every operating system must accomplish a few fundamental tasks. These include organizing files, launching programs to work on those files, allocating memory and other hardware resources, handling input and output, recording and replaying frequently-used sequences of operations, scheduling events like print queues or message exchanges, establishing data security and version control for the saved work, and providing an intelligible framework for presenting the state of all these activities. Not everyone grasps the importance of this: to organize your own work, and to become an effective computer user, you must learn to use these basic capacities of an operating system.

Like human managers, operating systems vary enormously in their styles, in the ranges of resources and tasks they can handle, and in the degrees to which tasks can be delegated to them for handling without explicit instruction. Some of these capabilities may interest casual users; others will remain best left to a systems administrator.

A particularly important distinction can be drawn between single-user and multi-user operating systems. Personal computers usually have single-user operating systems, but larger computers typically have multi-user operating systems that allow them to interact with many users simultaneously. Simple operating systems allow only one task to be performed at a time, but multitasking systems allow different tasks (such as editing one document and printing out another) to be executed simultaneously. Among popular operating systems of the 1980s and 1990s, for example, DOS is an example of a simple, single-task, single-user operating system, while Unix is a more complex and sophisticated multi-user, multitasking system.

Usually an operating system controls a single computer, but as networking technology has developed there has been growing interest in very sophisticated systems that can allocate the resources of an entire network. Such a system might, for instance, examine the network to find a processor that is not currently in use and allocate a task to it—without the user knowing or caring where the work is actually being done.

Early operating systems were instructed by means of typed commands. This provides great power and flexibility, but the commands can often seem cryptic and mysterious—particularly to a beginning user. Thus, as computing has ceased to be the domain mostly of technical specialists, there has been a strong trend toward providing more graphic and intuitively understandable means of communication between users and operating systems. The Apple Macintosh, for example, popularized the idea of communication by using a mouse to point at "icons" displayed on a "desktop." Earlier textual operating systems such as DOS and Unix quickly adopted this approach by means of adding on graphical "windowing" systems. The latter have the disadvantage of being working at arm's length from systems that are not inherently graphical in the first place, but they can compensate for this by allowing advanced users to resort to typing when that remains appropriate, such as for referring to items that are not immediatey visible on the limited area of the screen. An independent windowing system may also be adapted to a variety of host operating systems in order to standardize interaction formats. The X windows system developed at MIT in the 1980s is one prevalent example of this approach.

Data

When you look at a desktop display (figure 2.6) you will usually see a collection of icons representing files of information stored on disk. Some of these are data files containing information to be processed, and some of them are application files containing programs for doing the processing.

All the information stored in data files is in digital format. In other words, it is encoded as collections of 1s and 0s. These 1s and 0s are represented physically in computer memory by tiny devices (of various types) that can be switched between two different states.

Coding schemes are used to represent different types of data elements in this way. Most basically, strings of 1s and 0s can be interpreted as integer numbers. Combinations of integers can then be used to represent rational numbers and (to finite precision) real numbers. (In chapter 3 we will consider the digital representation of numbers in more detail.) They can also be used to represent alphabetic characters. Thus computer programmers habitually think in terms of instructions to perform operations on binary digits (bits), integers, real numbers, and alphabetic characters.

Structures of these basic data elements can be put together and stored to represent more complex things. Characters can be strung together into words and sentences. Sequences of numbers can be used to describe sounds, images, or physical objects. So, at a higher level of consideration, we can classify files according to the types of things they represent—as numeric data files, text files, sound files, image files, geometry files, and so on. The

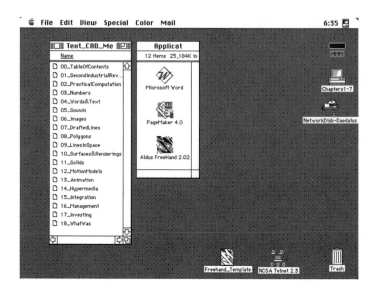

2.6
A desktop display

information that they contain is appropriately interpreted by output software and devices as tables of numbers, printed text, sequences of sounds, or displays of images. But if you try to output an image file as sound, or a text file as an image, you get nonsense.

Data Structures and Databases

If it is to be useful for some practical purpose, a collection of data elements (whether stored in a computer or not) must satisfy two conditions. First, it must contain what you need. Second, it must be structured in such a way that you can get at what you need with reasonable efficiency.

To illustrate the importance of data structure, let us consider the telephone directory. We use it for the purpose of converting information that we have (somebody's name) into information that we need (that person's number). Somewhere it contains what we need, and our task is to find this as quickly as possible. The procedure that we apply is simple and efficient, and it goes roughly as follows. First, open the book about half way through, and look at the first and last entries on the page. If the name that you want is alphabetically after the last entry, then divide the following pages roughly in half and return to the first step. If the name alphabetically precedes the first entry, then divide the preceding pages roughly in half and return to the first step. If the name lies alphabetically between the first and last entries, then scan down the page until you locate it, read the corresponding number, and terminate. Notice how the procedure exploits structure: we could not apply it if the directory were randomly ordered. Nor could we employ it if the entries were sorted in numerical rather than alphabetical order. But we could use the numerically ordered directory for a different purpose—finding the name and address corresponding to a given number.

You can access the information contained in this book in at least four different ways. First, you can scan through it in sequence—an efficient strategy if you want to absorb everything that it contains. Second, you can consult the table of contents and follow its page references to jump directly to the beginnings of particular chapters that happen to interest you. Third, you can consult the index and follow its page references to find information on very specific topics. Finally, you can follow cross-references from within the text to other parts of the text (see "cross-reference" in index). Notice, though, that only two basic access mechanisms are employed—scanning in sequence and following references to locations of information. Computers use the same two basic mechanisms for accessing data stored in memory. Thus organizing files of data for computer manipulation is largely a matter of putting elements in appropriate sequences and of creating useful structures of references to memory locations (usually known as pointers) analogous to the index or cross-references of a book. The resulting pattern of information organization is known as a data structure.

There are only a few basic types of data structures (though these can be combined and elaborated endlessly). They are illustrated in figure 2.7. Often elements are simply stored in sequences, like shopping lists. Relationships of elements may be represented by creating two-dimensional tables—as in printed mileage tables that show the distances between pairs of cities. The entries in a table may be all of the same type (in which case it is called an array), or they may be of differing types—as in a table of employee data that shows names, social security numbers, birthdates, and so on. The idea of a table may be generalized to structures of three or more dimensions. Pointers may be used to create hierarchies of information, as in a library catalog's decimal call number system, or to create networks, as in a dictionary with cross-references between entries.

A collection of information that has been stored semi-permanently in computer memory for some particular purpose, and given a structure appropriate to that purpose, is known as a database. Sometimes a simple database is contained within a single file, but a database typically consists of many interrelated files. A database to support the work of a business organization might, for example, contain files of employee data, financial records, customer orders, and so on. Design databases typically contain files of geometric, image, and text data describing a project.

One especially versatile approach to storing information is to classify it according to what may be done with it. This allows programmers to obtain better results by developing operations and data structures together and to use classes of these as basic building blocks for more ambitious software design. This approach, known as object-oriented programming, has several advantages. Obviously it encourages modularity (and therefore adaptability) of software: pieces can be recombined in unforeseen ways; large teams of programmers can divide up projects more efficently. It also helps programmers to adapt and maintain large pieces of software, and to modify them significantly without having to rebuild them from the ground up. Libraries of previously-developed modules can very conveniently be used as the foundation for building new modules, so that the more software has been written, the easier it is to write more still.

Application Programs

The essential function of a computer can now be defined, rather more precisely than before, as the application of algorithms (sequences of instructions) to data files and databases to achieve useful results. Programming is the design of algorithms and the data structures on which they operate. From a user's viewpoint, programs are tools for

Single value

*Array of values
of the same type*

*Table of records
containing values of
different types*

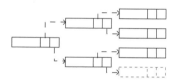

Linked list of records

Hierarchy of records

2.7
Basic types of data
structures

manipulating data files and databases. The following chapters of this book will primarily be devoted to introduction of the repertoire of computer tools available to designers and to discussion of their theoretical foundations, their capabilities, and their limitations.

In principle, programs can be expressed in many ways—in English, by means of flow diagrams (figure 2.8), or in specialized languages (known as programming languages) that have been developed expressly for this purpose. A programming language has rigorously defined syntax and semantics and so lends itself to very precise expression. Among the most popular current programming languages are Pascal, C++, Lisp, and Prolog. Historically, most practical software has been written in such languages, but as computers have become more powerful and as the discipline of programming has developed, it has become increasingly feasible to employ English-like and graphic formats for expression of programs.

Professional users of computers should have a critical understanding of the algorithms and data structures of the programs that they employ—their capabilities, their limitations, and the theory upon which they are based. It is as important to understand your intellectual materials and methods as it is to understand construction materials and methods. You do not yourself have to be skilled at the craft of programming, but you should have some practical acquaintance with it and be able to work effectively with those who are.

Interfaces

The physical interface between a computer system and you—the environment in which you do your work—is formed by some collection of devices for translating information stored in computer memory into visual or other sensorily accessible form (output devices), another collection of devices for performing the inverse function of getting information into computer memory (input devices), and software for structuring the back-and-forth flow of information. Usually these components are grouped and packaged into configurations referred to as terminals

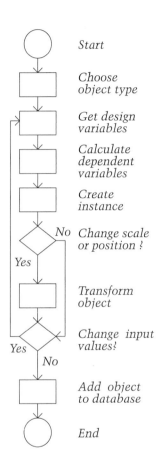

2.8
Flow diagram for a procedure

(if they have relatively little local memory and processing capacity), personal computers (if they have enough local memory and processing capacity to operate independently), or workstations (if they operate as nodes in a network).

Output devices are very diverse. They include displays and printers for text, graphic displays, audio output devices for music and speech, and robotic devices that execute movements. Input devices are similarly multifarious. These include keyboards for text, mouse and stylus devices for coordinates, microphones for speech and music, and scanners and video cameras for visual information.

The computers of the 1950s and 1960s frequently used as terminals devices such as teletypes and electric typewriters, consisting of a keyboard for input and a printer for output (figure 2.9). These allowed purely textual—question-and-answer or command-and-response—dialogues between the machine and the user: you gave a command to perform a task, then the software executed it, reported the result, and requested the next command. Printers were soon replaced by faster and quieter text display screens to produce a style of terminal that is still very popular in many applications and that was imitated in the earliest personal computers. In any case, one dimensional, text driven interfaces were very strict: you had to answer one question at a time in a sequence determined by the computer.

Later personal computers, particularly the Apple Macintosh and IBM-compatible machines running Windows, have popularized a more fluid, graphic style of interaction. These machines use two-dimensional graphic displays and gestural input with a mouse to supplement one-dimensional text strings and keyboard input, and they respond to actions (usually pointing and clicking) on windows, menus, and icons. Increasingly, dialogues combine text, graphic, and sound input and output (figure 2.10). The user of a computer-aided design system might, for example, view text and graphics on a screen, hear voice output, type in data, select objects on the screen with a mouse, sketch with a stylus, and give spoken commands.

Some interfaces, now, are even three-dimensional—using head-mounted three-dimensional display devices to

Method	Technology
Submitting batch jobs	Card deck
Sending text to timesharing system	Terminal
Answering menu questions	Hierarchy of menus
Pointing to initiate events	Screen and windowing system
Navigating object-based environment	Gloves and goggles

2.9
Evolution of human-computer interaction

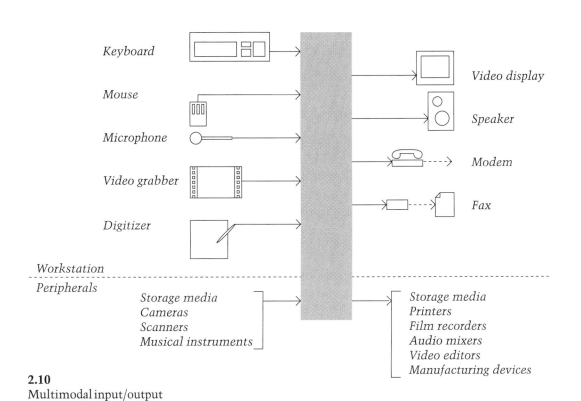

2.10
Multimodal input/output

place users inside virtual three-dimensional environments, and sensing gloves or complete sensing suits to read the user's gestures. These open the possibility of still less formalized, more natural interaction. Menus and icons may become obsolete, for example, as vocabularies of input gestures and three-dimensional "containers" expand, and as the data themselves become the working environment. You might, for example, access files by grasping "books" on "shelves," and you might pick up software "tools" from a "workbench."

The most important property of any human-computer interface is its responsiveness. Therefore, modern personal computer and workstation interfaces are organized to provide immediate feedback of output in response to input actions: when you hit a key you see a character displayed or you hear a sound, and when you move the mouse you see the cursor move on the screen. When you choose a different task, you see a different cursor change (figure 2.11). This not only lets you know what is happening, it helps you to understand and feel comfortable with your tools.

Different kinds of operations make different demands on the system's capacity to respond. Sometimes, as when typing characters or sketching with a mouse, users need to see responses within as little as a thirtieth of a second. At other times, as when saving work at the end of a session, they can readily tolerate delays of a few seconds as long as they can see that something is happening. As machines get faster, and response times get correspondingly shorter, software designers can provide increasingly sophisticated graphic and auditory feedback in response to a user's gestures. For example, fast graphics processors allow users to move about in complex three-dimensional environments in response to mouse or joystick gestures. Simple, early sketching systems interpreted mouse movements as displayed lines of uniform thickness, but more advanced ones that exploit greater processing power use a speed-sensitive, pressure-sensitive, tilt-sensitive stylus to produce lines much like those made by a sensitively wielded pencil, brush, or charcoal stick.

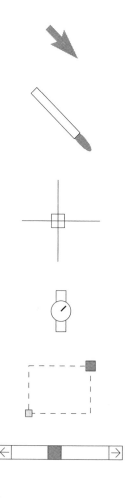

2.11
Different cursors

Environments and Metaphors

The interface to a computer system is usually presented as a hierarchy of nested work environments, each one of which is appropriate to the task at hand. The operating system interface is the outermost environment—the first thing that you see when you turn on the computer. Today, this is usually presented as a "desktop" with "documents" and "tools." Earlier, text-oriented operating system interfaces typically used the metaphor of a master/servant dialogue. Some of the most recent ones, such as Magic Cap, employ the metaphor of a "town" or "Main Street" filled with "shops" where you can find resources, and populated by intelligent "agents" that can be dispatched to perform tasks—perhaps in communication and cooperation with each other.

The operating system interface organizes and presents the resources of a computer, or network of computers, for convenient use. It provides access to data files, application programs, and facilities for allocating computer resources (memory space, peripheral devices, and so on) to tasks. Within this framework, the interface of each application program organizes a more specialized environment appropriate to the particular task at hand: word processing and page layout programs typically present simulated "sheets of paper," drafting programs present "drawing boards" and arrays of "drafting tools," three-dimensional modeling programs present three-dimensional "worlds," and so on. Then, within each application program, there may be even more specialized sub-environments, and so on to any depth.

In early operating systems and application software, the environments and tools that were presented derived very directly from the basic elements of computer hardware that were being employed. Users had to translate the tasks that they wished to perform into these often-alien terms. Today, with the availability of a lot more computing power to maintain sophisticated interfaces, environments are normally presented in terms of more familiar and comfortable metaphors of workplace, toolkit, and workpiece; the software automatically performs the necessary translation into computational terms. Furthermore, where early computing environments were often very rigid, most newer environments can be personalized to suit individual styles and tastes.

Computer hardware has become a commodity, while software has proliferated, diversified, and become more personalizable. So no two computing environments need be alike, and each one of us can put together a work environment that mirrors our own particular interests and talents. A personal, portable workstation can become a writing environment, a numerical computation environment, a musical composition and playback environment, a digital photography environment, or (of particular interest to us here) a superbly equipped and extremely efficient design environment that takes over many of the traditional functions of a drawing board and drafting interests and provides a growing array of new capabilities as well.

Suggested Readings

Foley, James, Andries van Dam, Steve Feiner, and John Hughes. 1989. *Computer Graphics—Principles and Practice (2nd Edition)*. Reading, Mass.: Addison-Wesley.

Kurzweil, Raymond. 1990. *The Age of the Intelligent Machine*. Cambridge: The MIT Press.

Laurel, Brenda. 1992. *Computers as Theater*. Reading, Mass.: Addison Wesley.

Laurel, Brenda, (ed.) 1990. *The Art of Human-Computer Interface Design*. Reading, Mass.: Addison Wesley.

Negroponte, Nicholas. 1989. "From Bezel to Proscenium: The Human-Computer Interface 25 Years Hence and Beyond the Desktop Metaphor." ACM Computer Graphics 23 (3): 19.

Von Neumann, John. 1959. *The Computer and the Brain*. New Haven: Yale University Press.

Weizenbaum, Joseph. 1976. *Computer Power and Human Reason*. New York: Freeman.

Williams, Michael R. 1985. *A History of Computing Technology*. Englewood Cliffs: Prentice Hall.

3

NUMBERS AND NUMERICAL MODELS

All practical computation is based upon the idea of letting numbers represent things that interest us—counts, measures, characters, words, sounds, positions, shapes, gestures, and so on. These things may, in turn, represent other things, which may represent yet other things, in potentially endless chains of reference. We often use computers to process very complex, multilevel representations of this sort, but these representations all reduce to collections of numbers in the end.

Binary Representations

An ordinary light switch illustrates the simplest type of numerical representation (figure 3.1). It has two positions, which we may designate 0 and 1 respectively. When the switch is in state 0 the light is off, and when the switch is in state 1 the light is on. In other words, we can write 0 to indicate that the assertion *the light is on* is currently false, and we can write 1 to indicate that the assertion is currently true. Thus we use a single binary digit to represent a state of affairs.

Now consider a house with a light in each room (figure 3.2). If there are two rooms we need a sequence of two binary digits to represent the current lighting conditions, if there are three rooms we need three binary digits, and so on. The position of a digit in the sequence tells us the room to which that particular digit refers. Technically, these

On: 1
Off: 0

3.1
A switch stores a
binary digit

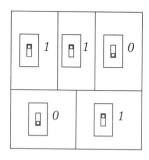

Status: 1 1 0 0 1

3.2
A bit vector encodes
information

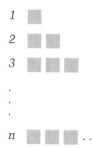

3.3
The natural numbers are
for counting

sequences of binary digits are known as bit vectors. Such vectors provide a system for describing situations in terms of the presence and absence of things, or the truth and falsehood of assertions. We can use them to describe situations of any complexity if we know an appropriate coding scheme and have sufficiently long bit vectors at our disposal to cover the possibilities.

At the most fundamental level of consideration, a computer is simply a device for storing bit vectors in memory and processing them with the CPU. Processing reduces to performing *and, or,* and *not* (Boolean) operations on pairs of binary digits, performing binary arithmetic on bit vectors, and testing bit vectors for equality.

Counts and Integers

The natural numbers {1, 2, 3, . . .} are used for counting (figure 3.3). In other words, they can represent collections of discrete things—the coins in your pocket, the columns of a building, the characters on a page, the chimes of a clock, or the clicks of a mouse. The basic computation on natural numbers is addition: you can, for example, add the number of coins in your right pocket to the number of coins in your left pocket to yield the total number of coins that you have. A second type of computation on natural numbers is multiplication: you can multiply the number of characters on a page by the number of pages in a book to yield an estimate of the total number of characters in the book.

When we add two natural numbers we always get another natural number: technically, the operation of addition is closed in the natural numbers. But if we subtract one natural number from another, we do not necessarily obtain a natural number, so the natural numbers cannot be used to represent things like overdrawn bank accounts or elevations below sea level. This deficiency can be remedied by adjoining zero and the negative integers to the natural numbers to yield the signed integers {. . . –3, –2, –1, 0, 1, 2, 3, . . .}. The operations of addition, subtraction, and multiplication are all closed in the signed integers (but division is not—a point to which we shall return). Thus the signed integers, together with

Base-ten	Base-two
1	1
2	10
3	11
4	100
5	101
8	1000
10	1010
20	10100
32	100000
50	110010
64	1000000
100	1100100

3.4
Decimal and binary
notation

the arithmetic operations that are closed in the signed integers, constitute a system for representing and reasoning about things that can be counted.

In everyday life we usually write the signed integers in base-ten notation, but it is also possible to write them in binary (that is, base-two) notation. That is, we can encode them as bit vectors. Figure 3.4 shows how this works. The most significant digit is always written on the left, and the least significant digit on the right. Notice how longer sequences of binary digits are needed to represent larger integers.

Computers sometimes use a single byte (eight bits) of information to represent a signed integer. One bit is needed to specify the sign (+ or −), so there are seven bits available to represent the magnitude. Thus the largest integer representable in this format is +1111111, or in decimal notation $2^7 - 1 = 127$. Clearly this is not sufficient for many practical purposes, so it is more usual to use sixteen bits, thirty-two bits, or even sixty-four bits.

Division and Rational Numbers

If we divide 4 by 2 we obtain an integer result, but if we divide 4 by 3 we do not. However, just as we can define the signed integers to obtain closure under subtraction, so we can define the rational numbers to obtain closure under division. A rational number is, then, any number (such as 4/3) that can be expressed as a ratio of two integers. Notice that the rational numbers include the signed integers, just as the signed integers include the natural numbers.

In architecture, design elements are often given integer lengths, widths, and heights, with the result that proportions are described by rational numbers. Andrea Palladio, for example, invariably proportioned rectangular rooms as ratios of small integers—1/1, 1/2, 2/3, 3/5, and so on (figure 3.5).

Roots and Irrational Numbers

Now consider the diagonal of a unit square (figure 3.6). We know from the Pythagorean theorem that its length is the square root of 2—a number that turns out to be irrational

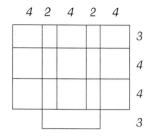

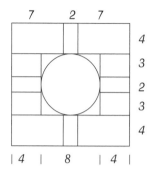

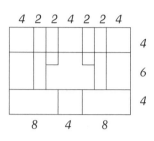

3.5
Integer ratios in
Palladio's villa plans

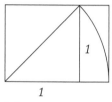

3.6
A root 2 rectangle

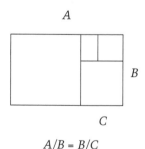

$A/B = B/C$

3.7
The golden rectangle

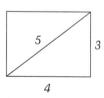

3.8
A rational rectangle

in the sense that it cannot be expressed as the ratio of two integers. (Discovery of this irrationality was profoundly distressing to the ancient Pythagoreans, who had developed a cosmology based upon integers and integer ratios.) Another well-known irrational proportion is that of the so-called golden rectangle (figure 3.7). Similarly, the circumference of a circle is described by the irrational number π. From an arithmetic viewpoint, these irrational numbers result from operations of extracting roots or evaluating infinite converging sequences of rational numbers.

In design, irrational numbers most frequently result from constructions of diagonals and circles, but they can emerge in many other ways as well. Since irrational numbers can be inconvenient in construction, designers sometimes try to avoid them by such devices as choosing rectangles in which the diagonals turn out to be rational (figure 3.8).

Real Numbers

The rational numbers together with the irrational numbers comprise the real numbers, in which operations such as extracting roots are closed. So the various types of real numbers are related as illustrated in figure 3.9. In general, we use real numbers for expressing the results of measurement operations and for describing and reasoning about the physical world in terms of lengths, widths, areas, volumes, masses, forces, temperatures, and so on.

Although real numbers cannot always be written exactly as ratios of integers, they can always be expressed with sufficient precision for practical purposes by rational

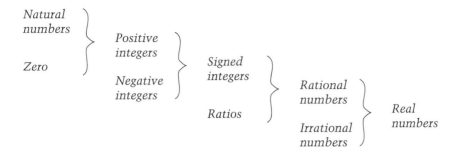

3.9
Types of real numbers

approximations. In other words, if we use a sufficiently large integer as the denominator of the fraction, we can come sufficiently close. The usual convention is to use a power of ten as the denominator and write the number using the radix point notation. Thus the length of the diagonal of a unit square can be expressed, with successively greater precision, as $1/1 = 1$, $14/10 = 1.4$, $141/100 = 1.41$, $1414/1000 = 1.414$, and so on indefinitely. (In this case ten is the radix, so the radix point is referred to as the "decimal" point.) For practical purposes, a few decimal places usually suffice, but we can go as far as we want: the number π, for example, has been evaluated (by computer) to tens of thousands of decimal places.

Fixed-point and Floating-point Representation

A given number may be stored in computer memory in either one of two modes: fixed-point or floating-point (figure 3.10). In fixed-point storage, the radix point is assumed to be at an invariant location in the stored sequence of binary digits. (Note that, in this case, the radix point is referred to as the "binary" point.) In floating-point storage, the number is represented as a fractional part and an exponent part, where the fractional part has the radix point at the left, and the exponent part is an integral power of the radix two. This arrangement allows the radix point to "float" depending upon the power of the exponent. With very large numbers the radix point floats far to the right (so that there are few digits remaining to the right of the point), but with very small numbers the radix point floats far to the left.

Sign bit	Exponent part	Fractional part
0	1 0 1 . . .	0 0 1 . . .

Binary point

3.10
Storage of a real number

Fixed-point representation has the advantage of compactness, and hardware for performing arithmetic operations on fixed-point numbers is the only kind available on some inexpensive, low-powered computers. It is particularly efficient where the numbers to be manipulated are all integers. But floating-point arithmetic is a necessity for many scientific and engineering computations, since it allows computations where the range of the magnitude of the numbers is very large (far larger than with fixed-point numbers occupying the same amount of storage), so high-powered personal computers and engineering workstations are invariably equipped with hardware for efficient performance of floating-point arithmetic as well.

Since floating-point arithmetic is carried out to limited precision on rational approximations to real numbers, it can produce unexpected or erroneous results under certain circumstances. An attempt to multiply a very large number by another very large number can generate a condition known as overflow—a number too large to represent in the space available. Conversely, an attempt to multiply a very small fraction by a very small fraction can generate underflow—a number too small to represent. In general, results of operations will have small round-off errors. Usually these do not matter, but they can become significant when lengthy sequences of floating-point operations are necessary to obtain a result, so careful programmers organize such sequences to minimize the effect of round-off errors. The presence of round-off errors can also mean that alternative sequences of operations which should produce exactly the same results do not always, in fact, do so. Consequently, a program cannot reliably test for equality of floating-point numbers. This has some important and rather unexpected consequences for practical computer-aided design: a system cannot, for example, be programmed to reliably recognize that two shapes represented by floating-point coordinates are identical, or symmetrical about an axis—even though you may be able to see easily from a display that they are (figure 3.11).

Fixed-point arithmetic on integers has fewer problems. Additions and multiplications of large numbers can, of course, produce overflow. And division by zero must be

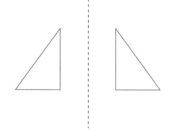

3.11
Undetectable symmetry
(when shapes are
represented in floating-
point coordinates)

avoided. But addition, subtraction, and multiplication cannot produce round-off errors, and results of division operations are always either rounded up or truncated (as specified in the program). Thus a program can safely test for equality of integers, and indeed this is a very common technique.

Numerical Variables

In computer programming a variable is a location set aside in computer memory for storage of a value. Most computing environments provide for storage of integer values in fixed-point mode, real values in floating-point mode, Boolean values (true or false) in binary mode, and characters (which we will consider in the next chapter). The basic operations associated with variables are declaration, assignment of a value, and accessing the value.

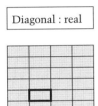

Declaration

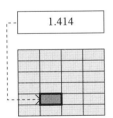

Assignment

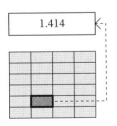

Accessing the value

3.12
Declaration, assignment, and access

Many programming languages, for example Pascal, require explicit declaration of variables before they are used (figure 3.12). The declaration specifies a variable's name and type—integer, real, Boolean, or character. A Pascal declaration of an integer variable called *Number_of_Columns*, for example, looks like this:

Var Number_of_Columns: integer;

And a Pascal declaration of a real variable called *Diagonal* takes the following form:

Var Diagonal : real;

Specification of a variable's type, as in these examples, tells the computer the storage mode that is required. It also allows automatic checking of programs for erroneous operations, such as attempts to perform floating-point arithmetic on character values. Some programming languages, such as Lisp, dispense with explicit declarations; this can allow quicker and more fluid program development, but has efficiency penalties and eliminates the possibility of checking for type errors.

Execution of an assignment operation results in storage of a value in the location identified by a variable name. Here, for example, are some Pascal instructions to perform assignment operations:

Number_of_Columns := 10;
Diagonal := 1.414;

The symbol := is called the assignment operator. It specifies that the variable on the left gets the value on the right.

Once a variable has been declared and assigned a value, that value can be accessed for use in computations and for output. In programming languages such as Pascal and Lisp, the value to be accessed is specified simply by writing the variable name. Thus a Pascal instruction to assign the value of *Diagonal* to another variable looks like this:

Height_of_Rectangle := Diagonal;

Notice that an attempt to execute this instruction would produce an erroneous result if the variable *Diagonal* had not been declared, since the computer would not know where to look for the value that is to be used in the operation. Similarly, if *Height_of_Rectangle* had not been declared, the computer would not know where to put the value. And the attempt would also produce an erroneous result if a value had not been previously been assigned to *Diagonal*.

Arithmetic Operations

The use of named variables makes it very easy to write instructions for performance of arithmetic operations. The basic arithmetic operators used in these instructions are usually written + (addition), − (subtraction), * (multiplication), / (real division), and *div* (integer divide and truncate). Thus the following are some typical Pascal instructions to perform arithmetic:

Area := Height_of_Rectangle * Width;
Perimeter := 2.0 * (Height_of_Rectangle + Width);

When the computer executes these instructions, it replaces the variable names in the arithmetic expressions with the values currently stored at the corresponding memory locations.

Numerical Functions

In scientific and engineering calculations it is often necessary to evaluate not only expressions constructed with the basic arithmetic operators, but also functions such as sines, cosines, square roots, and so on. So scientific hand calculators have function buttons (labeled with the abbreviated names of functions) as well as arithmetic operator buttons, and scientific programming languages provide similar repertoires of named functions. In Pascal, for example, an instruction to calculate the cosine of an angle might be written:

> *Result := Cos (Theta);*

The variable enclosed within the parentheses is the argument of the *Cos* function. When the computer executes this instruction, it accesses the current value of *Theta*, evaluates the cosine function for this argument, and replaces *Cos (Theta)* with the numerical result.

Similarly, a Pascal instruction to calculate the diagonal of a square from the Pythagorean theorem might be written:

> *Diagonal := Sqrt (2.0 * Width * Width);*

In this case, the function *Sqrt* returns the square root of the argument. Notice that the argument is itself an arithmetic expression.

Programming languages such as Pascal and Lisp go a step further than providing a repertoire of built-in functions by allowing a programmer to declare and later use new functions. A function declaration specifies the function's name and its arguments (there may be more than one argument) and contains a sequence of instructions specifying how to calculate the required value. Such homemade functions can then be used in exactly the same way as built-in functions. This feature provides enormous power and versatility: the language can, in effect, be extended with an unlimited number of new functions, and very complex functions can be built up from simpler ones. It is like having a scientific hand calculator with an indefinitely expandable set of function buttons.

Numerical Models

Numerical models describe the behaviors of systems that interest us in terms of input variables, output variables, and functions specifying how output variables depend upon input variables. A computer processes a numerical model by accepting values for the input variables, executing arithmetic operations and evaluating functions to produce corresponding values for the output variables, and finally displaying or printing the values of the output variables. A circle, for example, can be modeled numerically as a system in which *Radius* is the input variable, *Circumference* and *Area* are the output variables, the function specifying the dependence of *Circumference* on *Radius* is described by the arithmetic expression *2 * Pi * Radius*, and the function specifying the dependence of *Area* on *Radius* is described by the arithmetic expression *Pi * Radius * Radius* (figure 3.13). A computer might process this model by accepting a typed value for *Radius*, evaluating the arithmetic expressions to assign values to *Circumference* and *Area*, then displaying these values on the screen.

A numerical model may have any number of input and output variables and may also incorporate internal variables for use in storage of intermediate values produced during the process of evaluation. Consider, for instance, a numerical model of a rectangular box (figure 3.14). The input variables are *Length*, *Width*, and *Height*. The intermediate variables are *Front_Area* and *Side_Area*. And the output variables are *Surface_Area*, *Volume*, and *Surface_to_Volume*.

Since designers are concerned with physical systems, many of the numerical models they use involve geometric and physical variables and incorporate functions that express geometric and physical laws. Architects, for example, make frequent use of simple numerical models to calculate areas, volumes, and proportions. Landscape architects evaluate cut-and-fill and drainage models. Urban designers calculate plot ratios and floor area ratios. Engineering consultants often use very complex models based on physical laws to calculate values for structural,

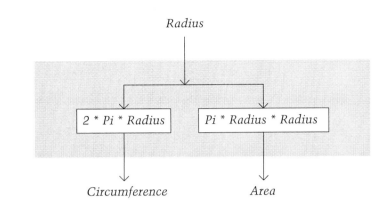

Input variable Radius

Functions 2 * Pi * Radius   Pi * Radius * Radius

Output variables Circumference   Area

3.13
Numerical model of a circle

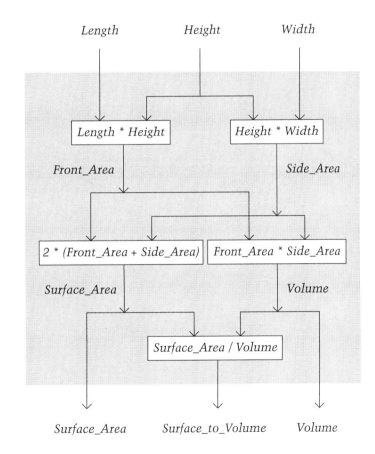

Input variables Length Height Width

Functions Length * Height   Height * Width

Front_Area   Side_Area

2 * (Front_Area + Side_Area)   Front_Area * Side_Area

Surface_Area   Volume

Surface_Area / Volume

Output variables Surface_Area   Surface_to_Volume   Volume

3.14
Numerical model of a
three-dimensional box

thermal, lighting, and acoustic variables. Sometimes these engineering models are so complex that they would be completely impractical to evaluate without the aid of a powerful computer. Design of high-rise buildings in earthquake zones, for example, requires evaluation of extremely complex numerical models describing dynamic seismic behavior: the availability of sufficient computer power to manipulate these models has allowed dramatic changes in the skylines of Los Angeles and San Francisco since the 1960s.

Modeling with Procedural Programming Languages

When you use a simple electronic calculator (or an abacus or a slide rule) to evaluate a numerical model, you execute a sequence of steps, and you probably jot down values of internal variables along the way. The complete sequence of steps constitutes a procedure for finding the required output values. A procedural programming language such as Pascal, Lisp, C, or Fortran provides you with the capability to write down an entire procedure, name it, and store it in computer memory for future use. Thereafter, the procedure may be invoked by name and applied to the input data that you have to produce the output values that you need. It becomes a specialized design tool. And a developing collection of such tools becomes intellectual capital that can be drawn on as needed when problems arise and need to be solved.

A procedure consists basically of declarations and instructions to perform actions—to accept input values, to perform arithmetic operations, and to store, display, or print output values. In addition, it must contain information specifying the sequence in which these actions are to be performed. Simple procedures are expressed as sequences of instructions, and the computer executes these instructions in the sequence in which they are written. More complex procedures incorporate control statements that specify loops and branches (figure 3.15). Procedures may invoke other procedures, so that complex procedures may be built up hierarchically from simpler procedures

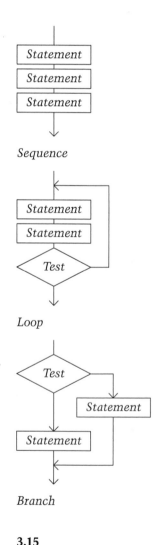

Sequence

Loop

Branch

3.15
Flow of control

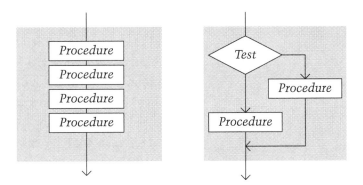

3.16
Procedures built from procedures

(figure 3.16). And some procedural programming languages even allow procedures to invoke themselves recursively.

Programming an efficient, reliable procedure to evaluate a numerical model can become a very demanding enterprise—one that is usually best left to specialists. But any designer who wants to make effective use of computer technology is well advised to learn the rudiments of procedural programming and to develop the skill of quickly crafting small programs to solve problems that emerge in the course of a design project. This is not difficult: it involves grasping the basic concepts of input and output, arithmetic operations, evaluation of functions, and the control constructs of looping, branching, hierarchies of abstraction, and recursion, together with the vocabulary and syntactic conventions of some suitable procedural programming language. If you have this skill you can modify design tools, customize them to meet your special needs more precisely, and even develop completely new tools where necessary. It also enables you to inspect an existing program to uncover the assumptions that it embodies and to see exactly how it works.

Modeling with Spreadsheets

Spreadsheet systems provide an alternative way of expressing and evaluating numerical models. Like procedural programming languages they provide for declaration of variables, input and storage of values, execution of arithmetic operations and evaluation of functions, assignment of values, and output of values. But they utilize radically different control constructs for organizing the

Value	$200,000
Interest	8%
Period	5

Year	Principal	Interest
1	-1765	-16000
2	-1907	-15859
3	-2059	-15706
4	-2224	-15541
5	-2402	-15364
6		
7		
8		
9		
10		

Total Prin.	Total Int.
10357	78470

Value	$200,000
Interest	8%
Period	**7**

Year	Principal	Interest
1	-1765	-16000
2	-1907	-15859
3	-2059	-15706
4	-2224	-15541
5	-2402	-15364
6	-2594	-15171
7	-2802	-14964
8		
9		
10		

Total Prin.	Total Int.
15753	108605

Value	$200,000
Interest	**10%**
Period	7

Year	Principal	Interest
1	-1216	-20000
2	-1337	-19878
3	-1471	-19745
4	-1618	-19598
5	-1780	-19436
6	-1958	-19258
7	-2154	-19062
8		
9		
10		

Total Prin.	Total Int.
11535	136976

3.17
Changing input variables in a spreadsheet

process of deriving output values from input values, and so engender different styles of programming and user interaction. They are especially well adapted to quick, ad-hoc development and application of simple models, but they are less general than procedural programming languages in their capabilities, and less suitable for handling large-scale, complex models.

Spreadsheet systems vary widely in their features and user interfaces, but they are all based on the same key idea. Variables are represented as locations (known as cells) in a two-dimensional table that is displayed on the screen. A value can be assigned to a variable by typing it into the appropriate cell. Functions that make the value of one cell dependent on the values of other cells may be specified. Then, whenever the value of a cell is changed, the values of dependent cells are automatically updated so that the effect of the change ripples through the table.

Figure 3.17 illustrates a simple, typical interest-payment model in spreadsheet format. The model uses the spreadsheet's built-in functions, including conditionals. Whenever any of the three input variables is changed, all the yearly calculations are reevaluated automatically, and the effect ripples through to the bottom line.

Modeling with Symbolic Mathematics Systems

Programs written in procedural languages are efficient tools for evaluating numerical functions, and spreadsheets provide a convenient way to construct and manipulate simple structures of variables and functions. But neither provides any help with symbolic mathematics—the transformation of mathematical expressions according to applicable rewriting rules. Consider, for example, the commutative laws of arithmetic. A procedural language or spreadsheet will evaluate the expression $(a + b)$, but it will not tell you that, since addition is commutative, you can replace it with the equivalent expression $(b + a)$. Nor will it tell you that, since subtraction is not commutative, you cannot replace $(a - b)$ by $(b - a)$. Construction of sophisticated mathematical models, such as those used in structural, thermal, lighting, and acoustic analysis of buildings, frequently involves derivation of formulae by applying rewriting rules—simplifying equations, using trigonometric identities, symbolically differentiating and integrating, and so on. You have to derive the required formulae manually before you can write a procedure or produce a spreadsheet model to evaluate these formulae. This can be an intellectually demanding task, requiring considerable mathematical sophistication and substantial effort.

Symbolic mathematics systems such as Mathematica provide powerful tools for automatic derivation of formulae by application of rewriting rules. In addition, they have large libraries of built-in mathematical functions (typically hundreds of them) so that they can perform like enormously sophisticated scientific calculators to evaluate these formulae. Finally, they provide versatile output capabilities: results can be displayed in numeric form, as two-dimensional and three-dimensional graphs of the values of functions, and even as sounds produced by interpreting functions as waveforms.

These systems were first conceived as tools for scientists and engineers. Of broader significance, though, is the way that they make centuries of accumulated mathematical expertise available to nonspecialists who have substantive problems to investigate. They will be increasingly widely used as tools for technical analysis and problem solving in design.

Feasibility and Optimality

So far we have considered the flow of information from values of independent variables of a model to values of the dependent variables. Sometimes, however, designers need to reverse this flow—to find values for independent variables that produce satisfactory values for the dependent variables.

Consider, for example, the design of a rectangular room in which *Length*, *Width*, and *Height* are the independent variables and *Plan_Proportion*, *Floor_Area*, *Perimeter*, and *Volume* are the dependent variables. We want to choose values for the independent variables such that certain constraints on the values of *Plan_Proportion*, *Floor_Area*, and *Perimeter* are satisfied. Figure 3.18 illustrates the logic of this situation. The space of possible solutions is represented by a three-dimensional Cartesian coordinate system in which each point stands for a combination of values for *Length*, *Width*, and *Height* (figure 3.18a). Reasonable upper and lower bounds for these independent variables are thus represented by horizontal and vertical planes that enclose a rectangular box-shaped subspace (figure 3.18b). Constraints on *Plan_Proportion* are represented by planes that bound a wedge-shaped subspace (figure 3.18c). Intersection of the box and the wedge yields a domain of feasible solutions (figure 3.18d). Further constraints on *Floor_Area* and *Perimeter* define subspaces as shown in figures 3.18e and 3.18f respectively. Intersecting all these subspaces yields the domain of feasible solutions with respect to all the constraints (figures 3.18g and 3.18h). We can then order these feasible solutions according to their values for *Volume*.

The flow diagram for a simple computer program to find a feasible solution with the largest possible value for *Volume* is illustrated in figure 3.19. It consists basically of three nested loops that enumerate combinations of values for *Length*, *Width*, and *Height*. Within the inner loop, corresponding values for the dependent variables *Plan_Proportion*, *Floor_Area*, and *Perimeter* are calculated and tested for feasibility. Whenever a feasible solution is found, the value of *Volume* for this solution is calculated. This value is compared to the largest previously found value of *Volume*, and if it is found to be larger it is recorded (together with the corresponding values of the independent variables) as the new largest value. On exit from the outermost loop, the currently recorded alternative is the solution to the problem. Generate-and-test procedures of this basic form provide a very general (but extremely inefficient) way to optimize systems subject to constraints.

More sophisticated constraint-solving and optimization programs use clever strategies to avoid exhaustive enumeration of feasible solutions, and, indeed, such enumeration is often impractical for realistic problems. For a system of real variables, linear constraints, and a linear function to be minimized, for example, it can be shown

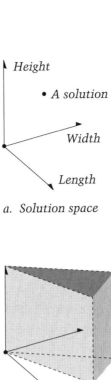

Height

• *A solution*

Width

Length

a. *Solution space*

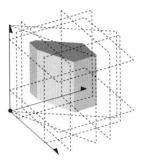

b. *Constraints on Length, Width, and Height*

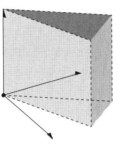

c. *Constraints on Plan_Proportion*

d. *Intersection of box and wedge*

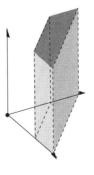

e. *Constraints on Perimeter*

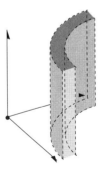

f. *Constraints on Floor_Area*

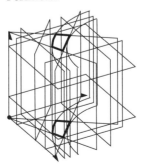

g. *All constraints*

h. *Feasible solutions*

3.18
A solution space and subspaces defined by constraints

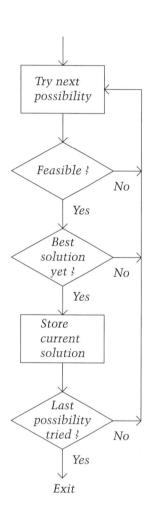

3.19
Simple generate-and-test
procedure

that the optimal solution will always be found at a vertex of a convex, plane-faced volume enclosing the feasible solutions. Linear programming procedures can take advantage of this fact to find (with great efficiency) optimal solutions to problems with thousands of variables and constraints.

Engineers frequently use programs written in procedural languages to perform specialized optimization tasks such as finding structural members with the minimum cross-sectional area needed to provide required strength, air-conditioning system configurations with the minimum capacity needed to handle anticipated climatic and occupancy conditions, and so on. Where a specialized program is not available for an optimization task, generalized optimization systems can often be used (with a bit more effort) to do the job. Many optimization problems require minimization of a linear function subject to linear constraints, for example, and general linear programming systems can be used for efficient solution of extremely large problems of this sort. Finally, if an appropriate general optimization system is not available, a symbolic mathematics system might be used to derive formulae for the objective function and constraints and to investigate the behavior of the objective function by plotting graphs for ranges of values of design variables or by setting the value of its first derivative to zero.

In the past architects, landscape architects, and urban designers have made little practical use of rigorous, formal procedures for finding feasible and optimal design solutions. Ad hoc trial-and-error has usually been preferred to carrying out lengthy, tedious numerical computations by hand. But the computer eliminates the need for this hand computation, and as designers realize the advantages of efficiency and rigor that search and optimization programs provide, such programs will become an increasingly important part of a designer's everyday tool kit.

Use of formal optimization techniques does not mean that design reduces to search and optimization. Formulation of the problem is the creative part: a search or optimization program just efficiently teases out the consequences logically implicit in a formulation and frees the designer from the totally mechanical task of deriving these consequences by hand. Nor does it mean that simplistic technical objectives replace subtle and complex design intentions: discovery of a technical optimum provides information about what is logically possible, but does not determine what should be.

Interpretation and Abstraction of Numerical Models

Early computer technology foregrounded numerical models and numerical computation. Computers were designed to serve primarily as number crunchers that accepted numerical data on punched cards or tape and printed out numerical results, and programming was largely a matter of expressing mathematical formulae in processable guise. (The name of a popular early programming language, Fortran, actually stands for "formula translator.") But this is, by now, a highly anachronistic conception of practical computing. Modern computer environments interpret and abstract underlying numerical models, thereby shielding users (and to an increasing extent programmers) from the intricate internal machinery of numerical data structures, formulae, and calculation procedures, and often completely eliminating the need to deal with numerical input and output (figure 3.20).

Output devices and associated software provide one important means of interpretation: they automatically convert streams of numbers generated by computations into pictures, sounds, text displays, robot motions, and so on. Conversely, input devices and associated software automatically convert keystrokes, mouse positions, audio and video signals, readings from scientific instruments, and the like into numbers. Thus input and output devices are like a cloak of disguise that wraps a computer and enables it to play many different roles. Figure 3.21 shows some of the roles and disguises that will concern us in the following chapters.

Abstraction has the effect of dividing a computer system into a hierarchy of levels, such that the elements and operations at the highest level are those that are

Input:
pictures
texts
sounds
gestures
etc.

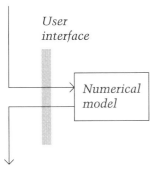

User interface

Numerical model

Output:
pictures
texts
sounds
gestures
etc.

3.20
Eliminating the need for numerical input and output

Role	Input	Output
Text processor	Character keyboard	Text display
Musical instrument	Musical keyboard	Sound synthesizer
Speech system	Microphone	Speaker
Read-aloud system	Text scanner	Speaker
Image processor	Video camera	Graphic display
Drafting system	Mouse or stylus	Graphic display
Virtual reality system	Dataglove	Head-mounted display

3.21
Roles and disguises

directly presented to the user via input and output devices, elements and operations at a high level are always implemented as structures of elements and operations at the next lower level, and the lowest level is the level of actual hardware operations. Figure 3.22, for example, shows the basic abstraction hierarchy for a computer drafting system.

The user of this system sees a graphic display of lines and arcs and uses a mouse to specify where such elements should be inserted, to select elements, and to select deletion and transformation tools to apply. The programmer of the underlying numerical model uses a language such as Pascal or C to declare data structures for storage of numerical coordinates describing these graphic elements and writes procedures that express graphic operations in terms of sequences of arithmetic operations on the coordinate data. The language compiler interprets decimal numbers as binary numbers and instructions expressed in the language as sequences of very basic operations on binary data. Finally, the hardware stores binary values as states of two-state electronic devices and performs operations by means of arrangements of registers and switching circuits.

Level	Basic elements	Basic operations
Drafting system	Lines, arcs, etc.	Insertion, selection, deletion, transformation
Numerical model	Coordinate vectors, transformation matrices	Addition, subtraction, multiplication, division
Binary model	Bits, bit vectors	Boolean operations, binary arithmetic
Hardware	Logic circuits	Switching

3.22
Abstraction hierarchy of a drafting system

The advantage of organizing a system in this way is that it enables you to work at any level without knowing or caring about what happens at the other levels—as long as the level-to-level interfaces are well defined. The user of a drafting system does not need to know the details of how coordinate vectors are stored in a data structure and multiplied by matrices to accomplish geometric transformations (unless some malfunction or failure requires investigation), any more than the driver of an automobile needs to know the details of how an internal combustion engine works. Conversely, if the programmer of a drafting system knows the functions that the system must provide, he or she need know very little about how the system is actually used to construct building plans, elevations, and sections.

Conclusion

Real numbers for expressing measures, integers for expressing counts and rankings, and binary digits for expressing the truth or falsehood of assertions together provide a precise and versatile medium for describing systems that may interest designers. Furthermore, structures of such systems may be specified by writing functions that interconnect the values of numerical descriptor variables. Then system behavior may be explored by assigning values to independent variables and evaluating functions. Programs may be written in procedural languages to do the work of evaluation, and spreadsheet or symbolic mathematics systems may also be used. These programs and systems replace hand algorithms (such as the long-division algorithm with which generations of schoolchildren have been tortured), slide rules, specialized analog devices such as planimeters and daylight protractors, nomograms and other graphical computation aids, mechanical calculators, and even electronic hand calculators.

Traditionally, scientists and engineers have worked directly with sophisticated numerical models (and have often used computers to help them), while designers have worked with graphic media and other nonnumeric representations. Now the distinction has disappeared: computers work internally with numerical models, but through their capacity for interpretation and abstraction they can accept input data and instructions and produce output in whatever form is appropriate to the task at hand.

Suggested Readings

Dantzig, Tobias. 1954. *Number: The Language of Science.* Fourth edition. New York: The Free Press.

Ellis, Brian. 1968. *Basic Concepts of Measurement.* Cambridge: Cambridge University Press.

Goodman, Nelson. 1976. "The Theory of Notation." In *Languages of Art.* Indianapolis: Hackett.

Radford, Antony D., and John S. Gero. 1988. *Design by Optimization in Architecture, Building, and Construction.* New York: Van Nostrand Reinhold.

Rucker, Rudy. 1987. *Mind Tools: The Five Levels of Mathematical Reality.* Boston: Houghton Mifflin.

Sterbenz, P. H. 1974. *Floating Point Computation.* Englewood Cliffs: Prentice Hall.

Tufte, Edward. 1990. *The Visual Display of Quantitative Information.* Cheshire CT: Cheshire Press.

4

WORDS AND TEXTS

Mies van der Rohe (a man of few words himself) admonished architects to draw, not talk. But modern design professionals cannot afford the luxury of silence: production of verbal information (often in large quantities) is a continual, inescapable necessity. Text processing, then, is one of the most obvious and mundane of computer applications in design practice—but careful examination of how computer resources are organized and applied to accomplish it provides a useful starting point for discussion of computer-aided design in general.

Characters

Printed texts like this one are, in essence, arbitrarily long strings of characters. These characters are drawn from some well-defined character set such as that of a standard English-language keyboard. (There are, of course, other standard character sets for texts in Greek, Hebrew, Sanskrit, Russian, Chinese, Japanese, Korean, and so on.) Each character in the character set can, through use of an appropriate coding scheme, be represented by a sequence of binary digits. The ASCII code, which is normally used for encoding text into binary format for storage in computer memory, employs eight bits (one byte) to represent each character (figure 4.1). Thus an ASCII text system can have a character set of up to 256 different characters—more than enough to allow construction of texts from uppercase

Char.	Code	Binary code
A	65	01000001
B	66	01000010
C	67	01000011
a	97	01100001
b	98	01100010
c	99	01100011
,	44	00101100
/	47	00101111
0	48	00110000
1	49	00110001
2	50	00110010
3	51	00110011
â	131	10000011
ä	132	10000100
à	133	10000101

4.1
ASCII coding of keyboard characters

the quick| fox

the|fox
⟵

the quick brown|fox
⟶

the quick dog|
⟶

4.2
Deleting, inserting,
overwriting text

and lowercase alphabetic characters, numerals, punctuation marks, accents, spaces, and a selection of special symbols. Larger character sets, for Kanji text processing for instance, require more complex coding schemes.

ASCII text files are simply sequences of encoded characters. Basic text-editing systems for operating on such files thus provide, at the very least, facilities for entering characters into the file by typing, for selecting character substrings, and for deleting, copying, and moving selected substrings (figure 4.2). Slightly more sophisticated systems also provide the capacity to search for instances of a specified substring (such as *Chicago*) and replace them with instances of some other substring (such as *Los Angeles*). Text editors of this sort are fairly cumbersome to use but very general in their application: they can handle standard English prose, extracts from *Finnegan's Wake*, Pascal or Lisp code, stanzas of *Jabberwocky*, or completely random character sequences like those produced by the scholars that Gulliver encountered at the Academy of Lagado.

Words

Word-processing systems are slightly more specialized than basic text editors, and as a result they more effectively perform the particular tasks for which they are intended. They exploit an elementary structural property of English (though not all) texts—that such texts consist of discrete words comprising short strings of characters separated by spaces and punctuation marks. Thus they can provide operations not just on characters, but on entire words. They can, for example, count and report the number of words in a file. More usefully, they can compare words in the file with those of a stored lexicon and report as possible spelling errors those that fail to match. Furthermore, they can provide the functions of a thesaurus by cross-indexing the lexicon so that the user can instantly retrieve lists of the synonyms and antonyms of selected words. (Notice, however, that a word processor with a standard lexicon would be defeated by the nonstandard spellings and meanings of the words of *Jabberwocky* or *Finnegan's Wake*.)

Or words in the lexicons of different languages (such as English and French) can be cross-linked to provide the functions of a translating dictionary.

A lexicon is usually much larger than a character set, so software that recognizes and operates on words (rather than just strings of characters) tends to require more computer resources. The lexicon must be stored (which consumes memory space) and searched (which consumes time).

Sentences

Most texts are not just arbitrary strings of words. If we take a higher-level view we find that they consist of larger units—sentences—structured according to the syntactic rules of a language such as English, French, Pascal, or Lisp. Since most interesting languages have very large or even infinite numbers of sentences, it is usually impractical to check these sentences for correctness by matching them against a list of allowable possibilities, but it is often possible to write software that will parse sentences to determine syntactic correctness. In particular, the syntax of a computer programming language is explicit, rigorously defined, and usually relatively simple, so specialized text processors designed for producing code in such languages normally incorporate syntax-checking capabilities.

The syntax of a natural language such as English tends to be more complex, and less consistent and explicit, but syntax checkers have been written for them with increasing success. As a result, some of the more sophisticated text processors intended for use by technical writers, journalists, and so on can report incorrect or undesirable syntax and even suggest ways to restructure problem sentences. They are of little help, however, to novelists who employ complex and nonstandard sentence constructions, and they break down completely when confronted with the unpredictably deviant structures that so delight poets: applying a syntax checker to lines by William Blake will not unravel their mysteries.

Sentence translation is a much more complex task than word translation, but it is routinely carried out for computer languages. The function of a computer language compiler or interpreter is to translate sentences in a language such as Pascal or Lisp into sequences of binary digits that specify sequences of processor operations. It is also possible to implement translators from, say, Pascal to Lisp. Sentence translation between natural languages such as English and French requires very sophisticated software, but this has been produced with increasing success. Such software cannot yet match the performance of skilled human translators on tasks such as translation of Racine into correspondingly elegant English (and perhaps never will), but it can often produce acceptable results when applied to technical papers, newspaper articles, and the like.

Complete Texts

Complete texts, like complete sentences, have definite limits. For example, books and Pascal programs mark their boundaries by means of a title at the beginning and the symbol *End* at the end. In between come the constituent sentences. These are arranged in a particular sequence, and they may be grouped into subunits such as paragraphs, stanzas, procedures, chapters, and sections. In some cases there are supplementary pointer structures (tables of contents, indexes, cross-references, footnotes, and so on) to facilitate navigation through the text. Some types of texts, like Pascal programs and haiku, must be structured according to very precise and explicit rules. Others, like novels, are more loosely structured.

The most specialized and powerful text-processing systems are those designed specifically for producing and editing texts of particular types. These exploit knowledge of the rules governing these texts to provide functions such as automatic checking for completeness and consistency, automatic construction and maintenance of supplementary pointer structures, and automatic infill of detail (for example, closing parentheses in Lisp programs). Some will provide suggestions through use of a built-in thesaurus or even rhyming dictionaries. Specialized editors for computer programs in particular languages are the most commonly encountered examples of this sort of system, but outline processors for producing hierarchically organized technical documents, text processors specifically intended for handling the apparatus of scholarly papers, and even processors for haiku, sonnets, and other structured poetic forms are all finding increasing application.

Formatting for Display and Printing

Text stored in computer memory is incorporeal and invisible, but a text-processing system makes it visible to us by displaying it on a screen or printing it on paper. When this is done, the text is shaped into a specific physical form: characters are given particular shapes and spacings, and the one-dimensional string of characters is arranged into some pattern on a two-dimensional surface. The crafts of typography and layout come into play (figure 4.3).

However, text-processing software allows us to pursue these traditional crafts in a fundamentally new way. With an old-fashioned typewriter, for example, you had to lay out a text on the page as you produced it. Decisions about typeface, margins, whether to single-space or

4.3
Format properties

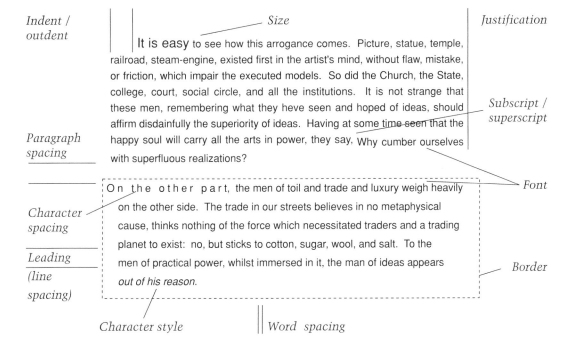

Indent / outdent

Size

Justification

It is easy to see how this arrogance comes. Picture, statue, temple, railroad, steam-engine, existed first in the artist's mind, without flaw, mistake, or friction, which impair the executed models. So did the Church, the State, college, court, social circle, and all the institutions. It is not strange that these men, remembering what they heve seen and hoped of ideas, should affirm disdainfully the superiority of ideas. Having at some time seen that the happy soul will carry all the arts in power, they say, Why cumber ourselves with superfluous realizations?

Subscript / superscript

Paragraph spacing

On the other part, the men of toil and trade and luxury weigh heavily on the other side. The trade in our streets believes in no metaphysical cause, thinks nothing of the force which necessitated traders and a trading planet to exist: no, but sticks to cotton, sugar, wool, and salt. To the men of practical power, whilst immersed in it, the man of ideas appears out of his reason.

Font

Character spacing

Leading (line spacing)

Border

Character style

Word spacing

double-space, and so on had to be made before you executed the keystrokes and could not be changed later. The computer reverses this. With a text processor you can make and alter format decisions at any time—before, during, and after input of a text file. Furthermore, you can produce differently formatted text documents, perhaps printed on different types of output devices, from the same file. Thus text processors provide many tools for specifying the way that an unformatted text file is to be translated into a formatted printed document.

Formatting tools operate at different levels of a hierarchy—typically those of the character, the paragraph, the section, and the complete document. At the character level, for example, you can usually specify a font (figure 4.4), a style (bold, italic, etc.), and a spacing (normal, condensed, or expanded). The most sophisticated software, for use with correspondingly high-quality printers, provides for precise control of refinements such as kerning and leading. At the paragraph level you need to control margins, indents, justification, and spacing. If a document is subdivided into sections or chapters, you need to specify

4.4
Examples of fonts

ABCDEFGHIJKLMNOPQRSTU
123456789
abcdefghijklmnopqrstuvwxy
abcdefghijklmnopqrstuvwx
ABCD abcd ABCD abcd

ABCDEFGHIJKLMNOPQRSTU
123456789
abcdefghijklmnopqrstuvwxy
abcdefghijklmnopqrstuvwxy
ABCD abcd ABCD abcd

ABCDEFGHIJKLMNOPQRSTU
123456789
abcdefghijklmnopqrstuvwxyz
abcdefghijklmnopqrstuvwxyz
ABCD abcd ABCD abcd

Body: indent first 0.25 in, justified, leading 15 pt

Quotes: justified, leading 10 pt, space 10 pt before 10 pt after

Captions: font 9 pt, leading 11 pt, first line bold

Illustrations: font 9 pt, italics, leading 11 pt

Subhead: font 12 pt, bold expanded 1 pt, leading 20 pt, space before 20 pt after 5 pt

Folio: font 8 pt, caps, width 120%, flush left

4.5
Text styles

4.6
Formation of characters
from dots

the conventions for beginning and ending these. Finally, at the level of the complete document, you need to control headers, gutters, positioning of page numbers, and numerous other details.

In everyday document production most people want to focus on content rather than details of formatting. In response to this, text-processing software usually provides a repertoire of standard formats (known as "styles") that can be selected from a menu for automatic application to specified pieces of text (figure 4.5). These styles may be edited, and new ones may be added to the repertoire. This is a powerful capability: you can change the format of an entire document, such as a book, simply by editing its style specification.

Producing Printed Output

There are many kinds of printers, but use of a laser printer of some kind has become the standard way to produce printed output of high typographic quality from a text-processing system. A laser printer deposits a matrix of microscopic black dots on the paper surface, and individual characters are built up from these dots (figure 4.6). Inexpensive models have a resolution of a few hundred dots per inch, while the more sophisticated models (which allow much greater typographic refinement) have resolutions of up to several thousand dots per inch.

To control a laser printer, text files and associated formatting information must be translated into instructions for depositing dots on the page. This translation is a surprisingly complex task, since it must take account of numerous subtle typographic issues, and it is usually accomplished by programs written in special languages such as Postscript. If you want to develop your own fonts, or customize other typographic details, you can write your own printer-control programs.

Page-layout programs can be used to control positioning of text blocks and illustrations on laser-printed pages (figure 4.7). (The pages of this book were produced with a layout program running on a personal computer.)

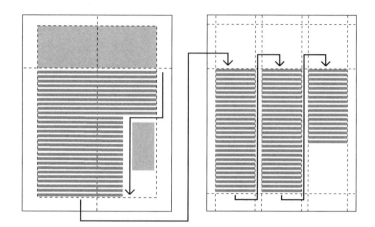

4.7
One-dimensional text
flowing into two-
dimensional fields

Textual Analysis

Many text-processing systems provide simple textual-analysis functions. General-purpose word processors, for example, can usually produce counts of characters, words, lines, and paragraphs in a selected fragment of text. More specialized systems, for use in literary stylistics, can produce elaborate statistical analyses of word frequencies.

Some much more elaborate systems can, with at least partial success, scan through texts to extract pertinent facts. Experimental systems have been developed, for example, to receive wire-service news text and sift out items on specified topics of interest. In the future designers and other professionals will probably depend heavily on the assistance of knowbots—systems that scan through building codes, technical reference manuals, and the like to find extracts relevant to a task at hand.

Automated Synthesis

Texts of various kinds can be synthesized automatically by recursive application of rewriting rules to strings of characters. Figure 4.8a shows a simple example of some rewriting rules for production of English sentences. The vocabulary of symbols manipulated by these rules consists of terminals (words that can appear in finished sentences) and markers that can be rewritten. (The markers are shown in italics.) The rules are applied recursively to a starting symbol to derive strings of words. A rule applies when its left-hand side matches a substring of the current string. A derivation

a. Rewriting rules

1. *sentence* → *nounphrase verbphrase*
2. *nounphrase* → *article noun*
3. *verbphrase* → *verb nounphrase*
4. *article* → a, the
5. *noun* → dog, cat
6. *verb* → chased, bit

b. Derivation of a sentence

sentence (starting symbol)
nounphrase verbphrase (by rule 1)
article noun verbphrase (by rule 2)
article noun verb nounphrase (by rule 3)
article noun verb article noun (by rule 2)
the *noun verb article noun (by rule 4)*
the dog *verb article noun (by rule 5)*
the dog chased *article noun (by rule 6)*
the dog chased a *noun (by rule 4)*
the dog chased a cat *(by rule 5. termination)*

4.8
Rewriting rules and their
application

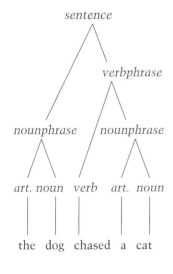

4.9
Syntax tree for a sentence

terminates when no further rule applications can be made. Figure 4.8b illustrates the derivation of a terminal string.

The vocabulary, starting symbol, and rewriting rules together constitute a phrase-structure grammar for a subset of English. The sentences derivable by this grammar constitute the language that it specifies. Each sentence in the language has a hierarchical structure determined by the rewriting rules, as shown in figure 4.9.

Instead of being run generatively, the grammar can be run in reverse to determine whether or not a given string is a sentence in the language. The rewriting rules now become reductions (figure 4.10a). If a sequence of applications can reduce a string of words to the starting symbol, then the string is a sentence in the language (figure 4.10b). Otherwise it is not.

As we shall see in later chapters, the idea of generative grammars consisting of rewriting rules is of very general importance in digital design media. Rewriting rules can specify and parse not only strings of words, but also strings of musical sounds, two-dimensional arrangements of shapes, three-dimensional arrangements of solid building blocks, and four-dimensional choreographies of solids moving in space.

a. Reductions

1. *nounphrase verbphrase → sentence*
2. *article noun → nounphrase*
3. *verb nounphrase → verbphrase*
4. a, the → *article*
5. dog, cat → *noun*
6. chased, bit → *verb*

b. Parsing a sentence with reductions

the cat bit the dog
article cat bit the dog *(by rule 4)*
article noun bit the dog *(by rule 5)*
nounphrase bit the dog *(by rule 2)*
nounphrase verb the dog *(by rule 6)*
nounphrase verb article dog *(by rule 4)*
nounphrase verb article noun (by rule 5)
nounphrase verb nounphrase (by rule 2)
nounphrase verbphrase (by rule 3)
sentence (by rule 1. termination)

4.10
Reductions and their application

Levels of Structure and Significance

We have now seen that text has a hierarchy of syntactic units, such that higher-level units are built up by stringing together lower-level units. Bits are strung together to make characters, characters are strung together to make words, words are strung together to make phrases, phrases are strung together to make sentences, and sentences are strung together to make texts.

At each level in this hierarchy there are structural rules and standards of correctness (though these are clearer at the lower levels than at the higher levels). Not every string of bits specifies an ASCII character, and it is trivial to check whether a given string does or does not. An arbitrary string of characters does not necessarily make an English word, and it is fairly easy to check a string against a (large) lexicon to determine whether it does or not. Sentences in a particular language may be indefinitely numerous, but they are governed by identifiable rules of syntax, and it is often possible to write software that will check for compliance with these rules. Some classes of complete texts composed of many sentences (sonnets, Pascal programs, and so on) are also governed by fairly well-defined structural rules.

Corresponding to the syntactic levels there are levels of meaning and of operations. A bit is the elementary, atomic unit of information: it can be understood as the answer to a yes/no question. You could write an ASCII file, bit by bit, using a keyboard consisting of just two keys—but this would be ludicrously tedious. A far more practical strategy is to work at the molecular level—that of characters—using a more extensive keyboard, software that translates keystrokes into ASCII code and ASCII code into displayed characters, and basic text-editing operations. When characters are combined into words, these words can, with appropriate software, be interpreted automatically through use of a dictionary, thesaurus, translating dictionary, or even rhyming dictionary. When words are combined into sentences, these sentences can, through use of various different kinds of software, be interpreted as other things—sentences in some other language, sequences of machine operations, melodies, or pictures. Just as the meaning of a sentence is determined by the meanings and relationships of the constituent words, so the meaning of a recipe, program, narrative, description, or dialogue is determined by the meanings and relationships of the constituent sentences. Highly specialized text processors—program editors for particular programming languages, outline processors for technical documents, automatic haiku generators, and so on—provide powerful tools for constructing, manipulating, and analyzing these sorts of structures.

Suggested Readings

Chappell, Warren. 1970. *A Short History of the Printed Word*. New York: Alfred A. Knopf.

Heim, Michael. 1987. *Electric Language: A Philosophical Study of Word Processing*. New Haven: Yale University Press.

Kenner, Hugh. 1987. *The Mechanic Muse*. New York: Oxford University Press.

Knuth, Donald E. 1982. "The Concept of a Metafont.". *Visual Language* 17 (Winter 1982) : 3–27.

Knuth, Donald E. 1986. *The Metafont Book.* Reading, Mass.: Addison-Wesley.

RACTER. 1984. *The Policeman's Beard is Half-Constructed: Computer Prose and Poetry by RACTER.* New York: Warner Books.

Rubintein, Richard. 1988. *Digital Typography.* Reading, Mass.: Addison-Wesley.

Smith, Peter. 1990. *An Introduction to Text Processing.* Cambridge: The MIT Press.

Smith, Ross. 1990. *Learning Postscript—A Visual Approach.* Berkeley: Peachpit.

White, Jan V. 1988. *Graphic Design for the Electronic Age.* New York: Xerox Press / Watson-Guptill.

5

SOUNDS

Sounds are rapid vibrations transmitted to our eardrums through variations in air pressure. If you were, for example, to plot air pressure (that is, sound intensity) as a function of time for a pure tone, you would produce an undulating line like that shown in figure 5.1. This is analog information: intensity varies continuously with time. But if you were to sample the intensity with some finite level of precision at finite time intervals, you would produce a stepped line. This is digital information: intensity varies in discrete steps. By recording intensities with greater precision, and sampling at closer intervals, you can make the digital representation of a sound approximate the analog representation as closely as you may wish.

Once sounds have been encoded digitally they can be stored in computer memory, manipulated by computer programs, and played back through sound output devices. Thus computers can be employed to process digitally encoded sound effects, speech, and music in ways closely analogous to their use in processing digitally encoded text.

Sampling, Quantization, and Compression

Some personal computers and workstations now have built-in microphones for direct input of sound. Others provide for connection of microphones as peripheral devices or for sound input from audio tape recorders. In any case,

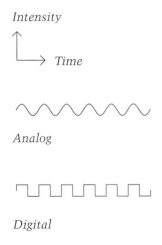

Intensity

Time

Analog

Digital

5.1
Continuous and discrete variations

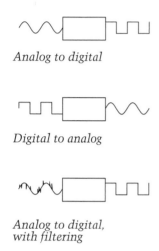

Analog to digital

Digital to analog

*Analog to digital,
with filtering*

5.2
Analog/digital conversions

special analog-to-digital conversion circuity is used to convert the analog audio signal into binary digits. Conversely, for output, digital-to-analog conversion circuitry is used to produce a signal that drives a speaker. The small, built-in speaker of a personal computer or workstation may be used, or (for better dynamic range and higher power) the computer may be connected to a high-quality sound system.

The functions of analog-to-digital conversion for recording and digital-to-analog conversion for playback are usually performed by special sound boards that contain the necessary circuitry (figure 5.2). These often perform additional signal-processing functions. They may, for example, filter input signals to remove unwanted hums, hisses, and pops.

The quality of digital sound depends on the sampling rate used in this analog-to-digital conversion (figure 5.3). Except for pure tones, sounds are mixtures of components of different frequencies, and Shannon's sampling theorem tells us that the sampling rate must be at least twice as high as the highest-frequency component present in the sampled signal. If this rule is not observed, then a phenomenon known as aliasing results: frequency components higher than half the sampling rate are recorded as other frequencies, and the sound is thus distorted. The rate of 48,000 samples/second, which is commonly used for making high-quality digital recordings of music, can capture without aliasing frequency components of up to 24,000 cycles/second—that is, above the upper limit of the audible range. However, much lower sampling rates can be used to produce understandable (though low-quality) recordings of speech.

Quality also depends on the number of bits used for quantization of each sample—that is, for expression of intensity as an integer number. Use of two bits per sample, for example, approximates each sample to one of only four different intensity levels. This usually results in gross distortion. Use of eight bits per sample, which allows distinction between 256 different intensity levels, produces much better results. The human ear can usually dis-

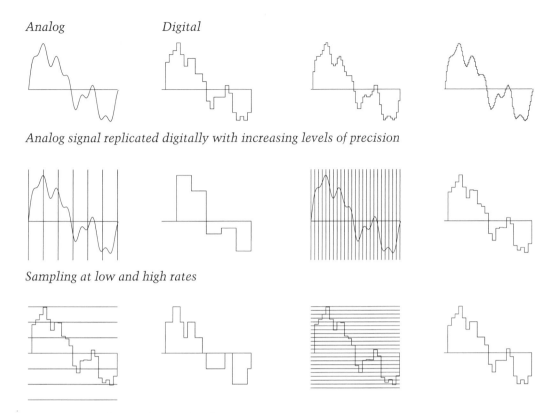

Analog　　　*Digital*

Analog signal replicated digitally with increasing levels of precision

Sampling at low and high rates

Quantizing at few and many levels

5.3
Digital sampling

criminate about 4,000 distinct levels (twelve bits/sample) and high-quality digital recordings are made at sixteen bits/sample.

The problem with high sampling rates and intensity resolutions is that they generate huge amounts of digital data. For example, one second of sound at 48,000 samples/second and sixteen bits/sample requires over eighty megabytes of storage—enough to completely fill the hard disk of a fairly powerful personal computer. There are several basic ways to solve this problem. The most obvious is to use some capacious, inexpensive digital storage medium such as CD/ROM. Another, which has been widely employed in personal computer applications, is simply to accept the quality limitations that follow from low sampling rates and intensity resolutions in order to achieve storage economy.

A third, more elegant approach to overcoming storage limitations is to compress digitally encoded sound for storage and decompress it for playback. One basic com-

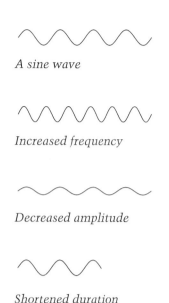

A sine wave

Increased frequency

Decreased amplitude

Shortened duration

5.4
Varying a sine wave

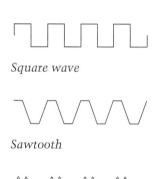

Square wave

Sawtooth

Harmonics

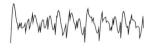

Random frequencies

5.5
A vocabulary of
waveforms

pression technique is based on the observation that the differences between successive intensities are usually much smaller than the absolute magnitudes. Thus a sequence of intensities can be encoded as a base intensity followed by a sequence of small integers specifying differences: the sequence 1024, 1025, 1025, 1026 would become 1024, 1, 0, 1. Since small integers can be expressed with fewer bits than large integers, this achieves storage economies. Future progress in computer processing of sound will depend directly on the ongoing development of fast compression/decompresion algorithms that achieve high compression ratios when applied to music and speech. But even using today's storage technology, it is already possible to amass enormous libraries of sounds for transformation and recombination in new and unforeseen ways.

Mathematical Specification of Sounds

Sounds can not only be recorded, but also synthesized from concise mathematical specifications. Consider a continuous pure tone. The corresponding sine wave can be produced by a simple program that repeatedly evaluates a sine function. Such a program can be controlled by three parameters—frequency, amplitude, and duration—to produce sounds like those depicted in figure 5.4. We can add sounds of different qualities to this basic repertoire by writing programs that generate square waves, sawtooths, white noise, and so on (figure 5.5).

Most interesting sounds, however, do not have uniform amplitude throughout their duration (figure 5.6). A piano note, for example, has attack and decay. Thus we might elaborate a sound-synthesis program by providing for variation of amplitude over a sound's duration. Different functions, controlled by appropriate parameters, can be used to produce different effects of amplitude variation. Similarly, frequency can be varied parametrically to produce siren sounds, sliding sounds, and so on.

Once we have a basic vocabulary of parametrically variable sound types, we can go a step further and provide for addition and subtraction of sounds, as illustrated in figure 5.7. Since the results of addition and subtraction

5.6
Decaying sound

operations can themselves be added and subtracted, this allows us to build up indefinitely complex sounds from simple components.

A piece of sound-generation software is, in effect, an artificial musical instrument. Instead of producing vibrations from a reed or string, it produces sequences of binary numbers that can be converted into an audio signal. And instead of providing keys, valves, and the like for control of sound production, it provides numerical parameters and mathematical operators.

Sequences and Notations

Sometimes we just want to specify production of a single sound—as a sound effect to punctuate a program, for example. Often, however, we want to specify sequences of sounds such as musical compositions and spoken sentences. This requires an appropriate notation system plus software (analogous to a text editor) for constructing, editing, and interpreting expressions in the notation.

A graphic notation system for a very simple artificial instrument is illustrated in figure 5.8. Each sound is represented by a rectangle. The type of sound is indicated by the pattern within the rectangle, duration by the length of the rectangle, frequency by the vertical position of the rectangle, and amplitude by the height of the rectangle. (More complex instruments have more parameters to control and hence require more elaborate notation systems.) Editing and playback software based on this notation might allow you to select sound types from a menu, shape and position the corresponding rectangles with a mouse, arrange rectangles into sequences, and play back the compositions that these sequences specify.

A regular rhythm might be depicted, in an extension of this notation, by vertical lines inserted at equal intervals—much like construction lines used to guide placement of columns in a building elevation (figure 5.9). The editing software might then snap sound rectangles to these lines so that sounds always start and stop exactly on the beat. Frequencies and amplitudes might similarly be constrained by snapping to equally spaced horizontal lines. To provide

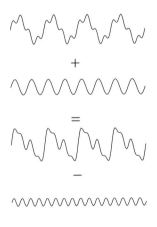

5.7
Addition and subtraction of waveforms

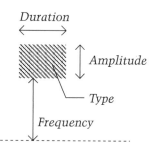

Duration

Amplitude

Type

Frequency

5.8
A simple graphical notation
for describing sounds

5.9
Snapping to locations in
time

5.10
Controls of a digital
sequencing system,
including real-time
note and track display

for multiple instruments, the notation system might be extended still further by introducing multiple tracks (figure 5.10). These tracks might be displayed in overlaid combinations as if on layers of transparent paper, or one beneath the other, to show relationships between the instruments. (Snapping to a regular grid and layering of information are ideas that we will encounter again when we consider drafting and geometric-modeling software.)

Traditional musical notation employs symbols that were designed for the pen rather than the mouse, and for specifying parameters of traditional instruments rather than digital synthesizers, but the principle is essentially the same. Sounds are represented by symbols that are arranged in sequences. Vertical position indicates frequency, and other graphic variables control additional parameters. Composition and playback software based on this notation allows you to select and arrange symbols and provides an artificial instrument that appropriately interprets the symbols as sounds.

One important distinction, however, is that digital sequencing notation can mix sound retrieved from memory with sound to be performed anew. Typical sequencers

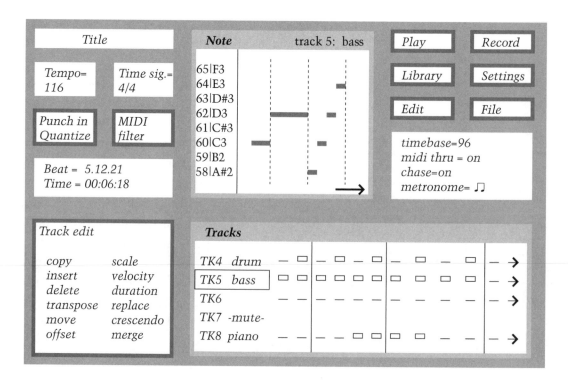

include notation for cueing samples and stored syntheses. Additional parameters specify duration, transformation, and overlay.

Figure 5.11 illustrates another kind of spatial notation of musical relationships, in the form of a villa by Palladio. Each room has a length, a width, and a height, which (as is well known) are usually related in harmonic ratios. These can be interpreted as frequencies of instruments in a three-track score, so that each room specifies a chord. Sequence and tempo are indeterminate, though constrained: you can take different paths at different paces from room to room. A playback device for this notation would interpret architecture as frozen music.

English text is also a notation (though a complex and not entirely consistent one); the human voice is a subtle instrument with many parameters; and reading text aloud is a particularly interesting case of a playback operation. There has been growing success in development of computer systems that can read aloud, either by processing text files or by scanning printed pages. Digital Equipment

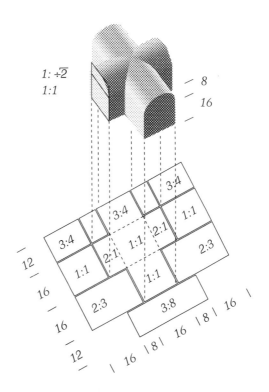

5.11
Architecture as frozen music

Corporation's DECtalk is an early example of a commercial system for this purpose. DECtalk uses a pronunciation dictionary of common words and a set of phonological rules to handle words not in the dictionary. More recently, the neural network NETtalk system developed at Johns Hopkins University by Terrence J. Sejnowski and Charles R. Rosenberg has demonstrated the capacity to learn correct English pronunciation from samples of text.

Transformations

A transformation is, in general, an operation that changes certain properties of an object while leaving its characteristic structure unchanged. Specifically, transformations of sound sequences leave certain relationships of the constituent sounds unchanged so that the sequence remains recognizable. Music is, to a large extent, a complex game of sound sequence transformation, so computer music software usually provides transformation operators as compositional tools.

One way to transform a sound sequence is to alter its tempo. This amounts to scaling the duration of the sequence so that all of the constituent sounds and the intervals of silence between them are shortened or lengthened in the same ratio (figure 5.12a). Similarly, the dynamic range can be scaled so that the whole thing becomes louder or softer (figure 5.12b). Adding a constant to every frequency value, or subtracting a constant, shifts the key of a sequence (figure 5.12c). Sequences can be reversed (figure 5.12d), and the scale can be inverted (figure 5.12e). These (and other) transformations can be combined with each other to produce extensive ranges of variations on a given theme.

Yet another way to transform a sound sequence is to play it on a different artificial instrument (figure 5.12f). This requires specification of a mapping from the sound repertoire of the first instrument to the sound repertoire of the second. The mapping might be arbitrary, but it will usually be chosen to preserve characteristic features of the sound sequence. Musicians use such mappings when they transcribe compositions written for one instrument into

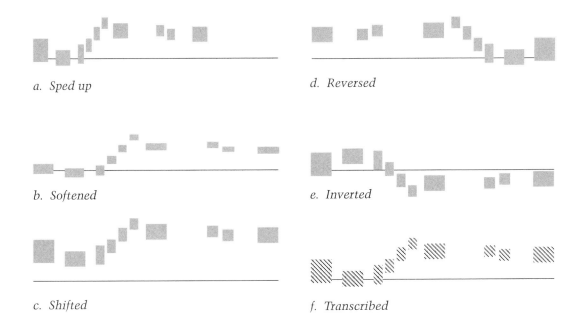

a. Sped up

d. Reversed

b. Softened

e. Inverted

c. Shifted

f. Transcribed

5.12
Transformations to a sequence

versions performable on other instruments. Closely analogous mappings are employed by word-processing systems when they transcribe text sequences into different fonts or transliterate Kanji into English characters, and by image-processing systems when they map color images on the computer screen to patterns of ink produced by a color printer.

Grammars and Syntax-directed Editing

We have seen that symbolic mathematics systems recursively apply rewriting rules to mathematical formulae to produce transformed formulae, and that systems for synthesizing sentences recursively apply rewriting rules to strings of characters. Similarly, rewriting rules can be used to produce sequences of symbols in musical notation systems—that is, grammatical compositions in a musical language.

Figure 5.13 illustrates a simple musical grammar based on our elementary rectangle notation system. The vocabulary consists of terminals (sounds of the instrument) and markers that can be rewritten. Markers define the frequency and duration boundaries of sequences of sounds and are depicted as empty rectangles. An initial marker defines the frequency and duration boundaries of the

B

Starting symbol

B → ABC

A →

B → ‖

C → ▐▄

Rewriting rules

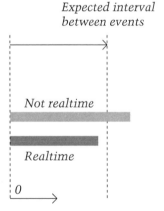

Some sound sequences in the language

5.13
A simple musical grammar

Expected interval between events

Not realtime

Realtime

0

Time required by computer to produce event

5.14
Realtime performance

entire composition. The rewriting rules are applied recursively to the initial marker to derive sequences of sounds that cannot be rewritten further—compositions in the musical language specified by the grammar.

Such grammars can be used for automatic generation and playback of musical compositions. Alternatively, they can support syntax-directed editing of scores. A syntax-directed editor might allow you to indicate a location in a score and then suggest sound sequences that could, according to the grammar, be substituted at that location. It might also allow you to select a sound sequence and then suggest locations for insertion of that sequence.

Playback

Playback software can either execute procedures to generate sounds as required or select from appropriately indexed repertoires of stored sounds. The former strategy makes heavy demands on processing capacity: you must have a sufficiently powerful processor at your disposal to generate complex sounds at high speed or must be content with simple sounds. The latter strategy makes heavy demands on memory capacity: you must have sufficient computer memory at your disposal to store a wide repertoire of sounds or you must be content with a restricted repertoire. In either case, the computer must reconstruct the signal at a rate that meets or exceeds the rate at which you expect to hear the sounds (figure 5.14).

Different playback techniques make the store-versus-compute trade-off in different ways and are thus suited to different computational environments and applications. Sounds generated by simple mathematical functions can usually be generated by software in real time. More complex musical sounds, and speech sounds, are often generated in real time by special chips. Some computer music systems depend on large repertoires of sampled sounds stored on hard disk.

Instead of synthesizing sound internally, a computer may send instructions to a separate synthesizer, much as it might send instructions to a printer, plotter, or milling machine. The synthesizer may employ any combination of analog circuitry, digital sound synthesis, and sampled sounds. MIDI is the standard language used to control synthesizers in this way, just as the Postscript language is used to control laser printers. Thus computer-controlled synthesizers are often referred to as MIDI instruments. They are modern equivalents of the player piano, controlled electronically rather than mechanically with a roll of punched paper.

Reconstructing sounds from digital rather than analog representations facilitates the elimination of noise. Any signal is degraded and distorted by transmission and storage media, all of which are ultimately analog. When an analog signal is played back directly, its imperfections are retained and show up as noise—bias on a tape or imperfections on a record, for example. When a digital representation is reconstructed, however, the signal is first converted from relative voltages to absolute zeros and ones. Minor deviations in the voltages—noise—thus have no effect. This characteristic makes digital representation useful not only in sound recording, but in any context where noise-free replication of information is required.

Sound Analysis

Digitally encoded sounds can be analyzed in many ways, and computer music systems typically incorporate some analysis capabilities. Many systems, for example, compute fast Fourier transforms (FFTs) to analyze a sound's harmonic spectrum and display the results graphically (figure 5.15). (Jean Baptiste Fourier discovered in the early nineteenth century that a complex waveform could be expressed as a sum of its frequency components—a fundamental basis for all telecommunications technology.) A Fourier transform breaks the waveform into its frequency components and shows how the amplitudes of the different frequencies vary over time. Results may be displayed either as a series of two-dimensional graphs of amplitude as a function of time or as a three-dimensional surface depicting amplitude as a function of frequency and time. Some systems allow FFT graphs to be edited interactively to specify new sounds.

Original sound

Component frequencies

5.15
A Fourier transform

Sound Recognition

A sound-recognition system is the inverse of a playback system: instead of converting notation into sounds, it converts sounds into notation. Thus a powerful sound-recognition system might (like a stenographer) take dictation to produce text documents or transcribe a musical performance into musical notation.

To accomplish such tasks, a sound-recognition system must segment a continuous stream of sound into discrete parts, then classify each part as an instance of some known type of sound. For example, a recognizer of continuous speech must segment input sound into phonemes (contrastive speech sounds), word sounds, and sentence sounds; classify word sounds as instances of words in its dictionary; parse sentences; and apply semantic rules to interpret sentences. These are all difficult computational tasks, especially when real-time performance is required.

By the early 1990s the technology of sound recognition had advanced to the point where systems capable of reliably recognizing single-word commands from a vocabulary of thousands were available as input devices for personal computers. An initial use for these systems in computer-aided design was to provide an extra input channel when both hands were occupied by keyboard and mouse.

Summary: One-dimensional Structures

Sound sequences and texts have much in common: from a computational viewpoint they are essentially one-dimensional structures of data elements in which each element has a unique predecessor and successor. Thus it is straightforward to translate back and forth between sounds and symbols. Sequences of spoken words can be written down, and a listener can record sequences of musical sounds in appropriate musical notation. Conversely, written text can be read aloud and musical scores can be performed. The designer's (author's, composer's) basic task, in each case, is to select elements and arrange them in sequence.

In the following chapters we will extend this idea to two-dimensional structures (images and drawings), three-dimensional structures (geometric models), and four-dimensional structures (animations). For each of these types of structures we shall examine the basic data elements and their digital representation, the ways that the data elements can be organized into larger structures (designs), and the computer tools that can be used to capture or create substructures and structures; to store, transform, and combine them; and to interpret them for output.

We shall find, however, that one-dimensional structures have a particular importance in computing, since computers (at least the sort that we shall consider here) are organized serially: their memories consist of serial-numbered locations, their programs are sequences of instructions, and their processors execute these instructions one by one. (The theoretical model on which practical computers are based, the so-called Turing machine, makes this basic serial organization very clear.) Thus, at some level (which may be invisible to the computer user) the two-dimensional, three-dimensional, and four-dimensional structures that concern designers must always be translated into one-dimensional structures.

Suggested Readings

Catalano, Fernando. 1990. "More Than Meets Our Ears: Voice Technology in CAD." *Architects' Journal* (14 November 1990): 59–62.

Goodman, Nelson. 1976. "Score, Sketch, and Script." In *Languages of Art.* Indianapolis: Hackett.

Holtzman, Steven. 1994. *Digital Mantras.* Cambridge: The MIT Press.

Mathews, Max V., and John R. Pierce (eds.). 1989. *Current Directions in Computer Music Research.* Cambridge: The MIT Press.

Moore, F. Richard. 1990. *Elements of Computer Music.* Englewood Cliffs: Prentice Hall.

Parker, Richard O. 1988. "An Introduction to Digital Signal Processing." *Journal of Engineering Computing and Applications* 2 (3): 6–10.

Roads, Curtis, and John Strawn (eds.). 1985. *Foundations of Computer Music.* Cambridge: The MIT Press.

Sejnowski, Terrence J., and Charles R. Rosenberg. 1988 [1986]. "NETtalk: A Parallel Network That Learns To Read Aloud." In James A. Anderson and Edward Rosenfeld (eds.), *Neurocomputing: Foundations of Research.* Cambridge: The MIT Press.

Stiny, George, and James Gips. 1979. *Algorithmic Aesthetics.* Berkeley: University of California Press.

Stawn, John. "Digital Audio Representation and Processing." Chapter 4 in John F. Koegel Buford, (ed.), *Multimedia Systems.* Reading, Mass.: Addison-Wesley.

Watkinson, John. 1988. *The Art of Digital Audio.* London: Focal Press.

6

IMAGES

Just as variations in sound intensity over time can be plotted as an undulating line, so variations in light intensity across a visual field can be plotted as an undulating surface (figure 6.1). The signal from a black-and-white video camera (which closely resembles the signal output by a microphone) describes this surface by taking a sequence of sections through it. When this signal is interpreted by an appropriate display device, such as a video monitor, a continuous-tone image results.

If a video signal is sampled with finite precision at discrete intervals, an approximation to the continuous-intensity surface results. This can be represented in computer memory as an array of integers, where each integer specifies an intensity (the height of one of the points making up the surface). By sampling intensities with greater precision, and at closer intervals, we can make this digital approximation approach the original continuous surface as closely as we may wish.

Pictures that are encoded and stored in this way are known as bitmapped images. The square array is called a raster grid (hence the term raster graphics), a single row from the grid is called a raster line, and a single square element is called a pixel (for "picture element"). Raster graphics display and printing devices interpret stored arrays of integers as visible arrays of square cells of corresponding intensities (figure 6.2). Systems for capturing, storing, manipulating, and displaying or printing such

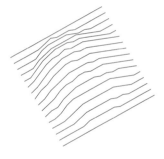

6.1
Variations in light intensity over a field

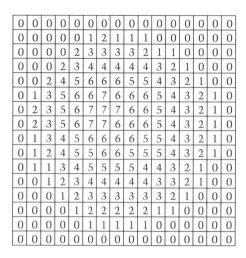

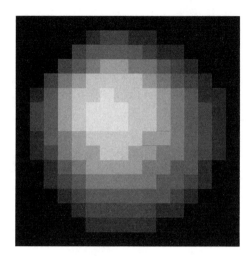

6.2
An array of intensity values
and its interpretation by a
display device

images (known as image-processing and paint systems)
have a wide and growing range of applications in design.

Scanning and Storage

The most immediate, least expensive way to capture a
bitmapped image is to translate a video signal into an array
of pixels. The signal may come directly from a video
camera, from a videocassette recorder, from a videodisc
player, or from a still-video player. The necessary analog-
to-digital conversion is accomplished through use of a
video frame grabber—a special board for a workstation or
personal computer (figure 6.3). A designer might, for
example, use a video camera for inexpensive, comprehensive site documentation, then capture important frames
from the resulting tape for further digital processing.

The disadvantage of video frame grabbing is that the
resulting bitmapped images are limited to video resolution—considerably less than one thousand pixels across
an image. Where better-quality images are needed, these
can be produced through use of the slower and more
expensive process of slide scanning. Devices for scanning
35 mm (and sometimes larger format) slides range from
desktop models designed for use with personal computers
to extremely expensive, high-precision models used in the
color printing industry. The more costly scanners are
capable of achieving higher resolution and greater fidelity
of tonal and color resolution, but even the least expensive

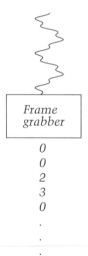

Video signal

Frame grabber

0
0
2
3
0
.
.
.

Intensity values

6.3
Frame grabber

desktop models can usually produce results that are adequate for most practical design purposes.

Flatbed scanners form an important link between traditional and digital graphic media. They look much like office copiers and convert ordinary drawings, photographic prints, or pages of text into high-resolution bitmapped images. The range of costs and performances is very wide: some are designed for black-and-white images, some for gray scale, and some for color; resolutions range upward from a few hundred points per inch; and formats range from letter size to the largest standard sizes of architectural and engineering drawings. In the future, as office copiers increasingly depend on digital rather than analog imaging technology, the distinction between flatbed scanners and copiers will largely disappear: you will be able to use an office copier as a graphic input device.

When bitmapped images are captured, they are stored temporarily on the hard disk of the workstation or personal computer connected to the capture device. But, since bitmapped image files tend to be large, they are usually transferred immediately to archival media such as floppy disk, optical disk, or tape. These media also serve for publication of collections of bitmapped images.

Low-resolution Images

The lowest precision at which intensities may be recorded is one bit per pixel. That is, intensities below a certain threshold are coded as zero and intensities above that threshold are coded as one to produce an array of bits. This array is interpreted by display devices as a stark black-and-white image, with no intermediate tones.

The quality of such an image depends directly on the spatial resolution (figure 6.4). If the spatial resolution is too low, then aliasing will result: diagonal straight lines will be stair-stepped, the shapes of contours will be unacceptably distorted, and fine textures will either clog up into black areas, burn out to white, or be rendered as spurious periodic patterns. These distortions are closely analogous to the distortions that result when sounds are digitally recorded at too low a sample rate.

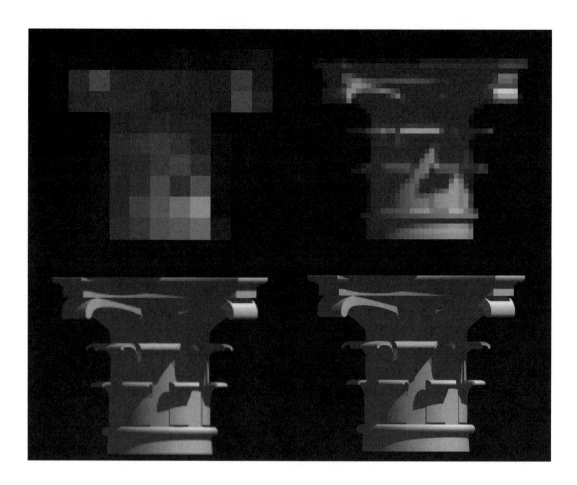

6.4
Increasing levels of
spatial resolution

High-resolution Images

Increasing the precision with which intensities are recorded
yields more intermediate tones (figure 6.5). Using two bits
per pixel yields a scale of four tones, three bits gives eight
tones, four bits gives sixteen tones, and so on. Achieving
completely smooth-looking gradations of tone requires
eight bits per pixel, which gives a scale of 256 discrete
tones. The effects of inadequate tonal resolution are
contouring in areas of continuous tonal gradation and the
muddying of fine detail.

For most practical purposes a spatial resolution of
about one thousand by one thousand pixels, with a tonal
resolution of eight bits per pixel, suffices to produce a gray-
scale image of good quality. Without compression, this
amounts to a megabyte of data. A two thousand by two
thousand image requires four megabytes. As with digital
sound, then, the storage requirements for digital images

are high, so inexpensive storage media and compression/decompression techniques become important.

Image Compression

One straightforward and popular compression technique for bitmapped images is known as run-length encoding (figure 6.6). It exploits the property of many (though not all) bitmapped images that long strings of successive pixels along a raster line have the same value. Thus it is more efficient to describe these strings by specifying the common value and the number of pixels in the string than it is to enumerate pixel values one by one. Procedures for converting bitmapped images into run-length encoded format, and converting back, are simple and quick.

Another common technique is known as quadtree encoding. This also exploits the property that there are often large, unbroken areas of uniform value. The procedure for constructing a quadtree is basically as follows. First,

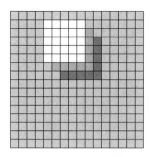

Uncompressed bitmap

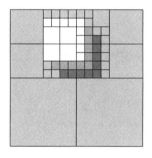

Run-length encoding

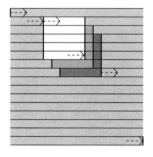

Quadtree encoding

6.6
Image compression

subdivide the entire bitmap into four quadrants. If any quadrant is nonuniform, then subdivide it again, and so on until there is no further need to subdivide or the level of individual pixels is reached. The result is a tree structure, each terminal of which can be labeled with the value of the corresponding area of the image.

Where images have smooth tonal gradients rather than large uniform areas, a version of the sound-compression technique discussed in chapter 5 can be used effectively. Since differences between successive intensities along a raster line are likely to be much smaller than absolute magnitudes, and thus do not require so much precision for their expression, it is more economical to store base values and sequences of differences than it is to store sequences of absolute magnitudes.

There are many other image-compression techniques—some of which are based on arcane mathematics. They vary in the types of images to which they are suited (since they exploit different properties of images), in the compression ratios they can achieve, and in the computational resources required by the associated compression and decompression procedures. A user of image-processing software does not have to know the details of available image-compression techniques but should take note of their characteristic capabilities and limitations and be able to choose an appropriate technique for a given task.

Tone-scale Adjustment

The dynamic range of an image-recording device, such as a video camera or a laser scanner, is the interval between the lowest and the highest intensities that it can record (figure 6.7). In general, high-quality recording devices have greater dynamic ranges than less sophisticated ones, but all have lower dynamic ranges than actual scenes (consider the intensity of a candle flame, for example, compared to the intensity of the surrounding blackness). Furthermore, display and printing devices often have even more compressed dynamic ranges than recording devices. Thus image recording presents the problem (of which painters and photographers have always been aware) of

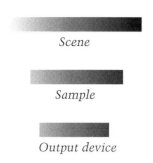

Scene

Sample

Output device

6.7
Dynamic range

6.8
Tone-scale adjustment

how to best use a medium's limited dynamic range to express the appearance of a scene having greater dynamic range.

As tools for handling this fundamental problem (and for producing other useful effects as well), image-processing systems provide tone-scale adjustment functions. These allow you to lighten an image (by adding a constant to each pixel value), to darken an image (by subtracting a constant from each pixel value), to expand and compress dynamic ranges (by multiplying and dividing pixel values), and to redistribute intensities to produce heightened contrasts and other effects. In general, tone-scale adjustments are conveniently specified by sketching a graph that shows the relationship between input and output intensities. Figure 6.8 shows some typical tone-scale adjustment graphs, their effects on an intensity histogram, and the corresponding appearances of the adjusted images.

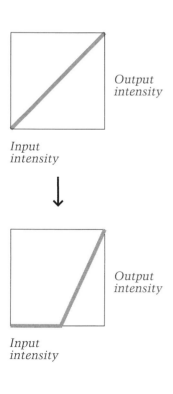

Output intensity

Input intensity

Output intensity

Input intensity

Tone-scale adjustment graphs

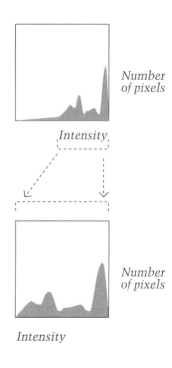

Number of pixels

Intensity

Number of pixels

Intensity

Histograms

Filtering

A screen for filtering gravel allows pebbles in a certain size range to pass through, an audio filter on a sound system allows components of certain frequencies to pass through, and in the same way a filter for digital images allows detail in certain ranges of granularity to pass through. One of the most commonly used is a smoothing filter that eliminates fine detail from an image. This is accomplished simply by replacing each pixel value by the mean value of the pixels in its neighborhood (figure 6.9): the larger the neighborhood, the greater the smoothing effect. Aliasing effects in images of inadequate spatial resolution can be mitigated by smoothing them to remove very fine detail: this is known as antialiasing. (Similarly, high-frequency components may be filtered out of sounds to eliminate aliasing effects.)

The converse of smoothing is sharpening, which accentuates edges and emphasizes fine detail. An interesting variant on the sharpening filter is one that extracts edges to convert a gray-scale image into a line drawing (figure 6.10).

6.9
Application of a smoothing filter

Original

0	0	0	4	0	0	0	0	0	0	0	0
0	0	4	4	0	0	0	0	0	0	0	0
0	4	4	4	4	4	0	0	0	0	0	7
0	0	4	4	4	0	0	0	0	0	7	0
0	0	0	4	0	0	0	0	0	7	0	0
0	0	0	0	0	0	0	0	7	0	0	0
0	0	0	0	0	0	0	7	0	0	0	0
0	0	0	0	0	0	7	0	0	0	0	0
0	0	0	0	0	7	0	0	0	0	0	0
0	0	0	0	7	0	0	0	0	0	0	0
0	0	0	7	0	0	0	0	0	0	0	0
0	0	7	0	0	0	0	0	0	0	0	0

Smoothed

0	0	2	2	2	0	0	0	0	0	0	1
0	2	3	4	3	2	0	0	0	0	1	2
0	2	4	4	4	2	0	0	0	1	2	3
0	2	3	4	3	2	0	0	1	2	3	2
0	0	2	2	2	0	0	1	2	3	2	1
0	0	0	0	0	0	1	2	3	2	1	0
0	0	0	0	0	1	2	3	2	1	0	0
0	0	0	0	1	2	3	2	1	0	0	0
0	0	0	1	2	3	2	1	0	0	0	0
0	0	1	2	3	2	1	0	0	0	0	0
0	1	2	3	2	1	0	0	0	0	0	0
1	2	3	2	1	0	0	0	0	0	0	0

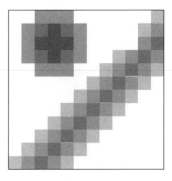

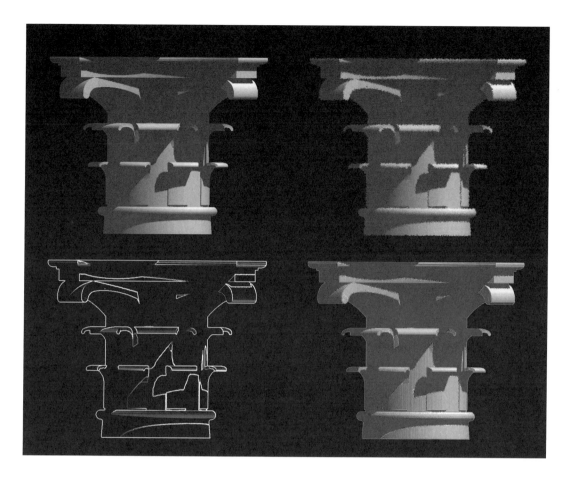

6.10
Examples of filtering:
original image, diffusion,
edge extraction, sharpening

Image-processing systems usually provide an extensive array of filters for eliminating undesirable features in images, emphasizing features of particular interest, and tuning them to match the requirements of particular situations. These filters may be applied in sequence. For example, a photograph might be passed first through a despeckling filter to remove dust spots and then through an edge-extraction filter to convert it into a line drawing.

Selecting, Cutting, and Transforming

Consider a rectangular fragment of a bitmapped image. It can be replicated at another location in the raster grid by a process picturesquely known as blitting—simply copying each pixel value in the fragment into a correspondingly translated location. Replications that are rotated by increments of ninety degrees, or reflected across horizontal or vertical axes, can be produced by means of obvious

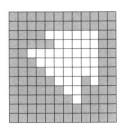

6.11
Replication

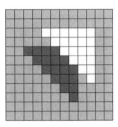

6.12
Cutting

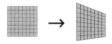

6.13
Refitting a transformed
image to the raster grid

extensions of this idea. This provides an efficient way to generate compositions of repeating parts (figure 6.11). The variant effect of cutting out and relocating a fragment can be produced by assigning values of zero to the pixels that have been copied to a new location, so that they appear black (figure 6.12). Not only can you internally rearrange an image by cutting, transforming, and reassembling its fragments, but you can also produce collages by combining fragments from different sources (see color plate 7).

Other transformations—rotations by arbitrary angles, scale transformations, shear and stretch transformations, and so on—are slightly more difficult to accomplish, since a single pixel in the original image does not necessarily map onto a single pixel in the transformed image (figure 6.13). The transformed image must be sampled and refitted to the grid before it is written back. Scale and distorting transformations provide a powerful way to manipulate the pictorial space of a photograph (figure 6.14).

Image-processing systems provide sets of tools for selecting fragments of images, cutting them out or replicating them, and performing a variety of transformations on them. Many different selection and cutting tools can be used. The simplest is a rectangle that can be shaped and positioned with a cursor. Some systems provide additional shapes such as circles, ellipses, arbitrary polygons, and freehand shapes and allow selection of pixel sets not only by location but also by value (all the white pixels within a specified circle, for example).

Image Combination

So far we have assumed that images are combined simply by copying new (foreground) pixel values over old (background) ones to produce the effect of pasting in a fragment that completely covers whatever was there before. But we can, in fact, combine background and foreground pixel values in any way we want. If we average the background and foreground values, for instance, we can produce the effect of a transparent overlay.

6.14
Manipulating pictorial
space using scale and shear
transformations

Such combination of background and foreground
values is usually controlled, in image-processing systems,
through use of mattes. These are bitmaps that "fit between" the background image and the foreground image.
Wherever a matte has a value of zero, the foreground value
replaces the background value; wherever it has a value of
one, the background value remains; for matte values in
between, the foreground and background values are aver-
aged correspondingly (figure 6.15).

Retouching and Painting

By taking advantage of the capabilities of a mouse or
stylus, you can extend an image-processing system to
encompass image retouching and even "painting" complete
new images. The basic idea is to treat the cursor as a
"brush" or "pen" that alters pixel values as it is dragged
across a displayed bitmapped image. Such simulated
brushes and pens can be astonishingly diverse (figure 6.16).
They can vary in size, shape, pattern, tone, and transpar-

6.15
Combining images with a
matte

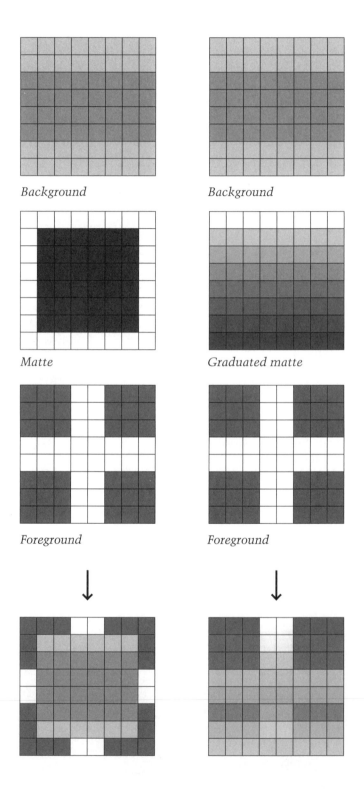

Background

Background

Matte

Graduated matte

Foreground

Foreground

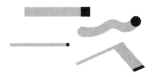

Simple application

Time-dependent

Graduated

Patterned

Transparent

Erasing

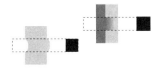

Smear and blend

6.16
A variety of brushes

ency to simulate all kinds of traditional graphic instruments and to become new kinds of instruments that have no direct counterparts in traditional media. A copy brush, for example, enables you to replicate patterns and textures within an image (figure 6.17) or paint parts of one image over parts of another (figure 6.18).

A flood operation changes the value of contiguous pixels (selected by indicating one of them) to a specified new value. This works well on images that consist of well-defined areas of uniform color, but it can produce unexpected results where this condition is not met. More precise control can be achieved by outlining areas and filling them (figure 6.19).

If you want to manipulate some portions of a bitmapped image while leaving others intact, you can can use an electronic mask. Like mattes, masks are bitmapped images superimposed on background images, but they control the application of brushes, flood operations, and so on rather than the combination of images. Wherever a mask has a value of zero, brush and other operations replace background pixel values by new ones; wherever it has a value of one, background pixel values remain unaffected; for in-between values, the background pixel values are modified proportionally. Thus a mask functions much like an airbrush frisket, an erasing shield, or the waxed pattern in batik printing. (The copy-brush effects shown in figure 6.17 were created with masks.)

The most obvious way to create a mask is by meticulously tracing outlines. But more efficient strategies are often possible. An object may be isolated from a uniform background, for example, by flooding the background with the mask color. (If the background is not completely uniform, it may often be made so by performing a posterization transformation.) The "hole" in the mask can itself be flooded to create a complementary mask fitting exactly over the object. The two masks can then be used for precise separation of operations on the object and its context.

6.17
"Erasing" elements by copy-brushing background textures over foreground objects

6.18
Copy-brushing textures from one image to another

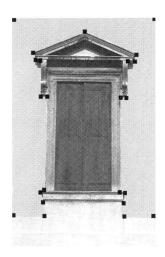

6.19
Fill operations on outlined
areas

The Generalization to Color

Techniques for digitally encoding and processing color
images are straightforward generalizations of those used
for monochrome images. They are based on the tri-
stimulus theory of color perception—that light of almost
any color perceivable by the human eye can be matched by
an appropriate mixture of red light, green light, and blue
light. Thus the color of a pixel can be specified by three
numerical values instead of just one—a red intensity, a
green intensity, and a blue intensity. This type of bitmap
is interpreted by a color display device (most commonly
a color video monitor), the screen of which is a mosaic of
tiny red, green, and blue dots that can be intensified to
specified levels. The eye integrates these distinct dots, so
that the effect of additive color mixture results.

It follows from this system of color specification that
any color has a location in a finite Cartesian coordinate
system, the axes of which represent red, green, and blue
intensities. This is known as the RGB color space or (since
the axes are of equal length) the RGB cube. The structure
of this cube is most easily understood if we imagine
allocating just one bit to represent each intensity: in other
words, each primary can be either on or off. When all of
them are off, the color specified is black, located at the
origin. Conversely, when all of them are on, the color
specified is white, located at the opposite vertex. Another
possibility is that just one of the primaries is on: this

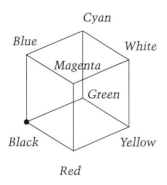

6.20
The RGB cube

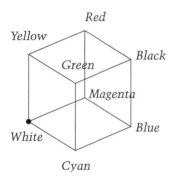

6.21
The CMY cube

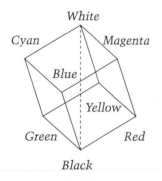

6.22
Black-to-white diagonal
becomes vertical axis

defines red, green, and blue vertices. The final possibility is that two primaries are on at once. This defines the colors of the three remaining vertices (which turn out to be the subtractive primaries): red and green give yellow, red and blue give magenta, and green and blue give cyan. Thus we have eight possible colors—black and white, the three additive primaries, and the three subtractive primaries—located at the eight vertices of the RGB cube (figure 6.20).

If we want to index the RGB cube less coarsely, to specify colors located along the edges, on the faces, and in the interior, we must use more bits for each intensity. By allocating two bits for each intensity we can specify four colors along each edge, sixteen colors on each face, and a total of sixty-four in the complete cube. By allocating still more bits, we can fill the cube with increasing density. The standard for full-color reproduction, with gradients composed of more distinct colors than the eye can separate, is eight bits per intensity for a total of twenty-four bits per pixel—indexing about seventeen million possibilities within the RGB cube.

There are some interesting ways to look at the RGB cube. If we spin it around so that the white vertex becomes the origin, we obtain the CMY (cyan, magenta, yellow) cube for specifying colors in terms of subtractive rather than additive primaries (figure 6.21). Painters and printers make more use of subtractive mixture of pigments than additive mixture of light, so they may find this a more convenient color-specification system. It is a trivial operation to convert CMY values back to RGB values for display.

We can also rotate the RGB cube so that the diagonal connecting the black and white vertices becomes vertical, with white on top (figure 6.22). This reveals some mathematical structure. Neutral, 50 percent gray is exactly at the center, and there is a neutral axis of grays from black at the bottom to white at the top. If we look straight down the neutral axis from the white end, we see the red, yellow, green, cyan, blue, and magenta vertices arranged in a color wheel (figure 6.23). Fully saturated, pure hues are along

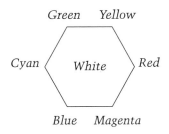

6.23
A view down the axis
reveals a color wheel

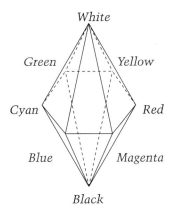

6.24
Double hexacone

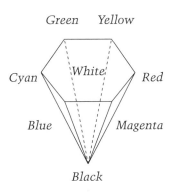

6.25
Single hexacone

the edges of the hexagon that they define, and each of these hues grades down through pastel tints to white at the center. Conversely, if we look down the neutral axis from the black end, we see the pure hues on the perimeter grading down through darker tones to black. This suggests another way of specifying color. We might specify hue by position on the color wheel (that is, an angle between 0 and 360 degrees), we might specify value (expressed as a percentage) by height along the axis from black to white, and we might specify saturation by proximity to the neutral axis. This is convenient for artists who are used to taking pigments in pure hues, mixing them to produce other hues, and producing tints and tones by mixing in white and black.

But this simple transformation of the RGB cube suffers from one important defect: the pure hues have varying value, as shown by the fact that they are on a zigzag line around the center of the color solid. One way to correct this problem is to straighten the zigzag into a plane hexagon such that all the pure hues have 50 percent value. This produces a double hexacone, as illustrated in figure 6.24. Another way is to straighten the zigzag such that all the pure hues have 100 percent value, to produce a single hexacone as illustrated in figure 6.25. Both single-hexacone and double-hexacone models are commonly used for color specification in computer graphics.

Mappings between points in single- and double-hexacone color spaces, and between these and color cubes, are straightforward, so automatic translation of color data from one system to another is easy to accomplish. Consequently, most color paint and image-processing systems allow users to work in whatever systems they wish. Notice, however, that conversion may have implications for color interpolation processes and the appearances of color gradients, since a straight line in a hexacone system does not, in general, map to a straight line in a cube system or in the other type of hexacone.

The tone-scale adjustment and filtering techniques that we considered for gray-scale images can readily be generalized to colored images, but they require more computation since they must be applied not just to a single value for each pixel, but to the red, green, and blue components. In addition, color image-processing software provides tools for color correction and transformation. If we consider them in terms of the RGB system, then color transformations amount to tone-scale adjustments of the red, green, and blue image "layers" to change their respective contributions to the overall effect. Alternatively, color transformations formulated in terms of the hexacone color systems can be used to redistribute hues, saturations, and values within an image.

Display and Printing

Bitmapped images are most commonly displayed on CRT monitors. These come in three basic varieties: bilevel, gray scale, and color. Bilevel monitors, such as that on the early Macintosh models, can display one-bit images. Gray-scale monitors can display monochrome images like those of black-and-white television sets, at intensity resolutions ranging from two bits per pixel to eight bits or more, depending on the capabilities of the circuitry that controls the display. Similarly, color monitors can display images at color resolutions of up to twenty-four or more bits per pixel.

Gray-scale images can be halftoned for display on bilevel monitors (figure 6.26). Digital halftoning is a process of replacing gray pixels in a gray-scale source image by patterns of black and white pixels in a bilevel target image. The viewer's eye then integrates these patterns to read gray tones. Many different procedures have been developed for accomplishing this efficiently and with minimum loss of important visual information. These procedures produce characteristic regular or random patterns; and they handle edges and fine detail in different ways, to yield different graphic qualities—much as with the different hatching patterns traditionally used to produce gray tones in ink line drawings. But they all sacrifice

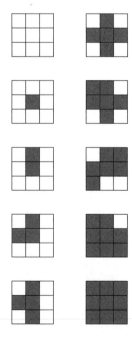

6.26
Halftone patterns

a little spatial resolution in order to achieve greatly enhanced intensity resolution.

The idea of halftoning can be generalized to allow display of twenty-four-bit color images on eight-bit color monitors. In this case, colored pixels in the source image are converted into patterns of eight-bit pixels in the target image—much as in an Impressionist painting. This process is known as dithering. Due to slight loss of spatial resolution, dithered images usually look a little softer than true twenty-four-bit images, but the color effect is excellent.

Images displayed on monitors can be successfully photographed with an ordinary 35 mm camera (if care is taken to avoid unwanted reflections and a sufficiently long exposure is used to avoid uneven scanning effects) or by using a special film recorder. A simple analog film recorder consists of a small CRT monitor located in front of a fixed-focus camera in a darkened box (figure 6.27). It takes a video signal directly from the monitor of a workstation or personal computer and produces an image of exactly what is currently shown on the screen—even the cursor, if you neglect to move it out of the way. A digital film recorder is a more elaborate and expensive device that can produce better results. It accepts an image file rather than a video signal, so it eliminates window borders, cursors, and other extraneous features of the screen display. And it incorporates a high-precision CRT, so that it can record images at higher resolution than can be displayed on a workstation or personal computer.

Photographic film is a high-resolution, continuous-tone medium, so loss of visual information in transfer from CRT to film is minimal. But color CRT displays and color slide or print film are imperfect color media and can reproduce differing ranges of colors (more technically, they have different color gamuts), so there is inevitably some color distortion. This differs with the type of color film. The effects of the distortion can be minimized by careful color correction of the image before it is photographed and by careful exposure, but they can never be eliminated entirely.

6.27
Film recording

Most other techniques for producing hard copy require halftoning or dithering before the image is transferred to paper. In particular, the inexpensive laser (or even impact) printers that are designed for use with personal computers can be used to produce halftoned gray-scale prints. But, due to their limited resolution, the results are often barely adequate. If small halftone dots are used for high spatial resolution, their limited range of size variation yields correspondingly limited tonal variation and a muddy appearance. Conversely, if halftone dots are made larger for an expanded tonal range, the dots become overly conspicuous.

Better results can be achieved by using higher-resolution image setters. These usually provide precise control of halftoning, so that you can use fine or coarse screens, rotated at various angles, as appropriate to the characteristics of the source image and (in the case of images that are to be reproduced further) of the printing process that will be used.

Inkjet, thermal wax-transfer, electrostatic, and dye-sublimation printers can all be used for direct production of color prints on paper. As the names suggest, they use different processes for transferring pigments to the paper: inkjet printers fire droplets of opaque liquid ink from small nozzles; thermal wax-transfer printers use sheets of cyan, magenta, yellow, and black wax film to produce small dots of opaque melted wax; electrostatic printers use electrostatic charges to control depositing of opaque colored toner; and dye-sublimation printers create mixtures of transparent dye on the surface of special paper. Inkjet, thermal wax-transfer, and electrostatic printers use dithering to generate wide ranges of intensities and colors from dots of just a few colors, but dye-sublimation printers actually create dots of many different colors. Formats, resolutions, color gamuts, and costs vary enormously—from inexpensive, letter-size, low-resolution printers with limited gamuts to much more costly large-format, high-resolution, full-color models. Considerable color distortion is inevitable when models with limited color gamuts are used.

For conventional color printing, bitmapped images can be digitally color separated—an increasingly attractive alternative to making a color photograph and then color separating it. The process involves making four halftoned images, for magenta, cyan, yellow, and black printing plates, on an image setter. Software for this is built in to many paint and image-processing systems.

In general, techniques for producing prints from bitmapped images extend the ancient tradition of printmaking. The image file is the modern equivalent of the etcher's plate or the lithographer's stone—a device for controlling transfer of ink to paper. The printmaker's task is to control the variables of the transfer process to achieve results with the desired graphic qualities. This is straightforward for processes with few variables, for example production of a monochrome print on a standard laser printer, but can become very complex when high-quality, carefully controlled color prints are needed.

Image Archives

Electronic image archives, consisting of bitmapped image files (not to be confused with analog images stored on videodisc), are an increasingly popular alternative to conventional photo archives and slide libraries. These have the advantages of compactness, of not being subject to problems of image deterioration, of supporting efficient search and retrieval, and of allowing production of displays, slides, and prints in many different formats as required.

Image archives are usually stored on an inexpensive, high-capacity, long-lasting medium such as optical disk (or magnetic tape if fast access is not required). Compression software may be used to minimize the amount of storage required. A common arrangement is to provide a large image server on a network and to allow users of personal computers or workstations on the network to download compressed image files from the server and decompress them at the destination. The effect is to make the resources of a slide library continuously available at every personal computer or workstation. Furthermore, the downloaded images can be manipulated, analyzed, inserted into text documents, and printed.

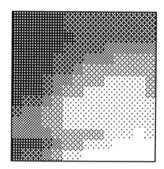

Elevation

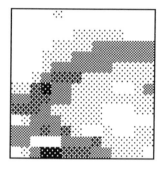

Slope

6.28
Visualization of spatial
distributions

Grid Mapping and Spatial Analysis

Two-dimensional arrays of numerical values are useful not only for recording light intensities in visual fields, but also for mapping temperatures, sound levels, smog pollution levels, topographic elevations, ocean depths, or anything of interest that varies spatially. The recorded values can then be interpreted and displayed as intensities or colors, so that the spatial distribution can be visualized. Figure 6.28, for example, depicts as intensities the changing values of elevation and slope over a portion of a topographic surface. Satellite and medical-imaging systems commonly record radiation intensities in a wider spectrum than that of visible light to produce bitmaps that are displayed as pseudocolored images.

Arrays of numerical values are often used by landscape planners and designers to describe distributions of soil types, ground cover, surface water, and so on. Specialized map-analysis software is used to construct such bitmaps from survey data or traditional maps, to perform various types of analyses, and to generate graphic output in specified formats.

Map-analysis software usually provides for mapping many variables on the same grid—in effect creating different map layers—together with flexible reporting capabilities that enable the user to display occurrences of whatever combinations of values are of interest. Assume, for example, that a site planner wants to find wetlands on middle slopes. These areas can be found and mapped through Boolean combination of slope and surface water maps as shown in figure 6.29.

Two-dimensional arrays of numerical values can also be analyzed statistically. A simple procedure can be used, for example, to scan through a selected portion of a bitmap, count pixels with specified characteristics, and thus report the total area covered by pixels with that value. A site planner might apply this procedure to estimate the total buildable area on a site. Sometimes it is useful to summarize gridded data by computing means and standard deviations and then producing histograms (figure 6.30). A site planner might characterize parts of a site by computing

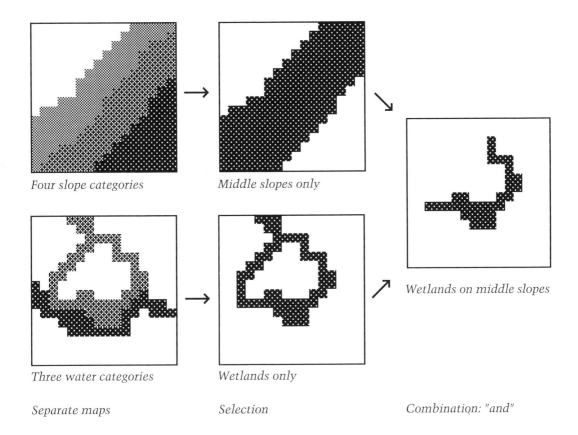

Four slope categories   Middle slopes only

Three water categories   Wetlands only   Wetlands on middle slopes

Separate maps   Selection   Combination: "and"

6.29
Boolean combination of
grid maps

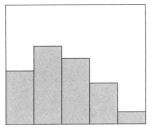

0-4 4-8 8-12 12-20 20+

6.30
Slope histogram for map
shown in figure 6.29

mean slope values, for instance. Detailed analyses might involve looking for correlations of spatial variables, looking for clusters of similar pixels, and so on.

Time-series analyses are possible when bitmapped representations of the same area at successive time intervals are available and can be registered with each other. Earth satellites repeatedly image the same areas, for example. One simple analysis technique, which is frequently used by ecologists and urban geographers interested in processes of growth and change, is to compare successive images and display those pixels which differ from their predecessors by amounts greater than some specified threshold.

Shape and Character Recognition

To recognize a shape in a bitmapped image is to classify it as an instance of some established class of shapes. We would normally classify the shapes shown in figure 6.31, for example, as instances of uppercase alphabetic characters. Character-recognition software can be applied to

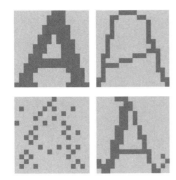

6.31
Bitmaps identifiable
as characters

bitmapped images of pages of printed text to classify such discrete shapes as instances of characters, and so translate an image file into a text file that can be manipulated with a word processor. If the recognition software is sufficiently fast and reliable, this provides a very efficient alternative to retyping existing text. It also supports text input by writing with a stylus on a tablet instead of typing at a keyboard—a useful strategy for very small laptop computers, for input of Kanji, and in other contexts where standard keyboards are not very effective.

It would similarly be useful to scan existing line drawings to produce bitmapped images, then automatically recognize walls, doorswings, dimension lines, and so on to produce a bill of materials or a structured geometric model of some kind. Unlike text, drawings do not consist of discrete graphic elements, and they must be segmented into such elements before recognition procedures can be applied. This vastly complicates the interpretation problem (in the same way that interpretation of continuous speech is far more difficult than recognition of single-word commands). As a result, practical sketch-recognition and drawing-interpretation systems have been much slower to emerge than character-recognition systems.

In general, standard computers have not proven to be as good at solving recognition and image-interpretation problems as was once hoped. A promising new avenue (more accurately, revival in a new guise of an idea that earlier seemed unpromising) is to use neural network devices that can be trained to recognize patterns in data.

Uses and Limitations of Bitmapped Images

Bitmapped images may be very beautiful, but their beauty is only skin deep. A bitmap is just a numerical equivalent of the thin skin of emulsion that covers the surface of a photograph or the thin layer of pigment that covers a painting. It follows that image-processing software can efficiently substitute for the traditional techniques of painting and photography, and it can extend and generalize these techniques in some interesting ways. The information in a bitmap of a three-dimensional scene is, however, merely a sample taken from a particular view-point at finite spatial and tonal resolution. The incompleteness of the sample limits what you can do: you cannot expect image-processing software to show you detail of indefinitely fine resolution, to show you objects in the scene from other than the original viewpoint, or to provide manipulative operations that depend on knowledge of the internal structure of the manipulated object.

Suggested Readings

Anderson, James A., and Edward Rosenfeld. 1988. *Neurocomputing: Foundations of Research.* Cambridge: The MIT Press.

Baxes, Gregory A. 1984. *Digital Image Processing: A Practical Primer.* Englewood Cliffs: Prentice Hall.

Castleman, Kenneth R. 1979. *Digital Image Processing.* Englewood Cliffs: Prentice Hall.

Cannon, T. M., and B. R. Hunt. 1981. "Image Processing by Computer." *Scientific American* 245 (4): 214–25.

Fiume, Eugene L. 1989. *The Mathematical Structure of Raster Graphics.* New York: Academic Press.

Foley, James, Andries van Dam, Steven Feiner, and John Hughes. 1990. *Computer Graphics: Principles and Practice.* Reading, Mass.: Addison-Wesley.

Hall, Ernest L. 1979. *Computer Image Processing and Recognition.* New York: Academic Press.

Holtzmann, Gerard J. 1988. *Beyond Photography: The Digital Darkroom.* Englewood Cliffs: Prentice Hall.

Mitchell, William J. 1992. *The Reconfigured Eye: Visual Truth in the Post-Photographic Era.* Cambridge: The MIT Press.

Pavlidis, Theo. 1982. *Algorithms for Graphics and Image Processing.* Rockville, Md.: Computer Science Press.

Pratt, William K. 1978. *Digital Image Processing.* New York: John Wiley.

Samet, Hanan. 1990. *The Design and Analysis of Spatial Data Structures.* Reading, Mass.: Addison-Wesley.

Tomlin, C. Dana. 1990. *Geographic Information Systems and Cartographic Modeling.* Englewood Cliffs: Prentice Hall.

7

DRAFTED LINES

It may be that the most rigorous exponents of Impressionism conceived of pictures as collections of colored points corresponding to light intensities reaching the painter's eye, but this was exceptional. Painters, drafters, and designers usually conceive of pictures in a much more highly structured way—as collections of geometric entities, such as straight lines, arcs of circles, and closed polygons. The artist composes by inserting these sorts of entities into a picture and relating them to each other in appropriate ways. In the creation of representational pictures the artist deploys these two-dimensional geometric entities on the picture plane to depict physical objects in three-dimensional space.

When an artist makes a freehand sketch, the intended entities and relationships are rendered only approximately by marks on paper. In technical drafting, though, geometric entities are rendered precisely through use of instruments such as straightedges and compasses, and relationships are formed accurately through execution of geometric constructions. Similarly, computer graphics software that is designed for use in technical drafting provides tools for precise manipulation and accurate presentation of geometric entities (figure 7.1).

The databases processed by this software contain digital representations of geometric elements and their relationships. A typical format is illustrated in figure 7.2.

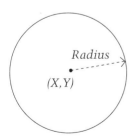

7.1
Geometric entities

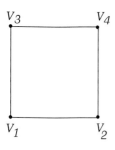

$V_1 (0,0)$

$V_2 (1,0)$

$V_3 (1,1)$

$V_4 (0,1)$

$L_1 (V_1, V_2)$

$L_2 (V_2, V_3)$

$L_3 (V_3, V_4)$

$L_4 (V_4, V_1)$

7.2
Numerical description of
a simple shape

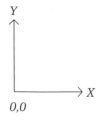

7.3
A rectangular Cartesian
coordinate system

There is a point table and a line table. The entries in the point table record x and y coordinates of points, and the entries in the line table specify which pairs of points are associated to define lines. Associated procedures translate the values in this table into lines on a display screen. Raster graphic displays produced from such databases may look much like displays produced from bitmaps, but they behave very differently since operations are defined on the lines themselves rather than on the pixels that make up the display of lines.

Coordinate Systems

The idea of a rectangular, two-dimensional Cartesian coordinate system provides the foundation for all drafting software (figure 7.3). Within such a system, points are specified by their coordinates—that is, pairs of numbers. These numbers are stored in binary format in computer memory.

Let us assume that one bit is used to specify each coordinate. This yields a 2 x 2 grid of specifiable locations, as illustrated in figure 7.4. Within this grid, then, six different straight lines may be specified by their end points. If we take a design to be a set of lines, this elementary coordinate system allows us to construct just $2^6 = 64$ different designs. However, this number increases very dramatically as we increase the number of bits used to encode each coordinate. With two bits per coordinate we have a 4 x 4 grid of sixteen distinct points, which provides a thousandfold increase in the number of different designs. Practical drafting systems employ eight-bit, sixteen-bit, or thirty-two-bit binary numbers to represent coordinates.

Usually, however, designers do not want to think in terms of integer coordinates. They want to use, instead, normal units such as feet and inches, meters, and so on. Hence a drafting system normally provides a menu of units from which the user can select and internally converts coordinates expressed in these user-selected units into binary integer form. It is straightforward to extend this idea to provide a unit-conversion capability so that,

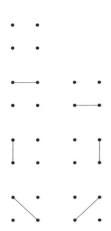

7.4
Lines in a minimum
coordinate system

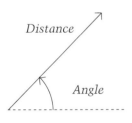

7.5
Polar coordinates

for instance, coordinates expressed in feet and inches can be reexpressed in meters and centimeters.

In some design contexts it is convenient to work in polar coordinates (figure 7.5) rather than rectangular coordinates. Many drafting systems provide this option. The translation between polar and rectangular coordinates is just a matter of some simple trigonometry and can be performed automatically.

The usual way to translate from user coordinates to the internal binary representation is automatically to set the maximum extent of the drawing (in either direction) equal to the full extent of the coordinate system (as determined by the number of bits used for each coordinate). This means that small objects can be represented with high precision or very large objects can be represented with lower precision. However, if very large objects (complete city plans, say) and very small objects (such as window details) are shown in the same drawing, the small objects may be represented with inadequate precision. Hence the user of a drafting system must keep in mind that coordinates are represented to finite precision and organize drawings so that precision problems do not develop.

Some systems simplify the issue of extent and precision by representing coordinates internally as floating-point rather than integer numbers. This yields a coordinate system of large and indefinite extent, in which small coordinate values have many significant decimal places and large coordinate values have few. In effect, small objects located near the origin of the coordinate system are represented with high precision, while small objects located far from the origin are represented more approximately. By contrast, an integer coordinate system provides a uniform density of spatial indexing throughout its extent.

Point Specification

The most fundamental operation that a drafting system provides is specification of a point within the coordinate system. The most precise but most cumbersome way to accomplish this is to type in numerical values. It is quicker and more convenient to place the cursor and click with a mouse, but this is much less precise. Where

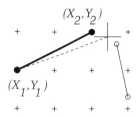

Snap to module

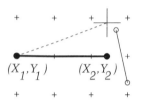

Snap to orthogonal axes

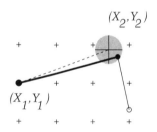

Snap to object

7.6
Geometric guides

coordinates are to be digitized from an existing drawing, use of a digitizing tablet with a stylus or digitizing puck is the most suitable technique. Since pointing and digitizing devices are inherently imprecise, geometric guides are frequently used to constrain their input (figure 7.6). These various numerical and graphical techniques have their strengths and weaknesses, which make them suitable for different applications, so many systems provide the means to use all of them quickly and interchangeably.

The capacity to specify any point in the coordinate system is clearly essential, but it does not, in itself, provide a sufficient basis for efficient construction of drawings. In most practical contexts a designer needs to select from among a very much smaller subset of points. A drafting system should, then, provide tools for specifying such subsets, constraining choice to them, and efficiently selecting from among their members. Many drawings, for example, are constructed under the discipline of some modular grid. The grid amounts to a specified subset of the points in the coordinate system, and the end points of lines are constrained to be in this subset. In response to this, drafting systems normally allow users to define grids with grid points at specified intervals and provide for efficient selection of grid points by automatically "snapping" an indicated point to the nearest grid point. This is particularly useful with mouse or stylus input, since it allows the user to indicate points quickly and approximately without paying the penalty of lost precision.

The minimal requirement is for a drafting system to provide square grids parallel to the coordinate axes (figure 7.7). More sophisticated systems may go beyond this to provide the other regular plane systems of points. They may also allow grids to be rotated and superimposed. Polar grids are appropriate where polar rather than rectangular coordinates are used.

As a drawing develops, a designer mostly needs to select significant points in the existing skeleton of lines—end points of existing lines, center points and tangent points of arcs, line intersection points, and so on (figure 7.8). Some of these points are represented explicitly in the data structure, and the rest are implicit but can be computed

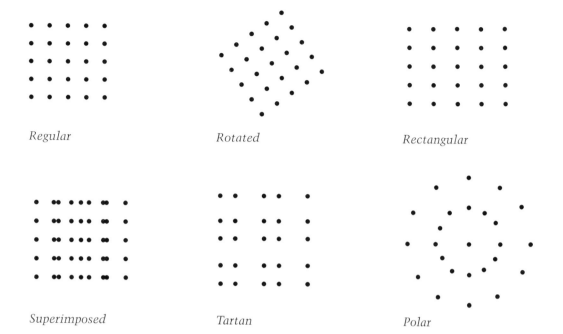

Regular

Rotated

Rectangular

Superimposed

Tartan

Polar

7.7
Grids

as required. Sophisticated drafting systems, then, provide for snapping to both explicit and implicit significant points.

Different sorts of points may, of course, seem significant in different design contexts at different moments. A drafting system can respond to this variability by allowing the user to specify the types of points that are to be considered and a diameter of attention. Then, as the cursor moves across the drawing, points of the specified types within the specified radius of attention can be highlighted (figure 7.9).

Experienced users of drafting systems usually take extensive advantage of constraint and snapping capabilities. They begin by building up skeletons of construction lines, then use these structures to snap further lines quickly into place, then use these lines to locate still finer details, and so on until the entire drawing is complete. By following this strategy they can almost entirely eliminate the need for painstaking location of points by calculating and typing coordinates or by precise stylus work. (This is consistent with good classical drafting technique, which depends on construction and avoids use of the graduated scale as much as possible.)

Nearest point to cursor

Equal division point

Center

End point

Intersection

Quadrant

Midpoint

*Perpendicular
(to last point)*

*Tangent
(to last point)*

7.8
Significant points on
existing lines

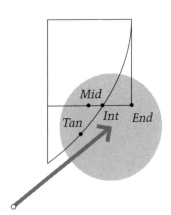

*Automatic highlighting of
significant points within
radius*

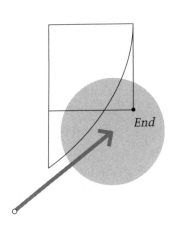

*Highlighting just one kind
of point*

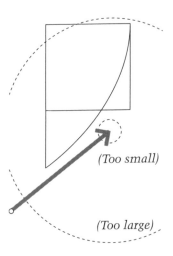

*The radius of attention
should match the scale of
the geometry*

7.9
Automatic highlighting
of significant points near
the end of a rubber-band
line

(X_2,Y_2)

(X_1,Y_1)

Simple input

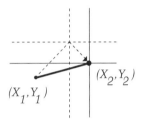

(X_2,Y_2)

(X_1,Y_1)

"Rubber-band" input

(X_1,Y_1)

(dx,dy)

Slope and intercept

7.10
Specifying a line

Repertoires of Line Types

The capacity to specify lines is built from the capacity to specify points (figure 7.10). Any two points define a straight line, for example, so all drafting systems allow a user to specify straight line segments by indicating their end points. When a mouse or stylus is used for this purpose, indication of the first end point fixes one end of the line and a "rubber-band" line then stretches from that location to the current location of the cursor and follows the cursor until the second end point is selected. This graphically demonstrates the mathematical equivalence of a second basic way to describe a straight line numerically—by its origin, direction, and length. An indefinitely long straight line (which might, for example, serve as a construction line) can be specified by slope and intercept.

Curved lines of various types can be specified by giving their end points plus sufficiently many additional points or parameter values to define the shape between the two ends. Any three points lie on (and therefore specify) a circular arc, for example. Mathematical equivalences multiply in this case: drafting systems normally provide for specification of arcs by end points and a center point, by end points and a point on the circumference, by end points and an included angle, by an end point, center point, and swept angle, and so on (figure 7.11). Any of these ways may be needed, depending upon the context into which the arc is to be snapped. Notice, incidentally, that a computer drafting system has no difficulty with handling arcs of large radius—a type of graphic element that causes problems in traditional drafting, where compasses are of physically limited radius and the drawing surface for location of center points is of limited extent (figure 7.12).

Any straight line is the radius of a circle, so complete circles are usually input by means of a variant of the rubber-band line. Furthermore, any arc specifies a complete circle, so any of the methods used for inserting arcs may be modified slightly to serve for inserting circles.

Any straight line may also be interpreted in yet another way, as the defining diagonal of a rectangle that bounds an ellipse (figure 7.13). So the rubber-band line technique can

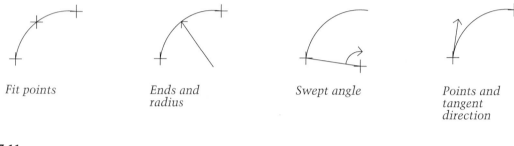

Fit points   *Ends and*   *Swept angle*   *Points and*
                      radius   *tangent*
                                                                  direction

7.11
Specifying an arc

7.12
Large-radius arcs: the
Sydney Opera House

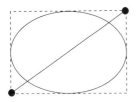

7.13
Ellipse bounded by a rectangle

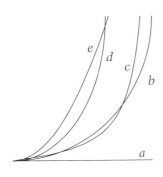

a. *Straight line*
b. *Circular arc*
c. *Hyperbola*
d. *Ellipse*
e. *Parabola*

7.14
Conic section curves

7.15
Splines

also be adapted to serve for convenient specification of ellipses. Whereas ellipses are difficult to handle with traditional manual drafting instruments, and so have often been approximated by ovals (constructions of tangentially connected circular arcs), they present no problems when even a very simple computer drafting system is used.

Straight lines, circular arcs, and elliptical arcs are all subclasses of conic section curves (figure 7.14). The repertoire of a drafting system can be expanded to the conic sections in general by providing for hyperbolic and parabolic arcs as well.

Since any curve can be represented by a sufficiently complicated polynomial expression, and other instances of the same type can be specified by varying the coefficients of that polynomial, the repertoire of different types of curved lines provided by a drafting system can be extended almost indefinitely. There is little practical need for this, however. Addition of a few basic types of spline curves to the conics suffices for most design purposes (figure 7.15). A spline curve, much like the pinned wooden splines used in manual drafting, is specified by an arbitrary number of control points, which (depending on the particular type of spline) may or may not lie on the curve.

A drawing from a drafting system, then, is essentially a two-dimensional arrangement of instances of the line types that the system provides (as a text is a one-dimensional arrangement of instances of characters from a character set, and a melody is a one-dimensional arrangement of sounds). The wider a system's repertoire of line types, the more versatile it will be in its representational capabilities.

Notice that, under this representational scheme, some lines in a drawing are explicitly represented in the underlying data structure but others are only implicit. Consider the simple drawing shown in figure 7.16, for example. The simplest way to input it and represent it in the data structure is as three long lines. This means that the three sides of the triangle are only implicitly represented. Alternatively, the figure might be input and stored as six shorter lines. Thus the three sides of the triangle are represented explicitly, but now the longer lines are only

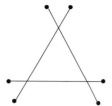

Three segments

Nine segments

7.16
Alternative representations
of a simple line shape

*Approximating a smooth
curve with short straight
segments*

*Incorporating straight and
curved segments*

7.17
Chains or polylines

implicit. (There are many other possibilities as well.) This has important practical consequences, since most drafting systems (at least among those commercially available at the time of writing) allow you to select and operate only on lines that are explicitly represented in the data structure. However, this is not a necessary restriction: it is feasible (although computationally more expensive) to extend the principle of constraint-based editing and allow a user to specify not only the types of points that are to be selectable, but also the types of lines—independently of whether they happen to be represented explicitly in the data structure. (You might, for example, happen to be interested in short horizontal and vertical lines that run between intersection points, or in long inclined lines that form tangents to arcs.)

Chains of Lines

Most drafting systems provide for representation of irregular lines, in piecewise fashion, as connected sequences of short line segments. In the simplest case, points on an arbitrary curve are connected by straight lines to produce a faceted approximation (figure 7.17); the corresponding input technique is to specify these points in sequence. In general, the segments might be of any line type provided by the system.

Such a chain, often called a polyline, is useful for describing a complex object or path, such as a boundary or contour line in a site plan, that is to be understood as a single entity. If a chain's last point is connected back to its first point, it forms a closed circuit—a structure of particular interest that will be discussed in detail in the following chapter.

Another kind of chain operation constructs irregular lines from straight lines by executing procedures to fractalize them, as shown in figure 7.18. The degree of irregularity that results can be controlled by a parameter. Some drafting systems include this type of line in their repertoires.

Basic Operations on Lines

Just as a text-processing system provides basic tools for inserting, selecting, and deleting characters, a drafting system always provides basic tools for inserting, selecting, and deleting lines—the visible elements of a drawing. These suffice for constructing and editing drawings, but it is convenient to have a wider range of manipulative capabilities at one's disposal. Sophisticated drafting systems are distinguished from simpler ones by the wider ranges of specialized tools that they provide.

Among the most commonly provided additional tools are break, extend, and trim operations. A break operation separates a specified line into two lines at a specified point (figure 7.19). (Notice that this does not change the appearance of the drawing, but it does change the underlying digital representation, and this can later cause the drawing to behave differently when you perform other operations.) An extend operation lengthens a selected line by a specified amount or to meet some specified line (figure 7.20). Conversely, a trim operation shortens a selected line by a specified amount or cuts it back to some specified line (figure 7.21).

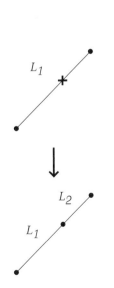

7.18
Fractalized lines

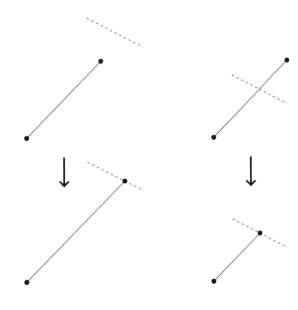

7.19
Break operation

7.20
Extend operation

7.21
Trim operation

Geometric Constructions

Traditionally, facility in technical drafting has depended upon knowledge of constructive procedures executed with traditional drawing instruments—procedures for constructing parallels and perpendicular bisectors to lines, tangents to circles, and so on. (The famous secrets of the medieval masons mostly consisted, in fact, of step-by-step descriptions of these procedures.) They can be replicated with the basic drafting system functions of snapping (equivalent, for example, to placing the point of compasses at the intersection of two lines) and insertion, deletion, division, extension, and trimming of primitives. There is no need, however, to burden the user of a drafting system with remembering all the steps of all these procedures. It is better to provide for automatic execution of commonly used constructive procedures, thus extending the tool kit with some higher-level operations.

The computer versions of these procedures depend not on finding points by intersecting lines or arcs (as in Euclid) but on evaluating formulae. Consider, for example, the problem of finding the midpoint of a straight line. The beautiful construction given by Euclid involves striking two arcs to locate a pair of points, then constructing a line through those points to locate the required midpoint (figure 7.22). In the computer version, the X-coordinate of the midpoint is calculated by taking the average of the X-coordinates of the ends, and the Y-coordinate of the midpoint is calculated by taking the average of the Y-coordinates of the ends. The generalization to division into any specified number of equal parts is obvious. Although the arithmetic becomes more complicated, further generalization to subdivision of arcs and splines is also straightforward.

In addition to procedures for subdividing existing lines, a draftsperson needs to know procedures for inserting new lines in specified orientations to existing lines. To show wall thicknesses on a plan, for example, an architect often needs to insert parallels to existing straight lines, arcs concentric with existing arcs, and even splines appropriately offset from existing splines. Other artifact

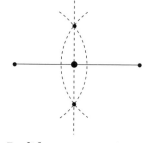

Euclidean construction

(X_1, Y_1) (X_2, Y_2)

$((X_1 + X_2) / 2 ,$
$(Y_1 + Y_2) / 2)$

Computer calculation

7.22
Finding a midpoint

geometries may be defined in terms of perpendiculars to straight lines, and normals and tangents to curves. Sophisticated drafting systems provide convenient tools for locating crucial construction points or for inserting lines directly in these relationships. These may be used for graphic problem-solving, in the same way that the mathematical functions provided by electronic calculators, spreadsheets, and symbolic mathematics systems may be used for numerical problem-solving. The larger its repertoire of useful geometric construction tools, the more effectively a drafting system can be used as a problem-solving rather than mere decision-recording medium.

Designers often want to avoid discontinuities in curved profiles, for example, and this necessitates locating curves in tangential relationships: a straight line may be tangent to a circular arc, an arc may be tangent to another arc, an arc may form a fillet between two straight lines, and so on. Unless your geometric knowledge is extensive, construction of these figures can present considerable difficulty. Thus many drafting systems emphasize tools for continuous connection of straight lines and curves.

This game can be elaborated endlessly, since entire construction procedures can always be used as steps in still more elaborate construction procedures—just as very complex mathematical functions can be built up from simple ones. In this way a whole hierarchy of drawing construction tools can be implemented (figure 7.23). At the bottom of the hierarchy are a very few simple, basic operations and at the top there are potentially many powerful, specialized procedures. Skilled users of drafting systems achieve maximum efficiency by avoiding low-level operations wherever possible and exploiting the power of whatever high-level operations are available.

It is worth noting, parenthetically, that traditional drafting (and hence design) practice is based almost entirely on the relatively simple constructions of lines and arcs that can be executed efficiently with straightedges and compasses and a basic knowledge of Euclid's *Elements*. But a computer can rapidly execute very complex constructions (for example, insertion of normals at equally spaced points

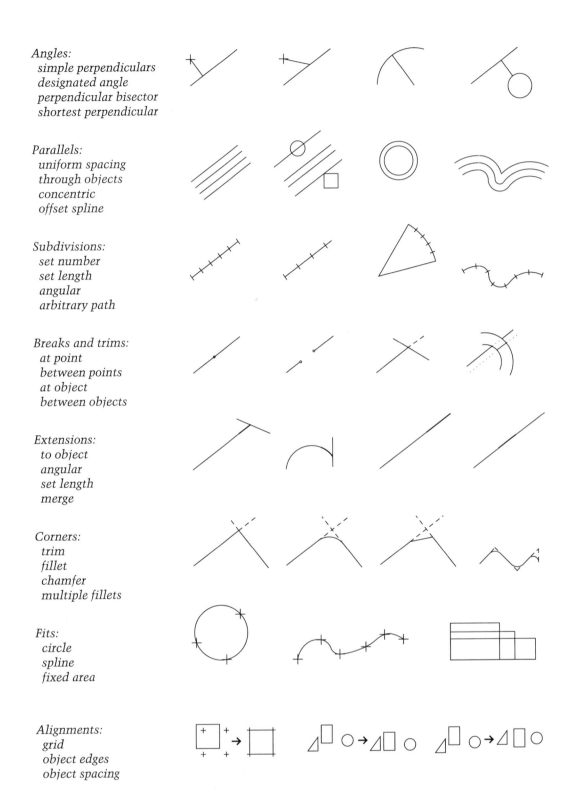

Angles:
  simple perpendiculars
  designated angle
  perpendicular bisector
  shortest perpendicular

Parallels:
  uniform spacing
  through objects
  concentric
  offset spline

Subdivisions:
  set number
  set length
  angular
  arbitrary path

Breaks and trims:
  at point
  between points
  at object
  between objects

Extensions:
  to object
  angular
  set length
  merge

Corners:
  trim
  fillet
  chamfer
  multiple fillets

Fits:
  circle
  spline
  fixed area

Alignments:
  grid
  object edges
  object spacing

7.23
A typical repertoire of
geometric constructions

along an arbitrary spline curve), so designers' geometric explorations no longer need be constrained by these ancient limitations. Some architects have begun to exploit this freedom.

Selecting, Transforming, and Duplicating Subshapes

Lines are put together (whether by hand or by using a computer drafting system) to construct more complex shapes such as rectangles, triangles, or complete building elevations. Any part of such a shape that can be traced is a subshape (figure 7.24). Computer drafting systems provide not only for selecting and operating on points and lines, but also for selecting and operating on arbitrary subshapes. This greatly enhances their power.

Most computer drafting systems formalize the concept of subshape by treating the complete drawing as a set of instances of line types, and subshapes therefore as subsets. These subsets form a Boolean lattice under the relation of shape inclusion, and the nodes in that lattice define all the possible subshapes (figure 7.25). It follows that subshapes can be selected either by selecting constituent lines one by one or by specifying an area of drawing surface and counting all lines falling within that area as members of the subshape

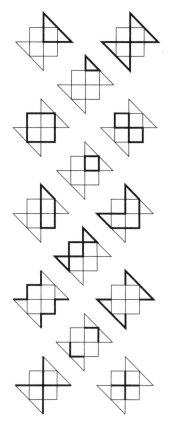

7.24
Some of the emergent subshapes of a simple shape

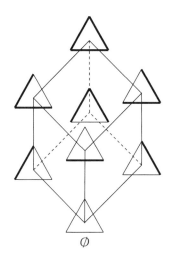

7.25
The Boolean lattice of a set of line segments

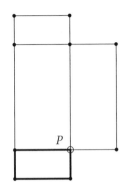

7.26
Point is not in the database, and the highlighted rectangle cannot be selected

(or selection set, as it is often called). More complex subshapes may be selected by adding lines to a selection set or deleting lines from it.

This approach is not entirely satisfactory, however, since many of the subshapes that may be of interest to a designer are not subsets of line primitives and cannot directly be selected in these ways (figure 7.26). The alternative is to extend the idea of constraint-based editing one step further and provide a facility for specifying the subshape types that are currently of interest and for automatically recognizing emergent instances of them.

Designers most frequently pick out subshapes because they want to transform them in some way (figure 7.27). Drafting systems provide tools for translating, rotating, reflecting, scaling, and distorting specified subshapes, and use of these tools to manipulate entire subshapes usually proves to be a much more efficient way of modifying a drawing than modifying lines one by one. Since values for transformation parameters are frequently defined by existing geometry, it is often very efficient to specify transformations by snapping or by pointing to existing geometric entities to describe distances and angles (figure 7.28).

Simple systems allow translation, rotation, reflection, and scaling operations to be performed individually. More sophisticated systems allow arbitrary sequences of these transformations (concatenated linear transformations) to be specified, named, and recalled and applied. For example, the operation of rotation about an arbitrary point is a translation followed by a rotation then a translation back (figure 7.29).

Internally, the task of performing geometric transformations is essentially one of multiplying the coordinate pairs that define the original shapes by transformation matrices to produce transformed coordinate pairs that define the transformed shapes (figure 7.30). This highly standardized and repetitive task can be performed by software or, for greater speed, by specialized graphics hardware.

Drafting systems also provide tools for replicating (and deleting) complete shapes. It is not very useful to replicate a shape directly on top of itself, so replication is usually combined with some transformation.

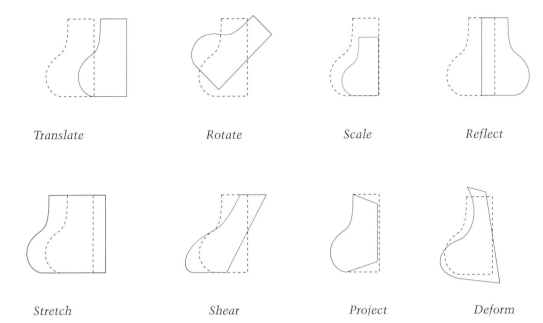

Translate   Rotate   Scale   Reflect

Stretch   Shear   Project   Deform

7.27
Basic geometric
transformations

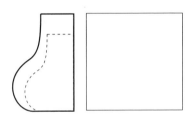

7.28
A transformation parameter
defined by an existing
object

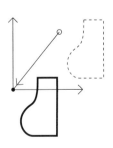

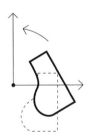

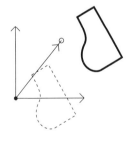

*Step 1: translate the
center of rotation*

Step 2: rotate about origin

Step 3: translate back

7.29
A concatenated
transformation: rotation
about an arbitrary point

$$\begin{bmatrix} P_x & P_y & 1 \end{bmatrix} \cdot \begin{bmatrix} 1 & 0 & 0 \\ 0 & 1 & 0 \\ t_x & t_y & 1 \end{bmatrix} \cdot \begin{bmatrix} r_{1x} & r_{2x} & 0 \\ r_{1x} & r_{2x} & 0 \\ 0 & 0 & 1 \end{bmatrix} = \begin{bmatrix} P'_x & P'_y & 1 \end{bmatrix}$$

Point   *Translation   Rotation*   *Transformed*
                                                       point

7.30
Matrix transformation of a
coordinate vector

Combination of replication with translation provides an extremely efficient way to generate rows and grids of shapes. Similarly, combination of replication with rotation and reflection is an effective way to generate figures with symmetry about points and axes (figure 7.31).

Repeatable Standard Shapes

Some types of subshapes are used very frequently in drawings, so drafting systems are often elaborated to provide for instantiation of complete subshapes selected from a standard menu—much as a drafter working by hand might trace stencils or cut and paste photocopies to produce instances of common shapes. Some simple shapes, such as rectangles, are used in many different contexts. But others are more specialized: doorswing symbols are commonly used in architectural plans, resistor symbols are commonly used in electrical diagrams, boxes and arrows are commonly used in flowcharts, and so on. So drafting systems usually provide small menus of repeatable standard shapes for general use, plus much more extensive custom menus for particular applications (figure 7.32). In the more sophisticated systems, users can extend and customize these menus themselves.

Documentation for different drafting systems refers to these standard shapes variously as cells, components, instances, and groups. However the IGES (International Graphic Exchange Standard) standard for graphic data transfer calls them segments, and this terminology is now widely used.

Segments are defined in their own local coordinate systems and are instantiated in drawings by specifying values for location parameters: X-coordinate, Y-coordinate, orientation, and handedness. The handedness parameter

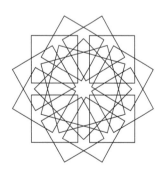

7.31
Symmetric figures
generated by geometric
transformations

allows an element such as a doorswing to be instantiated in both right-handed and left-handed versions.

Where a design is built up from repeating elements, use of segments provides a very efficient drawing construction method—particularly when it is combined with some of the other techniques that we have considered. Segments can be snapped into place on grids and skeletons of construction lines, and arrangements of segments can be replicated and transformed as higher-level subsystems.

As J-N-L Durand demonstrated in his *Précis* and other texts, complex designs can often be parsed into hierarchies of repeating subsystems. Skeletons of construction lines define the geometric relationships between subsystems. At the lowest level of the hierarchy there are very basic standard elements. A computer drafting strategy based on use of segments, snapping to constructed points and lines, and replication and transformation of increasingly complex subsystems is directly in the tradition of Durand.

Parametric Variation

The usefulness of a standard shape to a designer is much enhanced if instances of that shape can be varied appropriately to fit many different contexts: a doorswing that can fit to an opening of any width is more useful than one of fixed width. So standard shapes are usually parameterized for adaptability. Consider, for example, a semicircular arch (figure 7.33). Obvious parameters are span, thickness, and number of voussoirs. By varying these parameters, while preserving the essential form of the arch, we can produce a wide range of instances.

Drafting systems that provide vocabularies of parameterized shapes allow the user to specify parameter values and have the capacity to produce the corresponding instance automatically—a process known as parametric variation. This is accomplished by treating some of the entries in the data structure as variables rather than constants and by specifying that the values of some variables are dependent on the values of others. The form of the dependency is described by a numerical function. Figure 7.34, for example, shows the network of dependencies for our semi-circular arch.

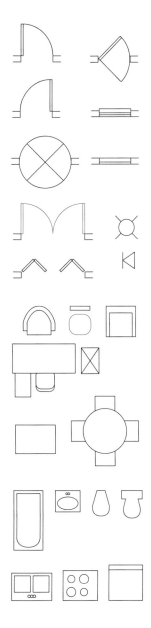

7.32
Part of a shape menu for interior design applications

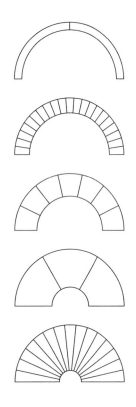

7.33
Parametric variations on a
simple arch

Independent variables

Thickness

Span

Number of
voussoirs

Height

Chord length
of voussoir

Angle swept
by voussoir

Dependent variables

7.34
Network of dependencies
for the arch

To instantiate or modify a parameterized shape, the designer simply specifies values for the parameters by typing them in, by moving a slider, or by selecting and moving a point on the shape itself. Values of dependent variables are then calculated, and the corresponding instance is displayed.

Drafting systems with simple data structures typically use parametric shape procedures merely as data-input tools—"adjustable stencils"—that create sets of lines and add them to the data structure. Under this arrangement, relationships between shape variables are not recorded as part of the design, and shapes cannot be varied parametrically after they are inserted. Systems with more sophisticated data structures store parameter values in the data structure and execute parametric procedures whenever instances of parametric shapes need to be displayed. Thus relationships between shape variables are permanently recorded, and shapes can be varied parametrically at any time.

The most comprehensive and rigorous approach to implementation of parametric variation capability provides for storage of relationships both *within* and *between* parametric shapes. In other words, the user can specify functions that make the parameters of one shape dependent on the parameters of another shape and can vary the parameters of this function to create different instances of the relationship. For example, a parameterized rectangle and a parameterized ellipse might be put into a coaxial relationship (figure 7.35). Thus the coordinates and orientation of the ellipse are made dependent on the coordinates and orientation of the rectangle, and the parameter of the relationship is the center-to-center distance along the common axis. The relationship can be depicted by drawing the axis and showing a dimension arrow. An interface might allow for selecting and dragging the tips of the dimension arrow to vary the relationship.

Many of the shape-to-shape relationships that designers need to define are quite simple and can easily be shown graphically by analogy with common mechanisms (figure 7.36). If a point on one shape is "pinned" to a point on the other, then the shapes can rotate in relation to each other.

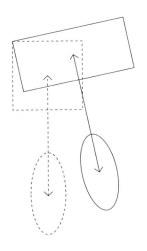

7.35
Maintaining a spatial
relationship

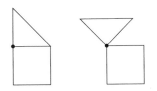

Pinned at a point

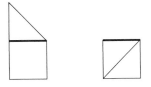

Hinged along a line

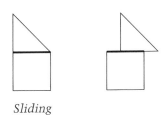

Sliding

7.36
Shape relationships as
mechanisms

If a straight line on one shape is "hinged" with a straight line on the other, then the two shapes can reflect in relation to each other. If a straight line on one shape can "slide" along a straight line on the other, then the two shapes can translate in relation to each other. And an adjustable pair of lines diverging from a center of scaling can be used to vary a proportion relationship. Tick marks can be placed on these regulating lines to show the limits of variation. The idea can be extended indefinitely by allowing locations and orientations of some regulating lines to control locations and orientations of other regulating lines. (The idea of regulating lines is, of course, an old one: both Durand and Le Corbusier relied heavily on it. But it becomes much more useful and interesting when lines are used not just as a rigid construction skeleton, but to regulate the behavior of a drawing and maintain its essential structure as parts are manipulated.)

Some drafting systems provide fixed vocabularies of parameterized standard shapes and regulating lines which you can "click together." Others allow you to extend the vocabulary as required by programming your own through spreadsheet interfaces or by providing a general-purpose programming language (such as Pascal or Lisp) that can access the data structure.

Constraint Solving

Now consider a relation of the form $a + b = c$ between three shape parameters (figure 7.37). Such relations are called constraints, since assignment of a value to any variable restricts or determines the values that can consistently be taken by the others. In this particular case, assignment of values to any two of the variables determines the value of the third, as we can see by transposing the expression to read $a = c - b$ or $b = c - a$. In general, any kind of arithmetic expression can appear in a constraint, and the relational operator linking the two sides may specify equality, that one side is less than the other, or that one side is greater than the other.

The most general and flexible way to provide for parametric shape variation in a drafting system is to allow the user to specify arbitrary constraints on the locations of

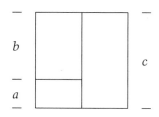

A parameterized shape

*Relationship of the
parameters*

7.37
Interdependent parameter
values

7.38
Possible behaviors of a
constrained object

line end points (and additional defining points in the case of curves) and automatically to adjust end-point locations as necessary to maintain consistency whenever the user selects and moves any one of the constrained points (figure 7.38). Software systems that perform the necessary calculations are known as constraint solvers, and these are an increasingly standard feature of advanced drafting systems.

Depending on the nature of the specified constraints, a shape may be underconstrained so that there are many ways to adjust it to maintain consistency, it may be uniquely constrained so that there is just one way to adjust it, or it may be overconstrained so that there is no way to adjust it. You can discover how much freedom there is in the shape by experimentally attempting to move points and letting the constraint solver adjust it in response.

General, efficient constraint solvers capable of handling realistic design problems are exceptionally difficult to implement: they can become formidably complex, and the computations required to find solutions to constraint problems can be extensive. So, although integration of constraint solvers into drafting systems was first proposed in the early 1960s, it was not until the late 1980s that robust, practical constraint solvers for drafting systems became commercially available.

*Moving a point on a
constrained object*

*Verticality and height
maintained*

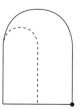

*Verticality and curvature
maintained*

End point maintained

Syntax-directed Editing

Just as the idea of constraint-based point selection and constraint-based line selection can be extended to constraint-based subshape selection, so the idea of geometric construction (putting lines in specified types of relationships with other lines) can be generalized to putting subshapes into specified types of relationships with other subshapes. Consider the possible relationships of a square to another square, for example. These include face adjacency, vertex adjacency, parallel-sided and concentric, rotated and concentric, and face to diagonal (figure 7.39). A simple syntax-directed drafting system that provided a square as the vocabulary element and tools for inserting squares in these relationships would support very efficient construction of the types of compositions shown in figure 7.40. (The term "syntax directed" is used because such relationships define the syntax of compositions made from vocabulary elements.)

Deletion of subshapes may also be syntax directed. In other words, the system may provide operations for deleting specified parts of certain types of subshapes. In general, a syntax-directed editing operation may be described as a rule for replacing one type of subshape with another (figure 7.41). The rule can be applied to any subshape that matches the left-hand side. The result of application may be insertion of a new subshape, deletion of part or all of the existing subshape, or some combination of insertion and deletion.

Syntax-directed editing rules customize a drafting system for very efficient construction of designs of a certain type. (They amount to shape grammars that specify languages of line compositions.) There may be rules for laying out floor plans, developing window details, and so on.

Interface Dynamics

Traditional drawings are static: lines remain fixed in place on the paper and can be altered only by laboriously erasing and redrawing. But the line structures maintained and displayed by a drafting system are dynamic: they can be

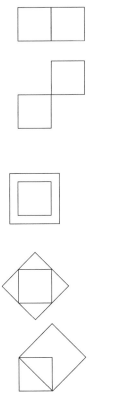

7.39
Possible relationships of
two squares

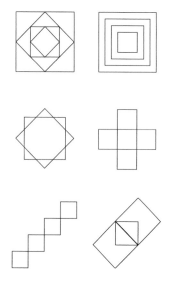

7.40
Some shapes made
by snapping squares
into standard spatial
relationships

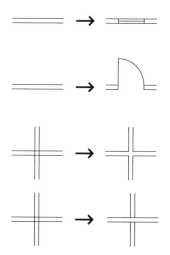

7.41
Examples of syntax-
directed editing rules

varied rapidly and continuously. Increasingly, as computers have become faster and display technology has become more sophisticated, drafting system software has reduced its reliance on metaphors carried over from traditional drafting and has exploited the potentials of dynamic interaction. Use of a highly dynamic drafting system not only is quicker than traditional drafting (or use of the older style of computer drafting system), but also provides a qualitatively different way to explore shape, dimension, and geometric organization.

The most elementary use of dynamic interaction is in line-insertion operations. Most systems provide rubber-band straight lines and variants of the same technique for inserting circular arcs, elliptical arcs, and rectangular boxes. More sophisticated systems also provide for real-time manipulation of spline curves by selecting and tweaking control points. The most sophisticated systems evaluate dependent variables or even solve constraint systems with sufficient speed to support real-time parametric variation of complex shapes.

In older systems geometric transformations of shapes were first specified by a typed command and then executed—often with significant delay. But in newer systems translations, rotations, and resizings of complex shapes are accomplished in real time by selecting the shape with a mouse or stylus then continuously dragging into position (figure 7.42). Even reflection operations can be performed continuously (although they actually amount to rotating a shape out of the plane) by dragging the corner of a selection rectangle back across one of that rectangle's edges. This lets a designer observe a continuum of possibilities.

But the real potential of dynamic interaction emerges when it is combined with snapping, geometric construction, and syntax-directed editing. In the simplest case, a rubber-band line or dragged shape snaps from grid location to grid location instead of varying continuously. In a more sophisticated syntax-directed system, the user specifies the spatial relationships that are of interest, and a line or shape snaps to the nearest one as the cursor moves around. As a rubber-band line moves across a complex drawing, for

7.42
Examples of continuous
geometric transformations

example, it might snap to the end points of existing lines, to the center and tangent points of existing arcs, and into parallel and perpendicular relationships with existing lines.

In traditional drafting, lines are fitted into place one by one—like the stones of a pyramid. But in dynamic drafting, a designer specifies the elements and constraints of mechanisms, then explores adjustments of those mechanisms to join them together and appropriately embed them in particular contexts. A drawing is not a fixed structure of lines, but the current state of a line mechanism that has been organized to behave in a particular way.

Structuring Drawings

Lengthy texts are usually subdivided into named parts, such as chapters, then these parts may be further subdivided into subsections, and so on. (This book, for example, has a two-level hierarchy described by a table of contents.) Similarly, it is convenient to subdivide a large and complex drawing into named parts that have related content. Each of these parts is a subset of the set of points and lines constituting the complete drawing.

One way to represent the assignment of entities to subsets is to store each subset of graphic entities in a separate, appropriately named file. Another possibility is to store all the entities in a single file, but to add a field for a subset name to each entity record. In either case, the effect is to assign each entity to one and only one subset. By analogy (though an imperfect one) with the traditional use in technical drafting of overlaid sheets of transparent paper, subsets of graphic entities are usually referred to as drawing "layers" (figure 7.43). Assigning an entity to a layer, then, is like drawing it on a particular sheet. Drafting systems provide mechanisms (which range from elementary to very elaborate and sophisticated) for organizing drawings in this way. At a minimum, they provide for creating and naming layers, working in specified layers or combinations of layers, shifting elements and shapes from layer to layer, and selecting layers or combinations of layers for display, editing, or printing. Flexible layer-selection capabilities become particularly important when

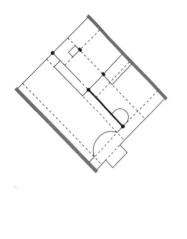

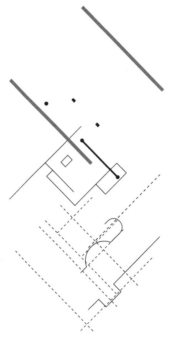

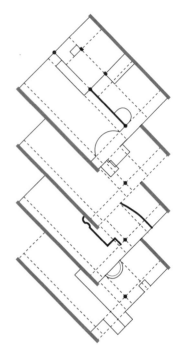

A plan . . .

Made up of several layers representing systems

As one of several layers representing building levels

7.43
Layers

Regulating lines
  rc
  1ere
  2eme
  3eme
Walls
  free walls
    rc
    1ere
    2eme
    3eme
  shared walls
Piloti
Windows
Rails

7.44
Example of layer hierarchy

large, complex drawings must be displayed and edited on small computer screens.

More sophisticated systems provide for partitioning of layers into sublayers, then further partitioning of sublayers, and so on to produce a hierarchy of graphic parts (figure 7.44). This provides the user with an efficient way to retrieve parts of a large drawing, in the same way that the hierarchical organization of a large library according to the Dewey Decimal System provides an efficient way to retrieve books. However, the simple "transparent paper" metaphor begins to break down when layers are organized in this fashion.

In general, a drafting system's drawing organization capabilities need not be constrained by the old-fashioned and inadequate "transparent paper layer" metaphor. A more flexible strategy is to allow association of multiple nongeometric attribute fields with each graphic entity (figure 7.45). Some of these fields may contain values needed to control graphic display and access. Others may be defined by the user for the purpose of associating

Geometric data			Nongeometric data (system-defined fields)				Nongeometric data (user-defined fields)			
ID#	Type	Points	Color	On/off	Access	Revision	Label	Floor	Room	Cost

7.45
Association of nongraphic data with geometric entities

identifiers—floor number, room number, subsystem, supplier, and so on—with each entity record. Entities may then be selected, sorted, and displayed by any specified combination of these identifiers. In other words, the drawing is treated as a graphic database from which different types of reports are generated for different purposes. Drawings organized in this way are content addressable rather than location addressable: you retrieve and display drawing elements according to what they are, rather than according to where you put them.

The idea of a drawing as graphic database can be taken one useful step further by allowing association with graphic entities of data fields for costs, specification clauses, text notes, and the like. This facilitates coordination of drawings, specifications, and other documents, and (with appropriate data-extraction software) allows the graphic database to serve as a source of input for costing, schedule production, and other programs. The approach is of limited utility, however, since drafted drawings typically do not provide a sufficiently complete, nonredundant, consistent description of a project. (Later we shall see that appropriately structured three-dimensional geometric models can do so.)

Different design tasks demand different organizations of a drawing. A simple diagram might be drafted on a single layer. An elementary organization into a small number of layers usually suffices for development of architectural plans and elevations. But very large, complex, technical drawings usually benefit from careful organization into sophisticated graphic databases. The drawing-organizational tools provided by drafting software are correspondingly varied. Inexpensive systems, designed for performing simple tasks on personal computers, usually provide only basic layering schemes. But systems designed for handling large and complex projects need to provide general, flexible database-management tools equal to such tasks.

Formatting Drawings

Recall the way that, in text processing, the stored text may be given particular typographic form and layout for display and printing. Similarly, with drafting systems, a file of abstract geometric information may be given specific graphic form. Shapes may be laid out at particular scales on surfaces of specified dimensions, lines may be given particular weights and styles, and details such as title blocks may be added. In traditional drafting a sheet size and scale must be selected before you begin drawing, and you cannot change the weight or style of a line once it has been drawn (except by laborious erasing and redrawing); but a computer drafting system allows you to make or change formatting decisions at any time and to generate displays and drawings at different scales and in different formats from the same file (figure 7.46). This yields large efficiencies. It also facilitates making graphic design decisions, since you can easily try out different line weights and so on, and judge their effect on the appearance of the complete drawing.

One important consequence of this separation between specification of geometric information and formatting of drawings is that you do not work (as you must, in traditional drafting) at a specific, fixed scale. Instead, you specify actual (full-scale) dimensions and coordinates, and map this information at any appropriate scale whenever you need to produce a display or plotted drawing. Display software treats the window in which the drawing is displayed as the viewfinder of a camera with which you can track and zoom freely across the surface of the drawing. You can zoom in to work on a detail, or you can zoom out to see the whole drawing. You may want to have

Scaling

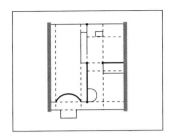 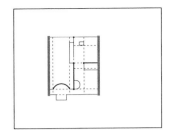

*Adding notation
(independent of scale)*

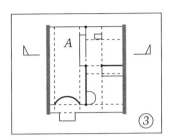 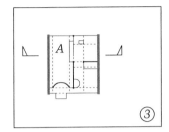

*Varying line types and
weights*

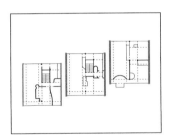 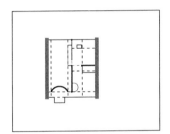

*Arranging multiple views
on sheet*

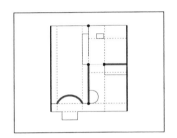 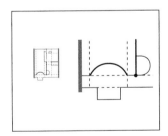

Selecting layers

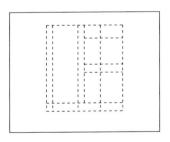 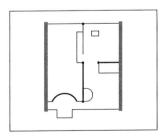

7.46
Formatting output

several windows open at once—one providing an overview of the entire drawing, and the others zoomed in to various details.

This separation of dimensional definition from scaling for display allows some useful freedoms in the handling of dimensional information. You can, for example, work in a dimensionless conceptual unit such as a module or bay and only later give a design definite dimensions by assigning a value to this unit. Or you can design a building in feet and inches but produce the drawings at a metric scale.

Another difference from traditional drafting is that you can precisely control the kind and amount of graphic information displayed at a particular moment or shown on a print that is made for a particular purpose. Where a layering scheme is used you accomplish this simply by switching layers on and off to yield different combinations: if your drawing is subdivided into n layers you will be able to display or print 2^n different combinations of layers. Where more sophisticated database-management techniques are used, you specify exactly what kinds of things you want to see and the software responds by searching the database to produce an appropriate graphic report. Selective display is not just a convenience, it can also be an important design-analysis tool. If you want to study the relationship between, say, the circulation system and the structure of a building, you can generate a display or print showing just the circulation and structural elements.

Printing and Plotting

Printers and plotters are, like traditional devices such as ruling, Graphos, and Rapidograph pens, devices for precisely placing ink on paper. The difference is that they are controlled by streams of commands sent from a computer rather than by a human hand and eye. They vary widely in cost, speed, reliability, sheet size, line quality, and the precision of control that they offer.

Electromechanical pen plotters, which emerged in the earliest days of computer graphics, provided for many years the standard way to produce output from drafting systems, and they still have their uses. They literally embody the idea that a line is the visible trajectory of a moving point, since they all work by moving a pen or marker across a drawing surface, though there is considerable variation in the specific arrangements of gantries, drums, and so on used to achieve this. The pen is moved in a raised position to locate it at the start of a line, then moved in a lowered position to draw the line. Different line weights and colors are produced through some arrangement for selecting different pens.

Pen plotters can produce large, precisely drafted ink drawings on standard drafting film, so they fit very easily into design offices that still make extensive use of traditional drafting and reprographic techniques. The plotted drawings can be stored and printed in the usual ways and can be finished or corrected by hand if this is desired. Since pen plotters have many mechanical components, however, they cannot be produced very inexpensively, and they are intrinsically limited in both speed and reliability. This means that they are increasingly being displaced as more fully electronic raster printing devices develop in capacity and sophistication and drop in cost.

Some people find the precise, mechanical quality of pen plotters unattractive and prefer the slightly wobbly line work and imprecise endings of hand-drawn lines. Pen-plotted drawings can be "humanized," in a disconcertingly convincing way, by mounting a pen loosely so that it shakes a little as it moves (figure 7.47).

Raster printers and plotters work by depositing tiny dots of ink to build up lines, characters, and halftone screens. Many different transfer mechanisms are used: impact, thermal, electrostatic, inkjet, and laser. Resolution varies (depending on the technology) from less than one hundred dots per inch to several thousand dots per inch, and paper formats range from letter size up to the sizes handled by the largest pen plotters.

In the past the use of raster printers and plotters was limited by the need to execute a slow and expensive process of rasterizing line data (converting it to patterns of dots) before printing. Large, high-resolution drawings

7.47
Results of varying plotter pen stability

presented a particular problem, since they translated into huge quantities of raster data. As processor and memory costs have dropped, however, rasterization processes have become quicker and cheaper—making raster printing and plotting increasingly attractive.

Raster printers and plotters are much more versatile than pen plotters, since lines, characters, and halftone screens can all be built up from dots. There is no need to use crosshatching to produce toned areas on drawings, and the characters used in annotation text can be in standard fonts (not constructed from small numbers of pen strokes). So many of the old conventions of technical drafting, which derive from the physical limitations of technical pens and the need to minimize penstrokes, can be abandoned when raster printers and plotters are used for drawing production.

Automated Measurement and Analysis

Designers do not just construct and produce drawings, they also measure and analyze them. (Indeed, one of the fundamental purposes of precise construction is to allow accurate measurement.) They measure lengths, angles, and areas, and they count instances of things. Traditionally, the have used tools such as graduated scale rules, protractors, and planimeters to accomplish these tasks, together with slide rules or electronic calculators to derive additional quantities from these basic measurements. Drafting systems provide measurement capabilities through application of arithmetic procedures to values stored in the data structure.

The most elementary capability is that of reporting the numerical coordinates of a selected point. The capability of a scale rule can be provided by a simple procedure that calculates and reports the distance between two selected points and that of a protractor by a procedure that calculates and reports the angle between two straight lines. More complex procedures can be implemented to calculate distances along the various types of curved lines provided by a system.

In systems that provide parametric shapes, parameter values can be processed not only to produce shape instances, but also to yield properties of those instances. If you know the length and width of a rectangle, for example, you can calculate its area, perimeter, proportion, area/perimeter ratio, and so on. The data structure can also be scanned to produce counts of the instances of specified types of subshapes. Note, however, that counting procedures that recognize emergent instances will, in general, produce different results from procedures that only take account of instances that are explicitly represented in the data structure.

The simplest measurement facilities merely report measured values on the screen. More ambitious systems provide interfaces to spreadsheets or programming languages so that further analyses can be developed from the extracted values. A spreadsheet might be used, for example, to apply cost coefficients to measured plan areas and report rough cost estimates.

Uses and Limitations of Two-dimensional Drawings

All models are abstractions from the full complexity of reality: they specify some properties and relationships of real objects completely and accurately, but distort others or leave them out entirely. An appropriate model for some particular purpose conveniently represents just those properties and relationships that are relevant to that purpose, but at the same time achieves clarity and economy by leaving out everything that is not. A model that consists of a set of two-dimensional line drawings of a building or other design is a particularly highly abstracted representation, and this is the source of both its major strengths and its most obvious weaknesses. When it explicitly presents and appropriately structures precisely the information that matters to an architect or engineer at a particular stage in the building design process, it is particularly convenient and economical. But because it deals with only a few aspects of a very complex reality, there are many important design activities that it cannot support.

Since the data structure of a two-dimensional drafting system represents surfaces and solids only by their edge lines, and most edge lines only by their end points, and since it represents three-dimensional objects only in two-dimensional projection, it has the virtues of parsimony. It is relatively quick and easy to construct (by comparison with the more complete three-dimensional representations that we will consider later), economical in use of memory, and rapidly manipulable. Since coordinates are stored with high precision it allows sizes, shapes, and locations of elements in plan, section, and elevation to be specified with great accuracy. (This is not possible in a paint system, where precision is severely restricted by the limited size of the raster grid.)

The main disadvantage of such an abstract and economical representation is that the viewer must "fill in" a great deal of information to interpret two-dimensional shapes as projections of three-dimensional objects and lines as boundaries of surfaces and solids. Misinterpretation is possible (especially if the delineator and viewer do not share a common understanding of architectural forms and construction processes), and there is considerable danger that ambiguities and inconsistencies will escape notice until it is too late to avoid damaging consequences. Furthermore, where a complete and consistent geometric description of a design is needed as input to a procedure that performs some design analysis or synthesis task, a drafting system model usually cannot provide it.

The value of models that have greater geometric completeness should not be overstated, however. Plan, section, and elevation drawn precisely in line are not just deficient representations of three-dimensional form (as proponents of more elaborate three-dimensional modeling systems sometimes like to suggest): they are, when properly constructed and used, powerful abstractions that allow the designer to focus on issues of central importance. As Le Corbusier remarked, in *Vers une architecture:*

To make a plan is to determine and fix ideas. It is to have had ideas. . . A plan is to some extent a summary like an analytical contents table. In a form so condensed that it seems as clear as crystal and like a geometric figure, it contains an enormous quantity of ideas and the impulse of an intention.

But, as he also emphasized, exploration of architectural ideas does not stop at this level of abstraction:

The plan is the generator, "the plan is the determination of everything; it is an austere abstraction, an algebrization, and cold of aspect." It is a plan of battle. The battle follows and that is the great moment. The battle is composed of the impact of masses in space. . .

Thus a two-dimensional drafting system is most appropriately used in design at a relatively early stage when, after some initial unstructured exploration (perhaps by freehand sketching on paper or with a paint system), it is time to "determine and fix ideas" with some precision. Then, to engage the "battle" that follows, it becomes more useful to employ less abstract models—models that represent lines, surfaces, and volumes in three-dimensional space and that show the effects of surfaces in light. Later, when a design has been completed, the precise, parsimonious character of drafted plans, sections, and elevations again becomes appropriate for expression of definitive construction information.

It would be a serious mistake to think that use of a computer for drafting such two-dimensional line representations merely results in quicker production of finished drawings. Indeed, efficiency in drawing production is no more than a useful byproduct. The real significance of computer use for drafting is that static, location-addressable, fixed-format, non-machine-analyzable design representations give way to dynamic, content-addressable, variable-format, machine-analyzable representations. This provides more effective support of design exploration, graphic problem-solving, and analysis.

Suggested Readings

Bowyer, Adrian and John Woodwark. 1983. *A Programmer's Geometry*. London: Butterworths.

Crosley, Mark Lauden. 1987. *The Architect's Guide to Computer-Aided Design*. New York: John Wiley.

Durand, Jean-Nicolas-Louis. 1802. *Précis des leçons d'architecture*. Paris: Ecole Polytechnique.

Durand, Jean-Nicolas-Louis. 1821. *Partie graphique des cours d'architecture*. Paris: Ecole Polytechnique.

Gross, Mark. 1990. "Relational Modeling: A Basis for Computer-Assisted Design." In Malcolm McCullough, William J. Mitchell, and Patrick Purcell (eds.), *The Electronic Design Studio*. Cambridge: The MIT Press.

Kroll, Lucien. 1987. "Computers. " In *An Architecture of Complexity*. Cambridge: The MIT Press.

Mitchell, William J., Robin S. Liggett, and Thomas Kvan. 1987. *The Art of Computer Graphics Programming*. New York: Van Nostrand Reinhold.

Mortenson, Michael. 1989. *Computer Graphics: An Introduction to the Mathematics and Geometry*. New York: Industrial Press.

Radford, Antony, and Garry Stevens. 1987. "Computer-Aided Drafting." in *CADD Made Easy: A Comprehensive Guide for Architects and Designers*. New York: McGraw-Hill.

Reynolds, R. A. 1987. "Computer-Aided Draughting." In *Computing for Architects*. London: Butterworths.

Schilling, Terrence G., and Patricia M. Schilling. 1987. "Drawing Organization." In *Intelligent Drawings: Managing CAD and Information Systems in the Design Office*. New York: McGraw-Hill.

Stiny, George. 1990. "What Designers Do that Computers Should." In Malcolm McCullough, William J. Mitchell, and Patrick Purcell (eds.), *The Electronic Design Studio*. Cambridge: The MIT Press.

8

POLYGONS, PLANS, AND MAPS

A map of the United States can be seen not just as a collection of lines depicting coasts and state borders but also as a collection of closed polygons—the states themselves (figure 8.1). Similarly, an outline floor plan can be seen as a collection of polygons corresponding to rooms (figure 8.2). For many practical purposes it is useful to extend the techniques considered in the previous chapter to provide for representation of plans, maps, and other two-dimensional designs as collections of polygons. This allows association of names, colors, and patterns with polygons; production of graphics with shaded, colored, and pattern-filled areas; automatic calculation of areas, perimeters, centroids, and other such geometric properties; and association of nongeometric data (such as population statistics) with polygons to produce spatially indexed information systems.

Specialized systems that model designs as collections of polygons have many important practical applications in architectural space planning, in urban design, in landscape analysis, and in facilities management. Tools for constructing and manipulating polygons are also frequently added to general-purpose drafting and paint systems. Some general-purpose graphics systems integrate all three types of graphic elements that we have considered so far—bitmaps, lines, and polygons—within a unified framework.

8.1
A map composed of polygons

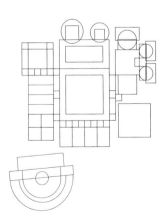

8.2
A plan composed of polygons

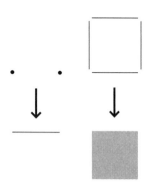

8.3
Points bound lines and lines
bound polygons

Representing and Manipulating Polygons

Just as zero-dimensional points can be associated to define one-dimensional lines, so one-dimensional lines can be associated to define two-dimensional closed polygons (figure 8.3). In each case geometric objects of lower dimensionality become boundaries of objects of higher dimensionality. The usual way to represent collections of polygons in computer memory, then, is to list the coordinates of vertices in order (figure 8.4): each pair of successive vertices thus defines an edge, and the sequence of edges bounds the polygon. The corresponding way for a user to specify a polygon is to click off the vertices, one by one in clockwise or counterclockwise sequence, with a mouse or stylus. To allow reshaping of polygons that have already been constructed, polygon-modeling software often provides vertex insertion, deletion, and displacement (tweaking) operations (figure 8.5).

Strictly speaking, the vertices of polygons are always connected by straight edges. But polygon-modeling software often generalizes by allowing polylines, arcs and other kinds of curves to form edges (figure 8.6) and by providing for vertices to be interpreted as spline control points instead of as end points of edges (figure 8.7). Chains of vertices form edges; chains of edges joined end-to-end in a ring form a polygon. (figure 8.8).

Chain representations of polygons, though adequate for many practical purposes, do suffer from some fundamental limitations. First, they do not guarantee that polygons are well formed: they allow edges to cross and form topologically inadmissable loops, as shown in figure 8.9. Secondly, they do not allow representation of polygons with holes (figure 8.10)—although this latter limitation can be overcome by introducing additional edges connecting holes to the exterior.

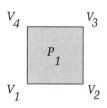

V_4 V_3

P_1

V_1 V_2

V_1 (1,0)	E_1 (V_1,V_2)
V_2 (1,0)	E_2 (V_2,V_3)
V_3 (1,1)	E_3 (V_3,V_4)
V_4 (0,1)	E_4 (V_4,V_1)

P_1 (E_1 , E_2 , E_3 , E_4)

8.4
Numerical description of a
polygon

Define chain

Displace

Remove

Add and displace

8.5
Adding, deleting, and
displacing vertices

8.6
Closed shapes with
straight and curved edges

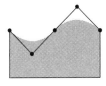

8.7
Interpretation of vertices as
spline control points

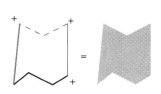

8.8
Joining chains to form a
closed polygon

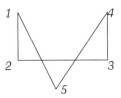

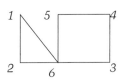

8.9
Invalid polygons
produced by tweaking
operations

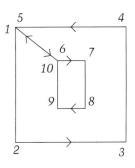

8.10
Representing a hole by
inserting additional edges

Union

Intersection

Subtraction (A–B)

Subtraction (B–A)

8.11
Area set operations

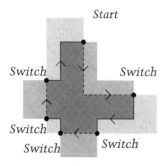

8.12
Finding a polygon of intersection

Union, Intersection, and Subtraction

Many polygon-modeling systems extend the basic repertoire of polygon-manipulation tools by providing union, intersection, and difference operations. These allow polygons to be used as "stencils" for cutting each other, like pieces of cardboard (figure 8.11).

The basic procedure for computing unions, intersections, and differences is first to identify the intersection polygon, then to delete edges as appropriate to produce the particular result required. The usual way to find the intersection polygon is to apply the right-turn rule: start at a point where an edge of one polygon crosses into the interior of the other polygon, then trace edges in clockwise fashion, switching from one polygon to the other wherever their edges intersect (figure 8.12). In practice, this simple and elegant procedure must be elaborated to deal with various special conditions that defeat it (as, for example, when a vertex of one polygon lies on an edge of the other) and to avoid finding spurious intersections or missing real ones as a result of round-off errors in coordinate calculations.

Displaying and Printing Polygons

Polygons represented in a data structure may be interpreted graphically in several different ways (figure 8.13). The most direct interpretation is produced by showing the edges as lines. Alternatively, polygons may be filled with tones or colors, or they may be hatched with line patterns. This is particularly effective when output is produced with high-resolution laser printers that can generate fine halftone screens and delicate patterns. Fill colors and patterns need not be uniform: many polygon-modeling systems provide for a variety of graduated fill effects, much like those produced by graded watercolor washes or by airbrushing within a polygonal boundary defined by a stencil.

Filling and hatching procedures all make use of a more basic procedure—the point-in-polygon procedure—for determining whether an arbitrary point is inside a specified polygon. This has many variants, but essentially it goes as follows (figure 8.14). Extend a ray from the point to another point known to be outside the polygon's boundary, and count the number of times that the ray intersects the polygon's edges. If the number of intersections is odd, then the point is within the polygon; but if the number of intersections is even, then the point is outside. (There is an ambiguous condition if the ray happens to pass through a vertex: this must be detected, and a new ray chosen.)

Many real polygons, such as that defined by the coastline of Australia, are of indefinite complexity; the more closely you look at them, the more complicated they become. However, it makes practical sense to simplify them for small-scale display on devices of limited resolution. So some polygon-mapping systems will automatically simplify complicated outlines (as represented numerically in the database) to match the resolution of the current view. Display conventions may also vary automatically with scale; a city might be shown as a simple dot on a large map, as a small circle in a closer view, as an outline polygon when closer still, and eventually as a collection of polygons representing actual city blocks.

Display software must also be designed to handle overlapping polygons appropriately. When opaque filled polygons are drawn on top of each other on raster displays, the later polygons occlude the earlier ones, and different drawing orders produce different graphic results—just as paper cutout polygons can be superimposed in different ways (figure 8.15). Thus polygon-modeling systems typically assign a definite drawing order by sending a selected polygon to the bottom, by bringing a selected polygon to the top, and so on.

When a transparent polygon is superimposed on another colored polygon, the color of the overlap should be determined by the colors of both the top polygon and the bottom polygon. The color mixture may be additive, as when one patch of colored light overlaps another, or subtractive, as with polygons of colored film on a light table or with layers of transparent watercolor wash. The data structures of polygon-modeling systems can straightforwardly be extended to allow association of transparency values with polygons, and the display software can then be modified to produce effects of transparent overlay (figure 8.16).

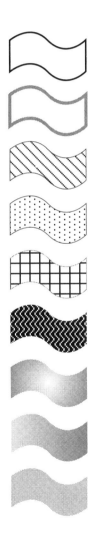

8.13
Varying outlines and fills

Compositions

It is often useful to model a building elevation or section as a collection of polygons (figure 8.17). These polygons can be filled with patterns or colors to represent different materials. Overlaid elements in a composition can be explored quickly using opaque polygons (figure 8.18). Cast shadows can also be represented by polygons. Shading of curved surfaces can be depicted by means of graduated fills, and glass can be represented with transparent colored polygons. This type of representation allows rapid experimentation with alternative color schemes, tonal relationships, and textural effects, since polygons can be selected and their colors or patterns redefined at will. The process is very much more efficient than the traditional ones of using watercolor wash to fill between inked boundaries or of cutting out and laying down pieces of adhesive colored film.

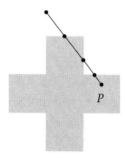

Odd: Inside

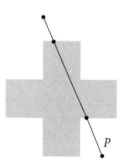

Even: Outside

8.14
The point-in-polygon test

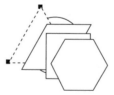

A stack of polygons (in order of their creation)

A move-forward operation

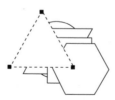

A move-to-front operation

8.15
Superimposition of opaque polygons

Opaque

Transparent (no fill)

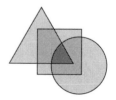

Partially transparent

8.16
Transparency

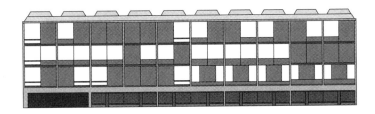

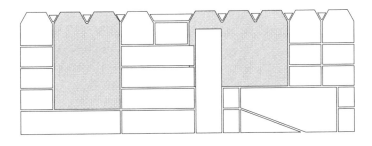

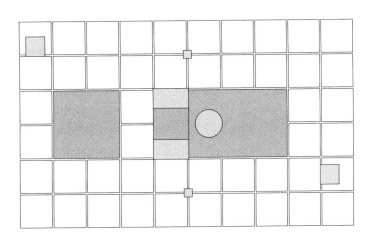

8.17
Elevation, section, and plan
composed of polygons

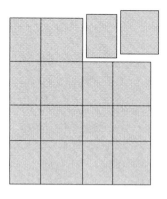 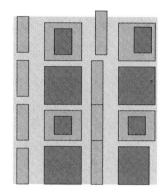 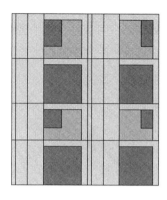

8.18
Composing by means of
opaque polygons

8.19
A site plan composed of
building footprint and
shadow polygons

Many schematic design issues can be explored through processes of shaping, sizing, and arranging polygonal elements, and polygon-modeling systems may effectively be used to support this. Site plans may be treated as collections of building footprint and shadow polygons (figure 8.19). These can quickly be selected and fluidly moved around, much as you might shuffle cardboard polygons. Similarly, floor plans may be modeled as collections of room polygons, and furniture and equipment layouts within rooms may be explored by arranging furniture footprint polygons. Later, when wall thicknesses, door and window openings, and other details of polygon boundaries become the focus of attention, polygon representations can become underlay layers for further development of the design using drafting system capabilities.

Maps and Tessellations

Many floor plans and maps are most appropriately modeled not just as loose-packed configurations of (maybe disjoint or overlapping) polygons, but as plane-filling mosaics in which polygons share boundaries. Such mosaics may be uniform like triangular or square grids, they may be regular like the many repeating tile patterns that are known (figure 8.20), or they may be completely arbitrary.

The first step in using a polygon-modeling system to design a repeating tile pattern is to define the tile shapes that are to be used. Combinations of copy, translate, rotate, and reflect operations can then be employed to build up regularly repeating structures. If there is a programming language interface to the system, some

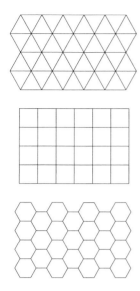

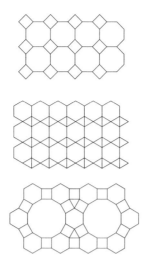

8.20
Types of mosaics: regular grids, repeating tile patterns, and a map composed of arbitrary polygons

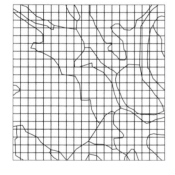

8.21
A square grid superimposed on a polygon map

simple code may be written to execute the repetitive operations that are involved. Once patterns have been produced, colors and shapes can be varied to yield many different figures and readings.

A political map of the United States is an example of an irregular mosaic of polygons; it consists of arbitrarily-shaped state polygons with the edges representing state boundaries. Similarly, a single-line floor plan is a mosaic of room polygons, with the edges representing dividing wall.

Cartographers frequently employ square coordinate grids (figure 8.21). This establishes a relationship between polygon and raster representations of features. If grid cells are significantly smaller than the polygonal features being mapped, then the polygon representation can be converted into a raster representation without much loss or distortion of shape information. But, if the grid cells are large relative to the polygonal features, then such conversion distorts shapes and loses small features.

Grids for large-scale maps may vary, since the problem of projecting from the spherical coordinates of the globe to the planar coordinates of a map has many different solutions (figure 8.22). Choice of a projection usually depends on the map's intended purpose. So correct registration of maps, especially ones of different scales and from different sources, requires knowledge of the projections used and the conversion formulae between them.

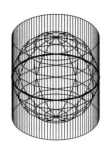
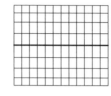

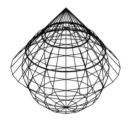
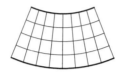

8.22
Different projections

Map and Plan Topology

To function correctly, software for processing polygon maps and plans must be designed very carefully to preserve the fundamental property that each point belongs to exactly one polygon. This is not as trivial as it may sound. Consider, for example, the floor plan shown in figure 8.23. If it is input by separately digitizing the boundaries of each individual room, each wall will be digitized and stored twice. This is inefficient, and small errors due to limited accuracy of the digitizing device will tend to produce slivers and gaps along boundaries that can lead to serious errors in processing polygons (figure 8.24). A standard way to overcome the problem is to employ a data structure based upon the idea of a vertex dictionary (figure 8.25). The coordinate records for vertices are serial numbered and referenced by a dictionary that records the vertices belonging to each polygon. Coordinates for each vertex are recorded only once, and boundaries dividing adjacent polygons are unique.

A second problem is that operations on mosaics of polygons often require access to information about connections and adjacencies of vertices, edges, and polygons, and this may be difficult to extract from representations as chains of edges or even vertex dictionary representations. Consider, for example, the simple operation of shifting a vertex (figure 8.26). In order to redraw the affected edges correctly, the system must determine the edges that are incident on that vertex. And, in order to refill the affected polygons, the system must determine the polygons that are bounded by those edges. In other words, an explicit representation of the mosaic's topology is needed.

The basic idea of a topological representation is illustrated in figure 8.27. The plan or map is treated as a network of vertices and edges. Vacant regions are bounded or partially bounded by edges. This structure may be represented as a square "adjacency matrix" in which non-zero entries signify that the corresponding vertices are connected by an edge. This matrix may be stored in highly compressed form, since it normally consists mostly of zero values. (That is, most pairs of vertices are not connected.) The topological dual of this network can usefully be represented as another adjacency matrix in which non-zero entries represent region-to-region adjacencies.

This representation allows mapping software to maintain topological consistency, as operations are performed, by enforcing some simple rules. Each edge must join two vertices and separate two regions (at least one of which must be completely enclosed). Each region must be surrounded by a cycle of alternating edges and vertices, and each vertex must be surrounded by a cycle of alternating regions and edges. Finally, each intersection of edges must be a vertex. Compliance with these rules assures that properties of polygon incidence, inclusion, and adjacency are not inconsistently or ambiguously represented.

Polygon-mapping software may automatically check for topological consistency when maps are digitized or translated from drafting systems (figure 8.28). When inconsistencies are detected, a system may automatically correct them (when the resolutions are obvious) or else prompt the user for further information.

Sophisticated polygon-mapping systems may allow different sorts of information to be represented in different map layers, as illustrated in figure 8.29. Layers may be overlaid automatically to produce new thematic maps with new polygon boundaries and topologies. These systems often combine polygon data with line and point data.

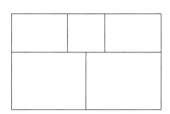

8.23
Plan as a mosaic of polygons

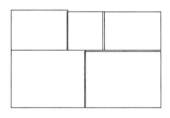

8.24
Redundancy and inaccuracy in a plan mosaic of polygons

8.25
A vertex dictionary

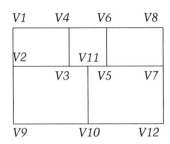

V1 (X1,Y1)
V2 (X1,Y1)
V3 (X1,Y1)
V4 (X1,Y1)
V5 (X1,Y1)
.
.
.

P1 (V1,V2,V3,V4)
P2 (V3,V4,V5,V6)
P3 (V5,V6,V7,V8)
P4 (V2,V11,V10,V9)
.
.
.

8.26
Moving a vertex

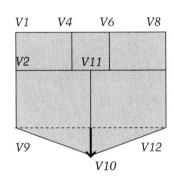

8.27
Topological representation
of a plan: a boundary
network and its dual

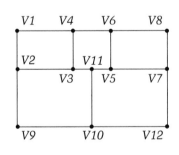
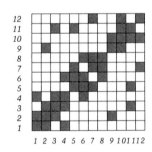

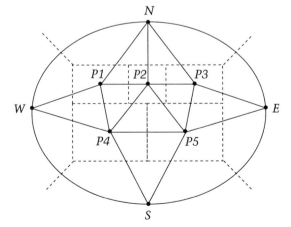

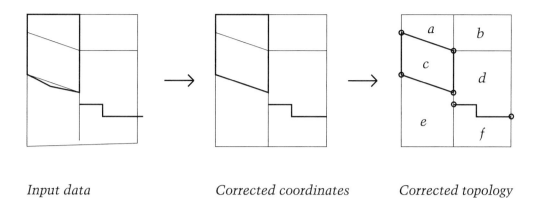

Input data   Corrected coordinates   Corrected topology

8.28
Correcting map input data
to maintain topological
consistency

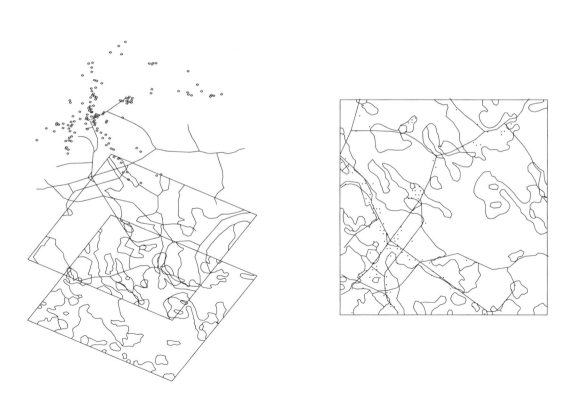

8.29
Creating a new thematic map by
combining layers

Space Planning

Many space-planning problems of the kind commonly faced by architects, interior designers, industrial engineers, and silicon chip designers (who must arrange components and their connections for optimum use of limited chip real estate) may be formulated as problems of arranging polygons or permuting their contents such that certain criteria are satisfied. In other words, the task is to assign appropriate values to variables in a polygon data structure. Several specific formulations of such problems have been investigated extensively, algorithms for solving them have been developed, and these algorithms are sometimes implemented as tools in computer-aided design systems.

One of the most straightforward of these formulations is illustrated in figure 8.30. A schematic floor plan, represented as a collection of room polygons, is given. Activities from a given list are to be assigned to rooms such that specified area requirements for activities and adjacency requirements between activities are satisfied. If there are *n* rooms and *n* activities, there will be *n*-factorial possible ways of assigning activities to rooms. The problem, then, is to search through possible assignments of activities to rooms to find at least one that satisfies the

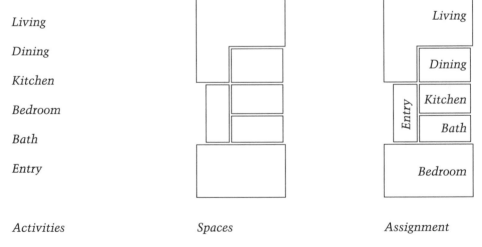

Living

Dining

Kitchen

Bedroom

Bath

Entry

Activities　　　　　*Spaces*　　　　　*Assignment*

8.30
Assignment of activities
to spaces

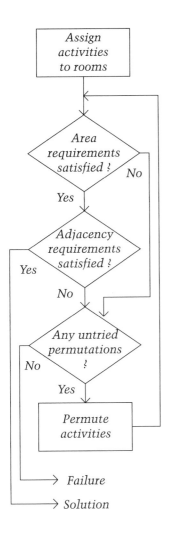

requirements. This can be a very tedious task to carry out by hand, but a computer can easily be programmed to enumerate solutions efficiently and exhaustively (provided that the adjacency and area requirements constrain the problem sufficiently and the number of rooms is not unreasonably large). The basic steps in a suitable search procedure are illustrated by means of a flow diagram in figure 8.31.

A variation on this formulation assumes that room-to-room distances and activity-to-activity traffic flows are known and that the objective is to assign activities to spaces such that circulation cost is minimized (figure 8.32). The resulting problem, known technically as a quadratic assignment problem, is much more difficult to solve since relocating an activity from one space to another affects its circulation relationships to *all* other activities. However, procedures do exist for finding good (if not necessarily optimal) solutions with a reasonable amount of computational effort. These procedures can also be used to solve analogous problems of locating warehouses within transportation networks, assigning departments of an organization to floors in a high-rise building, or laying out electronic components on a circuit board such that the total length of wiring is minimized.

8.31
Flow diagram for discovery of feasible assignments

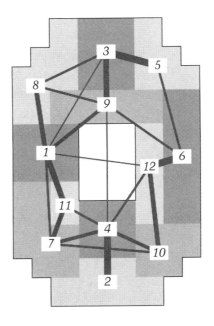

8.32
Solution to a quadratic assignment problem

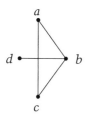

Adjacency requirements
graph

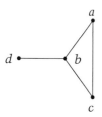

Planar embedding

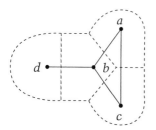

Bubble diagram

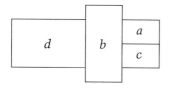

Plan satisfying area,
proportion, and shape
requirements

8.33
Development of a plan
from an adjacency-
requirements graph

But what if the layout of spaces is not given? Consider, for instance, a set of rooms, with specified adjacency requirements, and the problem of finding a plan that contains these rooms and satisfies these adjacency requirements (figure 8.33). The solution procedure, in this case, makes use of the idea of a dual graph representation of a planar mosaic of polygons (as discussed earlier). The first step is to search for a way of embedding the graph of the adjacency requirements in the plane such that no edges cross. There may be many ways of doing this, there may be just one way, or there may be no way. If there is no planar embedding, then the problem as formulated has no solution; but if there is a planar embedding, then a planar dual can always be constructed. The regions of this planar dual (with the exception of the infinite exterior regions) are the required rooms, and the edges are their walls. The final step is to adjust room shapes to satisfy any area or shape requirements. Notice how the design develops through a sequence of representations—set of spaces, topological description (the adjacency matrix), planar embedding, and final geometric realization—with information being added at each step.

Polygon Grammars

The idea of a shape grammar for two-dimensional line shapes can be extended to two-dimensional colored polygons (figure 8.34). In this case shape rules are defined on arrangements of colored polygons rather than on line shapes. Furthermore, they may include specifications of the orders in which polygons resulting from application of shape rules are to be layered. (Rules that are otherwise the same, but layer polygons in different ways, may produce very different graphic results.) Such grammars may be used to generate graphic compositions of colored areas and to produce floor plan and page layouts (figure 8.35).

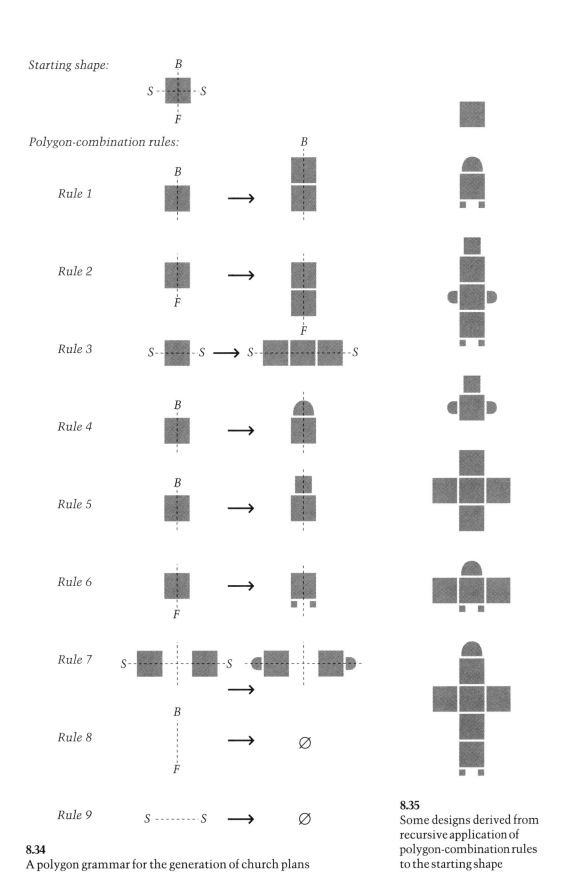

Starting shape:

Polygon-combination rules:

Rule 1

Rule 2

Rule 3

Rule 4

Rule 5

Rule 6

Rule 7

Rule 8

Rule 9

8.34
A polygon grammar for the generation of church plans

8.35
Some designs derived from
recursive application of
polygon-combination rules
to the starting shape

Geographic Information Systems

Powerful geographic information systems (GISs) can be produced by establishing cross-references between polygon geometric data and files of associated non-geometric data (figure 8.36). Thus non-geometric information can be accessed conveniently by selecting polygons. Conversely, reports produced by searching the non-geometric data can be presented graphically in the form of color-coded thematic maps.

Consider, for example, the screen display shown in figure 8.37. By clicking on a map polygon, the user of this system can retrieve an image of the corresponding building. Demographic and tax data, associated texts, recorded sounds, and video clips might be accessed in similar ways. Conversely, results of a database search for properties owned by members of a specified family might be presented by highlighting the appropriate polygons on the map (figure 8.38).

Similar systems are useful in facilities management. In this case, the facility is represented in plan as a collection of room polygons. The corresponding records of nongeometric information contain names of room occupants, telephone numbers, utility access points, furniture and equipment located in the room, and the like.

Polygon maps may also be used to provide access to collections of bitmapped images (or texts, sounds, movies, etc). For example, selecting a polygon from a city map might retrieve of an image of that building (figure 8.38). Such a system might also include historic data, so that depending on the time selected, different images (perhaps showing previous buildings at the location) could be retrieved. Indeed any electronic document can serve as a multimedia access structure—maps are just especially familiar guides for cross-referencing materials.

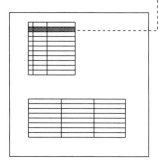

Drawing database

Relational database

8.36
Attaching nongeometric data to polygons

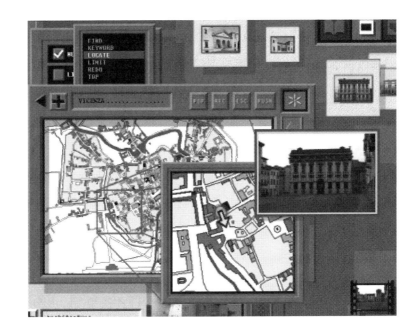

8.37
Map-based access
to images and
nongeometric data

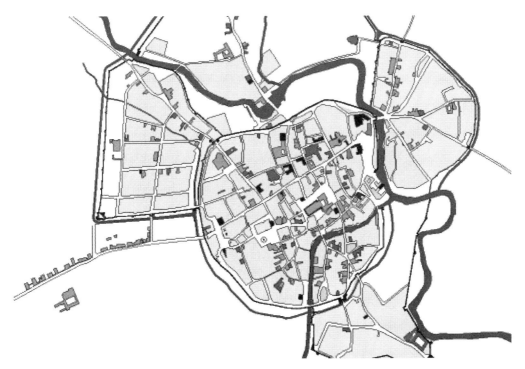

8.38
Graphical report on a
nongeometric data query

Area Analysis

The usefulness of polygon-based GIS and facility management systems can be extended greatly by adding facilities for counting polygons of specified kinds, calculating various properties of polygons, comparing polygons, and combining polygons.

Polygon area calculation capabilities allow automatic production of area reports and density and cost analyses of various kinds. One common method for computing polygon areas is illustrated in figure 8.39. A horizontal line is drawn beneath the lowest vertex, trapezoids are constructed as shown, and their areas are calculated and summed. Then the areas of the underside trapezoids are calculated and summed. Finally, the underside area is subtracted from the total area to yield the area of the polygon itself.

Another method is illustrated in figure 8.40. Triangles are constructed from a vertex as shown. The areas of each triangle are computed by a simple formula, and the total area of the outside triangles is subtracted from the total area of the inside triangles to yield the area of the polygon.

This procedure can be extended to yield polygon centroid coordinates as well. First, the centroid of each triangle is calculated as the average of its vertex coordinates. Then, the centroid of the polygon is found by taking the area-weighted average of the triangle centroids.

Computation of centroids is useful not only for technical purposes, but also in the generation of graphic displays. One good rule for placing text labels on polygons, for example, is to locate them at polygon centroids. But, since centroids of concave polygons may fall outside the polygon boundaries, this simple rule does not completely suffice, and it must be supplemented by others.

Sophisticated geographic information systems and facility management systems need the capability to combine results of area, density, and distance calculations with results of database searches to yield new graphic displays. For example, a user query might generate a display of all residentially-zoned parcels (as classified in

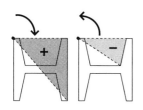

8.39
Calculating polygon areas by trapezoids

8.40
Calculating polygon areas by triangles

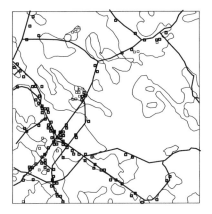 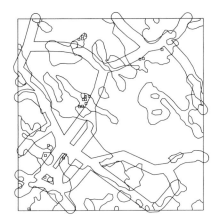

the non-geometric database) of population density (as calculated from parcel areas) of greater than some specified value. Decisions about which values to store in a GIS model and which ones to compute as needed are particularly important ones in GIS design.

Spatial analyses may also generate new polygons. For example, a planner might be interested in all the houses affected by the noise of a road (figure 8.41). Thus a "noise zone" might be calculated by computing distances, then added to the map as a new polygon.

Uses and Limitations of Polygon-modeling Systems

The uses and limitations of polygon-modeling systems are complementary to those of the line-modeling systems discussed in the previous chapter. Whereas drafting systems represent the boundaries of things by lines, polygon-modeling systems explicitly deal with the spaces between those boundaries (figure 8.42). Thus drafting systems are most appropriately used for tasks that require line constructions and precise delineation of artifact geometry, while polygon-modeling systems provide appropriate environments for producing drawings consisting of

8.42
Space between the
boundaries

areas of color and pattern and for working on space-planning, analysis, and management problems. In many design contexts, both lines and areas are of interest, so computer-aided design systems often combine line-drafting and polygon-modeling capabilities in a single software package.

Suggested Readings

Baglivo, Jenny A., and Jack E. Graver. 1983. *Incidence and Symmetry in Design and Architecture.* Cambridge: Cambridge University Press.

Boast, R. B., and J. P. Steadman. 1987. "Analysis of Building Plans in History and Prehistory." *Environment and Planning B: Planning and Design* vol. 14 no. 4. Special issue.

Bowyer, Adrian, and John Woodwark. 1983. "Areas." In *A Programmer's Geometry.* London: Butterworths.

Cowen, David J. 1988. "GIS Versus CAD Versus DBMS: What Are the Differences?" *Photogrammetric Engineering and Remote Sensing* 54 (11): 1551–55.

Ehrig, H., M. Nagl, and G. Rozenberg (eds.). 1982. *Graph Grammars and Their Application to Computer Science.* New York: Springer-Verlag.

Flemming, Ulrich. 1986. "On the Representation and Generation of Loosely Packed Arrangements of Rectangles." *Environment and Planning B: Planning and Design* 13: 189–205.

Grünbaum, Branko, and C. C. Shepard. 1987. *Tilings and Patterns.* New York: W. H. Freeman.

Laurini, Robert, and Derek Thompson. 1992. *Fundamentals of Spatial Information Systems.* London, San Diego: Academic Press.

Steadman, Philip. 1983. *Architectural Morphology: An Introduction to the Geometry of Building Plans.* London: Pion.

9

LINES IN SPACE

Renaissance texts on perspective frequently depicted buildings as "wireframes"—collections of lines in three-dimensional space that had been projected in perspective onto a two-dimensional picture plane (figure 9.1). Similarly, in computer-aided design, the idea of a two-dimensional drafting system can readily be generalized to that of a three-dimensional wireframe-modeling system. This is accomplished by representing lines within a three-dimensional rather than a two-dimensional Cartesian coordinate system (figure 9.2), providing corresponding editing operations, and providing software for producing perspective and other projections on the display screen from geometric information stored in the three-dimensional database.

Construction Planes

Techniques for specification of points and lines in a three-dimensional Cartesian coordinate system are straightforward extensions of those used in two-dimensional drafting. Points can be specified by entering numerical X, Y, and Z values from a keyboard or by snapping to previously established points. A special three-dimensional digitizing device can be used in place of a two-dimensional digitizing tablet, or (more commonly) some scheme can be used to adapt a standard mouse or digitizing tablet for specification of points in three-dimensional space.

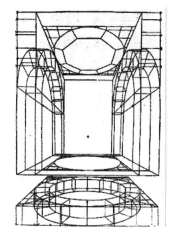

9.1
A Renaissance wireframe

157

The usual way to adapt a mouse or tablet for this purpose is to introduce the idea of construction planes (figure 9.3). Imagine a large sheet of glass located arbitrarily in space. You could locate points and lines in space by two-dimensional drafting on the surface of that sheet. Then, by inserting additional sheets at different locations, you could locate points and lines in other planes. Through use of enough of these construction planes you could build up a three-dimensional arrangement of lines specifying the geometry of a building.

Three-dimensional geometric-modeling systems usually provide a set of commands for specifying a construction plane—by giving the coordinates of three points on it or by tilting up from another plane, for example. Using these commands, you can make a construction plane coincide with any desired surface in a design's geometry (figure 9.4). Once a plane has been defined, you can name it and save it for future recall. By defining several construction planes, and moving back and forth among them, you can manipulate a three-dimensional model with ease.

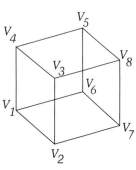

V_1 $(0,0,0)$ E_1 (V_1,V_2)
V_2 $(1,0,0)$ E_2 (V_2,V_3)
V_3 $(1,0,1)$ E_3 (V_3,V_4)
V_4 $(0,0,1)$ E_4 (V_4,V_1)
V_5 $(0,1,1)$ E_5 (V_5,V_6)
V_6 $(0,1,0)$ E_6 (V_6,V_7)
V_7 $(1,1,0)$ E_7 (V_7,V_8)
V_8 $(1,1,1)$ E_8 (V_8,V_5)
           E_9 (V_1,V_6)
           E_{10} (V_2,V_7)
           E_{11} (V_3,V_8)
           E_{12} (V_4,V_5)

9.2
Three-dimensional
coordinate system and
wireframe data structure

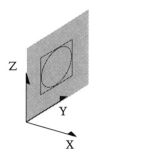

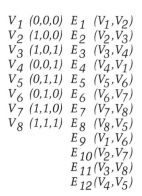

9.3
Construction planes

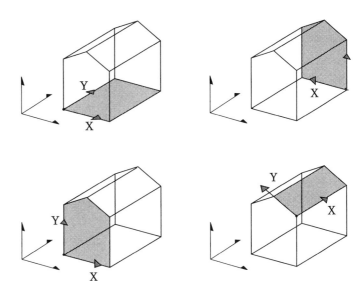

9.4
Construction planes
coincident with the faces
of a model

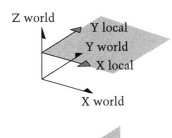

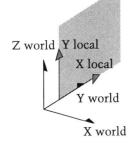

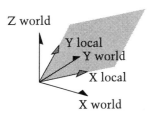

9.5
A construction plane is a
local coordinate system

Technically, a construction plane is simply a local two-dimensional coordinate system (figure 9.5). Two-dimensional coordinates from a mouse or tablet are interpreted by the software as points in the current construction plane and are automatically converted into three-dimensional global coordinates. In other words, coordinates are transformed as follows:

[X_local, Y_local] →
[X_global, Y_global, Z_global]

It is usually most convenient to organize the graphic interface so that the currently active construction plane coincides with the plane of the display screen. This is not essential, however (figure 9.6).

Glass-sheet Models

Dimensions and construction lines can be carried over from one construction plane to another. Consider, for example, a horizontal plan-construction plane intersected by a vertical section-construction plane as illustrated in figure 9.7. When the section-construction plane is being used, new lines can be snapped to the intersections of existing plan lines with the section plane. Similarly, when the plan-construction plane is being used, new lines can be snapped to the intersections of existing section lines with

A picture plane coincident with a construction plane

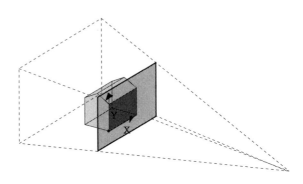

A picture plane not coincident with construction plane

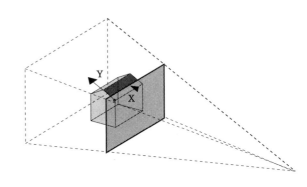

Multiple picture planes, but only one construction plane, may be active

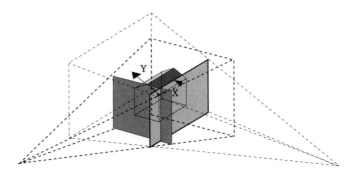

9.6
Picture planes and
construction planes

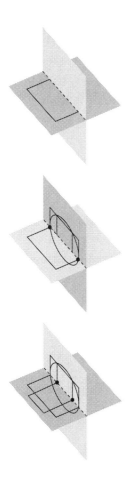

9.7
Snapping to elements in intersecting construction planes

the plan plane. This makes it very easy to work back and forth between plan, section, and elevation to produce a "glass-sheet" model in which a building's essential geometric organization is defined by shaping and positioning profiles and contours in intersecting horizontal and vertical planes (figure 9.8).

Three-dimensional Geometric Transformations

Just as a drafting system provides operations for copying, translating, rotating, reflecting, and scaling two-dimensional shapes in the plane, so a three-dimensional wireframe-modeling system provides these operations for constructing and arranging three-dimensional line shapes in three-dimensional space. They can be used to move shapes out of their original construction planes—to develop a glass-sheet model into a complete wireframe. In particular, a plan arrangement is often developed in the third dimension by translating shapes various distances in a direction normal to a horizontal plan-construction plane (figure 9.9). Similarly, elevations and sections may be developed by translating shapes in directions normal to vertical construction planes. In these cases the transformations that are applied record the designer's decisions about height, depth, and breadth. Another common move is to rotate elements about axes in their construction planes (figure 9.10).

9.8
Screen display of a glass-sheet model

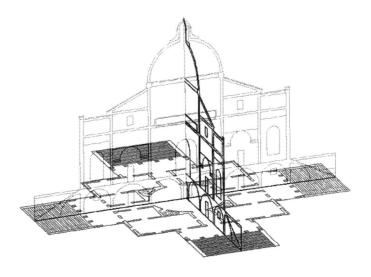

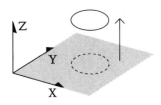

9.9
Translating a shape out of
the construction plane

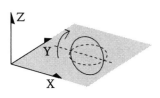

9.10
Rotating a shape out of
the construction plane

By setting up appropriate construction planes, by constructing plan, section, and elevation profiles and contours, by copying and transforming, and by inserting lines between established points, you can quickly delineate the boundaries of three-dimensional forms. For example, a vertical prism might be constructed by first setting out a polygon in a horizontal construction plane to define the base, then copying and translating to define the top, and finally inserting connecting lines to define the vertical faces (figure 9.11). Variants such as pyramidal forms, wedge-shaped forms, twisted forms, and antiprisms can be produced by simple variations of the transformation and connecting operations (figure 9.12).

Reflection operations in three dimensions take place across specified planes, rather than across lines as in two-dimensions (figure 9.13). Scale, stretch, shear, and perspective-distortion operations can also be applied to wireframe shapes to complete the repertoire of linear transformations (figure 9.14).

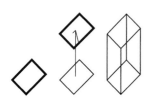

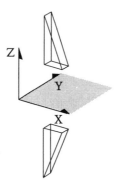

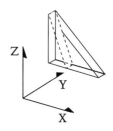

Stretch

9.11
Prism formed by connecting
base to translated copy

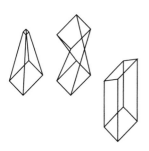

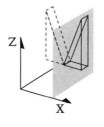

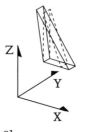

Shear

9.12
Other objects formed by
connecting base to
transformed copies

9.13
Reflection across a plane

9.14
Some additional geometric
transformations

Sweeping Points

When a straight line is translated out of a construction plane, its end points sweep out two new straight lines (figure 9.15). Thus the original line, the translated line, and these two new lines together describe the edges of a rectangle. This idea can be generalized: a translated polyline sweeps out the edges of a fence-shaped object, and a translated polygon sweeps out the edges of a prism. Many wireframe-modeling systems, then, provide the translational sweep operation for quick construction of "fences" and the edges of prismatic objects. (This operation eliminates the task of explicitly inserting connecting lines between the original and translated shapes.)

Similarly, when a straight line is rotated out of a construction plane, its end points sweep out two arcs (figure 9.16). The original line, the translated line, and the two arcs together describe the edges of a cylindrical surface. This rotational sweep operation is also commonly provided by wireframe modelers. If a profile consisting of connected lines and arcs is rotationally swept in increments, a surface mesh consisting of patches bounded by arcs and straight lines is the result (figure 9.17). A patch may bound a surface fragment of a cylinder, a sphere, a torus, or a cone.

When a three-dimensional object is scaled, it is sometimes useful to connect automatically the end points of the original and the resized lines. Thus, for example, the stones of a hemispherical dome can be constructed by first rotationally sweeping an arc to construct a mesh describing the inner surface, then scaling and connecting to construct the outer surface and the radial edges of the stones (figure 9.18).

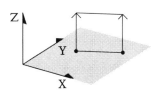

A swept point forms a line

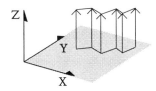

A swept line forms a rectangle

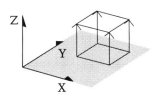

A swept chain forms a fence

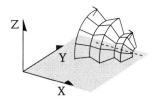

A swept polygon forms a prism

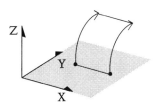

9.15
Lines translated out of their construction plane

9.16
A line rotated out of its construction plane

9.17
A profile rotated incrementally out of its construction plane forms a mesh

Inner surface

Outer surface

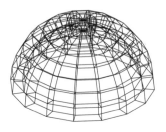

Connected surfaces

9.18
Construction of a
wireframe dome by scaling
and connecting

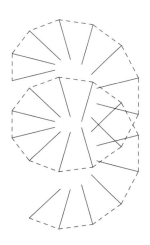

9.19
Translation and rotation of a
line sweeps out a helix

Space Curves

Most wireframe modelers provide only translational and rotational sweeps, but the idea can, in fact, be generalized endlessly. If a straight line is simultaneously translated and rotated, for example, each of its end points sweeps out a helix (figure 9.19). Whereas straight lines and arcs are plane curves (you can always fit construction planes through them), a helix is a space curve—one that exists only in three-dimensional space.

A limitless variety of space curves can be generated by procedures that calculate the coordinates of a point as some function of a parameter T. By incrementing the value of T through some range, a sequence of points on the curve is produced. Thus a procedure of this type is a tool for producing a space curve, in the same way that a straightedge is a tool for producing a straight line or a pair of compasses is a tool for producing an arc. If a wireframe-modeling system has an interface to a programming language, you can build your own tool kit of these procedures.

In the past it has been extremely difficult for architects to compose with space curves, since traditional drawing instruments work on planar surfaces to produce plane curves. Wireframe modeling removes this limitation.

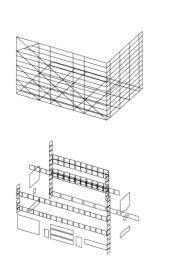

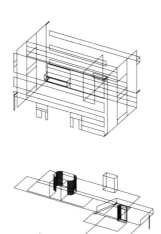

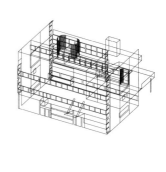

Structuring Wireframe Models

The ideas of grouping and layering generalize in a straight-forward way from two-dimensional drafting to three-dimensional wireframe modeling. The metaphor of a "layer" is less clear, however, since wireframes on different layers may intertwine in three-dimensional space (figure 9.20).

The idea of treating collections of lines as reusable vocabulary elements also generalizes. Lines may be grouped and copied, just as in two-dimensional drafting. And many wireframe modelers provide built-in vocabularies of basic shapes such as boxes, regular prisms, pyramids, wedges, spheres, cylinders, and cones (figure 9.21).

9.20
Different layers of a wireframe model intertwined in three-dimensional space

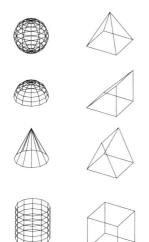

Viewing

A wireframe model might be realized in three-dimensional form—literally as a set of wires in space, for example—but it is usually more convenient to work with two-dimensional projections in which lines of the model are projected onto a flat surface for display. Geometric-modeling systems provide software for displaying and plotting specified projections.

Whereas a wireframe model is essentially a set of lines in three-dimensional Cartesian coordinate space, a draw-

9.21
A vocabulary of wireframe primitives

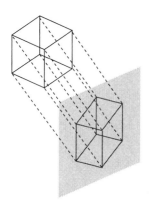

9.22
Picture plane and
projection rays

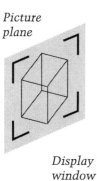

*Picture
plane*

*Display
window*

9.23
The picture plane is
mapped to the display
window

ing projected from that model is a corresponding set of lines in a two-dimensional Cartesian picture plane. Thus a projection method (such as orthographic, axonometric, or perspective) is simply a consistent rule for converting coordinate triples $[X,Y,Z]$ establishing line end points in the model into coordinate pairs $[X', Y']$ specifying corresponding end points in the projected drawing. (The idea can be extended, in a straightforward way, to allow for projection of curved as well as straight lines.) There are infinitely many such rules, but certain of them have particularly useful mathematical properties, have been sanctioned by tradition, and are widely accepted as standard conventions.

All the common projection methods produce linear transformations of the wireframe model: that is, they convert straight lines into straight lines—never into curves of some other kind. These projections can be visualized by imagining a picture plane located somewhere in the three-dimensional coordinate system and straight projection rays passing through the picture plane to connect end points in the three-dimensional model to end points of lines on the picture plane (figure 9.22). (Nonlinear projections involve curved picture surfaces and curved projection rays.) To produce a display on the computer screen, this picture plane is brought into coincidence with the plane of the screen to produce the effect of looking through a "window" into a three-dimensional world (figure 9.23).

To specify the location of the picture plane in the three-dimensional coordinate system, it is often convenient to take a specified point as the origin of an auxiliary polar coordinate system (figure 9.24a). The location of the picture plane can then be described in terms of azimuth, altitude, and distance. This is like moving a camera around a fixed object to produce views from different sides. Alternatively, the center of the picture plane can be taken as the fixed origin of a polar coordinate system, and translations and rotations of the three-dimensional model can be specified in this system to create the required relationship of plane and model (figure 9.24b). This is like holding the model in your hand and turning it around to look at it from different sides.

THREE-DIMENSIONAL MEDIA   166

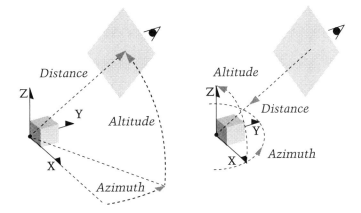

9.24
Controlling viewing
parameters

a. Like moving a camera   *b. Like holding the model*

The two ways of specifying the relationship between
model and picture plane are obviously mathematically
equivalent. Some wireframe modelers provide one, some
provide the other, and some provide both. Viewer-
centered viewing is natural when you want to think of a
design as an object, as is often the case in mechanical part
or product design. But object-centered viewing is natural
when you want to think of a design as an environment
through which you move, as is usually the case in architectural, landscape, and urban design. In either case the
internal operation is always one of moving the picture
plane rather than performing a three-dimensional transformation of the model itself.

Orthographic Projections

The simplest possible rule for converting three-dimensional coordinates into two-dimensional coordinates is to
throw away the Z values in the $[X,Y,Z]$ coordinate
triples while leaving the x and y values unchanged. This
rule may be expressed:

$$[X,Y,Z] \rightarrow [X,Y]$$

This produces an orthographic projection onto an *xy*
viewplane (figure 9.25). Similar rules can be used to
project onto XZ and YZ viewplanes.

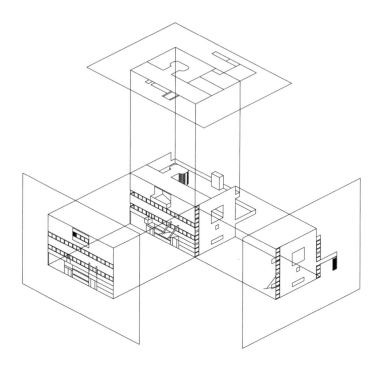

9.25
Orthographic projections

The most salient property of such an orthographic projection is that the image of a projected straight line will be the same length as that of the original line when the original is parallel to the viewplane. This means that contours, profiles, and faces parallel to the viewplane will be undistorted—the same sizes and shapes as the originals. But lines *not* parallel to the viewplane will be shortened when projected. The ratio of the projected length to the actual length is called the foreshortening ratio.

By changing view direction you can make different planes of a modeled building parallel to the viewplane—and thus present them in undistorted fashion. Furthermore, through multiplication by appropriate scale factors, you can produce views to any desired scale. In particular, by taking a top view with the viewplane parallel to a building's floor planes and applying an appropriate scale factor, you can produce a scaled plan projection. (Use of this convention in computer-aided design continues a tradition that goes back at least to 2150 BC and the reign of King Gudea of Lagash.) Most buildings also have many vertical wall planes, so it is also useful to produce elevations by setting the viewplane parallel to various important wall planes. (But this is not always the case: consider I. M. Pei's glass pyramid in the courtyard of the Louvre.)

Axonometric Projections

Often a designer needs to see the relationships between plans and elevations. The most obvious way to show these is to make an orthographic projection from an oblique view direction—such that horizontal and vertical faces are seen at once. This yields an axonometric orthographic projection (figure 9.26). Such projections can be subclassified according to the foreshortening ratios of the faces in the three principal directions: the projection is isometric if the three ratios are equal, dimetric if two of the three are equal, and trimetric if they are all different (figure 9.27). When a cube is drawn in isometric, the vertex angles in the drawing become 60 degrees and 120 degrees: this is the most common architectural convention.

The choice among viewing directions for axonometrics depends upon what is to be shown and emphasized. A worm's-eye axonometric shows how a plan organization develops into three-dimensional interior space, and a bird's-eye illustrates the relationships between elevations and roof forms (figure 9.28). Dimetrics are often appropriate for showing corner details. Trimetrics place the emphasis on just one of the faces.

Clearly the strengths and weaknesses of plans, elevations, and different kinds of axonometrics are complementary, so it is useful to have simultaneous orthographic views (figure 9.29). Whenever one view is altered in the course of a design process, then, the rest must correspondingly be updated. In manual drawing practice this process is laborious and a source of errors and inconsistencies. But a computer-aided design system can simultaneously update all the views whenever a change is made.

Orthographic-projection software is normally controlled by two viewing parameters. A direction-of-view parameter controls the distribution of foreshortening—that is, whether a plan, elevation, isometric, dimetric, or trimetric will result. And a scale (or zoom) factor determines the size of the projected image on the screen.

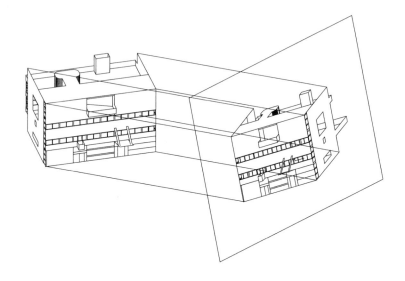

9.26
Axonometric orthographic
projection

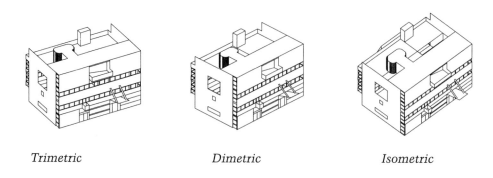

Trimetric *Dimetric* *Isometric*

9.27
Different foreshortening
ratios yield different types
of axonometrics

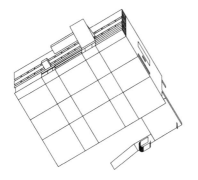
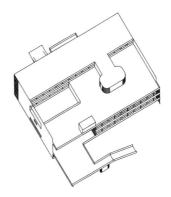

9.28
Worm's-eye and bird's-eye
axonometrics

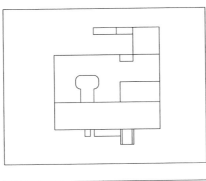
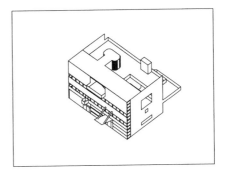
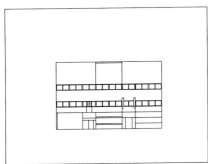
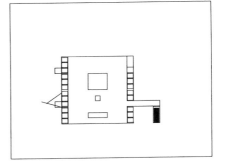

9.29
Simultaneous orthographic
projections

Oblique Projections

Sometimes an architect needs to keep one elevation of a building parallel to the viewplane (and thus undistorted) while showing something of the plan and faces of other elevations. This is impossible in orthographic projection, but it can be accomplished as shown in figure 9.30. The rule here is:

$$[X,Y,Z] \rightarrow [(X + Z/A), (Y + Z/B)]$$

The constants A and B control the foreshortening of the receding faces. In effect, depth information is encoded in the image by shifting points diagonally according to their depth back into the scene. Whereas the orthographic projections discussed earlier result from taking parallel projectors perpendicularly through the viewplane, this new type of projection results from using oblique parallel projectors. Chinese and Japanese painters have traditionally employed oblique parallel projection in architectural scenes, but it has been less popular in the West.

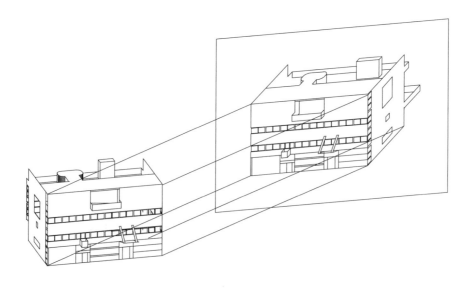

9.30
Oblique parallel projection
with true elevation

A variant of the same idea, which allows the plan of a building to remain undistorted, is sometimes preferred to the worm's-eye axonometric for showing how a plan develops into a three-dimensional interior space. It was popularized by Auguste Choisy in the nineteenth century, then widely used by twentieth-century modernists. It also enables a roof plan to be developed downward.

Software to produce oblique parallel projections requires specification of one more parameter than for standard parallel projections: the angle at which receding faces are to be taken back. This controls the foreshortening of the receding faces.

Perspective Projections

If X and Y coordinates are *divided* by an amount dependent on depth (rather than added to an amount dependent on depth as in oblique projections), then perspective projections are produced. The rule here is:

$$[X,Y,Z] \rightarrow [X/(C^*Z), Y/(C^*Z)]$$

The constant C controls rate of diminishment with depth back into the scene. This is simply another convention for encoding depth information in an image by distorting coordinates with depth. It is, however, related particularly closely to our optical experience, since the visual angle subtended at the eye (or a camera) by an object decreases with distance (figure 9.31).

As a famous illustration by Dürer long-ago showed, perspective projection can be understood as the result of taking projectors, diverging from the viewer's eye, through the picture plane (figure 9.32). The associated viewing parameters can readily be understood in these terms. First, the viewer's station point and direction of view establish the principal line of sight through the picture plane to the object (figure 9.33). By varying these parameters we can change the number and positions of vanishing points in an image and give emphasis to different faces of an object. A cube, for example, can be shown in one-point, two-point, or three-point perspective (figure 9.34). The horizontal and vertical angles subtended at the

9.31
The visual angle subtended by an object decreases with distance

9.32
Dürer's perspective
construction

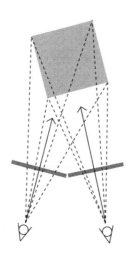

9.33
Principal line of sight

9.34
One-point, two-point, and
three-point perspective

apex of the viewing pyramid can also be varied. The effect is like that of manipulating a zoom lens. A narrow viewing angle produces an effect like that of a telephoto lens, and a wide viewing angle produces an effect like that of a wide-angle lens.

Clipping and Sectioning

When a parallel projection is displayed, lines must be clipped to the edges of the viewing box; in the case of a perspective projection they must be clipped to the edges of the viewing pyramid (figure 9.35). The effect is to terminate lines where they intersect the rectangular boundaries of the viewing window. This is called lateral clipping. Sometimes, as well, it is useful to clip lines to specified front (or hither) and back (or yon) planes. This is called depth clipping or z-clipping. It is analogous to the standard architectural technique of taking a plan or section slice through a building. Efficient procedures for clipping lines are well known and are standardly incorporated in wireframe-modeling systems.

It is a straightforward extension of z-clipping (though commercial wireframe-modeling systems rarely provide it) to clip lines to an arbitrary plane as a starting point for construction of a plan or section (figure 9.36). Lines need

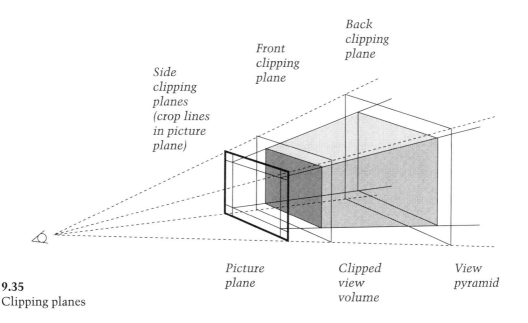

9.35
Clipping planes

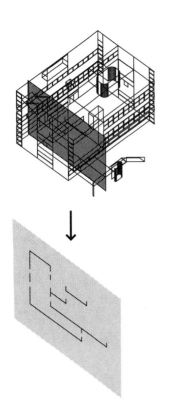

9.36
Cutting a section

to be broken at the section plane, and the break points highlighted. These can then quickly be connected to produce the required plan or section drawing. Usually it is best to assign the plan or section to its own layer, so that it can be shown in a different color, shown by itself, or switched off entirely. (This technique elaborates the idea of glass-sheet modeling, as discussed earlier.)

Spatial Ambiguity and Depth Cues

A common problem with wireframe images is the existence of spatial ambiguities. A cube in axonometric, for example, has two consistent spatial readings (figure 9.37). Selection of points and lines in projected wireframe views is inherently fraught with ambiguity, since a selected point on the picture plane actually specifies an infinite ray passing through the three-dimensional model (figure 9.38). These selection rays are parallel in orthographic projections but diverge in perspective projections—making accurate selection in perspective an exceptionally difficult task. Any ray may pass through multiple selectable entities. Good snapping capability, to compensate for selection inaccuracy, is thus essential in wireframe modeling.

Problems such as these can be mitigated or eliminated, however, through use of display techniques that provide additional depth cues to disambiguate an image. In hand drawing depth cues are often provided by breaking back lines, as shown in figure 9.39. This is not very practical in computer graphics (since it requires time-consuming calculation of intersection points), so alternative conventions are usually employed. Depending on the capabilities of the available display technology, line weight, intensity, or color may be varied to indicate depth.

The most common approach to removing spatial ambiguity, however, is to provide multiple, simultaneous projections. This is a straightforward computational task: the screen is subdivided into viewing windows, projections are performed, and projected views are mapped to windows (refer back to figure 9.29). Typically, one of these windows will provide a picture plane that is coincident with the current construction plane, and there will be at

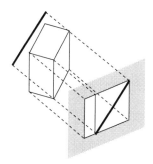

Ambiguous location of a line

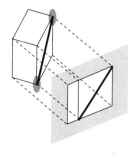

Snapping to existing objects relieves ambiguity

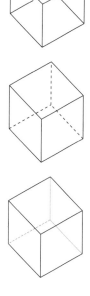

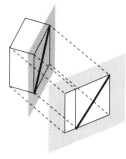

Snapping to grid in construction plane relieves ambiguity

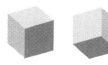

9.37
Two readings of a cube

9.38
Depth ambiguity in point selection

9.39
Graphic conventions for relieving depth ambiguity

least one other projection to relieve ambiguity. Operations, such as drawing a line, may be begun in one view and ended in another.

Multiple views also provide a designer with a way to keep multiple design issues in mind as a model is constructed and edited. One common technique is to set up several perspective views from crucial points in the approaches to a building from different directions. Then, whenever a design operation is performed in one view, the implications for other views can immediately be seen. This provides a way to escape from the myopic vision of a project that commonly results from working exclusively in plan or in section or in perspective from a particular viewpoint. And it completely eliminates the tedious task of constructing new views to see what a change made in plan or section means in perspective.

Fast computers allow real-time variation of viewing parameters to resolve spatial ambiguities, to reveal different aspects of an object's geometry, and to select telling viewpoints. This was rare in the past, but as sufficiently powerful computers have become increasingly available, it has come to be regarded as an essential feature of a good wireframe modeler. Figure 9.40 illustrates how azimuth and altitude of the picture plane may be varied continuously. Where available computer power is insufficient to handle a complete wireframe model in this way, a simplified version containing just enough information for orientation may be used for real-time viewing operations.

Yet another disambiguation technique (sometimes combined with real-time variation of viewing parameters in advanced systems) is to provide stereoscopic wireframe views. This requires computation of perspectives from slightly differing station points, together with use of a viewing system that recombines these views in some way. An ordinary color display can be used to display superimposed complementary-colored images which are viewed through complementary-colored pairs of filters. More advanced systems use cross-polarization, alternating views, synchronized shuttered goggles, and so on. With a stereo display, the cursor can be freed from the picture

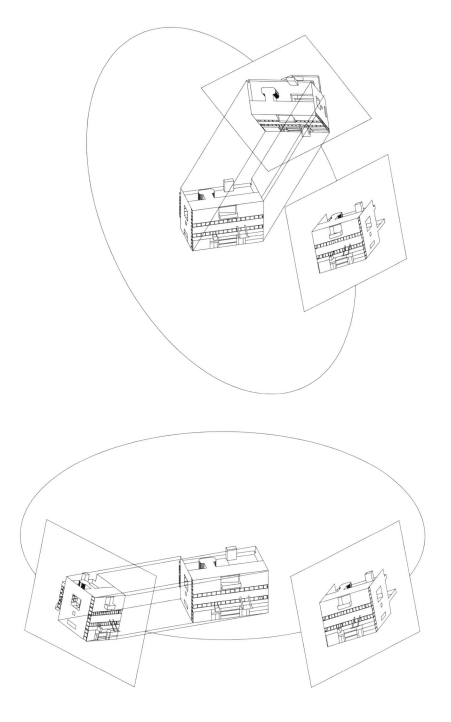

9.40
Dynamic viewing
transformations

plane and can move in three-dimensional space to select points and lines directly.

Stereo displays and three-dimensional cursors can also be used to construct wireframe models by digitizing from photographs. The starting point is a stereo pair of photographs. These are scanned and displayed on a stereo display screen. The three-dimensional cursor is then used to digitize points, just as a two-dimensional cursor can be used to digitize points from a two-dimensional bit-mapped underlay. A variant on this idea, which does not require use of a stereo display system, is to use two photographs, to digitize each point in each view, then to use a special reconstruction transformation of the form:

$$[[X_1,Y_1], [X_2,Y_2]] \rightarrow [X,Y,Z]$$

Producing Drawings from Wireframe Models

It might be thought (and it was once commonly suggested) that a plan could automatically be generated from a wireframe model by projecting it onto the ground plane and that a section could be produced by projecting onto an appropriate vertical plane. But a plan or section is a more subtle notation of design intention than a mere projection of lines from three-dimensional space. First, not all of the lines in a three-dimensional model are relevant in a plan drawing made for a particular purpose: some will have to be culled out by careful depth-clipping or sectioning operations or by explicit line-deletion operations. (This is particularly troublesome when distinct lines in space become coincident in plan projection.) Second, some lines in the plan will need to be given emphasis (by assignment of heavier line weight, or dashing, for example), and it is difficult to specify foolproof procedures for accomplishing this automatically. Finally, many plan notations are not, in fact, projections of three-dimensional shapes but conventional symbols: these must be inserted in place of the corresponding projected shapes.

The projection of a carefully layered and sectioned wireframe model is, however, useful as a starting point for construction of plans, sections, or elevations. It is best used as a reference layer that defines the "raw" geometry of a design and that serves as an underlay over which the two-dimensional expression is developed. One way to approach the task of further graphic development is to use drafting-system operations to edit the projected wireframe, define appropriate line weights, and lay out sheets. Another possibility is to transfer a projected wireframe to a paint system and there use flooding operations to define opaque and partially opaque surfaces. And a third possibility is to print on paper and then use pencil or watercolor (figure 9.41).

Dimensional Control

A particularly important technical use of wireframes is for dimensional control of a project—both in development and documentation of the design and in fabrication and construction. A carefully constructed wireframe can provide a three-dimensional skeleton of construction lines that establishes key dimensions and defines key locations as constructed end points and intersection points. This skeleton can be used as a basis for extraction of definitive coordinate and dimension values and as a framework for snapping design elements quickly and accurately into place. This generalizes the old idea (as developed, for example, in J- N-L Durand's famous series of architectural textbooks) of controlling development of a design by means of a two-dimensional skeleton of axes, arcs, and grids.

9.41
Pencil over wireframe

Zero points fixed:
free body

One point fixed:
pinned body

Two points fixed:
hinged body

Three points fixed:
fixed body

9.42
Fixing the position of a
wireframe object

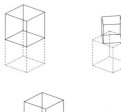

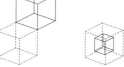

9.43
Some spatial relationships
of wireframe cubes

To snap a rigid wireframe element into position in space, three fixed points must be specified (figure 9.42). (If one point on the element is snapped to a point on the existing wireframe, then the element can rotate in three axes about the connection point. If two points are snapped, then the element can rotate about the axis passing through them. But if three points are snapped, no rotation is possible.) A system that supports point-to-point, point-to-line, and line-to-line snapping, together with real-time translation and rotation of elements (so that the remaining degrees of freedom for an element are always evident from its motion) makes accurate snapping together of wireframe elements particularly quick and easy.

Syntax-directed editing capabilities are also very useful. Rules for snapping three-dimensional wireframe elements together in commonly used spatial relationships can eliminate explicit performance of a lot of tedious and error-prone selection, translation, and rotation operations (figure 9.43).

Uses and Limitations of Wireframe Models and Views

A wireframe model takes its place in the image-production pipeline of a computer graphics system as shown in figure 9.44. Two-dimensional points are converted (through use of construction planes and so on) into a permanent three-dimensional geometric model consisting of points and lines. Projected views of that model become temporary display files that are used to drive display devices. And, when a raster display is used, the two-dimensional line data in the display files must be converted into bitmapped images.

A wireframe model provides a more complete representation of building geometry than a collection of two-dimensional drafted views—which are much like display files without a well-defined common reference. It is less of an abstraction away from three-dimensional physical reality (figure 9.45). Both its advantages and disadvantages follow from this shift in emphasis.

Data structures used to store wireframes tend to require more memory than those used to store two-dimen-

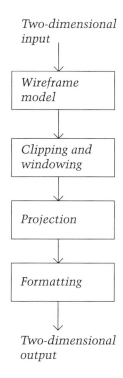

Two-dimensional
input

Wireframe
model

Clipping and
windowing

Projection

Formatting

Two-dimensional
output

9.44
The wireframe image
pipeline

sional drawings, since there will usually be more lines in the model (compare a wireframe of a cube with its plan or elevation) and since each coordinate is expressed by three numbers instead of two. More computational work must be done in manipulating these larger data structures, and considerable additional computation is required to produce perspective and parallel projections for viewing. There is more geometric information for the user to input, and many input and editing operations become more complex—both computationally and for the user. In general, construction of a wireframe model takes longer, and costs more, than construction of corresponding two-dimensional line models.

The additional trouble and expense can be justified when there is a genuine need for a higher level of geometric completeness and more systematic coordination of views—when the three-dimensional form is not readily evident from plans and elevations, for instance, or when views from many different directions are needed, or where animated movement through and around the building is required. Development of plans, elevations, and sections into a complete wireframe model can also provide the occasion for further resolution of a building's geometry and the basis for further elaboration into a surface or solid model—as discussed in the next two chapters.

Most importantly, a wireframe model can support forms of design exploration, geometric problem-solving, and measurement and analysis that are very difficult or impossible with two-dimensional representations. A designer can, for example, execute geometric constructions in planes that are not horizontal or vertical, perform constructions with space curves, and accurately measure shapes that would be foreshortened in plan or section.

9.45
Wireframe definition of
architectural geometry

Suggested Readings

Booth, Kellogg F. 1979. *Tutorial: Computer Graphics.* New York: IEEE.

Dewey, Bruce R. 1988. *Computer Graphics for Engineers.* New York: Harper & Row.

Edgerton, Samuel Y. 1975. *The Renaissance Rediscovery of Linear Perspective.* New York: Basic Books.

Evans, Robin. 1989. "Architectural Projection." In Eve Blau and Edward Kaufman (eds.), *Architecture and Its Image.* Montreal: Centre Canadien d'Architecture.

Foley, James D., Andries van Dam, Steven K. Feiner, and John F. Hughes. 1990. "Geometrical Transformations" (chapter 5) and "Viewing in 3D" (chapter 6). In *Computer Graphics: Principles and Practice.* Reading, Mass.: Addison-Wesley.

Kubovy, Michael. 1986. *The Psychology of Perspective and Renaissance Art.* Cambridge: Cambridge University Press.

Lotz, Wolfgang. 1977. "The Rendering of the Interior in Architectural Drawings of the Renaissance." In *Studies in Italian Renaissance Architecture.* Cambridge, Mass.: The MIT Press.

Newman, William M., and Robert F. Sproull. 1979. *Principles of Interactive Computer Graphics.* New York: McGraw-Hill.

Penna, Michael A., and Richard R. Patterson. 1986. *Projective Geometry and Its Application to Computer Graphics.* Englewood Cliffs: Prentice Hall.

Rogers, David F., and J. Alan Adams. 1976. *Mathematical Elements for Computer Graphics.* New York: McGraw-Hill.

Rooney, J., M. S. Bloor, and A. Saia. 1987. "Wire-Frame Modelling." In Joe Rooney and Philip Steadman (eds.), *Principles of Computer-Aided Design.* London: Pitman.

Salmon, Rod, and Mel Slater. 1987. *Computer Graphics: Systems and Concepts.* Reading, Mass.: Addison-Wesley.

White, John. 1987. *The Birth and Rebirth of Pictorial Space.* 3rd edition. Cambridge, Mass.: Belknap Press.

10

SURFACES AND RENDERINGS

10.1
Surfaces in light

In a famous passage of his *Ten Books on Architecture*, Leon Battista Alberti defined designs as abstractions separated from physical matter, but serving to specify how the physical matter of a building was to be organized and ordered. It followed, then, that a design consisted of "lines and angles" and that the designer's task was to make "a firm and graceful pre-ordering of the lines and angles." Correspondences between lines on paper and lines in space could be established systematically through use of projection techniques—in particular, perspective. This view provides the theoretical foundation for design by line construction in the plane (drafting) and for design by wireframe modeling.

In another of his works, *On Painting* (1435), Alberti pointed out that there was an alternative approach. "Mathematicians," he wrote, "measure with their minds alone the forms of things separated from all matter." But speaking as a painter, he then continued, "Since we wish the object to be seen, we will use a more sensate wisdom."

The Reception of Light

Alberti's concern as a painter was not with abstract geometry as specified by lines in space, but with the appearances of solid objects as they present themselves to the eye. Such objects, in his terminology, have "skins" composed of an outline (*orlo*) bounding a "plane" (*superficie*). The *superficie* is that "certain external part of a body which is known not by its depth but only by its length and breadth and by its quality." These external parts may, he says, be divided into four kinds according to their curvatures: flat ("that which a straight ruler will touch in every part if drawn over it"), spherical ("any part of that body is equidistant from its center"), hollowed ("as in the interior of an egg shell"), and compound ("in one part flat and in another hollowed or spherical like those on the interior of reeds or on the exterior of columns"). Appearances, he notes, are determined not only by properties of outline and curvature, but also by the positions of bodies relative to the observer: "as soon as the observer changes his position these planes appear larger, of a different outline, or of a different color." And there is one more thing "which makes the plane appear to change." It is "the reception of light." Alberti elaborates:

You see that spherical and concave planes have one part dark and another part bright when receiving light. Even though the distance and position of the centric line are the same, when the light is moved those parts which were first bright now become dark, and those bright which were dark. Where there are more lights, according to their number and strength, you see more spots of light and dark.

Thus the painter's fundamental intellectual program, as formulated by Alberti, was to study the appearances of surfaces in light (figure 10.1)—a matter of outline and surface geometry, lighting conditions, and observer position. In one important sense the history of European painting, over the span from Alberti to the Impressionists, can be understood as an elaboration and working out of this program. Successive generations of painters observed and found accurate ways to render increasingly complex and subtle effects of surface revealed in light.

Since the emergence of high-quality raster graphic display devices, which can render surfaces in light on a cathode ray tube as a painter does with pigments deployed on canvas, this intellectual program has been reconstructed in a new form. Software has been developed for modeling three-dimensional objects not just in terms of their edge lines, but as collections of surfaces described by their outlines and curvatures. (This requires a more elaborate data structure.) Such surface-modeling systems can produce not only wireframe images, but also hidden-surface views showing opaque surfaces in light. They allow information specifying surface properties (color, specularity, texture, and so on) to be associated with surface elements and allow the properties of light sources to be specified. From the geometric database, information about surface and lighting properties, and specified values for viewing parameters, they render effects such as shading, cast shadows, highlights, and reflections. The incorporation of increasingly sophisticated rendering algorithms, taking advantage of increasingly powerful computer resources, has enabled them to produce images that more and more closely approach photorealism.

Just as drafting and wireframe-modeling software enables us to explore architectural composition as Alberti conceived it in his *Ten Books on Architecture*—as the organization of lines and angles that specify the essential geometry of a building—so surface modeling supports architectural composition as it was defined in another way by Le Corbusier (himself a painter) in *Vers une architecture:*

Architecture is the masterly, correct and magnificent play of masses brought together in light. Our eyes are made to see forms in light; light and shade reveal these forms.

Insertion of Surface Facets

Figure 10.2 illustrates two plates from Sebastiano Serlio's *Architettura*, which was published just a few years after Alberti's treatise on painting. The first shows an octagonal well in wireframe perspective. In the second, opaque surfaces have been inserted into the wireframe such that polygons found within the frame have become outlines of surface elements. Serlio remarks that the solid body thus shown "is the same that is before shewed, both form and measure, but all the lines which cannot outwardly be seen are hidden." The wireframe has served as an ordering skeleton over which the solid has been constructed: Serlio notes that they who "well understand and perfectly bear in mind the hidden lines shall better understand the art than

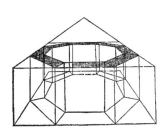
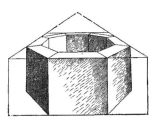

10.2
Wireframe and surface representations in Serlio's *Architettura*

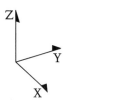

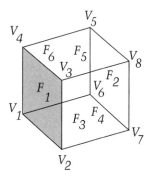

V_1 (0,0,0) E_1 (V_1,V_2)
V_2 (1,0,0) E_2 (V_2,V_3)
V_3 (1,0,1) E_3 (V_3,V_4)
V_4 (0,0,1) E_4 (V_4,V_1)
V_5 (0,1,1) E_5 (V_5,V_6)
V_6 (0,1,0) E_6 (V_6,V_7)
V_7 (1,1,0) E_7 (V_7,V_8)
V_8 (1,1,1) E_8 (V_8,V_5)
E_9 (V_1,V_6)
E_{10}(V_2,V_7)
E_{11}(V_3,V_8)
E_{12}(V_4,V_5)

F_1 (E_1 , E_2 , E_3 , E_4)
F_2 (E_5 , E_6 , E_7 , E_8)
F_3 (E_1 , E_{10}, E_6 , E_9)
F_4 (E_2 , E_{11}, E_7 , E_{10})
F_5 (E_3 , E_{12}, E_8 , E_{11})
F_6 (E_4 , E_9 , E_5 , E_{12})

10.3
A simple data structure
for surface description

others who content themselves with the outer superficies." So it is with surface-modeling software: the user first constructs lines, then employs these to guide development and positioning of surfaces.

The most basic surface-insertion operation is a generalization of the basic line-insertion operation. Just as a one-dimensional straight line segment is specified by its zero-dimensional boundaries (end points), so a two-dimensional plane polygon is specified by its one-dimensional boundaries (edge lines). Thus an obvious way to insert a plane polygon into a surface model is to indicate its boundary points in sequence.

A typical database format for a simple surface-modeling system, which is closely related to the basic surface-insertion operation, is illustrated in figure 10.3. There is a vertex list, an edge list, and a facet list. The vertex list records X and Y coordinates of vertices, the edge list specifies pairs of vertices linked by edges, and the facet list specifies sequences of edges bounding surface facets.

Sweep Operations

Another way to look at a straight line (as we saw earlier) is as the path swept out by a translated point. Similarly, we can regard a rectangular surface as the shape swept out by a translated straight line. It follows that we can specify such a surface by indicating a straight line and specifying a translation. More generally, we can specify assemblages of surfaces by sweeping arbitrary chains of lines (figure 10.4). Most surface-modeling systems provide such translational sweep operations for surface insertion. (Notice how they differ from wireframe translational sweep operations, which only create and insert lines.)

Figure 10.5 shows how a combination of facet-bounding and translational sweep operations can be used to model an open rectangular box. First the rectangular plan is constructed and swept to create the four upright sides. Then the vertices of the plan shape are picked off in sequence to create the top facet.

Singly curved surfaces (sometimes known as generalized cylinders) can be constructed by performing translational sweep operations on plane curves. Sweeping a

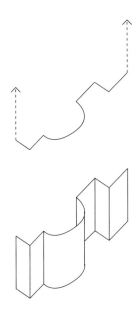

10.4
Translational sweep

circle, for example, constructs an open-ended cylinder (figure 10.6). More complex profiles can be swept to construct the forms of architectural moldings (figure 10.7).

In addition to translational sweeps, surface-modeling systems usually provide rotational sweep operations in which line shapes are swept along arcs of circles (figure 10.8). Cylindrical and conical surfaces, for example, can be produced by sweeping straight lines. Both spherical and toroidal surfaces can result from rotational sweeps of arcs.

The combination of translational and rotational sweep operations is very powerful. Almost all classical and Gothic architectural elements (columns, piers, entablatures, arches, moldings, etc.) can, for example, be modeled by applying translational and rotational sweep operations to profiles constructed from straight lines and arcs: this is closely analogous to the stonemason's technique of using a template to mark a profile on a block of stone, then cutting this shape through the mass (figure 10.9).

But some more general sweep operations are needed to construct certain types of surfaces and are thus provided by advanced surface-modeling software. One

Facet bounding

Translational sweep

Facet bounding

10.5
Modeling a box

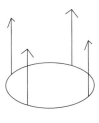

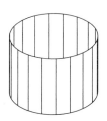

10.6
Sweeping a circle to
produce a cylinder

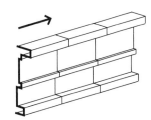

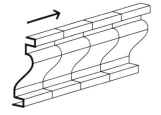

10.7
Sweeping profiles to
produce moldings

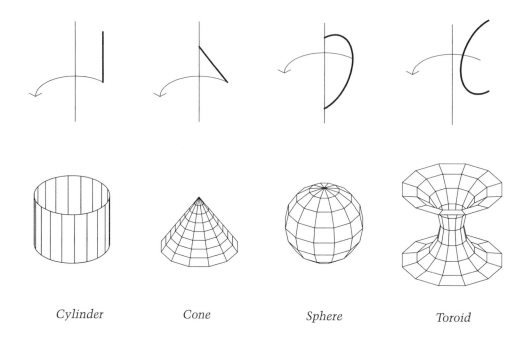

Cylinder   *Cone*   *Sphere*   *Toroid*

10.8
Rotational sweeps

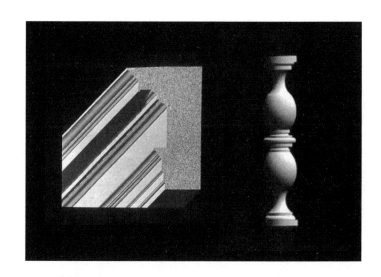

10.9
Classical elements formed
by sweeping profiles

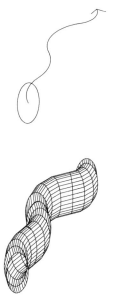

10.10
An ellipse swept along a
spline

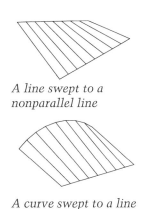

*A line swept to a
nonparallel line*

A curve swept to a line

A curve swept to a curve

10.11
Ruled surfaces

generalization is to allow sweeping of arbitrary curves along arbitrary curves—an ellipse along a spline, for example (figure 10.10). Some systems allow the two ends of a line to be swept along different curves. In particular, ruled surfaces may be specified by sweeping straight lines in this way (figure 10.11). Two particular types of ruled surfaces are fairly common in architecture (figure 10.12): the hyperboloid of revolution (which is produced by sweeping the ends of an inclined straight line around circles) and the hyperbolic paraboloid (which results from sweeping the ends of a straight line along non-coplanar straight lines).

A cone may be constructed not only by rotationally sweeping a straight line, but also by sweeping a diminishing circle along a straight line (figure 10.13). By analogy, some advanced surface-modeling systems provide generalized cone operations that define complex surface shapes by sweeping arbitrarily changing curves along arbitrary curves. This operation, for example, is useful for modeling human limbs.

Faceted Approximations of Curved Surfaces

Some surface-modeling systems represent curved surfaces internally by storing parameter values. A sphere can be represented by its center coordinates and radius, for example, and a cylinder can be represented by the end-point coordinates of its axis together with a radius (figure 10.14). These parameters can be used, in conjunction with appropriate mathematical formulae, to generate accurate images of surfaces as required.

An alternative approach is to approximate curved surfaces by small planar facets (figure 10.15)—just as a curved line may be approximated by small, straight segments. Often these facets are triangular, since triangles are always planar, but facets of other shapes may be used as well. This technique proves to be adequate for many practical purposes, and it simplifies many of the computational tasks that a surface-modeling system must perform, so it is widely used in contexts where precise representation of surfaces is not critical and where computational resources are limited.

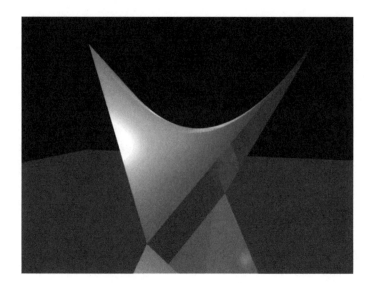

10.12
A hyperbolic paraboloid
surface

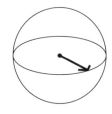

X_c , Y_c , Z_c , *Radius*

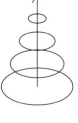

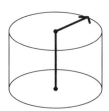

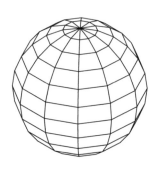

X_1 , Y_1 , Z_1,
X_2 , Y_2 , Z_2,
Radius

10.13
Constructions for a cone

10.14
Representation of
surfaces by parameter
values

10.15
Approximating a curved
surface by planar facets

Surface Patches

Where a surface is approximated by a mesh of triangles, linear interpolation between the vertices of any triangle produces points within that triangle. If a surface is approximated by a mesh of quadrilaterals, however, the vertices of a given quadrilateral do not necessarily lie in the same plane, and if they do not, linear interpolation between them will produce a bilinear curved surface (figure 10.16). Thus quadrilateral bilinear patches provide an alternative to triangular plane facets for representation of curved surfaces.

The idea of curved surface patches may be extended in various ways to provide curved surface representations that are appropriate for different practical purposes. An obvious generalization of the bilinear patch, for example, is a patch bounded by four arbitrary curves (figure 10.17). This type of patch, which provides more precise control of slopes, is known as a Coons patch. These patches are commonly used by boat and aircraft (and occasionally architectural) designers for skinning shapes that have been specified as sequences of profiles or ribs (figure 10.18).

10.16
A bilinear surface patch

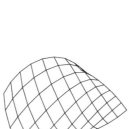

Edges of equal 2nd-order curves; vertices regular

10.17
Coons patches

Edges of arbitrary 2nd-order curvature; vertices regular

Edges of arbitrary 2nd-order curves; vertices arbitrary

Parameters

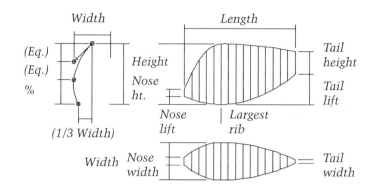

*Parametric variations
showing ribs in plan and
section*

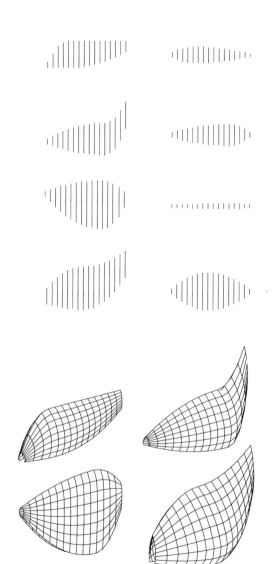

*Shapes skinned with
bilinear patches*

10.18
Parametric surface
definition using
control points

Variants on these shapes can readily be produced by manipulating the parameters that control profile curvature and spacing.

A specialization of the Coons patch, which has some attractive mathematical properties, is the bicubic patch: this has parametric cubic polynomials as the four boundary curves. Similarly, Bézier patches have Bézier curves as boundaries, and they can thus be manipulated by displacing Bézier control points—a particularly useful capability in CAD systems used for design of automobile bodies and similar sculpted forms.

Just as a smoothly curved line may be produced by bending a thin, elastic strip of wood or metal, so a smoothly curved surface may be produced by bending a thin, elastic sheet of material. And just as a drafting system's analogy to a physical spline is a mathematical spline curve manipulated by deploying control points on the drafting plane, so the surface-modeling system's analogy to a twisted elastic sheet is a mathematical spline surface manipulated by deploying control points in space. B-spline surfaces, which extend the idea of a B-spline curve, are especially widely used. A particular type of B-spline surface, known as a NURBS (non-uniform rational B-spline) has formal properties that make it attractive in many practical modeling applications.

A typical NURBS curved-surface modeler provides a vocabulary of basic shapes modeled as NURBS surfaces with meshes of control points (figure 10.19). These control points may be pulled and twisted (usually in real time) to sculpt the shape as required (figure 10.20).

A particular concern in using bicubic, Bézier, B-spline, and NURBS modelers to design curved objects is maintaining smooth curvature—not only of the surface itself but also, sometimes, of its first and second derivatives. Discontinuities in smoothness show up as unattractive bulges, wrinkles, kinks, and dimples. Sometimes they can also cause engineering problems.

Appropriate curved-surface vocabularies and modeling strategies are sometimes determined by the materials and fabrication processes that are to be used to produce the

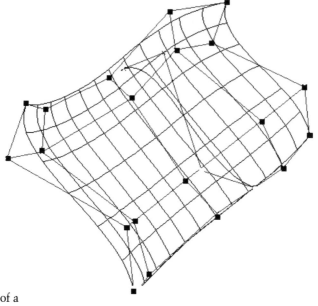

10.19
Control points of a
NURBS surface

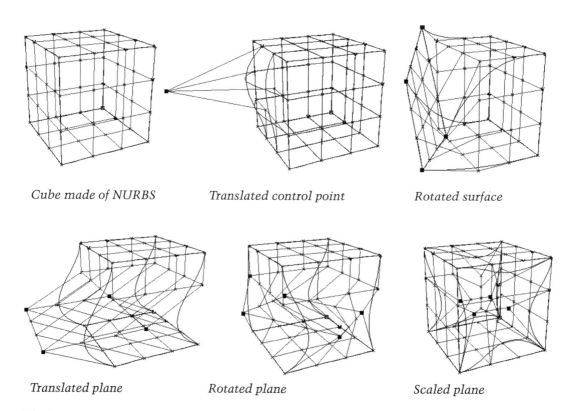

Cube made of NURBS   *Translated control point*   *Rotated surface*

Translated plane   *Rotated plane*   *Scaled plane*

10.20
Sculpting a NURBS surface

surfaces. Stiff sheet materials that are to be fabricated by cutting out facets suggest use of a faceted modeler. Flexible sheet materials such as plywood and sheet metal can be bent into cylindrical and similar singly curved (translationally swept) surfaces or twisted into ruled surfaces such as hyperbolic paraboloids. Flexible boards can be used to form lofted surfaces such as those of boat hulls. Pressed metal and injection-molded plastic can be formed into many doubly curved B-splined shapes, but this is usually an expensive industrial process.

Fractal Surfaces

Fractal surfaces are the opposite of smooth surfaces. They commonly result in nature from growth and erosion processes, and they are produced computationally by recursive subdivision of surface patches, as illustrated in figure 10.21. A surface is first approximated by a mesh of triangles. Then, using a random-number generator, each triangle is subdivided into four smaller triangles. This process is carried out recursively until a microstructure of tiny irregular facets is produced. By controlling the parameters of this process it is possible to construct fractal surfaces that depict various types of terrain and different sorts of textured materials with varying types and levels of roughness.

Topographic Surfaces

Topography varies arbitrarily, so representation of topographic surfaces is a matter of sampling and interpolation. Frequently, for example, elevations are recorded at points on a square plan grid. The surface can then be modeled by bilinear or bicubic patches (figure 10.22). Increasingly accurate representations can be produced by sampling elevations at finer resolutions. Relatively coarse sampling and curve interpolation produces very smooth surfaces, finer sampling allows small bumps and depressions to show up, and very fine sampling reveals that natural topographic surfaces are actually fractals. (Notice the close analogy with scanning a visual field to produce a square grid of intensity levels.)

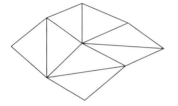
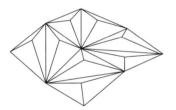

10.21
Recursive construction of a fractal surface

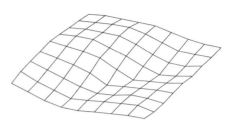

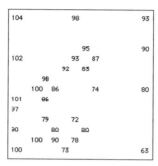

a. Grid

b. Spot elevations

10.22
Topographic surfaces
obtained from elevation
data

Another common technique is to record elevations of arbitrary points (spot levels) on a surface, then to employ a triangulation procedure to construct a mesh of planar facets known as a TIN (triangulated irregular network) model (figure 10.23). This is efficient, since data points can be concentrated where necessary to record abrupt changes and fine detail, but can be sparser elsewhere.

Topographic surface-modeling software usually provides for use of a variety of interpolation strategies and production of several different types of surface representations. Thus a set of spot levels supplied by a surveyor might be translated into a contour map, a drainage direction map, a grid of bilinear patches, a set of parallel section curves, and a TIN model.

Surface Intersecting and Cutting

In two-dimensional drafting it is often necessary to find line intersections and to divide or trim lines at intersection points. Earlier we saw how two-dimensional drafting software provides operations for accomplishing

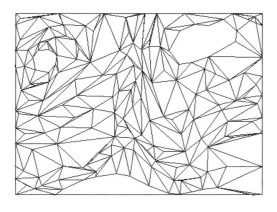

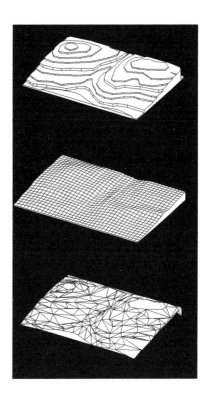

10.23
A TIN surface model,
compared with contour
and grid models

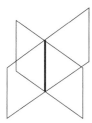

*Generating an
intersection line*

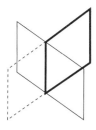

Cutting a surface

10.24
Cutting with intersecting
planes

this. Similarly, in surface modeling it is frequently necessary to find surface intersections and to divide or trim surfaces at intersection lines.

The simplest case is intersection of a plane surface by a plane surface—which always results in a straight line (figure 10.24). Efficient procedures to find such intersection lines are not difficult to implement, so surface-modeling systems often provide plane-cutting operations. In software that relies on faceted approximations to curved surfaces, it is easy to go a step further and provide a generalized surface-cutting operation. But where curved lines and surfaces are represented accurately, by equations and coefficient values, it is necessary to compute the equations describing intersection lines. This can be a very complex mathematical task, so software for true curved-surface manipulation is much more elaborate (and usually more expensive and demanding of computational resources) than software based on the idea of faceted approximation.

Systems that represent all kinds of surfaces by means of NURBS patches can provide general surface-cutting and

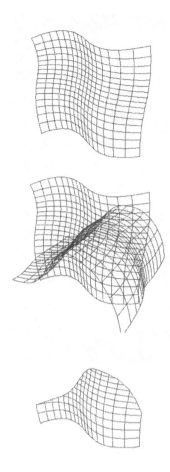

intersecting tools. This means that designers can use complex curved surfaces as cutting tools to sculpt other curved surfaces (figure 10.25). Furthermore, complex surface-intersection problems (as when complex profiles meet at awkward angles) can be resolved with ease.

Section drawings can be produced from surface models by cutting to a plane (or sometimes a more complex surface) to produce a collection of lines—in effect a wireframe model, which may be stored on a separate layer. Where closed facets of such wireframes indicate the interiors of solids, these facets can be fitted with surfaces to indicate *poché*.

Rendering

When a building or other artifact has been modeled as a collection of plane or curved surfaces in space, it can be rendered realistically in line, tone, or color. This is a three-step process. Rendering software must first generate a perspective or other projection: as in production of a wireframe view, each element in the geometric model is projected onto the viewplane and clipping is performed. Next, the visible surfaces must be determined: only those closest to the viewer will be displayed. Finally, some surface-rendering computation must be executed to determine how the visible surfaces will look. Thus the rendering pipeline, which provides the way to go from a surface model to a rendered image, is as shown in figure 10.26.

Visible-surface Determination

The problem of visible-surface determination is simply stated: given an object modeled as a collection of opaque surfaces, determine which edges and surfaces are visible to an observer at a specified location (for perspective projection) or viewing from a specified direction (for parallel projection). The solution principle is also simple: edges and surfaces in back will be obscured by opaque surfaces in front. Thus the problem is, in essence, one of sorting surfaces in depth.

The practical difficulty is one of computational complexity: as the number of surfaces in a model grows, the computer time required to determine the visible surfaces also grows (perhaps exponentially), and at some point the computation becomes impractical. For several decades, then, a great deal of research effort has been devoted to development of efficient visible-edge- and surface-determination procedures, and various clever approaches have emerged. But the details of these are now mostly of little concern to designers: with increasing availability of very fast processors, increasing sophistication of visible-edge- and surface-determination algorithms, and a growing tendency to incorporate standard algorithms in hardware, quick and reliable visible-surface determination for large geometric models has become commonplace.

One detail that *is* of practical concern is the distinction between hidden-line and hidden-surface procedures (figure 10.27). Hidden-line procedures perform accurate floating-point arithmetic to determine where lines are cut by edges of opaque polygons. This is a relatively slow and expensive process, but it yields coordinate data that can be used to produce large, accurate, pen-plotted or laser-printed line drawings. Hidden-surface procedures are used to produce bitmapped images. One common, simple procedure of this type is known (with little respect for the intelligence of painters) as the painter's algorithm. This is just the procedure of sorting polygons by depth back from the picture plane, then drawing from the back forward so that later polygons overwrite earlier ones. Since it does not require explicit determination of intersection coordinates, it is extremely efficient.

Simple depth-sorting, hidden-surface procedures are defeated by conditions such as cyclical overlap of surfaces (figure 10.28) and will produce inaccurate results when these conditions are encountered. The procedures can be elaborated to deal appropriately with these conditions, but the amount of computational work that they must do goes up accordingly, and it takes longer for them to produce results. Some rendering software allows the user to make the trade-off—to choose a quick sorting procedure that

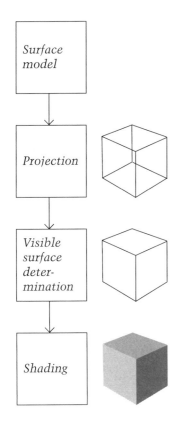

10.26
The rendering pipeline

Surface model

Projection

Visible surface determination

Shading

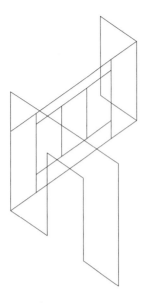

Wireframe view

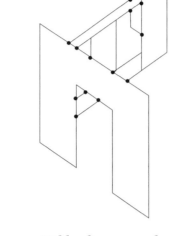

*Hidden-line removal:
64 line segments
calculated, 20 hidden*

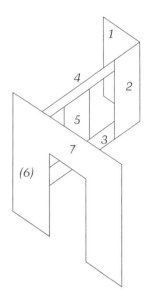

*Hidden-surface removal:
7 surfaces depth sorted*

10.27
Hidden-line removal
versus hidden-surface
removal

10.28
Cyclical overlap of surfaces

may produce flawed results due to sorting errors, or to choose a foolproof sorting procedure that takes longer. Quick sorts often suffice for a designer's own working purposes, since minor sorting errors are unlikely to cause confusion in this context. But they should never be used for presentations, since spatial ambiguities due to sorting errors can easily make a view incomprehensible to somebody who is not already familiar with the scheme.

A rendering process can be terminated following hidden-surface determination to produce an unshaded view. This highly economical sort of view represents in a way that is fundamentally different from shaded views. As Heinrich Wölfflin remarked, in a famous passage in *Principles of Art History*, "If we wish to reduce the difference between the art of Dürer and the art of Rembrandt to its most general formulation, we say that Dürer is a draughtsman and Rembrandt a painter." He took these artists as representative of two "radically different modes of vision"—the linear and the painterly—and suggested that these were "two conceptions of the world, differently oriented in their taste and in their interest in the world, and yet each capable of giving a perfect picture of visible things." In summary: "linear style sees in lines, painterly in masses." In a drawing composed of edge lines, as Wölfflin further commented, "the eye is led along the boundaries and induced to feel along the edges." This is a form of representation useful to a designer when "the sense and beauty of things is first sought in the outline."

Basic Shading

To produce more painterly images, light intensities at points on visible surfaces must be computed and rendered. To produce a monochrome shaded image, a single intensity is computed for each point; and to produce a colored, shaded image, intensities of red, green, and blue components are computed.

In general, intensity at a point is a function of many parameters: the spatial and spectral reflectivity properties of the surface at that point, the spatial and spectral emission properties of the light sources that are to be taken into account, the location of the viewer, and the relation of the surface to other surfaces in the scene. Simple, quick intensity-determination procedures take only some of these factors into account, and so produce only approximate results. More complex and costly procedures consider more of them to render wider ranges of optical effects and subtler nuances. The most sophisticated surface-rendering algorithm is not necessarily best for a designer's purposes. It is important to understand the basic properties of the various available algorithms, the kinds of results that they produce, and their demands on computer resources.

The most important effect of surface shading is to create pictorial space. Leonardo da Vinci put the matter thus:

The first business of the painter is to make a plane surface appear to be a body raised and standing out from this surface, and whoever excels the others in this matter deserves the highest praise. And this study, or rather this summit of our learning, depends on lights and shades.

Leonardo made endless careful studies of the reception of different kinds of light by different kinds of surfaces. Later scientists were to produce quantitative laws describing the distribution of light reflected from surfaces, and these eventually provided the basis for surface-shading algorithms used in computer graphics.

The most elementary of these laws is Lambert's cosine law, discovered by the sixteenth-century physicist and astronomer Johann Lambert. It reduces to a precise formula the fact long known to painters, and explicitly noted by Leonardo, that the intensity of reflected light from a plane surface is related to the angle at which the light is incident. If we simplify the situation by assuming a dull, matte surface (so that there are no highlights) and directional diffuse light (so that no shadows are cast), diffuse reflection will result—energy arriving from the light source will be scattered uniformly in all directions. Lambert's law states that the intensity of light reflected in this way is proportional to the cosine of the angle of incidence (figure 10.29). Thus intensity diminishes as the surface is tipped obliquely to the light source. Light incident perpendicular to a surface is reflected with maximum intensity, while light parallel to a surface will leave the surface in darkness. The s-shape of the cosine function assures that the drop-off in intensity is rapid in the middle ranges, but it flattens out at both extremes. The amount of light reaching a viewer is independent of that viewer's position: apparent intensities of surfaces will not change as the viewpoint changes.

A simple and remarkably effective way to shade plane surfaces, then, is to specify lighting direction, calculate surface normals, then use a cosine function to calculate surface intensities. This is usually known as Lambert or cosine shading: figure 10.30 gives an example. Old-fashioned drawing books demonstrate how to do it by hand with tonal media like charcoal and watercolor wash; simple software can perform it efficiently to produce bitmapped images from surface models; and special-purpose graphics hardware can now accomplish it at very high speed. The effect is very much like that achieved by painters of illusionistic architectural decoration and backgrounds at Pompeii or by a photographer who places a matte gray architectural model in diffuse light.

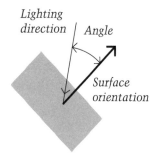

Lighting direction | *Angle*

Surface orientation

10.29
Lambert's cosine law

10.30
A simple Lambert-shaded image

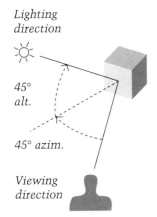

Lighting direction

45° alt.

45° azim.

Viewing direction

10.31
A simple convention for relation between lighting direction and viewing direction

The simplest way to perform Lambert shading is to adopt a standard convention for the direction of light and to let surface intensities vary over the full range from white to black. A common architectural convention, for example, is to let light arrive from over the viewer's shoulder, at angles of 45 degrees horizontally and vertically from the line of sight (figure 10.31). If the shaded object is then placed on a black ground, the light faces and their profiles will be emphasized; if it is placed on a white ground, the dark faces will be emphasized; and if it is placed on a mid-gray ground, the emphasis will be evenly distributed (figure 10.32).

More control over visual effects can be gained by introducing additional parameters into the basic shading equation. Most obviously, it is useful to be able to vary the direction of the incident light to change the distribution of darks and lights on the object. Control of lighting can be elaborated by providing for multiple light sources with different directions and intensities and by allowing specification of not only light source direction, but also actual position. Where position can be controlled it becomes possible to locate sources within buildings for night views and to simulate effects of artificial light (rather than sunlight) by diminishing intensity of illumination with distance according to the inverse square law (figure 10.33).

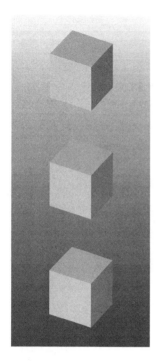

10.32
The effect of the ground

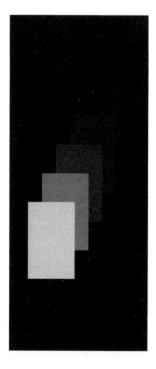

10.33
Diminishing the intensity
of illumination according to
the inverse square law

Surfaces can be differentiated by associating a surface reflection coefficient K with each one. This coefficient varies between 0 (black) and 1 (white). Thus the basic Lambert-shading equation is written

$$Id = Ip\ K\ cos(Theta)$$

where Id is the intensity of the reflected light, Ip is the intensity of the incident light, K is the surface-reflection coefficient, and $Theta$ is the angle of incidence. By varying surface-reflection coefficients the effect of a black-and-white photograph can be produced.

Objects rendered by this equation seem to exist in cold and harsh light like that of a flash photograph taken outdoors at night. This is because no account is taken of effects of nondirectional ambient light, which in the real world usually softens shadows and reduces contrasts (particularly in interior spaces, where there is much interreflection of light between surfaces). It is easy, however, to elaborate the basic Lambert-shading equation as follows

$$I = Ia\ Ka + Id$$

where I represents the surface intensity resulting from both ambient light and directional light Id. The ambient contribution is simply the product of ambient intensity Ia and the ambient reflection coefficient Ka. If the ratio of ambient to directional components Ia/Id is high, then contrasts between differently oriented surfaces will be reduced and the model flattened (figure 10.34), but if it is low then contrast will be high and modeling will be accentuated (figure 10.35).

Where color displays are available the idea of Lambert shading can be extended, in a very straightforward way, to provide a technique for producing colored, shaded images from surface models. Surface-reflection coefficients and source intensities are specified for red, green, and blue components, then used to compute reflected intensities for these components. The result is a color, specified in the RGB system, for each surface. Relationships of lighting and surface color can be adjusted to produce different types

10.34
High ambient light
reduces the contrast
between differently
oriented surfaces

10.35
Low ambient light and
directional light normal
to the front facade
produce high contrast
and dramatic modeling

10.36
Parallel surfaces of the
same reflectivity are
not distinguished by
Lambert shading

of images. If there is relatively little variation is surface color but dramatic, directional lighting, then images that emphasize modeling and chiaroscuro (like the paintings of Rembrandt) will result. But if local color is dramatically varied while lighting is kept flat, then images that cling closer to the picture plane (like Japanese prints or the paintings of Manet) can be generated.

The essential result of Lambert shading is to add to an image information about the orientations of surfaces. This clarifies angular relationships between surfaces and enhances the illusion of pictorial depth by reinforcing the depth cues provided by foreshortening. Lambert-shaded images, then, are often particularly useful for studying issues of massing: they clearly present just the information that is of interest, but they suppress irrelevant and distracting effects.

A characteristic disadvantage of Lambert shading is that parallel surfaces with the same reflection coefficients will have the same intensity. Thus the shading does not, in this case, convey depth information, and if the surfaces overlap in the image their outlines will be confused (figure 10.36). Similarly, if the incident light bisects the angle between two faces, definition of the separating edge will be lost. Even worse, if the incident light equally divides the solid angle at a vertex, definition of that vertex will be lost. These effects are particularly troublesome in one-point perspectives of buildings with parallel elevation planes and in plan and elevation projections. Often they can be avoided or minimized by careful adjustment of viewpoint or view direction or by movement of the light source. But in many cases introduction of additional graphic information is needed to disambiguate the image.

An obvious expedient is to combine Lambert shading with edge outlines. This produces a particularly crisp, clear image since it defines with precision both shapes and orientations of surfaces. However, such images direct the viewer's attention less precisely to profile and contour than do pure line images, and less precisely to tone and mass than do pure shaded images.

Smooth Shading of Curved Surfaces

10.37
Lambert-shaded faceted
spheres

When Lambert shading is applied to a faceted approximation of a curved surface, the results are reasonably satisfactory when the facets are small enough (figure 10.37). But the results may not be acceptable to a designer who wants to study fine nuances of curvature and the resulting modulation of light. Furthermore, distracting Mach bands—perceived exaggerations of intensity changes at edges of facets—are likely to appear. (That the dark side of an edge will often appear darker, and the light side lighter, was known to painters such as Leonardo and Mantegna, but the illusion is named after the physicist Ernst Mach, who studied it in the nineteenth century.)

A better approach to curved-surface shading is to distribute intensities smoothly, rather than to change them abruptly at edges of facets. In his treatise on painting Alberti formulated this task and suggested a way to proceed:

Remember that on a flat plane the color remains uniform in every place; in the concave and spherical planes the color takes variations; because what is here light is there dark, in other places a median color. This alteration of colors deceives the stupid painters, who, as we have said, think the placing of the lights to be easy when they have well designed the outlines of the planes. They should work in this way. First, they should cover the plane out to the outlines as if with the lightest dew with whatever white or black they need. Then above this another and thus little by little they should proceed. Where there is more light they should use more white.

The computational equivalent of this little-by-little procedure for smooth tonal distribution was first developed at the University of Utah by Henri Gouraud. His essential idea was to calculate surface normals at facet vertices, then calculate intensities at these points, and finally, linearly interpolate intensities between these points to render a smoothly shaded surface. Linear interpolation is the numerical version of grading a wash or smearing charcoal with your finger. The calculations are simple (and Gouraud shading is often now implemented in special-purpose hardware for even higher speed), but the results can be very convincing (figure 10.38).

However, Gouraud-shaded objects never sparkle. They always look as if they are made of some dull, matte material. This follows from the fundamental assumption, made in both cosine and Gouraud shading, that light is reflected equally in all directions. But most real surfaces reflect light somewhat unequally in different directions, with the result that specular highlights—more or less definite reflections of the light source—appear. These highlights move and change as the viewpoint alters.

This effect has long been known and exploited by painters: E. H. Gombrich has suggested that its use might go back to the great Greek Apelles; there certainly was extensive use by Roman and Byzantine painters; and Jan Van Eyck and the Flemish illusionists deployed it with exquisite mastery. The scientific basis for calculation of specular highlights is provided by the law of the perfect mirror: the angle of reflection is equal to the angle of incidence (figure 10.39). Thus the viewer can see specularly reflected light from a perfect mirror only when the angle alpha in figure 10.39 is zero. For imperfect reflectors the intensity of specularly reflected light gradually diminishes as alpha increases, so that the viewer sees a fuzzy highlight rather than a perfect reflection of the light source. Thus the principle of cosine and Gouraud shading can be modified to take account of specular reflection by making intensity a function not only of the angle of incidence, but also of the angle alpha between the angle of reflection and the angle of view.

A popular method for shading shiny curved objects in this way, to render specular highlights, was first developed by Bui-Tuong Phong. Phong shading not only deals with specular highlights, but also uses a more accurate interpolation technique than Gouraud shading. Consequently it is a more complex and expensive process than Gouraud shading, and it is difficult to compile into silicon. More recent research has focused on the accuracy and the speed of this type of rendering. Blinn shading procedures, and other more recent refinements of the idea, provide better results in some contexts. Figure 10.40 compares Gouraud, Phong, and Blinn shading.

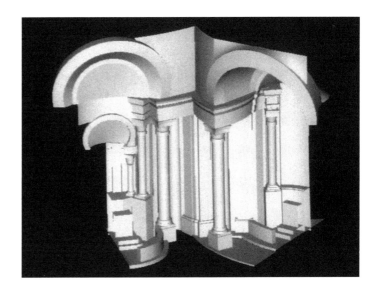

10.38
Gouraud-shaded curved
surfaces

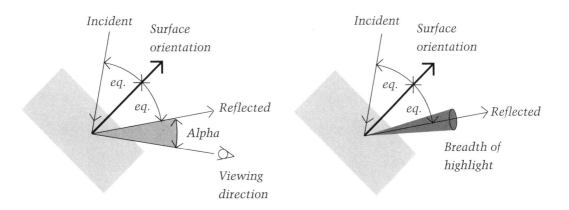

Specular reflection

Partial specular reflection

10.39
Specular reflection

10.40
Comparison of Gouraud
(back), Phong (middle), and
Blinn (front) shading

For Phong shading the angle alpha is calculated from the position or direction of light and the position or direction of view. The value of a specularity coefficient must be specified for each surface in the model. High specularity values yield the effect of very shiny surfaces with intense, concentrated highlights; lower values yield more diffuse highlights; and very low values yield the effect of a matte surface with almost imperceptible highlights. The center of a highlight will appear at the point where the angle of incidence equals the angle of reflection. The color of the highlight will be that of the light source, not that of the surface. Multiple light sources will produce multiple reflections. The overall effect is very much like that of a careful airbrush rendering with highlights. Figure 10.41 shows an array of Phong-shaded spheres: diffuse reflectivity varies along the vertical axis, while specularity varies along the horizontal axis.

With a surface modeler and a Phong-shading system an architect can conduct parametric studies of potential building appearance by systematically varying diffuse and specular reflectivities (to approximate effects of different

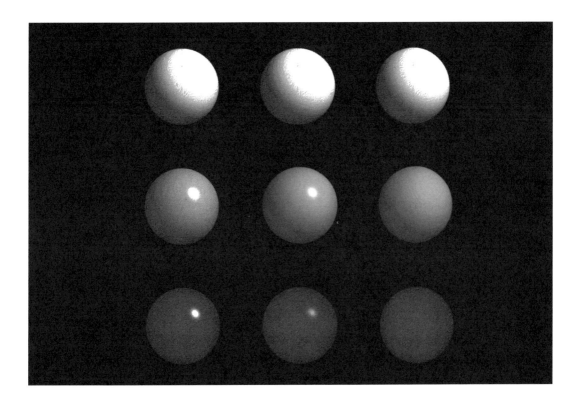

10.41
Varying the ratio of
specular to diffuse
reflection

materials and finishes) and lighting parameters. This sort of investigation would be impossibly laborious using conventional rendering techniques, but it is quick and inexpensive with computer-aided design.

Cast Shadows, Transparency, and Reflections

The advanced chapters of traditional treatises and textbooks on perspective usually consider the topics of cast shadows, transparency, and mirror reflections. These effects can all be investigated and rendered by extending the basic idea of tracing the paths of rays to determine foreshortening and occlusion.

A cast shadow, for example, can be treated as the darkness thrown on a surface by an object that intercepts light. It falls on the side opposite to the light source and can only become visible when the light direction differs from the view direction. In the simplest case there is a single, infinitely distant point light source—approximately the case of the sun shining out of a cloudless sky. This idealized situation was extensively treated in Gaspard

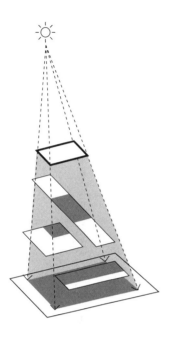

10.42
A shadow volume

Monge's *Géométrie descriptive* (1799), and Monge's projective methods developed into the traditional architectural subject of sciagraphy.

From a more modern computational viewpoint, the task of determining the shapes and locations of cast shadows turns out to be very closely related to the task of producing a hidden-surface perspective, and many of the same procedures can be employed. Surfaces produce shadow volumes from a point light source in just the same way that they produce occlusion volumes from eye points (figure 10.42). A cast shadow, then, is the intersection of a surface with a shadow volume. To put this another way, every surface that the light source "sees" is in light, while every surface occluded from the light source is in shadow. So addition of shadows to a hidden-surface scene can be accomplished by specifying a point light source and performing some extra surface-projection and depth-sorting operations. Shadow-casting procedures based on this principle can be used to add shadows to hidden-line, cosine-shaded, Gouraud-shaded, Phong-shaded, and Blinn-shaded scenes (figure 10.43).

Transparency effects are the inverse of cast-shadow effects. Where an opaque surface casts a patch of darkness, a transparent opening like a window casts a patch of light. And where an opaque surface occludes part of a scene, a transparent surface reveals part of a scene: it creates a view volume rather than an occlusion or shadow volume. Thus surface descriptions can be extended by specifying opacity coefficients (in addition to diffuse and specular reflection properties), and effects of surface transparency can be rendered through further generalization of surface-projection and depth-sorting procedures (figure 10.44).

Computations of mirror-reflection effects are based on the mirror law—that the angle of incidence equals the angle of reflection (figure 10.45). In the simple case of a plane mirror, then, the effect is to "double" the geometric model about the mirror plane. This double can then be projected in perspective in exactly the same way as the original, unreflected part of the model (figure 10.46).

10.43
Scenes with cast shadows

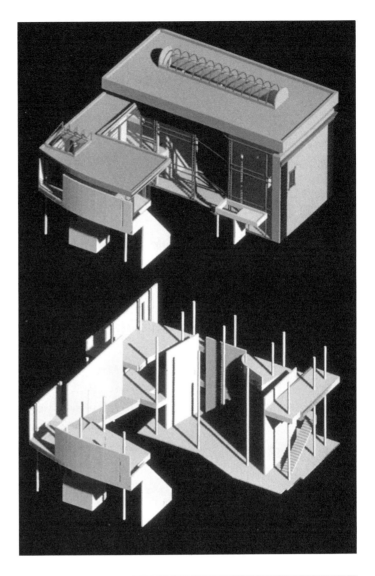

10.44
A scene with transparent
surfaces

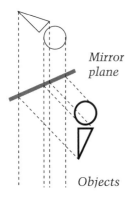

Virtual objects

Mirror plane

Objects

10.45
Effect of a mirror plane

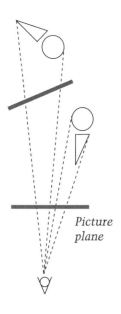

Picture plane

10.46
Reflected objects are
treated like real objects
in perspective projection

These principles of geometric optics are elegantly combined with the principles of shading that we considered earlier in a computationally intensive but increasingly popular technique known as raytracing. Raytracing procedures consider the picture plane as a fine grid of pixels placed between the viewer's eye and the scene, and they send a ray from the eye through each pixel to the scene (figure 10.47). By computing the red, green, and blue intensities reaching the eye along each ray, the color of each pixel can be established. Clearly this can become a very large task. If the grid has a resolution of one thousand by one thousand pixels, for example, it will be necessary to trace one million rays.

The color of each pixel is calculated as follows. The ray through the current pixel is traced to its first intersection with a surface in the scene. The color of the light coming from the surface at this point will be the color of the pixel. This color is due to the combined effect of three things: shading resulting from light directly incident on that point from light sources in the scene (calculated by one of the shading procedures that we have considered), reflections of other objects in the scene, and the color of any object seen through the surface at that point. To account for cast shadows, a shadow ray is fired from the point to each of the light sources in the scene (so the amount of computation goes up rapidly when multiple shadowing light sources are introduced into complex scenes). And to account for the reflection and transparency effects, the ray is split into a reflected ray and a transmitted ray, and these two spawned rays are continued until they, in turn, intersect surfaces. The color coming from these surfaces is then calculated in the same way. Of course the process need not stop here. The two spawned rays may themselves be split in two, and so on recursively to construct an intersection tree of reflected and transmitted rays for each pixel (figure 10.48). The intersection trees are developed to whatever depth is judged necessary to account adequately for cast shadow, transparency, and reflection effects. The computation required to render a scene grows exponentially with the depth to which spawned rays are traced.

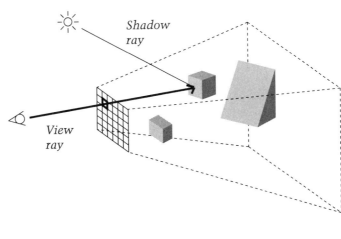

*The first intersection
of a ray with a surface*

Shadow
ray

View
ray

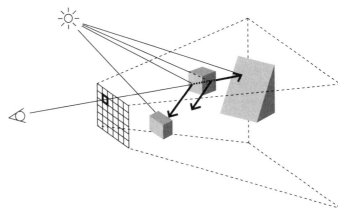

*Reflected and
transmitted rays*

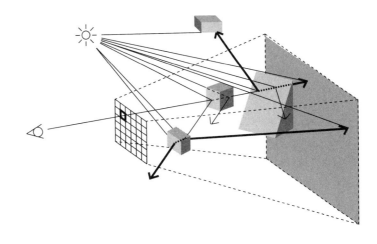

*Increasing complexity.
Many surfaces affect the
color of a pixel*

10.47
Raytracing

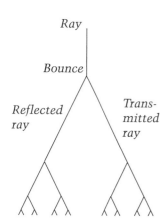

Ray

Bounce

Reflected ray

Trans-mitted ray

10.48
Exponential growth of the
number of spawned rays in
raytracing

Raytracing amounts to a strategy for discretizing and point-sampling the scene. Discretizing is accomplished by dividing the picture plane into pixels, and sampling is accomplished by constructing the intersection trees. Like any such strategy raytracing has characteristics that make it effective in some contexts but not in others. It works very well for highly specular scenes with point light sources, where it renders mirror reflections, highlights, sharp cast shadows, and refraction by transparent solids with breathtaking fidelity. It is least effective for rendering scenes that consist mostly of matte surfaces with spot, line, and area light sources, since evaluation of integrals rather than point sampling is needed for accurate rendition of diffuse shading and interreflection effects. Effects such as soft penumbrae and "bleeding" of colors due to diffuse interreflection between surfaces are not present in raytraced images. These limitations can be overcome, to some extent, by elaborating the basic raytracing procedure, but this tends to make the computations even more complex and expensive.

Raytracing was first applied to perspective rendering of architectural scenes by Arthur Appel in the late 1960s. During the 1970s and 1980s the technique was much elaborated, but production of raytraced images was regarded as a supercomputer application, and there was little practical application in design. By the beginning of the 1990s, though, it was becoming increasingly feasible on inexpensive personal computers. It will have a growing role to play in design contexts where effects of cast shadow, transparency, or mirror reflection are important and require close investigation.

Diffuse Global Illumination Effects

The qualities of many architectural interiors depend more on diffuse interreflections and soft shadows than they do on the specular reflections and point-source cast shadows that are rendered so effectively by raytracing. (Raytracers usually account for diffuse interreflection, in very approximate fashion, by introducing an ambient light term into shading equations.) To study such diffuse effects, radiosity-rendering procedures (which derive from thermal engineering techniques for studying radiant energy) are more effective.

Radiosity procedures begin by dividing the surfaces in the scene, rather than the picture plane, into small discrete elements (figure 10.49). Thus they are based on a different discretization strategy from that of raytracing—one that is independent of observer position. They do not distinguish between light sources and reflecting surfaces: any element of a scene may act as an emitter of light energy. This makes them very suitable for rendering scenes with area sources of light (such as the panes of a window) and scenes in which large, brightly lit surfaces contribute substantially to interreflection effects (figure 10.50).

Interreflection is handled by solving a set of simultaneous equations describing energy balance—the effect of which can be visualized as follows. Assume that light reaches a given surface patch in two ways: directly from the light sources in the scene and indirectly by reflection from other surface patches. Assume at the outset that all surface patches have zero intensity. A first iteration of the shading calculation establishes the amount of light reaching each patch directly from the light sources. Some of this will be absorbed, some of it will be transmitted, and some of it will be reflected. A second iteration calculates the amount of light reaching each patch on the first bounce

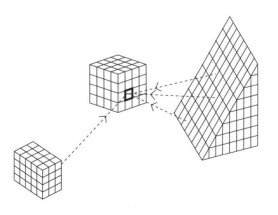

10.49
Radiosity techniques consider the transfer of light between discrete surface patches

Light source

Object

Umbra

Penumbra

10.50
Production of a penumbra
by an area source

from other patches. Again, some of this will be absorbed, some of it will be transmitted, and some will be reflected back into the environment. A third iteration calculates the effects of this second bounce, and so on. Since the light energy leaving a patch is always less than the light energy incident on a patch (unless the patch is a light source), the effects of additional bounces eventually become negligible. Thus successively more accurate approximations are constructed.

The geometric relation between a pair of patches determines the fraction of the light leaving one that reaches the other. This fraction is dependent on the shapes and areas of the two patches, their orientations, their distance apart, and any occlusion by intervening surfaces. The fraction for a given pair of patches is known as that pair's form-factor. The form-factors for a scene can be computed independently of viewer and light-source positions. Basically, this amounts to computation of a hidden-surface fisheye view (spherical perspective) from the center of each surface patch. For complex scenes computation of the form-factors is a massive task. However, this need not be repeated when viewing parameters are changed. Thus the radiosity method is expensive for producing a single view, but very efficient for producing large numbers of views.

In nondiffuse environments radiosity calculations become much more complex and time-consuming to carry out, partly because the intensity equations become more complicated when directional reflection must be considered and partly because smaller surface patches must be used to achieve satisfactory results. For scenes where both diffuse and specular effects are of interest, radiosity can be used to compute diffuse effects, raytracing can be used to compute specular effects, and the results can be summed to produce the final image.

Although the principles of radiosity have been exploited in various contexts since the 1960s (in the GLIM lighting analysis program, for example), radiosity rendering has been slower than raytracing to find practical application in design—mainly because it is even more demanding of computational resources. For a designer interested in close study of effects of light and surface, however, a radiosity renderer (particularly when calibrated carefully to produce accurate results) is an exceptionally powerful simulation tool and a necessary complement to a raytracer. In many contexts, for example, a raytracer can appropriately be used to produce studies of a building's exterior in crisp sunlight, while a radiosity renderer is used to study interior spaces with diffuse artificial light, window areas that function as light sources, and light-colored walls and ceilings that produce extensive diffuse interreflection.

10.51
Radiosity-rendered interior showing diffuse lighting and shadow effects.

10.52
Rendering surface texture
in increasing levels of detail

Surface Details and Textures

All the rendering procedures that we have considered so far make the assumption that surfaces (whether planar or curved) are uniform within their boundaries. In other words, reflectivity, specularity, and transparency values describe *whole* surface facets. This assumption greatly simplifies modeling and rendering, and is entirely appropriate when a designer is interested in studying basic interrelationships of surface geometry and lighting in a scheme. At another level of consideration, though, microstructural variation *within* surfaces becomes important.

Consider, for example, a brick wall (figure 10.52). As a first approximation, we might model and render it as a uniformly colored rectangle. For more accurate rendering to support closer consideration of design issues like the effects of different bonding patterns, we might next model it as a collection of smaller rectangles—the bricks themselves. Next, we might want to study the subtle but important effects of different ways of raking the mortar joints: this requires a three-dimensional model of surface relief and a rendering procedure that shows the shadow lines under individual bricks. Finally, we might recognize that individual bricks are not in fact uniform, but display variations of color and shininess across their surfaces. The appropriate level of consideration, modeling, and rendering depends on the design issue that is of current interest.

Finer and finer details of a design can always, in principle, be studied by building more and more intricate surface models—but this approach requires enormous modeling effort, consumes excessive amounts of memory for model storage, and makes huge demands on rendering systems. Fortunately, it is not always necessary. Approximate techniques for specifying and rendering surface detail will often suffice, and these are frequently provided by advanced rendering software.

The simplest approach is to provide for surface-detail polygons that are coplanar with base polygons in the surface model. These suffice for painted signs and decoration, and often for shallow-relief detail like brick and tile

Procedure to generate or sample texture

↓

Texture unit cell

Texels

Texture coordinate system

↓

Geometric transformations

↓

Texture mapped to local coordinate system of object

10.53
Texture mapping

patterns or curtain wall fenestration. This is economical, since the base polygons rather than the surface-detail polygons are depth sorted in hidden-surface and shadow-casting calculations.

Finer surface detail can be approximated by scanning an appropriate pattern or texture and mapping it onto a plane or curved surface (figure 10.53). Many raytracers and radiosity renderers can produce texture-mapped renderings in this way. The process is one of selecting an image (often taken from a library) to be mapped and specifying how the four corners of the image are to be placed on the surface. This can produce very effective results (figure 10.54), but developing libraries of scanned textures, selecting textures to apply to surfaces, and specifying mappings are all very time-consuming processes. Furthermore, great care must be taken to avoid unconvincing distortion of textures when they are mapped onto nonrectangular and curved surfaces, to keep textures in correct scale and orientation, and to avoid perceptible repetition when small texture samples are tiled over large surfaces.

A far more practical approach, for many classes of textures, is to generate the required surface variation by application of procedures that are controlled by just a few parameters (figure 10.55). One obvious parameterization approach is to adapt from two-dimensional paint systems the idea of a gradient fill operation. Another possibility is to apply a random speckling procedure. Sine functions can be used to generate ripple effects of various kinds. Recursive fractalization procedures can generate very realistic woodgrain, marbling, clouds, and other natural patterns. Regular tessellations and other repeating patterns can be produced by procedures that instantiate and transform standard motifs.

Wood-grain and many other surface textures vary characteristically from surface to surface of an object (the end grain looks different from the side grain, and so on) because they result from cutting oriented three-dimensional patterns. These textures are often most effectively generated by using procedures that produce three-dimensional "solid" textures and intersect them with object surfaces to produce variant surface

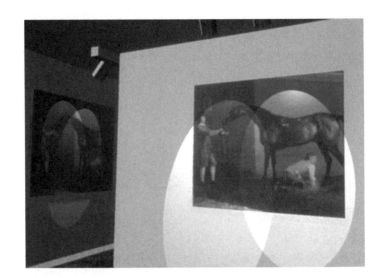

10.54
Application of a
sampled texture

10.55
Procedural textures

10.56
Bump-mapped texture

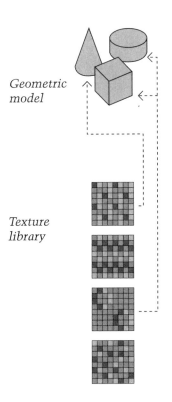

Geometric model

Texture library

10.57
Assigning textures from a library to surfaces of a geometric model

qualities. Such procedures can also be used by designers to study (without expensive experimentation on actual materials) effects of cutting wood, stone, and other materials in different ways.

Texture maps (either captured or procedurally generated) can be used to control not only variation in local surface color, but also variation in specular reflectivity, transparency, and relief. Effects of relief, such as those of orange skin or incised patterns, are produced by perturbing surface normals to approximate the shading of microfacets (figure 10.56). This strategy has some limitations (particularly in rendition of edges), but it can often produce very effective results. It is particularly useful for studying architectural compositions, such as those of H. H. Richardson, in which relationships of surface relief and roughness play an important role.

In summary, textures are functions of spatial coordinates: a two-dimensional texture is a function of X and Y in a surface-coordinate system, and a three-dimensional texture is a function of X, Y, and Z in a three-dimensional coordinate system. Such a function may have a single number as its value at specified coordinates, or it may have a vector of numerical values. Its values may be interpreted by a shading procedure as diffuse reflectivities, specular reflectivities, transparencies, surface normal perturbations, or anything else that the procedure takes into account in computing intensities. Depending on the character of the function, it may be represented as a stored array of values (sampled texture) or as a procedure that takes coordinate values as input (procedural texture): this is basically a store-versus-compute trade-off. Sophisticated rendering systems provide extensive libraries of textures, together with facilities for assigning textures to surfaces or solids in geometric models (figure 10.57).

Natural Phenomena and Landscape Composition

The techniques that we have considered so far yield a powerful tool kit for modeling, rendering, and studying landforms, architectural proposals, and urban design proposals. But landscape designers (and architects who want to study buildings in natural settings) need to extend this repertoire still further with tools for modeling and rendering vegetation, water, and atmospheric effects.

A simple but frequently very effective way to handle trees (particularly distant ones) is to texture map scanned photographs of trees onto transparent rectangles arranged parallel to the picture plane. For greater realism, and to provide greater flexibility in choice of viewpoint, such planes can be crossed as shown in figure 10.58.

An alternative approach is to employ growth-simulation procedures for construction of vegetation forms (figure 10.59). These can be designed either to produce two-dimensional images for texture mapping onto transparent planes or to produce full three-dimensional surface models that are then inserted into a scene and rendered in the usual way. (Three-dimensional vegetation models can become extremely complex, however, so rendering times can easily become excessive.) Very simple recursive procedures often suffice to produce convincing results, and adjustment of a few parameters of these procedures can yield wide ranges of variants. More sophisticated procedures can be based on the concept of a Lindenmayer system (a special type of grammar for describing growth and differentiation processes) to produce detailed, accurate models of particular plant species.

Still, horizontal water surfaces can be approximated in raytraced renderings by reflective planes, and ripple effects can be added with a sinosoidal texture-generation procedure and bump mapping to perturb surface normals (figure 10.60). Moving streams, waterfalls, and fountains are more difficult: the usual approach is to model them not as surfaces, but as procedurally generated configurations of discrete particles. The generative procedures incorporate laws of particle propagation and motion. This approach can be extended to modeling many other natural phenomena, such as swirling fog and smoke, clouds, flames and fireworks, and masses of foliage.

Effects of aerial perspective, haze, and mist can be approximated in landscape scenes by attenuating surface colors according to some exponent of the distance back

10.58
Representing trees approximately by texture maps on crossed planes

10.59
A procedurally
generated tree

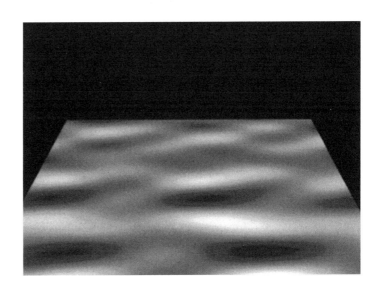

10.60
Water surface rendered
using bump mapping

10.61
Atmospheric perspective

from the picture plane (figure 10.61). A high exponent produces rapid attenuation, as in dense fog, while a lower exponent yields more gradual attenuation. A shift toward white produces a fog effect, a shift toward blue produces aerial perspective, a shift toward brown produces Los Angeles smog, and a shift toward black generates gathering gloom.

Retouching and Painting Shaded Images

Images rendered from surface models are not always perfect. Sometimes there are small modeling errors, such as omission of a surface, which yield blemishes. Sometimes there are polygon sorting errors or other undesirable artifacts resulting from the limitations of or bugs in rendering procedures. Or there may be problems of contrast and color balance. Usually these sorts of problems can be fixed by correcting the model or regenerating the rendering with slightly different viewing or lighting parameters. But if the problems are minor, it is often quicker and easier to move the bitmap to a paint and retouching program for correction—exactly as a scanned photograph might be retouched.

More interestingly, a synthesized image can be used as the base for hand sketching and rapid exploratory development of a design idea. One approach is to make a plot of a hidden-line view as a base for further development with colored pencil or watercolor. Another approach is to move a simple shaded image to a paint system, then to sketch over the top of it with paint tools.

Combining Synthesized and Captured Images

When two perspectives are overlaid, objects are brought together into definite relationship within the same frame of reference. This technique is sometimes used for piecewise synthesis of very large and complex perspectives. It can also be used for combining synthesized shaded images with scanned photographs.

To show a building in site context, for example, a perspective is synthesized with viewing parameters that match the camera position and settings for a site photograph. Then the synthesized image is carefully positioned

10.62
Matting a synthesized
image into a
captured image

relative to the photograph and electronically matted into it (figure 10.62). Various subtleties need attention if a convincing result is to be achieved. First, the lighting of the synthesized image must be matched as closely as possible to the lighting of the photograph. Foreground elements such as foliage must be replaced. (Use of a copy brush makes replacement easy.) Shadows and reflections may need to be adjusted by careful painting. And edges may need to be blended through use of a smoothing brush.

Variations on existing buildings and urban settings can also be depicted effectively in this way. Figure 10.63a, for example, is a photograph of Palladio's Villa Rotonda near Vicenza. This project was completed after Palladio's death, and the dome was not built to his original design. Figure 10.63b shows the villa as Palladio originally intended it. This image was generated by producing a surface model of the dome from Palladio's drawing, rendering the model from an appropriate viewpoint, and matting the rendered image into the photograph.

All the usual entourage elements can be cut out of scanned photographs and then matted into synthesized perspectives. A library of bitmapped people, automobiles, and trees, at different scales and under different lighting conditions, can be developed to facilitate this.

Output and Presentation Technology

For individual working purposes and small conferences, the bitmapped images produced by shading a surface model can be displayed directly on a color monitor. For

a. Villa Rotonda as completed

b. Villa Rotonda as intended

10.63
Historical reconstruction
using image-matting
techniques

presentation to larger groups, a video projector can be connected to the monitor. Alternatively, slide or print output can be generated.

High-quality results can be obtained by making high-resolution 35 mm slides on a digital film recorder. If these are projected at a large enough size to extend to the edges of the viewer's visual field, and if the viewer is located at a position corresponding to the station point from which the perspective was generated, a startling effect of three-dimensional realism is produced.

Adequate working prints can be generated from monochrome shaded images by halftoning and laser printing, and publication-quality halftones can be produced with a laser image setter. Inexpensive inkjet and thermal wax-transfer color printers usually produce disappointing results, since they lack the color and spatial resolution needed for accurate reproduction of the subtleties and complexities of sophisticated shaded images. Much better prints can be obtained (usually at correspondingly higher cost) with dye-sublimation printers, by making photographic negatives on a film recorder, or by making digital color separations on an image setter.

Uses and Limitations of Surface Modeling and Rendering

Surface models obviously contain substantially more information than corresponding wireframe models (figure 10.64). The complexity of the data structure increases too, since associations must be maintained not only between vertices and edges, but also between edges and surface facets. Thus storage and manipulation of data structures for surface models makes heavier demands on computational resources. There are more commands for a user to learn, and there is usually more work to do in constructing and editing a surface model, since surface shapes and properties must be specified. Generation of images can become significantly more time-consuming and expensive—particularly if detailed surface descriptions, sophisticated lighting models, and advanced rendering techniques are used.

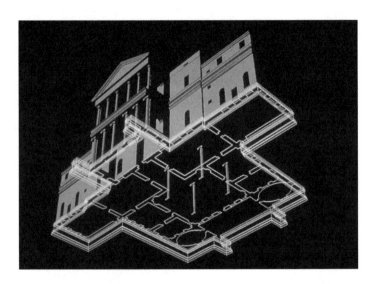

10.64
Surfacing adds information to a wireframe model

The advantages of surface modeling over wireframe modeling for many purposes are also considerable, however, and these frequently justify the additional effort and cost. (Furthermore, the cost difference is of decreasing significance as basic computational costs continue to drop and as hidden-surface and shading algorithms are increasingly embodied in silicon.) Much more realistic images than a wireframe view can be produced from a surface model, and subtle effects of light and shade, color, texture, transparency, and reflection can be explored. Furthermore, you can get just the level of realism that you need by applying different types of rendering procedures to a model.

Shaded images generated from surface models usually play a complementary role to plans, sections, and wireframes in design investigation. A plan or section provides a highly abstracted summary of a project's essential organization, a wireframe image gives an overview of its three-dimensional geometry, but a shaded or hidden-surface view is, by contrast, partial and fragmentary: it depicts only one of a project's indefinitely many aspects. A surface-modeling system can, however, inexpensively produce many such views—so that a project can be studied as a composition of revelations and concealments unfolding as an inhabitant moves through it.

Architects of the past often looked with a painter's eye: many of the greatest Renaissance architects were also painters, and Beaux-Arts architects were adept at the use of graded watercolor wash to study qualities of shade and shadow. But architects of the twentieth century have, for both ideological and pragmatic reasons, tended to rely on line drawings that abstract away from color, texture, and shading to emphasize pure geometry. Surface modelers and renderers create the possibility of recapturing the subtle understanding of surface and light that has, as a result, been lost.

Surface modelers are often marketed to designers merely as presentation tools. But that misses the most important point about them. When they are quick and cheap enough for everyday use they support graphic problem-solving by constructing, tweaking, and intersecting surfaces and by encouraging trial-and-error exploration of potential visual qualities in a cycle of modeling, rendering, modifying the model again, and so on until the desired effect is achieved.

Suggested Readings

Booth, Kellogg F. 1979. *Tutorial: Computer Graphics.* New York: IEEE.

Foley, James D., Andries van Dam, Steven Feiner, and John Hughes. 1990. *Computer Graphics—Principles and Practice.* Reading, Mass.: Addison-Wesley.

Freeman, Herbert. 1980. *Tutorial and Selected Readings in Interactive Computer Graphics.* New York: IEEE.

Glassner, Andrew. 1989. *An Introduction to Ray Tracing.* New York: Academic Press.

Greenberg, Donald P. 1986. "Computer Graphics and Visualization." In Alan Pipes (ed.), *Computer-Aided Architectural Design Futures.* London: Butterworths.

Greenberg, Donald P. 1989. "Light Reflection Models for Computer Graphics." *Science* 244: 166–73.

Greenberg, Donald P. 1991. "Computer Graphics and Architecture." *Scientific American* 264 (2): 104–9.

Hall, Roy. 1989. *Illumination and Color in Computer Generated Imagery.* New York: Springer-Verlag.

Hilbert, David, and S. Cohn-Vossen. 1952. *Geometry and the Imagination.* New York: Chelsea Publishing Company.

Jankl, Annabel, and Rocky Morton. 1984. *Creative Computer Graphics.* Cambridge: Cambridge University Press.

Joy, Kenneth I., et al. 1988. *Computer Graphics: Image Synthesis.* Washington: IEEE.

Kajiya, James T. 1986. "The Rendering Equation." *ACM Computer Graphics (SIGGRAPH 86)* 20 (4): 143–50.

Lord, E. A., and C. B. Wilson. 1984. *The Mathematical Description of Shape and Form.* New York: Halsted Press.

Magnenat-Thalmann, Nadia, and Daniel Thalmann. 1987. *Image Synthesis: Theory and Practice.* Tokyo: Springer-Verlag.

Newman, William M., and Robert F. Sproull. 1979. *Principles of Interactive Computer Graphics.* New York: McGraw-Hill.

Rivlin, Robert. 1986. *The Algorithmic Image.* Redmond, Wash.: Microsoft Press.

Rogers, David F. 1985. *Procedural Elements for Computer Graphics.* New York: McGraw-Hill.

Rogers, David F., and J. Alan Adams. 1976. *Mathematical Elements for Computer Graphics.* New York: McGraw-Hill.

Salmon, Rod, and Mel Slater. 1987. *Computer Graphics: Systems and Concepts.* Reading, Mass.: Addison-Wesley.

Upstill, Steven. 1989. *The Renderman Companion.* Reading, Mass.: Addison-Wesley.

Watt, Alan. 1989. *Three-Dimensional Computer Graphics.* Reading, Mass.: Addison-Wesley.

11

ASSEMBLIES OF SOLIDS

11.1
Solid building blocks

Sometimes designers want to conceive of three-dimensional compositions not abstractly in terms of lines in space, nor more visually as collections of surfaces in light, but spatially, as arrangements of volumes—both solids and enclosed voids (figure 11.1). Indeed, as Le Corbusier pointed out in *Vers une architecture*, this characterizes some architectural styles (figure 11.2). "Egyptian, Greek or Roman architecture," he wrote, "is an architecture of prisms, cubes and cylinders, pyramids or spheres: the Pyramids, the Temple of Luxor, the Parthenon, the Coliseum, Hadrian's Villa." By shaping and arranging blocks of wood or polystyrene an architect can compose directly in volumes, but this is slow and cumbersome. An increasingly attractive alternative is to employ solid-modeling software that provides prisms, cubes, cylinders, spheres, and so on as geometric primitives, together with tools for inserting, deleting, transforming, and combining these.

The displays produced by solid-modeling systems look much like the displays produced by wireframe- or surface-modeling systems (depending upon the way that solids are rendered), but the underlying geometric databases are very different. As a result, there are powerful geometry-editing operations not available in wireframe or surface systems, there are additional data extraction and analysis possibilities, and the process of design exploration with a solid modeler tends to evolve in different ways.

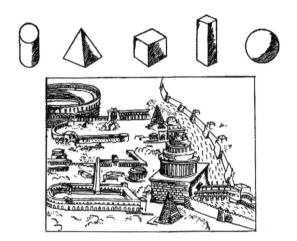

11.2
Volumetric composition
according to Le Corbusier

Voxel Representation

Just as sounds can be represented by one-dimensional arrays of data points and images can be represented as two-dimensional arrays of data points, so compositions of solids can be represented as three-dimensional arrays of data points. For this purpose we employ a cuboid subdivided into cubic voxels (volumetric elements) rather than a rectangle subdivided into square pixels (figure 11.3). We can then represent the forms of solid objects, using one bit of information per voxel, by coding a voxel outside the solid as zero and a voxel inside the solid as one.

As with sampling sounds and sampling images, we need a sufficiently high density of samples to avoid unacceptable aliasing effects. But high sample densities are particularly hard to achieve in this case: whereas halving the interval between sound samples doubles the total number of data points and halving the distance between image samples quadruples the number of data points, halving the distance between solid samples produces an eightfold increase in the number of data points.

However, voxel representations can usually be compressed effectively through use of a technique known as octree encoding (figure 11.4). This is a three-dimensional version of the quadtree technique for compressing bitmapped images, which was discussed in chapter 6. An octree is constructed by first subdividing the voxel array

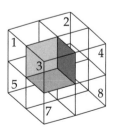

11.3
Pixels and voxels

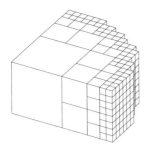

11.4
Octree representation of a
quarter cylinder

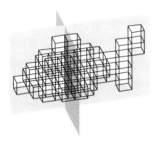

Wireframe

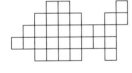

Sections

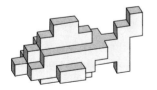

Shaded surfaces

11.5
Output from a voxel model

into octants, then further subdividing any nonuniform octants, and so on until there is no need for further subdivision or the level of individual voxels is reached. Each terminal node of the octree can then be labeled with the value of the corresponding volume.

We can generate output from voxel representations in several ways (figure 11.5). Horizontal or vertical slices through the voxel array are one-bit bitmaps that can be displayed as sections. We can also produce hidden-line and shaded images by interpreting the faces of voxels as opaque square surfaces. Raytracing techniques can be adapted to render solids as transparent volumes—a particularly popular technique in medical-imaging applications. And we can employ special devices to produce actual three-dimensional solids. A stereolithography device, for example, operates on a tank of liquid to produce laser-induced solidification at locations corresponding to occupied voxels.

Use of one bit per voxel suffices to distinguish between solid and void (which is enough for many design purposes), but we can introduce more distinctions if we wish. Use of two bits per voxel, for instance, provides for distinction between four different occupancy conditions—different materials, say, or different densities of material. This is useful when we need to represent the internal structures of solids, as geologists do when they represent geological structures, as oceanographers and atmospheric scientists do in their domains, and as medical imagers do when they investigate the internal structure of the human body. As sensing and sampling techniques develop, and as the growing availability of inexpensive memory and processing power increases the feasibility of handling large, high-resolution voxel representations, processing of voxel data for scientific visualization purposes is becoming an increasingly important field.

Boundary Representation

For designers' purposes, however, voxel representations suffer from the same sorts of limitations as the bitmapped images that we considered in chapter 6: they are low-level, unstructured, imprecise, and inefficient in use of available computational resources. We saw that, for greater precision and economy and to provide for higher-level design operations, we could use sparser and more structured representations in terms of lines—the boundaries of things. An analogous approach can be taken to solid modeling.

The basic idea here is to generalize and extend the techniques of surface representation that we considered in chapter 10. Connected pairs of zero-dimensional points (vertices) define finite one-dimensional lines, connected sequences of three or more one-dimensional lines can be used to define two-dimensional closed polygons, and connected assemblies of four or more closed polygons can be used to define closed polyhedral solids (figure 11.6). Thus data structures for boundary representation of polyhedral solids can be structured as illustrated in figure 11.7. These can be generalized, if desired, to provide for curved as well as planar faces.

These sorts of data structures consume more memory and are more cumbersome to manipulate than data structures for wireframe or even surface models of the same forms. This is partly because they must maintain a richer network of associations between geometric elements and partly because the associated operations for transforming and combining solids (which are, of course, implemented as operations on values in the data structure) must be prevented from producing invalid solids—self-intersecting ones, ones with "missing" faces, and the like (figure 11.8). The data structures and associated repertoires of operations of solid modelers are usually organized to maintain the topological properties of closed polyhedral solids as specified by Euler's theorem (figure 11.9).

Vocabularies of Solid Building Blocks

Drafting systems and wireframe-modeling systems provide operations for inserting various types of lines; surface-modeling systems provide operations for inserting various types of surfaces; and, as we might expect, solid-modeling systems provide operations for inserting various types of closed solids. A very simple system might, for example, provide operations for inserting, selecting, and deleting

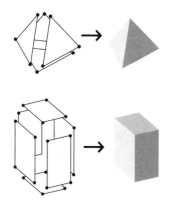

11.6
Surfaces form "watertight" boundaries of closed solids

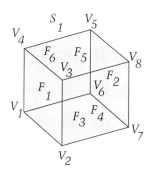

S_1

V_5

V_4

F_6 F_5 V_8

V_3

F_1 F_2

V_6

V_1

F_3 F_4

V_7

V_2

Not closed

V_1 (0,0,0)	E_1 (V_1,V_2)
V_2 (1,0,0)	E_2 (V_2,V_3)
V_3 (1,0,1)	E_3 (V_3,V_4)
V_4 (0,0,1)	E_4 (V_4,V_1)
V_5 (0,1,1)	E_5 (V_5,V_6)
V_6 (0,1,0)	E_6 (V_6,V_7)
V_7 (1,1,0)	E_7 (V_7,V_8)
V_8 (1,1,1)	E_8 (V_8,V_5)
	E_9 (V_1,V_6)
	$E_{10}(V_2,V_7)$
	$E_{11}(V_3,V_8)$
	$E_{12}(V_4,V_5)$

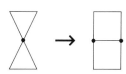

Infinite

F_1 (E_1 , E_2 , E_3 , E_4)
F_2 (E_5 , E_6 , E_7 , E_8)
F_3 $(E_1 , E_{10}, E_6 , E_9)$
F_4 $(E_2 , E_{11}, E_7 , E_{10})$
F_5 $(E_3 , E_{12}, E_8 , E_{11})$
F_6 $(E_4 , E_9 , E_5 , E_{12})$

S_1 $(F_1 , F_2 , F_3 , F_4 , F_5 , F_6)$

Self-intersecting

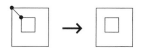

Nonmanifold

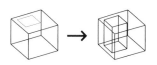

11.7
Boundary representation of
a closed polyhedral solid

11.8
Invalid solids

11.9
Euler operators for
manipulating vertices,
edges, and faces are
closed in the polyhedral
solids

rectangular boxes, of specified dimensions at specified locations and oriented parallel to the axes of the coordinate system (figure 11.10). This structures a useful but very restricted domain of formal possibilities. An obvious and simply implemented generalization is to allow placement of boxes in any orientation.

Vocabularies of polyhedra can be extended indefinitely—just as the Froebel blocks that Frank Lloyd Wright played with as a child came in sets of increasing variety, opening up increasingly extensive compositional possibilities. It is common, for example, to provide simple "pitched roof" forms such as appropriately parameterized triangular wedges, gables, hips, and pyramids (figure 11.11). And, just as drafting systems customarily provide circles and circular arcs as primitives, so solid-modeling systems frequently provide the basic solid derivatives of circles: cylinders, spheres, cones, and doughnuts (figure 11.12).

Solid-modeling systems that rely entirely on creating and locating instances of vocabulary elements are known as primitive instancing systems. They are very effective in contexts where the kit of parts that a designer deploys is, in fact, strictly limited (as is sometimes the case in the manufacturing industry). In most design contexts, though, it is necessary to extend the repertoire of possibilities by providing operations for constructing solids from points, edges, and surfaces, and for combining simple solids to make more complex solids.

Sweep Operations

Sweep operations are very commonly employed in solid-modeling systems to create new solids. When a closed polygon is translated along an axis, its zero-dimensional vertices sweep out one-dimensional edge lines, its one-dimensional edges sweep out two-dimensional facets, and its two-dimensional surface sweeps out a three-dimensional volume (figure 11.13). Solids can also be constructed by means of hierarchical sweep operations: a point might be swept to generate a straight line, that line might be swept to generate a square, and that square might be swept to generate a cube (figure 11.14).

Orthogonal

Non-orthogonal

11.10
Assemblies of boxes

11.11
A vocabulary of simple
roof forms

11.12
Solid derivatives of a
circle

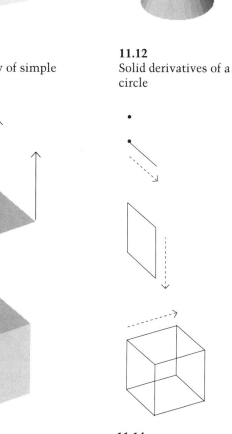

11.13
A swept polygon

11.14
Hierarchy of swept
primitives: point, line,
face, cube

ASSEMBLIES OF SOLIDS 241

11.15
Solids of translation and revolution produced from the same profile

11.16
A solid swept by a polygon moving along an arbitrary path

The usual approach to sweep operations is to provide for drafting profiles in a construction plane, then translational sweeping of closed shapes to produce prismatic forms, and rotational sweeping of open profiles to produce solids of revolution (figure 11.15). More sophisticated systems provide for sweeping closed shapes along arbitrary curves (figure 11.16). These operations have their counterparts in fabrication operations, so they often serve well for modeling physical construction components: extruded, planed, and rolled elements such as steel sections and wooden moldings can be modeled by translational sweeping; lathed elements and turned pottery can be modeled by rotational sweeping; and bent elements can be modeled by sweeping along curves. Sweep operations can also be used to model the envelopes swept out by moving cutting tools, and hence the volumes of material that they will remove.

Skinning and Tweaking Operations

Closed solids can also be constructed in surface-by-surface fashion, as illustrated in figure 11.17. This operation is known as skinning. The user must select the surfaces that are to be assembled into a solid. The software then checks that the specified surfaces do indeed enclose a volume (that they are "watertight"), and if so the surfaces are appropriately associated in the data structure. This method of solid definition is well suited to describing cast construction elements: indeed, the operation of constructing and positioning surfaces, checking for watertightness, and converting the hollow shell into a solid is very closely analogous to building and positioning form work and filling it with concrete. It is also good for describing the exterior volumes of buildings (since these are bounded by waterproof assemblies of surfaces) and the interior volumes of rooms (since these are often bounded by surfaces closed to keep in the warmth).

A closely related operation is known as tweaking—selecting and moving a vertex, control point, edge, or face to adjust the shape of a solid (figure 11.18). This operation must be controlled very carefully (either by the user or by the software), since it can produce inadvertent conversion of planar faces into nonplanar ones and conversion of closed solids into self-intersecting objects (figure 11.19). Tweaking vertices and control points is particularly effective for describing shapes such as those of tents, which are controlled at various points by poles and ropes. Objects that are formed by bending, twisting, and other such distortion operations can sometimes be modeled by taking a simple shape and tweaking it.

Features and Geometric Constructions

You can instantiate solids and locate them in space by specifying parameter and coordinate values, much as you can insert lines by specifying their end-point coordinates. But, just as drafting is more efficient when we take advantage of capabilities to snap to existing points and perform geometric constructions, so assembly of solids is more effectively performed by snapping new solids into specified relationships with existing ones. This requires definition of the features of the new solid that we want to relate to the environment (other solids), definition of the features of other solids to which they need to be related, and definition of the nature of the relationship.

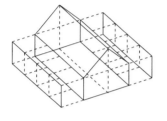

Wireframe

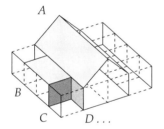

A

B

C   D...

Surfaces

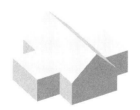

*Completed boundary
evaluated as a solid*

11.17
Skinning

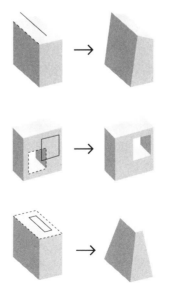

11.18
Tweaking

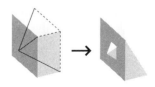

11.19
Invalid object produced
by tweaking

The complexity (and interest) of this issue is that solids have a great many definable features (figure 11.20), and the ways to relate solids in terms of these features can be extraordinarily varied. Potentially significant points associated with a solid include, for example, end points and midpoints of edges, center points of arcs, and centers of symmetry. Potentially significant lines include edges of faces, axes of symmetry, and surface normals. Potentially significant surfaces include not only faces, but also tangent planes to curves such as cylinders and spheres, and planes of reflective symmetry. Points may be snapped together; lines may be snapped into collinear, parallel, or perpendicular relationships; the bottom surface of one solid may be snapped into a coplanar relationship with the top surface of another one; and so on. It is, in fact, a nontrivial exercise to enumerate all the definite spatial relationships of design interest that can be formed between one type of solid and another (figure 11.21).

The realities of construction assembly often determine the potential spatial relationships of solid elements. If they are to be glued together, for example, they need face-to-face connection of sufficient area. If they are to be welded, they need edge-to-edge or edge-to-face connection of sufficient length. If a column is to support a beam without use of some sort of shear connection, then the column must go underneath the bottom face of the beam, and there must be sufficient bearing area. If you want to make a recessed joint (such as those common in timber construction), you must cut out a housing so that you can intersect one element with the other.

Similar practical constraints apply to the spatial relationships of closed volumetric elements such as rooms. If doors are needed between them, they usually need face-to-face connection of sufficient area. Alternatively (and less commonly), one might fit inside the other to form an aedicule. In classical composition, rooms were related concentrically, with coaxial axes of symmetry, or with coplanar planes of symmetry. But Frank Lloyd Wright overlapped interior volumes in ways that (in his later work) carefully avoided these classical relationships. And many of Frank Gehry's compositions juxtapose

11.20
Some of the features of a
simple solid

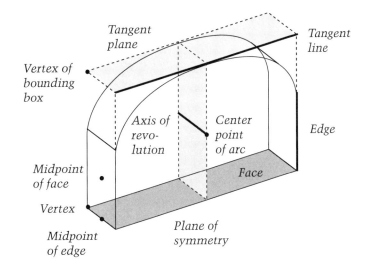

Tangent
plane

Tangent
line

Vertex of
bounding
box

Axis of
revo-
lution

Center
point
of arc

Edge

Midpoint
of face

Face

Vertex

Plane of
symmetry

Midpoint
of edge

11.21
Some of the possible spatial
relationships between a
cube and a cylinder

Coincident volumes

Coincident surfaces

Surface to edge

Surface to vertex

Partial inclusion

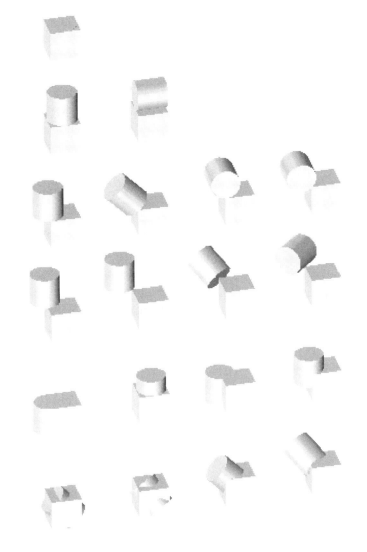

volumes in ways that conspicuously avoid concentric, coaxial, coplanar, parallel, and perpendicular relationships while still achieving the basic functional connections that are needed.

The simplest solid modelers avoid the issue of geometric construction altogether and merely provide for direct location of solids in the coordinate system. Some more ambitiously provide snapping and geometric constructions in construction planes, but not in three-dimensional space. Only the most sophisticated so far provide generalized capabilities for selecting features of solids and executing constructions in terms of these features. However, feature-based editing capabilities allow a designer to specify not only a vocabulary within which to work, but also a rudimentary syntax. As solid modelers are used more extensively in design exploration, this capability will be regarded as increasingly essential.

The Spatial Set Operations

Since lines, surfaces, and solids can be regarded as sets of points, we can define the set operations of union, intersection, and subtraction (relative complement) on them. Figure 11.22 shows their effects when applied to pairs of elements of increasing dimensionality. They can be implemented in line-, surface-, and solid-modeling systems, but they are of greatest utility in solid modeling because they provide a very elegant, powerful way to construct complex volumes from simple ones (figure 11.23). They provide the necessary path from the simplicity of a vocabulary of elementary closed solids to the complexity of many real three-dimensional solid objects.

Some interesting design strategies follow directly from combining these operations with specific geometric constructions. Perhaps the most obvious is to locate solids so that their faces are coplanar, then to perform union operations to build complex solids from simple ones (figure 11.24). This is closely analogous to gluing wooden blocks together or assembling pieces of cut stone.

But these logical solids, unlike actual pieces of wood, can overlap in space. Unioning overlapping solids can

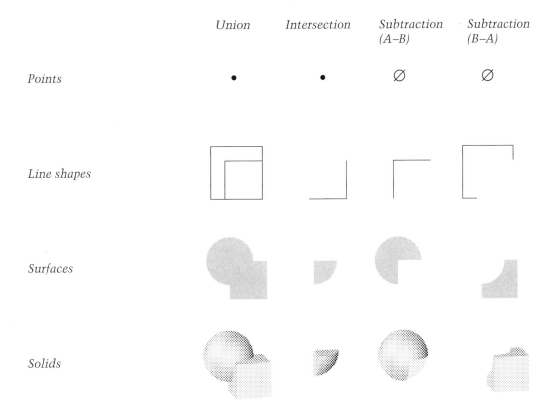

	Union	Intersection	Subtraction (A–B)	Subtraction (B–A)
Points	•	•	∅	∅
Line shapes				
Surfaces				
Solids				

11.22
The spatial set operations applied to elements of increasing dimensionality

11.23
Complexity from simplicity

produce surprising results. Figure 11.25, for example, shows the effect of snapping two cubes together at a vertex, rotating one of them, then taking the union. If a third cube is unioned in the same relation to the second as the second is to the first, and so on recursively, a complex symmetrical polyhedron soon emerges.

When the subtraction operation is used, one shape becomes a "cutting tool" on the other—much as a drill bit is a tool for subtracting a cylindrical solid from a piece of material. In general, subtraction can be used effectively to model construction components that are produced by material-removal operations such as drilling, sawing, carving, planing, and milling.

At a larger scale, architectural elements that are *conceptually* subtracted (even though they may actually be formed in some other way) can appropriately be modeled by means of subtraction operations. Consider, for example, a rectangular solid representing a wall. By locating translationally swept solids so that their sweep axes are

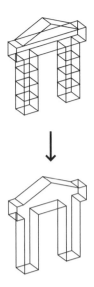

11.24
Gluing

perpendicular to the vertical faces, then subtracting, you can quickly cut out the usual sorts of simple door and window openings. The principle can be generalized, to produce a much richer variety of openings, by locating the subtracted solids in nonperpendicular positions, by subtracting nonprismatic solids such as cones and spheres, and by subtracting from more complex wall solids. Thus the famous window openings at Ronchamp, for example, can quickly be produced by subtracting angled pyramids from a wedge-shaped wall (figure 11.26).

Subtraction can also be used to hollow out interiors. For example, locate a rectangular box in plan, locate a smaller box inside it, and subtract to produce an interior room (figure 11.27). What remains of the original box becomes the wall *poché*. Or subtract a smaller hemisphere from a concentric larger one to generate a hollow dome. If you take a strict modernist attitude you will probably want the subtracted interior form to be similar to the exterior form, so that the exterior reveals the interior. But if you think more like a baroque architect you will probably want to subtract a dissimilar interior form—leaving a complex *poché* to mediate the differences between interior and exterior. Sir Christopher Wren's dome for Saint Paul's Cathedral in London, for example, has one shape on the exterior, a very different shape on the interior, and a vast *poché* volume taking up the difference (figure 11.28).

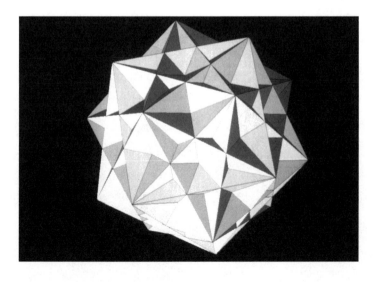

11.25
Complex solid produced by copying, rotating, and unioning cubes

11.26
Solid model of window
forms in south wall at
Ronchamp

11.27
Interior volumes hollowed
out by copying, scaling,
and subtracting

Wren, the great mathematician, would certainly have enjoyed the possibility of exploring geometric possibilities with a solid modeler.

Now imagine cutting a prismatic shape from the center of a rectangular block of polystyrene with a hot wire, cutting another prismatic shape from another direction, and removing the resulting core from the interior of the block. This core is formed by the intersection of the two prismatic shapes. The stonemason's strategy of projecting prisms from profiles drawn on the surfaces of a block, then removing everything except the intersection, illustrates the same idea.

Strategies for volumetric design by intersection generalize this idea. You can construct the basic form of Helmut Jahn's State of Illinois Center in Chicago, for example, by fitting a cone (resulting from setback requirements) into the corner of a rectangular box (defined by the Chicago street grid) and then intersecting (figure 11.29). Similarly, you can construct the form of pendentives making the transition between a square plan and a hemispherical dome by fitting a rectangular box into the equator circle of a sphere and then intersecting (figure 11.30). This construction can be generalized for production of column capitals and many other kinds of transitional solids: the plan shape can be not just a square but any polygon, and the intersected solid can be almost anything that is nonprismatic—an elliptical spheroid, a cone, a pyramid, or whatever.

11.28
Exterior volume, *poché*,
and interior volume in a
solid model of the dome of
Saint Paul's Cathedral

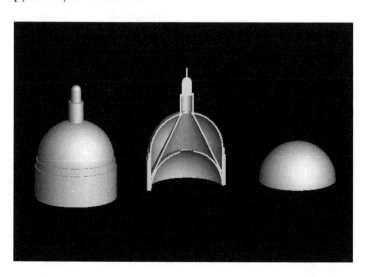

11.29
Basic form of the State of
Illinois Center modeled by
intersection and union

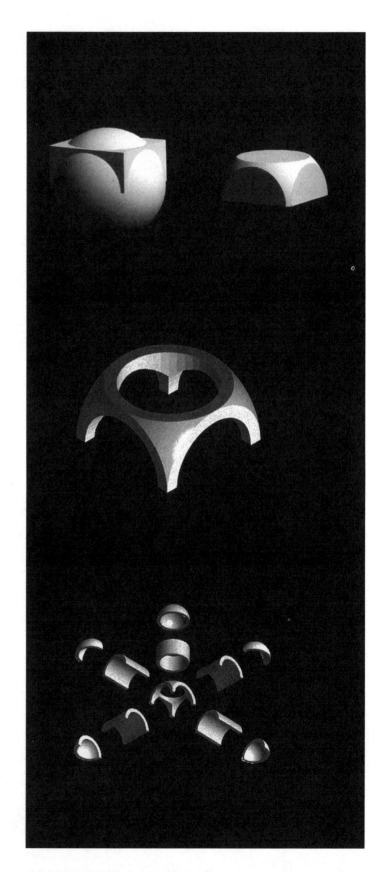

11.30
Pendentive and vault forms
modeled by intersection
and subtraction

Regularizing the Spatial Set Operations

A difficulty with the spatial set operations on solids is that they are not closed—they do not necessarily yield solids. In general, the intersection of two solids may yield a solid, a face, an edge, a vertex, or the empty set (figure 11.31). Some solid-modeling systems leave it to the user to make sure that operations are specified so as to produce nondegenerate solids, but a better approach is to eliminate the problem by regularizing the spatial set operations.

The basic idea is to partition a solid (considered as a point set) into interior points and boundary points (figure 11.32). Boundary points are defined as those whose distance from the solid and the solid's complement are zero. In general, boundaries may include dangling and floating edges and the like—the undesirable sorts of things that can result from ill-specified spatial set operations. These blemishes can be removed by the operation of regularization, which amounts to removal of every boundary point that is not adjacent to at least one interior point. The regularized union, intersection, and subtraction operations

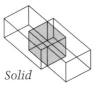

Solid

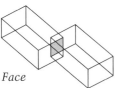

Face

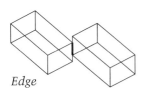

Edge

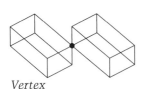

Vertex

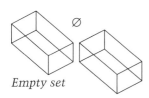

Empty set

11.31
Possible results of
intersection operations

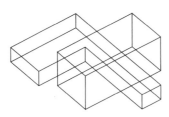 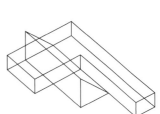

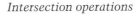

Intersection operations

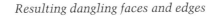

Resulting dangling faces and edges

Regularized results

11.32
Regularization

can then be defined so that they apply to regularized solids, and are closed in the regularized solids.

A related problem results from the round-off errors inherent in floating-point arithmetic. Faces that appear to be coplanar may overlap to produce intersection slivers and the like. Careful dimensional control, by snapping to grids and so on, is the best way to eliminate this possibility.

Constructive Solid-geometry Representations

Spatial set operations can be applied to the results of spatial set operations to produce trees of derived shapes. These are known as constructive solid-geometry (CSG) trees. At the terminal nodes of a CSG tree are instances of solids in the basic vocabulary of the solid-modeling system (figure 11.33). Each higher node is a union, intersection, or difference of two lower nodes. At the root node is the complete three-dimensional composition (figure 11.34).

Solid-modeling software evaluates specified CSG trees by converting them into boundary or voxel representations that can be used to generate displays and for other computational purposes. There are two basic ways to handle this, and in choosing between them the software designer must evaluate a trade-off between making demands on memory and making demands on processor capacity. The first approach is to evaluate each union, intersection, or subtraction as soon as it is specified and then store the resulting boundary representation. This is profligate in use of memory, but has the advantage that the tree is always fully evaluated: it is not necessary to reevaluate in order to display a node or perform some other computation that requires explicit boundary information. The converse approach is to store only the parameters of the lowest-level solids and the sequence of combination operations, and to reevaluate the tree to a specified node whenever the boundary information is needed. This is extremely economical in use of memory, but makes much greater processing demands and can result in very slow generation of displays. The first approach is usually appropriate when processor speed constrains performance more than memory limitations, and the second tends to be appropriate when the converse is true.

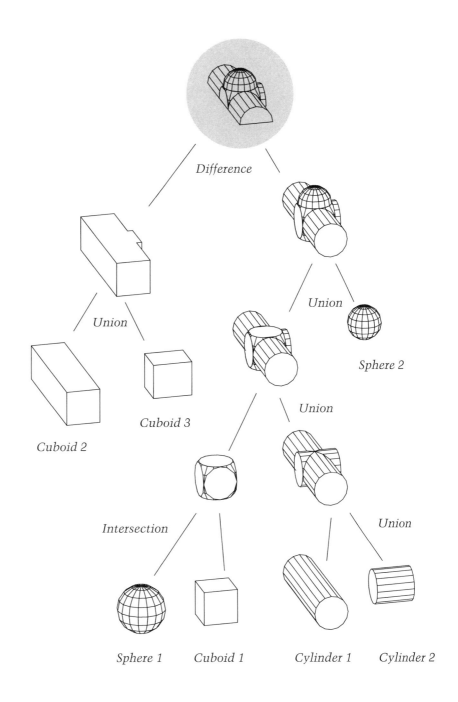

Difference

Union

Cuboid 2

Cuboid 3

Union

Sphere 2

Union

Intersection

Union

Sphere 1

Cuboid 1

Cylinder 1

Cylinder 2

11.33
Lower branch of a CSG
tree showing modeling of
a ceiling void from
geometric primitives

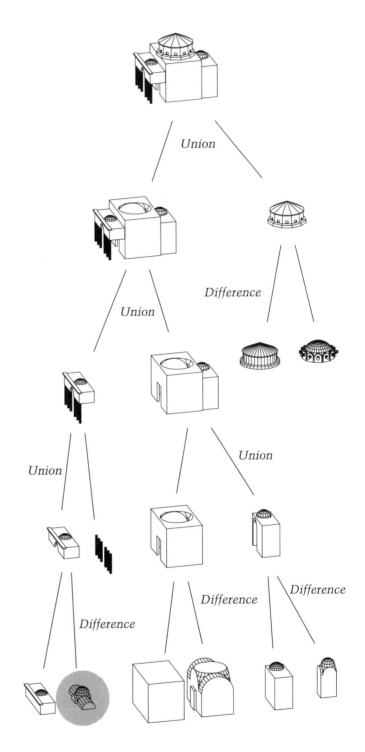

11.34
Root of a CSG tree showing
complete assembly (lower
branch from previous figure
attaches at the node
marked with a circle)

From a designer's viewpoint, however, the evaluate-as-needed approach has an additional advantage. It permits fluid variation of a design by manipulating the parameters of the lowest-level solids, by substituting different types of solids at the lowest level, and by pruning off whole branches of the tree and replacing them with new branches (figure 11.35). These capabilities turn a solid-modeling system into a particularly powerful tool for design exploration.

Power Sets of Solids

How many different solids can you produce by locating some elementary solids in space and performing union, intersection, and difference operations? The answer follows from the observation that overlapping closed solids always divide space into distinct closed regions. Each of these regions may, as a result of spatial set operations, become either solid or void. The set of all subsets of the set of regions (its power set), then, is the set of all possible solids. The power set forms a lattice under the relation of inclusion, as illustrated in figure 11.36. The spatial set operations provide a convenient way to explore this lattice.

11.35
CSG tree editing

CSG model

Primitive variation

Primitive substitution

Branch substitution

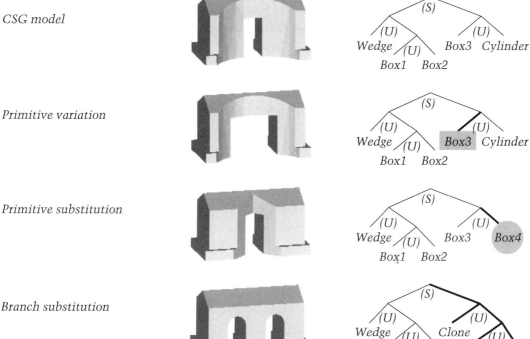

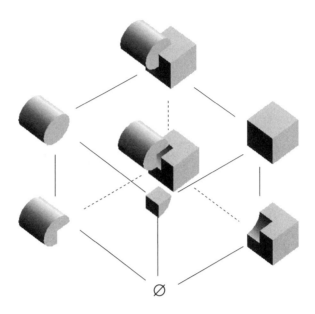

11.36
Power set of the closed
regions formed by two
overlapping solids

Volumetric and Engineering Analysis

Just as polygon-modeling systems are particularly useful
for urban design, space planning, and other work that
requires careful analysis of areas, solid models are correspondingly useful for design work that requires careful
analysis of three-dimensional forms. In particular, closed
solids have definite volumes, surface areas, centers of
gravity, and moments of inertia. These properties are
tedious to calculate by hand for any but the simplest cases,
but solid-modeling systems can be equipped with efficient,
general algorithms for deriving them from voxel or
boundary representations. (This is not possible with less
complete wireframe and surface models.) Thus you can
use a solid-modeling system to measure the amount of
material to be cast in a form, to measure the volume of an
auditorium for heating and cooling or acoustic analysis, or
to measure the volume of a building for urban design
analysis.

Volumetric analysis can be combined with spatial set
operations to provide some very powerful problem-solving
capabilities. Imagine, for example, that you need to design
a room with a specified volume. Instead of choosing some

simple shape (such as a rectangular box) to make the volume calculations easy, you might write a procedure to push two complex solids together along an axis, generate their intersection at each step, and calculate the volume at each step. If you did not like the shapes of appropriate volumes that resulted from this, you could try pushing them together along another axis.

Furthermore, the data structures of solid-modeling systems can be extended to provide for association of material properties such as density with solids. Associated algorithms can then derive additional properties. From volume and density, for example, the mass of a solid can be calculated. And if you know the location of the center of gravity, you know where this mass acts.

For detailed analysis of engineering properties, solids may be broken up into small pieces, known as finite elements, as illustrated in figure 11.37. Advanced solid-modeling systems provide algorithms for automatically constructing finite-element meshes from boundary models. Once this has been accomplished, finite-element analysis procedures can be used to produce detailed and accurate analyses of structural properties, thermal properties, and so on.

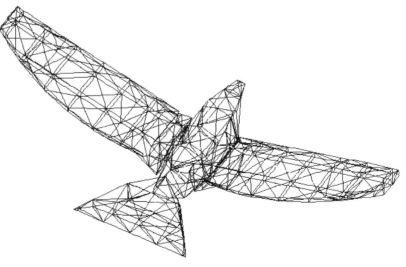

11.37
A finite element mesh

Assemblies

In the same way that a three-dimensional physical model can be assembled from wooden or plastic components, a digital model of a building can be assembled from discrete solids (figure 11.38). Such a model is the three-dimensional equivalent of the polygon maps that we considered in chapter 8: it exhaustively and unambiguously describes the occupancy of space by subdividing space into bounded pieces.

Before constructing a solid model of a building you must decide how to use solids to represent architectural elements. If you are making an exterior massing model, for example, the solids in the model will stand for major volumetric elements—much as blocks of wood or polystyrene stand for these elements in physical massing models. You may want to use such models not only to generate images, but also to analyze basic geometric properties of massing alternatives: you can compute volumes and surface areas, cut horizontal slices to reveal floor plates, and section vertically to study profiles.

For urban design purposes you can assemble simple exterior massing models of buildings into three-dimensional models of urban fabric. You can include in the model not only actual building volumes, but also notional volumes such as allowable building envelopes, air-rights volumes, view pyramids, and shadow volumes. These models are quicker to build, easier to modify and update,

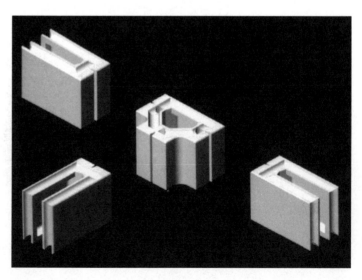

11.38
Components of a solid assembly

build, easier to modify and update, and much more compactly stored than the physical models that have traditionally been used for this purpose. With appropriate associated software you can use them to generate aerial, skyline, and street-level views, to analyze sightlines, and to study the shadowing effects of buildings. You can use spatial set operations to combine height, setback, and other constraints into allowable building envelopes for sites, and you can check for spatial clashes between proposed building forms and these envelopes. And by associating space use and ownership information with volumes, you can develop three-dimensional versions of the polygon-based geographic information systems that we discussed in chapter 8.

At the individual building scale you can use solids to represent closed volumes such as rooms, passageways, and elevator shafts. This is a useful type of model for preliminary studies of spatial organization and for generating input to programs analyzing heating, cooling, and acoustics. Its spatial complement is a model of the physical fabric. If you put these complementary models together, you obtain a close-packed assemblage of bounded forms, some of which are habitable spaces and some of which are tectonic elements.

A tectonic model represents a building as a collection of solid construction elements (figure 11.39). Such models are particularly useful for exploring not only ways to combine physical elements in space, but also ways to sequence their assembly in time on the construction site. By taking account of mass properties, tectonic models can be used to calculate dead loads for input to structural-analysis programs.

One of the hazards in design of a tectonic assembly is that you may inadvertently position solid elements such that they intersect. A duct may pass through space already occupied by a beam, for example. Fortunately, however, the procedures used to perform spatial set operations can be adapted to provide an efficient way of automatically checking for such spatial clashes. Essentially, a spatial clash checker looks for pairs of solids that have nonempty intersections.

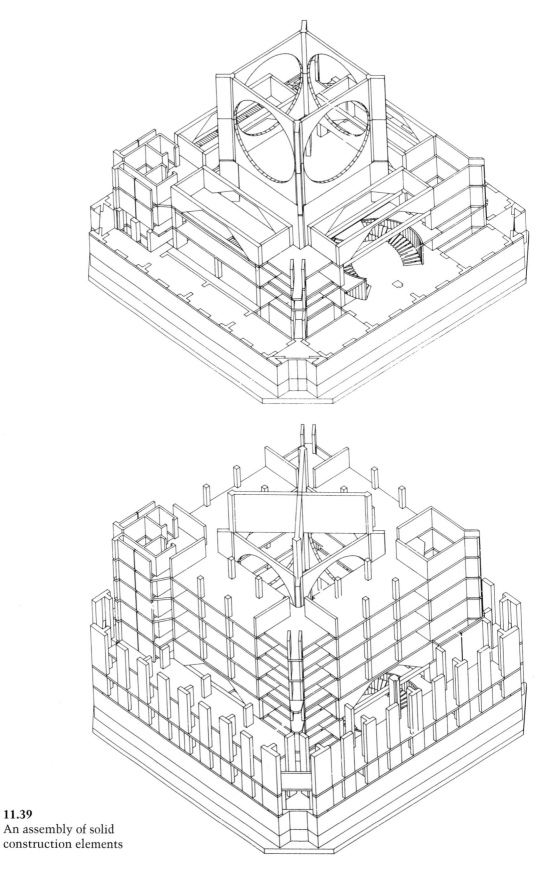

11.39
An assembly of solid
construction elements

The task of modifying an assembly of solids to reflect design changes can become laborious and frustrating, since changes in the position or dimensions of one solid element may propagate long chains of necessary adjustments to other elements. If columns are moved further apart, then you need to lengthen the beam that they support, then the slab supported by the beam must be correspondingly lengthened, and so on. This process of adjustment can be automated if component solids are defined as parametric objects and their relationships are described by formulae that relate parameters so that, in effect, the whole assembly is programmed to behave appropriately in response to changes in dimensions or locations of parts. Some advanced modelers provide for this. Specifying an appropriate structure of relationships for a complex three-dimensional assembly may, however, prove to be a very difficult problem.

Nonmanifold Assemblies

For some purposes, solid-assembly models may be too realistic. A designer might, for example, want to include freestanding wireframes and floating surfaces (as well as closed solids) in an assembly model to serve as a construction skeleton (figure 11.40). Furthermore, it may be useful to have operations that combine elements of different types—slicing solids with surfaces, extracting medial axes from solids, and so on. The data structure of a typical solid-assembly modeler is, unfortunately, not designed to allow this.

More technically, solid modelers are usually based on the assumption that solids have enclosing shells of surfaces and that these enclosing surfaces are two-manifolds (figure 11.41). Such shells always obey Euler's polyhedron law, which may be stated:

$$V - E + F - R = 2 (S - H)$$

where V, E, and F are, respectively, the numbers of vertices, edges, and faces, H is the number of holes, and R is the number of rings. This means, it turns out, that each edge must be incident at exactly two vertices, and each face

11.40
Constructions and stages
in the evolution of a solid
model

Two-manifold shell

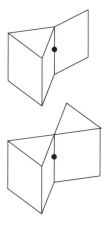

Nonmanifold assemblies of surfaces

11.41
Manifold and non-manifold shells

must be incident at exactly two edges. The data structures of solid modelers are designed to accommodate objects that obey this law, and operators that manipulate those data structures are designed to preserve consistency with it. This excludes stand-alone and dangling faces and edges (the explicit intention of the regularized spatial set operators)—an appropriate exclusion if the intention is to model a world of solid objects, but not if the intention is to model a designer's nonmanifold world in which such abstractions play an important role.

Nonmanifold geometric modelers, then, are systems that provide for assemblies of vertices, edges, faces, and solids into configurations that do not satisfy Euler's law. They include in their repertoires not only the usual operators for transforming and combining elements in each of these classes, but also operators that are not closed in one or another of the classes. These include operators that assemble edges to produce faces, that assemble faces to produce solids (the skinning operation discussed earlier), and that reduce solids to more abstract representations (which do not obey Euler's law) by pulling off faces, performing medial axis transforms, and so on. Thus they provide environments for incremental transformation of an abstract three-dimensional *parti*—a skeleton of lines and freestanding faces—into a complete, consistent solid-assembly model.

A full-featured, design-oriented geometric modeler might support four submodels: a point model, a wireframe model, a surface model, and a solid model. In the data structure, entities of lower-level models are associated to define entities of higher-level models: points bound lines, lines bound surfaces, and surfaces bound solids. Models at each level are regularized: the wireframe has no isolated points, the surface model has no isolated or dangling lines, the solid model has no isolated or dangling faces, and regularized union, intersection, and subtraction operators are used at each level. However, there may be points in the point model that do not bound lines in the wireframe, lines in the wireframe that do not bound surfaces in the surface model, and surfaces in the surface model that do not bound

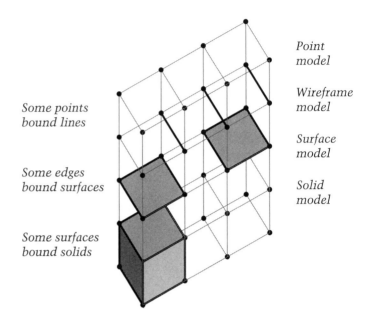

Point
model

Wireframe
model

Some points
bound lines

Surface
model

Some edges
bound surfaces

Solid
model

Some surfaces
bound solids

11.42
Entities in a full-featured
geometric modeler

solids in the solid model. Association operations are used to create higher-level entities: points are connected to make lines, lines are connected to make surface facets, and solids are skinned by surfaces. Conversely, cutting operations are used to create lower-level entities: solids are cut by surfaces to make surfaces or by lines to make lines, surfaces are cut by surfaces to make lines or by lines to make points, and lines are cut by lines to make points.

Producing Graphic Output

Solid-assembly models implicitly embody surface and wireframe models, so all of the types of renderings that can be produced from these less spatially complete models can be produced from solid-assembly models as well. Some additional types of graphic output are also made possible by the additional spatial information that a solid-assembly model contains.

First, you can cut arbitrary sections—at any location and angle and to complex section surfaces as well as to planes. Sectioning to a vertical plane to produce a traditional architectural section, to a horizontal plane to produce a plan, or to an inclined plane, is accomplished by subtracting a half space or a very large box. A thin slice can be cut out by intersecting the model with a slab-shaped object. Sometimes it is useful to intersect with more complex shapes to produce cylindrical cores, and so on.

Sectioning by intersection with a plane, rather than by subtraction or by intersection with a thin solid, is a good example of the use of a nonmanifold modeler. The result of sectioning a solid-assembly model by intersection with a plane is a set of two-dimensional *poché* polygons. These might be kept on a separate layer, since they are not really part of the basic geometric model, or they might be transferred to a two-dimensional drafting system for use in production of a section drawing.

Sectioned three-dimensional models may be shown in perspective or axonometric projection, or they may be projected orthographically onto planes parallel to the section planes to produce more traditional plan and section drawings. Section-cutting software can be extended to keep track of the new faces generated by the cut so that these faces can be shaded or outlined to show the *poché*. Many different rendering techniques may be used, depending on what you want to emphasize: among the options are wireframe with *poché*, hidden line with *poché*, hidden line with cast shadows, shaded, and shaded with cast shadows (figure 11.43).

11.43
A sectional perspective

Automated Production of Physical Models

The CAD/CAM techniques that have been developed for use in the manufacturing industry can sometimes be adapted effectively for production of physical topographic and architectural models from numerical data describing solids. If a model is broken down into planar surface facets, for example, then a computer-controlled laser cutter can be used to cut the facets from thin sheet material: finely detailed wooden models of buildings and contoured topographic surfaces can be produced in this way. Alternatively, the computer-controlled milling machines that now find wide application in the manufacturing industry can be employed to produce complex solid parts in metal or high-density foam. Stereolithography is perhaps the most versatile technique, and despite its technical complexity and high cost it has rapidly found a niche in medical imaging and mechanical parts design. A stereolithography system employs a computer-controlled laser to solidify liquid resin, in layer-by-layer fashion, to build up a solid.

All of these techniques make use of complex, expensive machinery that most designers are unlikely to have in-house. They will increasingly be made available by model-making and prototyping service bureaus, however. There are also some inexpensive alternatives. One effective way to streamline model production is to print facet shapes with a laser printer, mount them on cardboard, and cut them out with a matte knife.

Uses and Limitations of Solid Models

Solid models of parts and solid-assembly models have a higher level of geometric completeness than corresponding bitmapped images, drafted drawings, wireframe models, and surface models. This is the source of both their advantages and disadvantages.

In contexts where completeness and consistency of geometric representation are crucial, where it is necessary to integrate a wide range of applications around a geometric model, or where designers want to work in a directly sculptural way (rather than rely on abstractions like plans and sections), solid and solid-assembly models are particularly appropriate. But, since they must store more coordinate information and keep track of more topological relationships, solid models of artifacts tend to be much larger and more complex than less complete types of representations. This means that they make heavier demands on memory, computational capacity, and software engineering technique. A designer must consider whether the advantages of greater completeness justify the higher associated costs.

There is also a more subtle issue of representational economy. At an early stage in a design process a designer is usually interested in rapid, unencumbered exploration of ideas. Ambiguities do not cause major problems and may even become sources of creative ideas. Many inconsistencies can safely be ignored on the assumption that they will be dealt with later if the idea turns out to be a good one, but they are not worth attention if the idea is to be abandoned anyway. In this context sparse, economical representations that are easy to manipulate and do not mire the designer in demands for detail usually work better than representations that emphasize completeness and consistency. Later, when the focus shifts to resolving problems, working out details, analyzing cost and performance precisely, and producing complete documentation, abstract representations become less appropriate and techniques like solid modeling become more attractive.

The practical usefulness of solid-modeling technology has grown with the availability of computing power and the sophistication of available software engineering techniques, and this trend will continue. Prototype solid modelers emerged in the 1970s, but the commercially available systems that followed in the 1970s and 1980s were limited, slow, expensive, and often unreliable. By the end of the 1980s, however, robust and effective solid modelers were available on inexpensive personal computers and workstations, and they were becoming increasingly popular. As solid-modeling software exploits the capacities of increasingly powerful computers, it will be bound by fewer limitations on the topologies and geometries that it can process, it will be capable of handling larger and more complex projects, and it will increasingly emphasize real-time geometric transformation and spatial set operations, stereo and virtual reality interfaces, and other features that support swift, fluid manipulation of designs.

Suggested Readings

Foley, James D., Andries van Dam, Steven K. Feiner, and John F. Hughes. 1990. "Solid Modeling." In *Computer Graphics: Principles and Practice.* Reading, Mass.: Addison-Wesley.

Goult, R. J. 1987. "Finite Element Analysis." In Joe Rooney and Philip Steadman (eds.), *Principles of Computer-Aided Design.* London: Pitman.

Hoffmann, Christoph M. 1989. *Geometric and Solid Modeling: An Introduction.* San Mateo: Morgan Kaufmann.

Jared, G. E. M., and J. R. Dodsworth. 1987. "Solid Modeling." In Joe Rooney and Philip Steadman (eds.), *Principles of Computer-Aided Design.* London: Pitman.

Kalay, Yehuda E. 1989. *Modeling Objects and Environments.* New York: John Wiley.

Koenderink, Jan J. 1990. *Solid Shape.* Cambridge: The MIT Press.

Mantyla, Martti. 1988. *An Introduction to Solid Modeling.* Rockville, Md.: Computer Science Press.

Mortensen, Michael E. 1985. *Geometric Modeling.* New York: John Wiley.

Mullineux, Glen. 1986. *CAD: Computational Concepts and Methods.* New York: Macmillan.

Raper, Jonathan (ed.). 1989. *Three Dimensional Applications in Geographical Information Systems.* London: Taylor & Francis.

Weiler, Kevin J. 1986. "Topological Structures for Geometric Modeling." PhD. thesis, Rensselaer Polytechnic Institute.

Yessios, Chris. 1987. "The Computability of Void Architectural Modeling." In Yehuda E. Kalay (ed.), *The Computability of Design.* New York: John Wiley.

12

MOTION MODELS

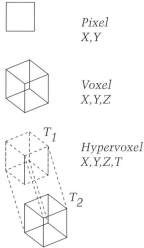

Pixel
X,Y

Voxel
X,Y,Z

Hypervoxel
X,Y,Z,T

12.1
A hypervoxel in a four-dimensional coordinate system

Consider a generalization of the idea of spatial and temporal sampling that was introduced in the discussion of digital sound, then developed further in our explorations of bitmapped images and solid models. You will recall that, in a digital sound recording, each data point has one time coordinate. In a bitmapped image each data point (pixel) has two space coordinates, and in a voxel representation of a solid each data point has three space coordinates. In an analogous digital model of a three-dimensional solid in motion over some time interval, then, each data point (hypervoxel) will have three space coordinates and one time coordinate (figure 12.1).

Assume, now, that we use one bit per hypervoxel to specify whether points in space are occupied at moments in time. The result is a description of a four-dimensional hypersolid. Such four-dimensional objects are very difficult to visualize directly, but, just as we can collapse a spatial dimension to produce a two-dimensional image of a three-dimensional scene, so we can collapse a hypersolid to a three-dimensional voxel model. One way to do this is to collapse the time dimension, so that versions of the solid overlap in the three-dimensional spatial coordinate system (figure 12.2): the effect is much like that of the famous multiple-exposure photographs made by Harold Edgerton to study motion.

12.2
Collapsing the time
dimension

A second approach is to select a plane, then collapse the three-dimensional scene onto that plane at successive moments (figure 12.3): this produces a sequence of two-dimensional bitmapped images—frames of a digital movie. If we display these frames side by side, we can obtain a sequence like the well-known photographic ones made by Eadweard Muybridge. And if we show them one after the other in rapid succession, we will see, from a particular viewpoint, the solid in motion.

Both of these visualization techniques have their uses. An urban designer might be interested in the three-dimensional envelope swept out by a building's shadow volume as the sun moves across the sky. But if we want to see the exact positions of the shadow volume at specific times of the day, we will prefer the sequence of frames.

As you might expect, adequate sampling rate is as important in digital representation of motion as it is in digital sound recordings, bitmapped images, or voxel models of solids. If the spatial sample rate is inadequate, then the familiar effects of spatial aliasing will show up in digital movies in particularly objectionable form. Sawtooth patterns will appear to crawl along profiles, for example. If the temporal sample rate is inadequate, then temporal aliasing effects—visual equivalents of frequency aliasing in sound recording—will also appear. Motion will appear jerky, spoked wheels may seem to revolve at spurious rates (or even to revolve backward), fine details of gesture may be lost, and so on.

Keyframes

Just as we can generalize the idea of pixel and voxel representation to hypervoxel representation of solids in motion, so we can also generalize the idea of boundary representation to four dimensions. Recall that, in a simple boundary model of a solid, zero-dimensional points with specified coordinates are associated to define one-dimensional lines, one-dimensional lines at specified positions are associated to define two-dimensional polygonal faces, and two-dimensional polygonal faces at specified

12.3
A succession of snapshots

positions are associated to define three-dimensional solids. Three-dimensional solids at specified time coordinates, then, form the boundaries of four-dimensional hypersolids (which may be depicted in two or three dimensions in the ways that we have considered).

In practice, software for modeling solids in motion typically provides the operation of keyframing for specifying such hypersolids. A pair of keyframes shows a three-dimensional solid at two moments in time—its states at the beginning and end of a motion sequence. Just as the translational sweep operation moves a two-dimensional shape through the third dimension to define a solid, the keyframe operation moves a three-dimensional solid through the fourth (time) dimension to sweep out a hypersolid. To visualize how this works for a simple case, consider a rectangular box at a specified position in space and time $T = 0$ (figure 12.4): this is the first keyframe. Now imagine the box translated and rotated to a different position at time $T = 1$: this is the second keyframe. When two keyframes have been specified, and we assume motion over the time interval $T = 0$ to $T = 1$, then it is straightforward to calculate a frame for any intermediate value of T. By incrementing values of T in discrete steps through the range 0 to 1, we can interpolate as many intermediate frames as we may wish to see.

When the box is moved in this way, each vertex sweeps out a line in four-dimensional space/time, each edge sweeps out a surface, and each surface sweeps out a solid. Thus we obtain a complete hierarchy of bounding elements defining a hypersolid. (If a wireframe or surface box instead of a solid box is keyframed, we obtain a correspondingly less complete space/time model.)

Any property of a three-dimensional solid may vary between keyframes. If only position varies, then pure translational motion results. If only orientation varies, then the solid rotates in place. When position and orientation both vary, the solid tumbles along a path like a baseball. Scale may also vary, so that the transformation from one keyframe to the next is a general similarity transformation—describable by a 4 x 4 transformation

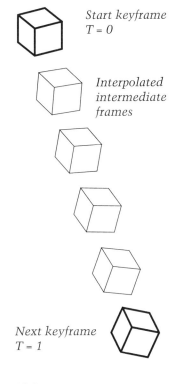

Start keyframe
T = 0

Interpolated
intermediate
frames

Next keyframe
T = 1

12.4
Interpolating positions
between keyframes

matrix. Finally, there may be parametric variation of shape and variation in surface properties such as color, specularity, transparency, and roughness.

Translational Motion Paths

The simplest translational motion path between two keyframes is a straight line in the three-dimensional spatial coordinate system. This can be interpreted as the locus of the origin of a local coordinate system (sometimes called a pivot point) in which the shape of the moving solid and its rotational motions are described.

More complex translational motion paths can be described by specifying not just pairs but sequences of keyframes, just as polylines can be specified by sequences of points. Then intermediate frames may be interpolated linearly (to produce jerky, segmented motion) or along arcs or splines to produce smooth motion (figure 12.5). Many motion-choreography and computer-animation systems rely heavily on the idea of splined interpolation of translational motion paths between keyframes.

Rates of Change

If positions along a translational motion path are interpolated by dividing the path into equal intervals, then translation at a uniform rate results (figure 12.6). But, if the path is divided into unequal intervals, then an object will speed up and slow down (like a roller-coaster car) as it moves along the path.

Another way to show this variation is to plot displacement along the path against time (figure 12.7). The first derivative of this curve shows the variation of velocity with time; the second derivative shows acceleration. Rates of change in size, color, transparency, and other keyframed variables can be plotted in exactly the same way. The interfaces of motion-modeling and computer-animation systems sometimes display all of these curves and allow for graphic editing by selecting and moving control points. When any curve (for example, an acceleration curve) for a variable is changed, all of the other curves for that variable are automatically adjusted.

12.5
Some basic types of
motion paths

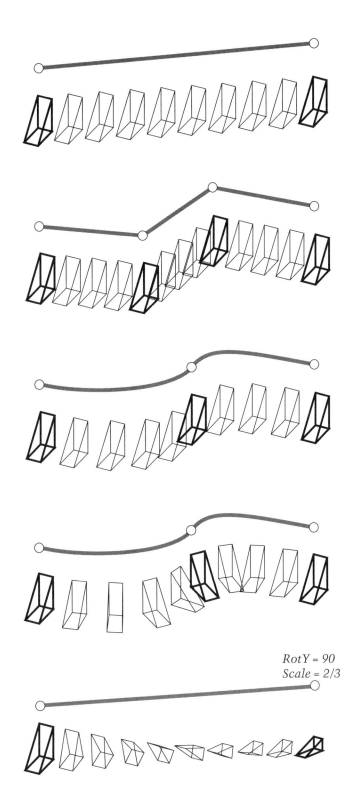

Straight line

Segmented

Spline

*Spline with rotation (to
maintain consistent
orientation to motion path)*

*RotY = 90
Scale = 2/3*

*Straight line with rotation
and scaling (unrelated to
path)*

Linear interpolation (sometimes called lerping) can be used to show movement of an automobile at constant speed, uniform rotation of a wheel, or light fading at a uniform rate. To achieve smooth initiation and termination of changes, s-shaped (slow-in / slow-out) curves are often used: these have zero derivatives at their end points and constant derivatives in the middle (figure 12.8). Other types of curves describe constantly accelerating motion (a rocket taking off), constantly decelerating motion (a rolling ball coming to rest), and sharp discontinuities (a ball struck by a baseball bat).

Motion Vocabularies and Compositions

These techniques extend the fundamental idea, which has evolved throughout this book, of a designer's vocabulary. A writer's vocabulary is a set of words, a musician's vocabulary is a set of sound types, a draftsperson's vocabulary is a set of line types, a sculptor's or architect's vocabulary is a set of surface types or a set of solid types, and a choreographer's or robot programmer's vocabulary consists of forms in motion.

Each element of such a vocabulary combines a three-dimensional solid object with a translational motion path and rate curves for rotations, size changes, color changes, and so on. The element can be instantiated by locating its defining keyframes in a four-dimensional coordinate system and by specifying values for other parameters. Motion compositions can be produced by instantiating elements within the same four-dimensional coordinate system.

Variations on motion themes can be produced by giving the same motions to different forms: thus a uniformly moving sphere might be substituted for a uniformly moving cube in a composition. Alternatively, the same form might be moved along different paths, or along the same path at different rates. Most importantly, the synchronization of individual motions may be varied so that different three-dimensional figures develop at different moments (figure 12.9).

Uniform   *Slow-in/*
Slow-out

T=0

T=1

12.6
Uniform and non-uniform
rates of translation

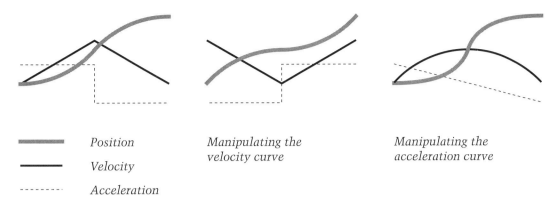

Position	
Velocity	*Manipulating the velocity curve*
Acceleration	*Manipulating the acceleration curve*

12.7
Manipulation of motion
curves to control
displacement along a path

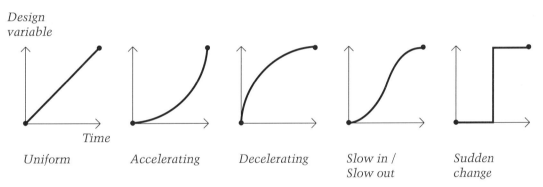

Design variable

Time

| Uniform | Accelerating | Decelerating | Slow in / Slow out | Sudden change |

12.8
Different rates of change of
a design variable between
two states

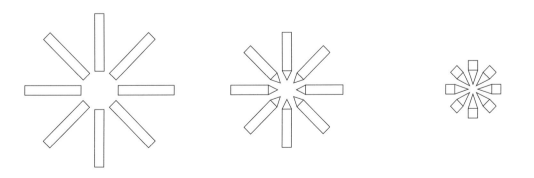

12.9
Forms emergent in
synchronized motion

Hierarchies of Motions

In an assembly of solids, some or all of the solids may move at once. The solar system, for example, is an assembly of spheres that spin on their own axes and also revolve around each other. We could specify these motions, in a model of the solar system, by constructing a sequence of keyframes for the entire system, but this would be very cumbersome. It is both clearer and more concise to specify movements of some objects relative to others. The obvious place to begin is with the sun, which we can locate at the origin of the global coordinate system (figure 12.10). Then we can specify the orbit of each planet in the sun's coordinate system. Next, we can take the center of each planet as a local coordinate system in which the orbits of moons are specified. Finally, if we want to specify orbits of satellites around each moon, we can center lower-level local coordinate systems on the moons. Thus we obtain a hierarchy of nested coordinate systems, together with motions described in terms of paths and rates in each one.

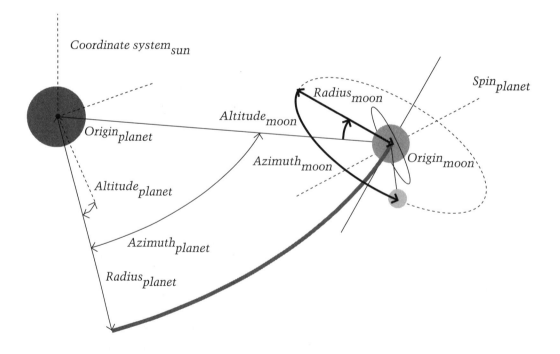

12.10
Hierarchy of parts,
coordinate systems, and
motions in the solar system

You can construct such hierarchies and motion descriptions in different ways, but (as Copernicus noticed) some ways are better than others. You might, for example, center the global coordinate system on the earth instead of the sun—a natural enough choice, since the earth provides the usual frame of reference for describing small-scale motions. Then, however, you would have to specify in this system the orbit of the sun around the earth and the epicycles of the planets.

Very complex motions can be choreographed by concatenating simple motions in nested coordinate systems. Consider, for example, a horse on a carousel. Relative to the carousel, the horse translates up and down along a straight path (figure 12.11a). Relative to the ground, the carousel rotates about a single axis (figure 12.11b). Concatenating these two simple motions yields the more complex path of the horse relative to the ground (figure 12.11c).

To support this sort of motion choreography, many motion-choreography and computer-animation systems organize three-dimensional elements and subsystems in hierarchies instead of layers. Each subsystem in the hierarchy is selectable and has its own local coordinate system. Motions of lower-level subsystems can be specified and synchronized at any level, within any of the local coordinate systems.

Articulated Motion of the Human Body

As dancers, choreographers, and robot designers know, the movements of the human body are organized in a hierarchy similar to that of the solar system. These movements may be described schematically as follows (figure 12.12). We center the origin of a body coordinate system (which moves within a global "stage" coordinate system) on the lower torso. The upper torso moves relative to the lower torso. Legs move relative to the lower torso, and arms and head move relative to the upper torso. The movements of each arm are organized in a hierarchy from the shoulder to the elbow to the wrist and so on down to the tips of the fingers. Similarly, the movements of the legs are organized

a. Motion of horse (relative to carousel)

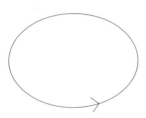

b. Motion of carousel (relative to ground)

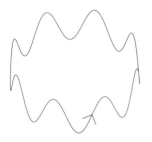

c. Motion of horse (relative to ground)

12.11
Concatenation of motions

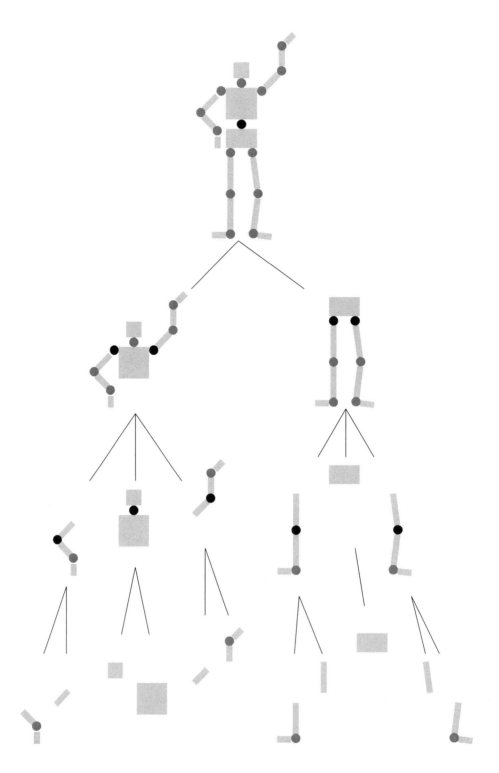

12.12
Hierarchy of parts,
coordinate systems, and
motions in an articulated
model of the human body

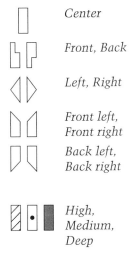

Center

Front, Back

Left, Right

Front left,
Front right

Back left,
Back right

High,
Medium,
Deep

Vocabulary

in a hierarchy from the hip joint down to the tips of the toes. Relative to the head, there is rolling of the eyes, wagging of the tongue, and wiggling of the ears. Although the motion of each body segment is relatively simple, the path of a point relative to the stage can become extraordinarily complex: consider, for example, the path of a Balinese dancer's fingertip.

An obvious difference between the human body and the solar system, however, is that the parts of the body are connected by joints. These joints, by their particular physical natures, constrain the motions of the parts that they attach to other parts. The middle joints of fingers, for example, are essentially hinges allowing rotation in one axis through a limited angular interval. But the shoulder is a ball joint allowing rotation in three axes.

The notation systems that choreographers have developed for specifying the articulated motion of limbs connected by joints can be adapted for use in programming computer models of the human body. One of the best known of these is the Labanotation system. This employs simple two-dimensional shapes to specify horizontal movement directions, combined with shading to specify vertical movement (figure 12.13). Some simple dance motions are shown, in this notation, in figure 12.14.

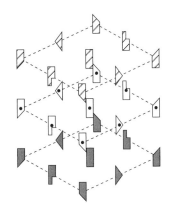

Configuration

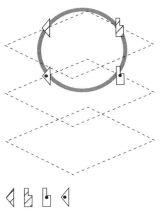

Port de bras

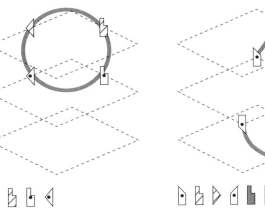

Tortillé

12.13
A notation system for dance: Labanotation

12.14
Simple examples of Labanotation

Mechanical Joints and Kinematic Chains

Motions of solids connected by joints that constrain (but do not, in general, prohibit) those motions are the particular concern of designers of mechanisms. As Franz Reuleaux systematically showed in his famous nineteenth-century textbook on kinematics, mechanical joints can be classified into types according to the ways in which they constrain motion (figure 12.15). (A single joint constrains the relative motion of two solid parts, so may be referred to as a kinematic pair.) Each type of joint can be described more precisely as a transformation (usually in 4 x 4 matrix form) specifying the constraints on relative motion of the parts that it connects. The joint matrix has variables, so particular possible spatial relationships of the parts can be specified by assigning values to these variables, and values can be incremented with time to simulate possible motions (figure 12.16).

Complete mechanisms can thus be described schematically as kinematic chains—stick-figure diagrams in which nodes stand for solid parts and connecting lines stand for joints. (For theoretical reasons related to techniques of motion analysis, mechanical engineers draw a basic distinction between open-loop mechanisms, in which the chain has no closed cycles, and closed-loop mechanisms, in which closed cycles do occur.) The motion choreography of a complete mechanism can, then, be explored by defining the geometry of each part in the kinematic chain and the transformation matrix for each joint, by choosing some of the variables as independent variables and incrementing their values with time, and by computing the values of dependent variables. Results can be shown either as sequences of animation frames or as diagrams of motion envelopes (as was illustrated in figures 12.2 and 12.3).

Advanced computer-aided mechanical design systems extend the idea of solid-assembly modeling by providing not only for modeling part geometry, but also for specifying joint types and parameter values. Motion of the mechanism can then be simulated by incrementing the joint

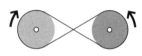

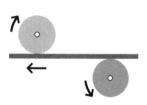

12.15
Constraint of motion by mechanical joints

12.16
Simulated motion of a four-bar linkage

12.17
A Calder mobile exhibits a hierarchy of pivoting motions

variables at specified rates through specified ranges. Spatial clash checking can be generalized to collision checking for moving parts.

The joints and mechanisms found in the built environment are generally fairly simple and can readily be described and simulated in this way. Doors and windows pivot on hinges or slide on tracks. Elevators and escalators also slide on tracks. Drawbridges and seesaws pivot vertically, swing bridges pivot horizontally, and lift bridges slide vertically. Cranes combine pivoting and sliding motions in various ways. Stadium and auditorium roofs sometimes have sections that slide or pivot to open and close. Folding awning frames, roof structures, bleachers, and chairs may be simple multibar linkages. The kinetic sculptures of Alexander Calder are articulated and jointed to produce hierarchies of pivoting motions (figure 12.17).

Simulation of Physical Behavior

The idea of detailed physical modeling of assemblies by describing solids and the interfaces between them can be developed still further by introducing laws of dynamics into motion simulation. In this sort of simulation, solids have mass and elastic properties; initial conditions of position, velocity, and acceleration are specified; and the laws of dynamics are used to work out physically possible sequences of events (figure 12.18). In 1986 Pixar Corpo-

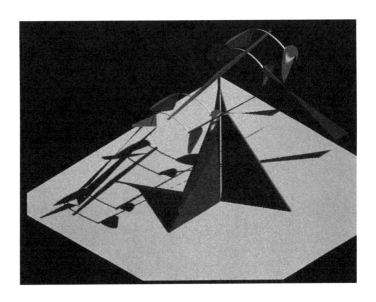

12.18
Simulated motion of a
bouncing ball

ration demonstrated this possibility with an animated film (called *Luxo Jr.*) in which an articulated drafting lamp jumps from one position to another.

Joint descriptions of the same kind as those used in dynamic simulations of mechanisms provide the basis for static and dynamic structural analysis of assemblies that are *not* mechanisms—those that are of particular interest to architects and civil engineers. The possibilities of joint constraint in a composition of solids actually define a continuum of mechanism and structure types (figure 12.19). At one extreme, all the solids in a composition can be isolated free bodies—each with three degrees of translational freedom and three degrees of rotational freedom. Next, the solids can be connected together in a minimal way (by a few wires, for example, as in a Calder mobile) to produce a mechanism with many degrees of freedom. Joint constraints can be added to produce a much more constrained mechanism in which movements are strictly limited. When exactly the right amount of constraint is added to the system, a statically determinate rigid structure results. If yet more constraint is added, the structure becomes statically redundant. Finally, the components may be completely fused together to produce a monolithic structure.

Free body

Mechanism

Determinate structure

Redundant structure

Monolithic structure

12.19
The continuum of
mechanism and structure
types

Uses and Limitations of Motion Models

Motion models of three-dimensional assemblies are relatively costly to build, modify, and maintain, so designers must consider whether the time and cost expended on them will be justified by the value of the visualization and analysis results obtained from them. Certainly they are not always necessary: adequate structural and kinematic analyses can often be produced from much more abstract network representations, for example.

They are most likely to be justified at a late stage in a design process (when details of geometry, materials, and connections have largely been resolved) rather than at an early one, when the organization and behaviors of an assembly are particularly difficult to understand (as in a complex piece of machinery) and when the penalties for design inadequacies are particularly severe (as in nuclear power plants). The costs of building and maintaining motion models are likely to drop as the technology advances, however. And at the same time, demands for more thorough evaluation of designs are likely to grow. (Many cities, for example, are now demanding detailed analyses of the shadow volumes produced by proposed new buildings.) So we will probably see much more widespread use of such models by designers in the future. Increasingly, they will take the place of physical prototypes.

Suggested Readings

Angeles, Jorge. 1982. *Spatial Kinematic Chains: Analysis, Synthesis, Optimization.* New York: Springer-Verlag.

Edgerton, Harold E. 1987. *Stopping Time: The Photographs of Harold Edgerton.* New York: H. N. Abrams.

Giedion, Siegfried. 1948. "Movement" in Mechanization Takes Command. Oxford: Oxford University Press.Hertel, Heinrich. 1966. *Structure—Form—Movement.* New York: Reinhold Publishing Company.

Hilbert, David, and S. Cohn-Vossen. 1952. "Kinematics" in *Geometry and the Imagination.* New York: Chelsea Publishing Company.

Hunt, Kenneth H. 1978. *Kinematic Geometry of Mechanisms.* Oxford: Clarendon Press.

Kepes, Gyorgy. 1965. *The Nature and Art of Motion.* New York: George Braziller.

Laban, R. 1966. *Choreutics.* London: MacDonald and Evans.

Muybridge, Eadweard. 1955. *The Human Figure in Motion.* New York: Dover.

Pratt, M. J. 1987. "Kinematic Analysis." In Joe Rooney and Philip Steadman (eds.), *Principles of Computer-Aided Design.* London: Pitman.

Reuleaux, Franz. 1963 [1876]. *The Kinematics of Machinery.* New York: Dover.

Rooney, Joe. 1987. "Geometry in Motion." In Joe Rooney and Philip Steadman (eds.), *Principles of Computer-Aided Design.* London: Pitman.

Shigley, J. E., and J. J. Uicker. 1980. *Theory of Machines and Mechanisms.* New York: McGraw-Hill.

Souriau, Paul. 1983. *The Aesthetics of Movement.* Amherst: University of Massachusetts Press.

Suh, C. H., and C. W. Radcliffe. 1978. *Kinematics and Mechanism Design.* New York: John Wiley.

Tilove, R. B. 1983. "Extending Solid Modeling Systems for Mechanism Design and Kinematic Simulation." *IEEE Computer Graphics and Applications* 3 (3): 9–19.

Zuk, William, and Roger H. Clark. 1970. *Kinetic Architecture.* New York: Van Nostrand Reinhold.

13

ANIMATION

13.1
Motion blur

An animated picture is a sequence of two-dimensional images (known as frames) that are displayed in fixed order. The frames may be produced by using a movie or video camera to sample a real scene, by drawing each one individually (either by hand or with a paint system), or by generating a sequence of projected and rendered views from a three-dimensional wireframe, surface, or solid model.

If there is sufficient similarity between each frame and the next (temporal coherence) and the frames are shown at a sufficiently rapid rate, then the illusion of smooth motion in the scene is produced. If there is little motion and a scene does not change much from one moment to the next, then a low sample rate suffices to achieve temporal coherence; but if there is a lot of motion then a higher sample rate is needed to avoid effects of jerkiness, flicker, or even complete incomprehensibility. When the playback rate is the same as the sample rate, motion in the scene unfolds at a normal rate. But temporal scaling occurs when the playback rate differs from the sample rate: action unfolds at a slower or faster rate than normal. For scenes with everyday levels of motion velocity and frequency, sample and playback rates of 24 to 60 frames per second (fps) suffice to produce good results. Normally, motion picture film is shown at 24 fps and videotape at 30 fps. The Showscan system produces very high spatial and temporal resolution by projecting 70 mm film at 60 fps.

If there is significant motion in a scene while a frame is being exposed by a movie or video camera, then motion blur will result (figure 13.1). Motion blur can also be simulated by rendering software. This blurring is a useful form of antialiasing: it smooths out jerkiness in the same way that spatial antialiasing smooths out jagged edges.

Projection and Animation

Plan and elevation, axonometric, oblique, and perspective views generated from a three-dimensional model can all be animated. By virtue of the different ways that these projections collapse three spatial dimensions into two, each one provides different motion possibilities.

In plan or elevation views, object motions parallel to the picture plane are undistorted, object motions perpendicular to the picture plane cannot be shown, and object motions oblique to the picture plane show up as temporally scaled motions across the picture plane (figure 13.2). The observer's viewpoint can translate across the picture plane to produce the effect of tracking, it can rotate to produce the effect of tilting, and the framing can be changed to produce the effect of zooming (figure 13.3). A lengthy horizontal pan can be used to show elevations along a street at a scale sufficient to reveal detail, a lengthy vertical pan can be used to show the progression of detail in a high-rise elevation, a closely framed pan along a linear design element such as a corridor in plan can be used to focus attention on a sequence of spatial incidents, and a zoom in or out can be used to show a detail in context. In any of this, changes in the observer's viewpoint never affect the way that foreground objects occlude background objects: in other words, there is no parallax effect.

When parallel-projected objects are allowed not only to translate, but also to rotate, an animated axonometric is generated. In other words, foreshortening becomes time-varying. Exactly the same effect is produced by rotating the picture plane around. A particularly useful technique (known as turntabling) is to cycle an object repeatedly through a full 360-degree rotation to show it from all sides (figure 13.4).

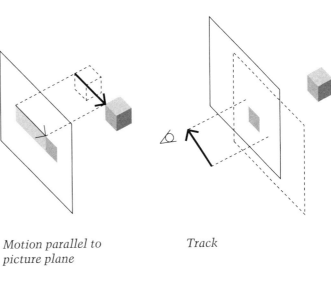

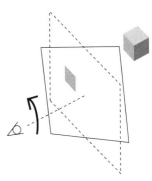

*Motion parallel to
picture plane*

Track

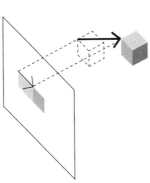

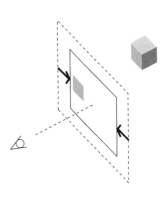

*Motion oblique to
picture plane*

Tilt

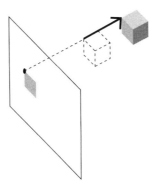

*Motion perpendicular to
picture plane*

Zoom

13.2
Motions in parallel
projection

13.3
Viewing parameter changes
in parallel projection

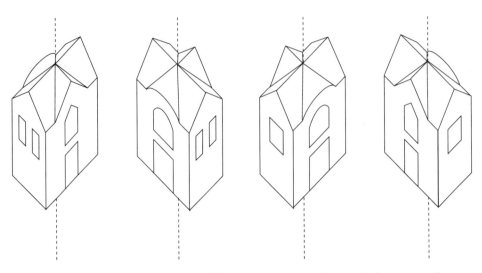

13.4
Turntabling an
axonometric

In oblique projections the angle between the viewing axis and the picture plane normal can be time-varying. For example, a roof plan might be kept constant from frame to frame while the viewing axis is cycled through 360 degrees to show all the different elevations.

In animated perspective projections not only the size of an object but also the temporal scaling of its translational motion varies with distance back from the picture plane (figure 13.5). This produces a complex interaction between foreshortening and apparent motion (figure 13.6), and creates a rich flow of visual information that allows us to perceive object sizes, positions, and motion directions and speeds.

The Virtual Video Camera

The viewing parameters for an animated perspective scene define a virtual video camera. These parameters (like the position and settings of a real video camera) may be varied with time (figure 13.7). The effect of camera tracking can be produced by translating camera position, the effect of panning and tilting by rotating (hence pointing the viewing axis in different directions), and the effect of zooming by varying the cone of vision. More complex effects can be produced by combining these basic ones in various ways (figure 13.8). A combination of tracking and panning can be used to keep the eye directed at a fixed point as the

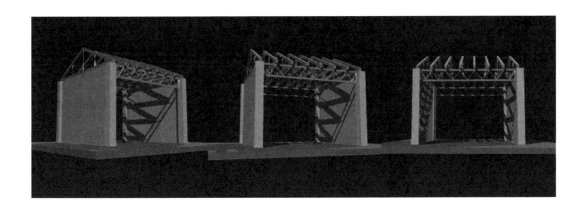

13.5
Turntabling a perspective

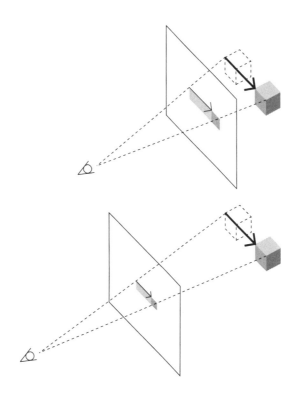

13.6
Temporal foreshortening

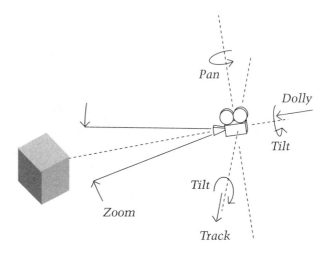

13.7
Time-varying parameters of
a virtual video camera

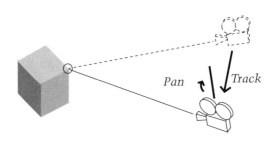

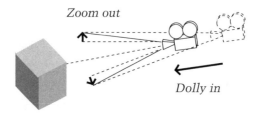

13.8
Combinations of camera
motions

camera position changes. And a combination of tracking in while zooming out can be used to keep framing constant while increasing foreshortening and deepening the pictorial space.

In a typical computer-animation system, these camera motions can be choreographed like any other kind of object motion. Camera-motion choreography is very commonly accomplished, today, through a combination of keyframing and splined interpolation.

Real video and movie cameras are relatively large, heavy, cumbersome objects with severely constrained movement and adjustment possibilities. They cannot fit through very narrow openings or pass through solid objects or move at high speed or accelerate and decelerate very rapidly or (usually) fly through the air. This gives live-action video and movie film a very characteristic look. But virtual cameras are dimensionless, weightless points with unlimited freedom of movement. So, unless you are trying for some reason to simulate live video or film footage, there is no need to move and adjust a virtual camera in traditional patterns: computer-generated animations can have a completely different look. (The virtual camera should not, however, sweep around aimlessly like a bumblebee on speed.)

Frames of Reference

Some scene and viewing variables change in value when parts of a scene are animated while others remain constant. Those with changing values are the action variables, while those that remain constant provide a frame of reference for the unfolding action. Divisions between action and frame-of-reference variables can be drawn in many different ways to facilitate the study of different design issues. Choice of the right frame of reference is as important an issue for a designer studying a project through animation as it is for a scientist studying some natural phenomenon through observation and experiment.

The most common way to draw the division between action variables and the frame of reference is to keep the geometry and lighting of a scene constant while changing

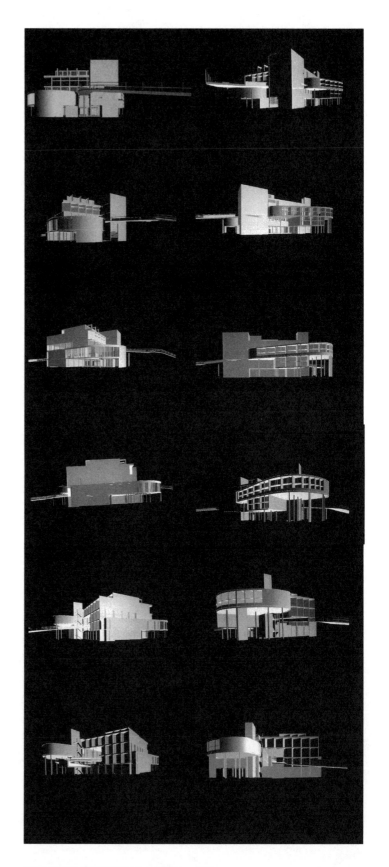

13.9
Moving the camera around
a fixed object

camera position and viewing direction (figure 13.9). The result is an animated walkthrough that simulates the experience of a visitor or inhabitant, or an animated flythrough that does not necessarily comply with constraints on plausible physical movement but serves to reveal the geometry and spatial organization of a design proposal.

Another possibility is to adopt the frame of reference of a stage director or choreographer. In this case, the basic geometry of a scene (ground) remains fixed, as does the camera, but certain objects (figures) move within the scene. Automobiles might move along a street, the hands of a clock might sweep around the face, doors and windows of a building might open and close, and so on.

The frame of reference of a lighting designer keeps scene geometry and camera position fixed but varies the light source parameters of shading procedures (figure 13.10). Thus light intensities may be faded up and down, hues may be transformed, and positions may be shifted. The effects vary, of course, depending upon the type of shading procedure used: varying the lighting of a raytraced or radiosity-rendered scene usually produces more complex effects than varying the lighting of a Gouraud-shaded scene.

Correlating Object and Camera Motion

A less obvious way to establish a frame of reference is to correlate some aspect of camera motion with some aspect of scene motion so that their relationship remains fixed as action unfolds. A camera may, for example, track, pan, and zoom to keep pace with an object moving through a scene (a favorite strategy of directors of sports videos). Furthermore, light source movement can be correlated with camera or scene motion: a spotlight can be held on a moving object, the effect of a handheld flashlight can be simulated in a walkthrough by moving a light source along with the camera position, and a cowboy can ride off into the fading sunset.

Where scene motion is defined in a hierarchy of coordinate systems, any one of those systems can serve as a frame of reference for camera location and motion.

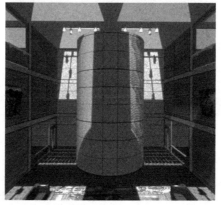

13.10
Varying lighting over time

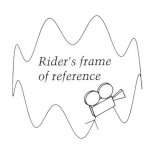

Rider's frame of reference

Spectator's frame of reference

13.11
Frames of reference for
depicting carousel motion

Consider, for instance, the problem of depicting the motion of a carousel (as discussed in chapter 12). The camera can be fixed in the coordinate system of the rider, or in the coordinate system of the setting, to depict the relative motion in different ways (figure 13.11). The complementarity of these motions can be shown by a split-screen presentation.

The Time Dimension

Temporal frames of reference (time frames) can also be shifted and nested. Whenever a simple animation sequence is run, the moment at which the action starts is shifted to the present. And, if the sequence contains a flashback, one time frame is nested within another. The time frame can also be expanded by running the sequence more slowly, compressed by running it more quickly, and reversed by running it backward.

Different time frames are useful for different design purposes. A landscape designer might make time-compressed animations of a proposal over a day to study variation in lighting, over a year to study seasonal mutations of foliage, and over a decade to study long-term growth and change. An architect might adopt the viewpoint of a building user moving up an escalator at natural speed. A construction manager might make a time-compressed simulation of the erection of a building. A machine designer might need to slow down the action to see how certain rapidly moving parts are interacting.

Design Vectors

From a designer's viewpoint, a particular three-dimensional configuration represents only one of many possibilities. Any one of the position, shape, and material variables in the data structure that describes the configuration might take a new value to yield a new design alternative. Furthermore, different states of the data structure may be taken as keyframes, and values may be interpolated between them in the usual way to yield sequences of design alternatives. These sequences may be played as animations, at any convenient speed. Any interpolated frame of the

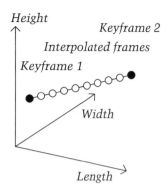

13.12
Solution space

animation presents a design alternative in the context of similar alternatives before and after.

More technically, the Cartesian product of the ranges of the variables in the data structure is the multidimensional solution space that the designer explores (figure 13.12). A keyframe corresponds to a point in that solution space. Linear interpolation between keyframes, then, yields a vector in the solution space.

Availability of sufficient computing power to allow rapid interpolation and playback of these sequences opens up the exciting possibility of extensive, high-speed design exploration by vectoring through a solution space. An exploration begins with specification of two keyframes at widely separated points in the solution space and interpolation of alternatives between them (figure 13.13). Next, one of these alternatives is selected as the most promising starting point for a new vector, and so on until a satisfactory alternative is discovered.

Computational Strategies

Generation of animation sequences makes very heavy demands on both computer memory and processing power. A single frame of 1024 x 1024 pixels, with 32 bits of color information per pixel, consumes four megabytes of memory in uncompressed form. At a rate of 30 fps, then, a second's worth of animation frames takes up 120 mb of memory. Furthermore, each frame may take a significant amount of computation to render—especially if sophisticated techniques such as raytracing and radiosity are employed—so generation of even a short sequence of frames can be a lengthy process. This means that animation processes often must be organized very carefully in order to obtain the results that are sought within the boundaries of available computational resources.

The most obvious way to avoid using up too much disk space for storage of frames is to write frames out to an inexpensive archival medium (such as digital audiotape) as soon as they are generated. Thus only a small buffer area needs to be set aside on disk. Since frames will normally be retrieved in sequence, storage on a sequential medium

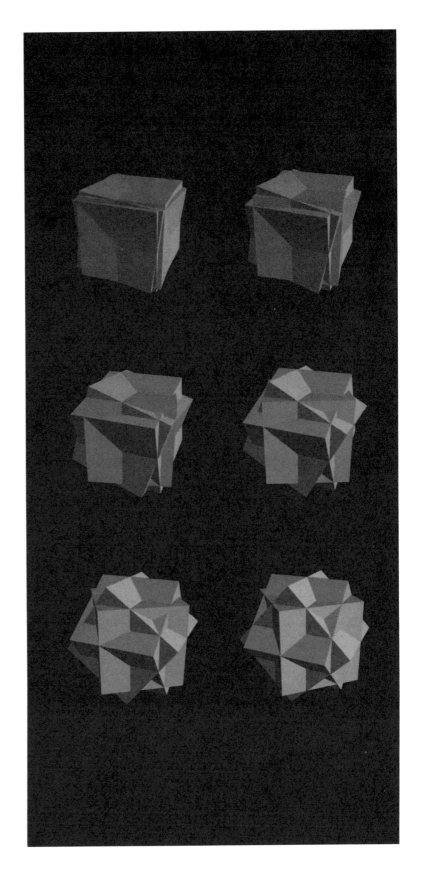

13.13
Animated vector of
design alternatives
(three cubes rotating
about a common
center point)

serves just as well as storage on a more expensive random-access medium.

Computation time can be saved by using inexpensive wireframe views instead of fully rendered frames for testing ideas about object and camera motion. Similarly, very small "postage stamp" raytracings can be used for quick, inexpensive testing of ideas about color and light. Yet another approach is to interpolate only a few frames, which produces jerky motion but often suffices at an early exploratory stage. (Computer-animation systems typically provide these "preview" modes.) Then, when motion, color, and lighting parameters have been finalized, the lengthy production of fully rendered frames at full resolution can be carried out in an overnight run or on a powerful compute server.

The time required to render a frame depends, of course, on the size and complexity of the three-dimensional model. Thus models that were developed for production of still images must often be simplified for animation. With limited computational resources available, there is a three-way trade-off to consider between the level of detail that is to be incorporated in the model, the sophistication of the rendering technique that is to be used, and the number of frames that can be produced.

Raytraced and radiosity-rendered animations are particularly time-consuming to produce. But radiosity procedures do offer one computational advantage that can often be exploited. Once a large initial computation of energy transfer paths between surface patches has been executed, it is relatively inexpensive to produce animation sequences in which scene geometry remains constant but view parameters change or lights switch on and off. (If scene geometry is altered, however, the initial large computation must be repeated.) Thus radiosity procedures are particularly well suited to producing walkthroughs of static architectural interiors.

Of course the most effective solution to the problem of computational constraints is to eliminate them by obtaining access to a sufficiently powerful computer. Indeed, much computer animation work is done on high-speed graphics workstations and on supercomputers. Special chips for efficient production of raytraced and radiosity-rendered frames are beginning to play an important role in this. As the technology develops, even inexpensive personal computers are becoming powerful enough to do useful animation work.

Real-time, Stored, and Recorded Animation

Where sufficient computing power is available to compute frames at a rate of at least 20 to 30 fps, real-time animations of three-dimensional scenes can be produced. This technique has a long history in specialized applications: by 1970 very expensive special-purpose graphics computers were being used to produce real-time shaded animations for flight simulation purposes, and some designers had begun to explore their potential. High-speed refreshed-vector displays have also been used, since the 1960s, for real-time animation of wireframes. By 1990 realtime animation of simple three-dimensional objects was possible on many personal computers, and sophisticated three-dimensional animation was becoming commonplace on more powerful graphics workstations. In the future exploitation of growing computational power will allow increasingly widespread, everyday use of real-time motion interfaces to geometric-modeling systems.

Realtime motion interfaces support design exploration processes that are qualitatively different, in significant ways, from those that are possible with static drawings and physical three-dimensional models. Like physical three-dimensional models, they allow translation and rotation of elements—but free from gravity and the constraints of physical solidity. They also allow the operations of three-dimensional scaling and reflection (scaling by a factor of minus one), which are impossible in the world of material three-dimensional objects. Other manipulative possibilities include realtime translational and rotational sweep operations to develop profiles, realtime surface sculpting by moving NURBS surface control points, and realtime union, intersection, and subtraction operations as objects are continuously pushed together.

Where real-time animation is infeasible, but sufficient disk storage is available, animation frames can be generated, stored on disk, then displayed in sequence at a rapid enough rate to produce the illusion of smooth motion. Since a frame may take upward of a megabyte of storage, and the local disk capacity of a personal computer or workstation is fairly limited, this technique is best suited to production of animation loops that last just a few seconds. Such loops can be particularly useful for studying specific design issues, such as the experience of approaching and entering a building or the evolution of a complex object's profile as an observer moves around it (figures 13.14-13.15). The interface can be arranged to allow precise control of playback speed, inspection of single frames, and movement forward or backward through the loop.

Where a noncomputer playback device is to be used, animation frames must be recorded on a transportable medium. Usually, the quickest, simplest, and least expensive way to record an animation is on standard videotape. This requires a video card to produce a NTSC or PAL video output signal and a video recorder of some kind. A consumer half-inch VCR can be used, but better results can be obtained (at higher cost) with industrial or broadcast-quality equipment and larger formats. To produce frame-accurate editable tape, a video deck that identifies each frame with a SMPTE (Society of Motion Picture and Television Engineers) time code is needed.

Even when excellent video equipment is used, videotapes of computer animations are plagued by some characteristic forms of image degradation. With care, these can be minimized, but they can rarely be eliminated completely. First, the resolution of a video image is normally less than that of a good digital image, and the video image is not as sharp. Second, the difference in resolutions can accentuate stair-step aliasing problems (particularly with text characters). And the video image may flicker perceptibly where there is high contrast.

Much better results can be obtained by using a film recorder for frame-by-frame transfer to 16 mm, 35 mm, or even 70 mm film. This technique is commonly employed

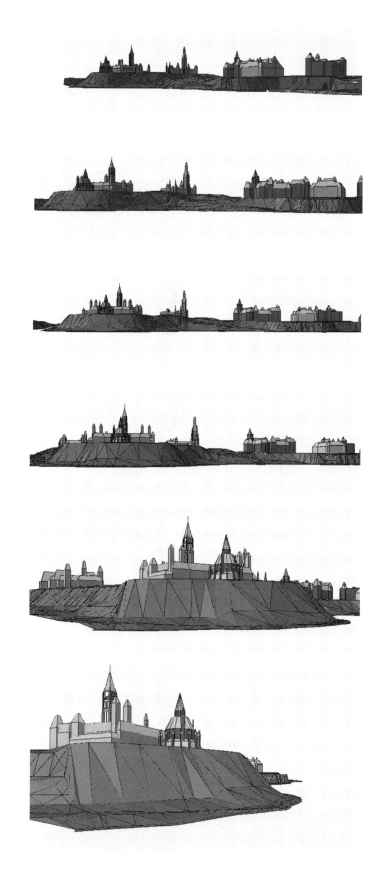

13.14
Evolution of a profile

13.15
Approaching, entering, and
moving through a building

in the film industry, where very high image quality is essential. However, it requires a high-quality film recorder equipped with an appropriate film back, it is slow and expensive, and it requires playback equipment that is not as readily available as VCRs and video monitors.

In the future high-resolution digital video will probably replace both analog video and movie film. At that point, there will be no need to record computer animations on nondigital media.

Video Postproduction

The task of combining animation sequences into complete film or video productions is closely analogous to that of combining sentences and paragraphs into complete texts or combining sound sequences into complete musical compositions, and so requires an analogous kit of editing tools. More specifically, the basic operations are those of traditional film and video editing: selection of a sequence from an archive of available sequences, specification of the sequence's start and finish frames, insertion of the sequence at a specified location in a longer sequence, and production of a print or copy of the completed work.

One obvious way to edit computer animations is to use traditional film or video postproduction technology. In other words, animation sequences are first recorded on film or videotape and then edited (figure 13.16). This has all the usual disadvantages: the necessary equipment is specialized and expensive, film reels and videotapes are fragile and cumbersome to handle, splicing can be difficult, and making successive copies degrades image quality. Another possibility is to edit in digital format and only afterward convert to nondigital format. Fully digital postproduction systems do not need to cut, shift, and splice sequences physically, but can represent playback orders simply as lists of pointers to subsequence locations in storage. So editing operations are executed merely by changing pointer values. However, this approach demands either very large amounts of high-speed digital storage or very effective image-compression technology. A third possibility is to record all the sequences on computer-

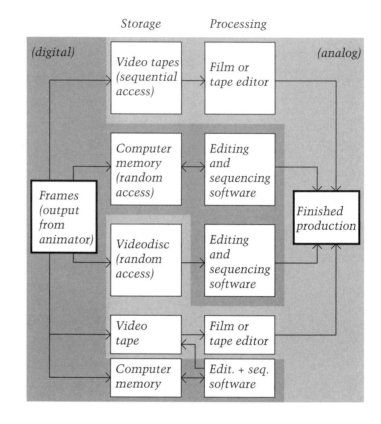

Storage   Processing

Traditional
postproduction

Digital postproduction

Videodisc postproduction

Hybrid system

13.16
Editing options

controlled videodisc (a random-access analog medium)
and use sequencing and playback software that maintains
lists of pointers to locations on the disc. The problem here
is that standard videodiscs cannot be erased and rerecorded.
A fourth possibility is to use a desktop video controller
that employs a combination of special hardware, sequence
editing software, and traditional video postproduction
techniques.

One pioneering desktop edit controller, the Video F/X,
uses a Macintosh II personal computer and two frame-
accurate computer-controlled video decks. Video clips are
represented on the Macintosh screen by small still images
of the first frame of each one. Assembling clips into
sequences is accomplished by selecting, inserting, deleting, and moving these first-frame images. Transitions
such as fade-ins and fade-outs can be specified. When a
sequence has been assembled, the system retrieves clips
(by SMPTE time code) in order from the first deck and
writes them on the second deck.

Blending Computer Animation with Live Video

Video postproduction usually includes not only sequence editing, but also titling, chroma-keying, and other special effects. These can usually be replicated very effectively in a digital environment.

One special effect of particular interest in many design contexts is chroma-key combination of computer animation and live video. This extends the idea of inserting a synthesized image of a project into a captured image of a site (which we discussed in chapter 10). For example, a computer-animated building may be shown in the context of a live street scene—with traffic going past, people going in and out, and so on. Alternatively, a live street scene may be visible through the window of a computer-animated building interior. Or videotaped people may walk through an animated interior space.

This sort of special effects work may be accomplished by first preparing the live footage and the animation footage and then using a traditional video chroma-key system to combine them. Alternatively, an appropriate video board or frame-by-frame video capture and image matting may be employed to produce the effect digitally.

It is fairly easy to produce convincing combinations if the camera position remains motionless. If the camera moves, however, the live camera must be coordinated precisely with the virtual camera of the animation system—a very difficult task when specialized, expensive devices such as computer-controlled camera cranes are not available.

Virtual Reality Systems

One of the most interesting playback devices for computer animation is a pair of eyephones (figure 13.17). These devices are analogous to earphones (and often used in conjunction with earphones), but instead of presenting sounds to each ear, they present animated images to each eye. And, like earphones, they can present slightly differing information on the left and the right to yield a stereo effect. Prisms can be incorporated, so that stereo images of three-

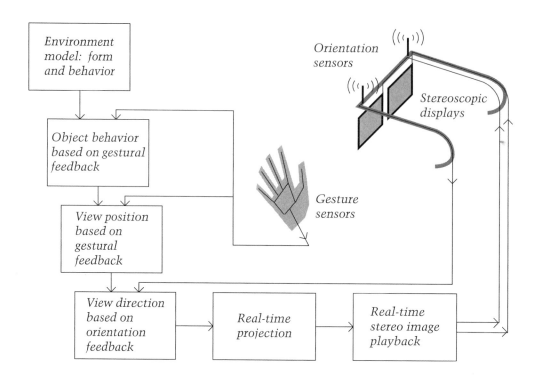

13.17
A cyberspace system

dimensional objects can be seen within real environments. (They are, however, much more complex in construction than earphones and much more cumbersome to wear, and these disadvantages have greatly limited their practical applications.)

Eyephones are usually combined with three-dimensional position-sensing devices (like those used in three-dimensional digitizers) so that the system can keep track of the position and viewing direction of the wearer's head. As the wearer moves around, a real-time stereo animation is adjusted in accordance with the varying coordinates and view direction. Thus the wearer can, for example, be placed "inside" a building, and can walk around to explore it. Other frames of reference are possible: the wearer might walk in giant strides across a terrain model of the entire United States or crawl along the tiny pathways of a silicon chip.

Further extensions are possible if the wearer also dons a dataglove or datasuit, so that hand gestures can be sensed. This allows the wearer to "grasp," "carry," and "throw" objects in the simulated environment, to sculpt them by moving NURBS control points, and so on. The simulated environment does not have to be programmed to behave like the real three-dimensional world but can become a medium more suited to a designer's needs. Objects might not move according to the laws of gravity and Newtonian dynamics, for example, but through a gravity-free environment to snap into place at grid points and other significant locations. A designer with a sure aim might stand at a fixed location, gesture instances of design elements into existence, and toss them along straight trajectories to stick like darts at distant locations. If the location for an element is too distant, it might simply be beckoned forward, so that the whole design translates around the designer.

The basic idea is a fairly old one (a prototype head-mounted stereo display was demonstrated by Ivan Sutherland, at the University of Utah, in the 1960s), but interest in it has slowly gathered momentum as technological advances have made it seem increasingly practical. By 1990 several research and development groups were actively working on it, and some commercial products were even being promised.

Animation and Holography

Another old idea slowly approaching practical application is holographic presentation of animations. An appropriately constructed sequence of computer-generated animation frames can be converted into a white-light hologram. When the hologram is appropriately illuminated, the combined effect of the frames is to produce a stereoscopic image that displays correct motion parallax as the viewer's head is moved from side to side. The hologram-production process is, however, one requiring complex and expensive setups and tedious hand crafting. It will remain cumbersome and expensive until special printers are developed to do the job automatically.

Conclusion: Unfreezing Images

The real world moves and changes, but designers have worked for centuries with frozen images—static structures of lines embedded in paper fibers. Now those images can be animated—brought to life—as, according to legend, was Pygmalion.

Suggested Readings

Arnheim, Rudolf. 1957. *Film As Art.* Berkeley: University of California Press.

Aukstakalnis, Steve, and David Blattner. 1992. *Silicon Mirage.* Berkeley: Peachpit.

Auzenne, Valliere Richard. 1993. *The Visualization Quest: A History of Computer Animation.* Rutherford, NJ: Fairleigh Dickinson University Press.

Badler, Norman I., Brian A. Barsky, and David Zeltzer. 1990. *Making Them Move: Mechanics, Control, and Animation of Articulated Figures.* Palo Alto: Morgan Kaufman.

Lederman, Susan J., and Bill Nichols. 1981. "Flicker and Motion in Film." In Bill Nichols, *Ideology and the Image.* Bloomington: Indiana University Press.

Magnenat-Thalmann, Nadia, and Daniel Thalmann. 1985. *Computer Animation: Theory and Practice.* Tokyo: Springer-Verlag.

Magnenat-Thalmann, Nadia, and Daniel Thalmann (eds.) 1992. *Creating and Animating the Virtual World.* Tokyo: Springer-Verlag.

14

HYPERMEDIA

14.1
Memex, 1945
"We cannot hope to equal
the speed and flexibility
with which the human
mind follows the
associative trail, but it
should be possible to beat it
decisively in regard to the
permanence and clarity of
the items resurrected from
storage."
—Vannevar Bush

In the everyday world, paths to needed data are often
frustratingly long and slow. You might have to walk to the
library to get a book, search through the card catalog to find
its call number, look up a floor plan to find the location of
that call number in the stacks, walk into the stacks to lay
your hand on the book, look up in the index the page
number of the item that you want, flip to that page, and
finally scan down the page. At each stage you follow a
pointer to a storage location or search a structure to find
what you need next. A computer system can vastly speed
this process, and bring needed data instantly to your
fingertips, by doing the work of pointer-following and
searching for you. This allows you to find your way rapidly
through all the kinds of computer-maintained structures
that we have considered in this book—one-dimensional
text and sound sequences, two-dimensional images and
drawings, three-dimensional geometric models, four-dimensional kinematic models, collections of such structures, and various multimedia combinations of them.

The idea was first intimated, in the 1940s, by Vannevar
Bush. His proposal was for an electromechanical device,
called the Memex, for flexibly accessing large amounts of
text and visual information stored on microfilm (figure
14.1). The Memex was never built, but as increasing
amounts of information have become available in digital
format, and as computer power has become inexpensive

and widely distributed, various digital versions of the Memex idea have emerged. They have become known as hypermedia systems.

Access Structures

The heart of any hypermedia system is an access structure. This can be thought of as a network in which reference links associate locations (known as nodes) in texts, files of structured data, plans and maps, three-dimensional models, and so on (figure 14.2). Software for creating hypermedia representations provides tools for defining nodes and for specifying reference links between them.

Conversely, software for using hypermedia representations provides tools for following links from node to node—much as you might follow a reference from a card catalog to a book in a library, but a lot faster. By choosing different paths through the network you can explore the nodes in different sequences. The network of references thus functions as an access structure to a body of knowledge.

In general, a link in an access structure has a direction (one-way or two-way) and a label. Two-way links consume more storage but permit reverse navigation—from an instance of a particular type of plumbing fixture in a plan

14.2
Nodes and links

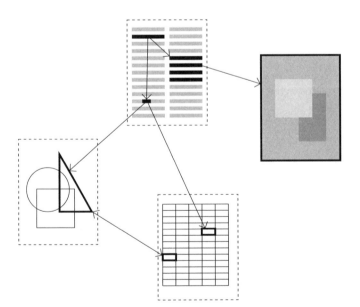

to its catalog entry, for example, and back from the catalog entry to *all* the instances of that fixture in the plan. Labeled links can be used to provide different access structures for different users with different interests and needs.

In practice, only a few basic types of access structures turn out to be widely useful (figure 14.3). We have encountered most of them before, in other contexts, since they represent very general modes of organization. The simplest is a linear list, in which each node has a single predecessor and a single successor: this is a suitable structure for connecting episodes in a narrative or instructions in a step-by-step recipe. Obvious variants are the two-way linked list, in which you can move both forward and backward, and the cycle, in which the end node points back to the start node.

If each node has a single predecessor and multiple successors, then the access structure becomes a tree—suitable for guiding you to information about increasingly specialized subtopics, as in a medieval summa or in the modern Dewey Decimal indexing of a library. If paths through a tree can reconnect, so that there are alternative ways to reach a node (as is usually the case in a Pert chart, for example), then the structure is a re-entrant tree. Finally, if there are no restrictions on the ways that nodes can be linked, the structure is a free-form network—a maze in which it is very easy to wander in circles, retrace your path, cross it, or reverse it. Hypermedia systems sometimes keep track of the path that a user has followed through a network, like Ariadne's thread through the Cretan labyrinth, so that steps can easily be retraced. More sophisticated systems can simplify use of free-form networks by identifying link labels and presenting just those paths appropriate to particular users or conditions (figure 14.4).

There is nothing new in use of these structures to navigate through data. They have long been used internally in computer programs to provide efficient access to data needed for computations. And this book provides access structures in the form of a hierarchical table of contents, an alphabetically sequenced index, cross-references from text to illustrations, and a (fairly sparse) network of cross-references within the text. Furthermore, technical books

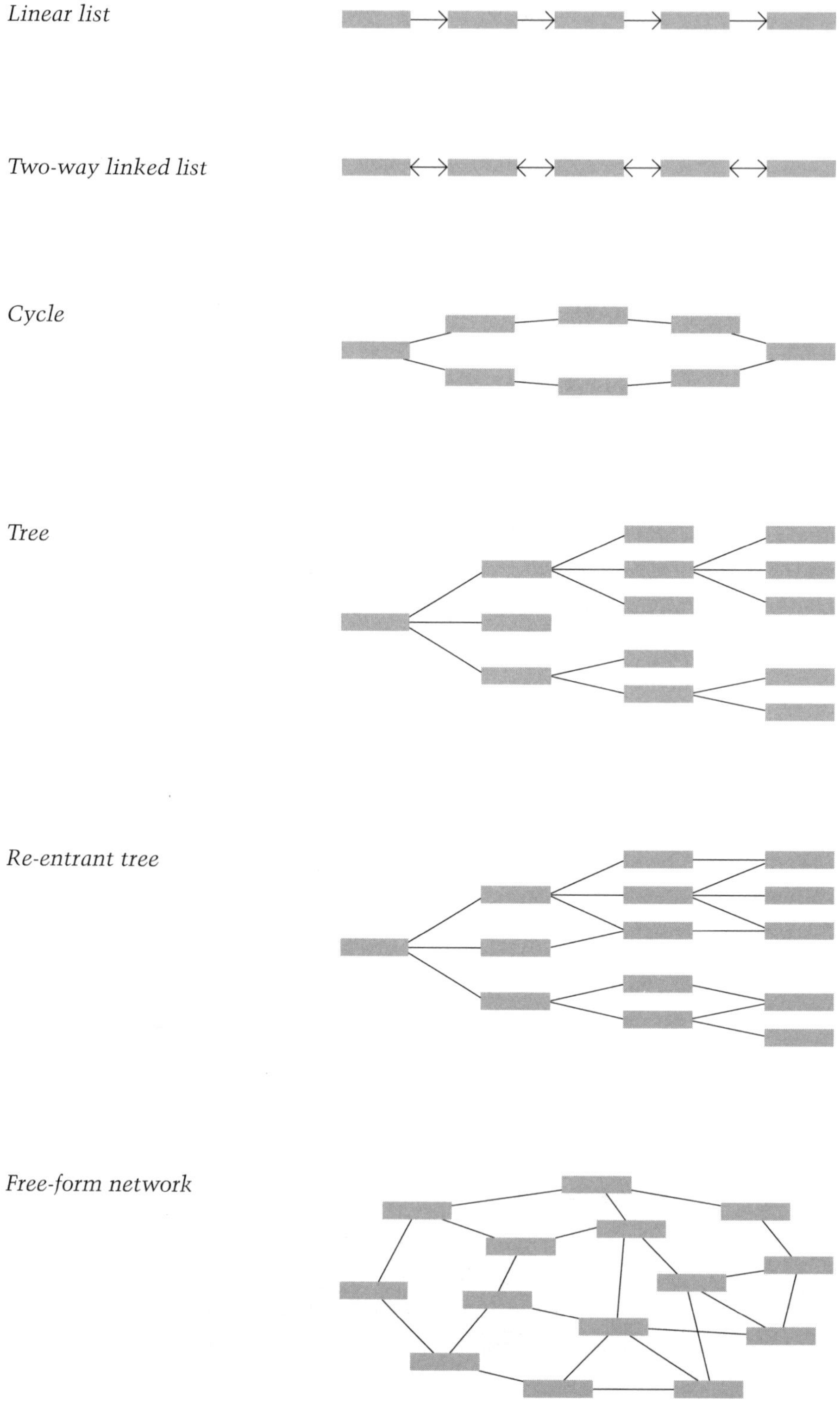

Linear list

Two-way linked list

Cycle

Tree

Re-entrant tree

Free-form network

14.3
Basic types of access
structures

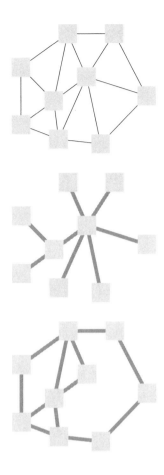

14.4
Subsets of paths through a labeled network

and papers cite each other to create enormous networks of cross-references. But hypermedia systems make these structures explicitly available to users for fast navigation through large bodies of data to find needed items and to support exploratory browsing.

Very similar strategies for indexing and cross-referencing information (in nonelectronic implementations) are commonly employed in traditional design documentation. A set of working drawings usually has, on the face sheet, an index telling you the sequence number of the specific drawing that you want. A plan drawing may contain references to detail sheets and (on section lines) to section drawings. Symbols in drawings are cross-referenced to door and window schedules, to fixture schedules, and to paragraphs of specification text. The specification text, in turn, refers to standards documents and product catalogs. The standards documents and product catalogs have their own indexing and cross-referencing systems. When information describing a design is stored in electronic form, then, there is obvious potential for replacing these relatively slow and cumbersome access structures by their electronic counterparts.

Indexing from One-dimensional Structures

The simplest sort of hypermedia system embeds nodes in a linear structure, just as this text embeds figure references (figure 14.5). If you were reading this text in a hypermedia system, you could click on the figure reference to retrieve the corresponding drawing instead of looking for it at some nearby location on this page or the next. Or you might click on a footnote or bibliography reference to retrieve the cited text.

Texts and text collections that are stored in digital form and provided with access structures for quick navigation through them have become known as hypertexts. They can provide convenient access to huge amounts of textual information: some massive hypertexts like the *Thesaurus Linguae Graecae* (with associated software like *Ibycus* and *Pandora*) take as their subject the entire literary discourse of a culture.

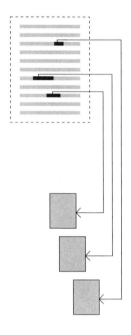

14.5
A simple one-dimensional
index: nodes in a text point
to other documents

The reader's experience of such hypertexts is not just quantitatively different from that of a book, but qualitatively different, since hypertext shifts the emphasis from scanning of text in physically fixed sequence to exploring chains of association. Furthermore, as poststructuralist literary critics never seem to tire of pointing out, the meanings of complete texts are largely a matter of intertextual relationships. Hypertext software, then, provides tools for defining intertextual linkages and exploring structures of intertextual relationship.

Since designers must often navigate through massive amounts of technical reference material—building codes, product catalogs, technical handbooks, and so on—to find items that are relevant to a particular task at hand, there is potential for expanding use of large, richly cross-referenced hypertexts in place of print versions of these materials. Depending on size, frequency of update, and frequency of access, these hypertexts might be published and distributed on floppy disk or CD/ROM, or they might be maintained centrally and accessed via a network. A milestone in electronic distribution and accessing of design reference material was reached in the late 1980s, when McGraw-Hill Information Systems introduced an electronic version of the widely used Sweet's construction products catalog.

Many of the more advanced word-processing systems provide tools for construction and automatic maintenance of common text-access structures. These can be used to produce indexes and to maintain correctly numbered sequences of footnote and figure references as pieces of text are added, deleted, and moved (figure 14.6). Hypertext structures can also provide a convenient framework for editorial annotation of texts and for modular development of multi-author texts (figure 14.7).

Branching Sequences

Linear structures can be combined into branching sequences by providing several nodes linking the end of each linear segment to the beginnings of other linear segments. This allows production of interactive text narratives in

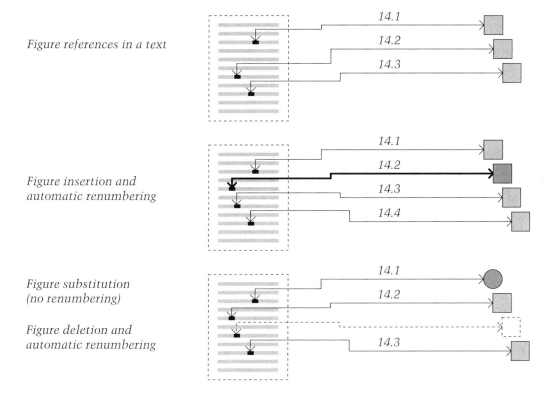

Figure references in a text

14.1
14.2
14.3

Figure insertion and automatic renumbering

14.1
14.2
14.3
14.4

Figure substitution (no renumbering)

14.1
14.2

Figure deletion and automatic renumbering

14.3

14.6
Reference maintenance

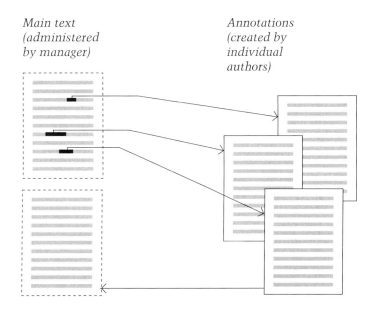

Main text (administered by manager)

Annotations (created by individual authors)

14.7
Annotation

which the reader chooses between alternative continuations at various points. When multiple authors work on a text, alternative versions of the parts and editorial comments can be fitted together in similar fashion. The final version, then, is specified by deleting the editorial comments and choosing a single path through the segment network.

Interactive musical compositions and interactive videos can also be constructed in this way. (Editing of segments into a network structure is really a generalization of the traditional idea of sequence editing to produce a special case of a network—that is, a chain of segments with no branch points.) The constituent segments may be stored either on disk (if there is enough space available) or on a computer-controlled videodisc or CD-ROM player. Videodisc has been a particularly popular interactive video medium since it has represented an attractive trade-off between image quality, storage capacity, retrieval time, and cost. Storage of compressed digital video on magnetic disk will be an increasingly attractive alternative.

Interactive video has initially been most popular in educational applications. In design its most obvious application is in production of interactive walkthroughs. The street network of a town, for example, can be documented by tracking a video camera down each street (in both directions). The resulting segments can then be connected to generate a movie map in which the user chooses a direction at each intersection (figure 14.8). Thus the user can explore the town by choosing paths through it—just as you would if you were exploring on foot.

Indexing from Two-dimensional Structures

Nodes may be embedded not only in linear, one-dimensional structures like texts, but also in two-dimensional structures like maps and plans (figure 14.9). Consider, for example, the problem of providing access to a large collection of slides of a historic town. A street map might show small graphic icons at the locations where the slides were taken. These icons serve as nodes linked to the image database, so that clicking on a node retrieves and displays the corresponding slide image.

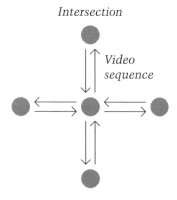

Intersection

Video sequence

14.8
Choices at an intersection in a branching moviemap

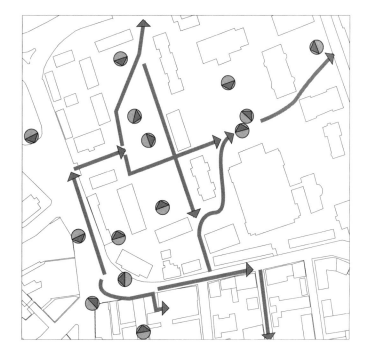

Still images

Video sequences

14.9
Indexing from a two-
dimensional map

Furthermore, maps and plans can be organized in a hierarchy of areas shown in increasing detail, from a map of the world down to detailed plans of particular rooms in particular buildings (figure 14.10). This suggests a hypermedia access structure in which two-dimensional maps and plans present sets of selectable locations. Whenever a location is selected, either a slide taken at that location or a smaller-scale map or plan is retrieved. With this structure, you could literally search the world for the slides that you need.

Just as points can be used to indicate locations of still images, so lines on plans and maps can be used to indicate video or movie camera paths. These can serve as nodes providing access to video sequences stored on videodisc or to sequences of walkthrough perspective views. The user clicks on one point to indicate the start of the sequence that is to be retrieved, then on a second point to indicate the end. The corresponding sequence is then retrieved from the archive and played.

Nodes on plans and maps can also provide access to text, audio, or bitmapped sketch annotations. These annotations might be permanent: a plan of a historic town might be audio annotated with short lectures by archi-

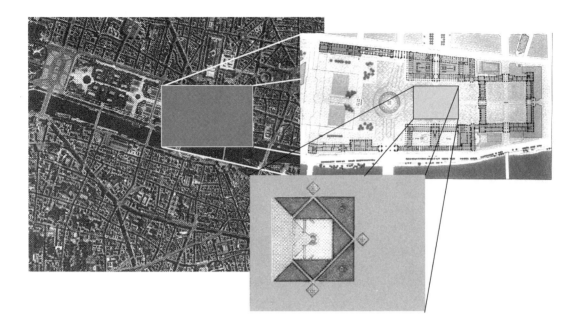

14.10
Hierarchy of areas

tectural historians, for example, or a design proposal might be text annotated with notes recording the reasoning behind design decisions (figure 14.11). Or they might be temporary: a design project leader might annotate a drawing with sketches and audio comments specifying corrections to be made and details to be integrated—an electronic version of the traditional practice of marking up a print with a red pencil.

Indexing from Three-dimensional Structures

In much the same way that maps and plans can be organized in hierarchies of areas depicted in increasing detail, three-dimensional geometric models can be organized in hierarchies of ever more finely detailed volumes. The corresponding interface allows a user to explore a model of a building or urban area (perhaps in real-time walkthrough mode) at a particular level of detail and to select a volume to explore at a higher level of detail. The hierarchy might have a very rough massing model at the highest level, with detailed models of construction subassemblies at the lowest level. If the three-dimensional model represents an existing building, landscape, or urban environment, then access to still images (point samples) and video sequences (linear samples) can potentially be provided within the

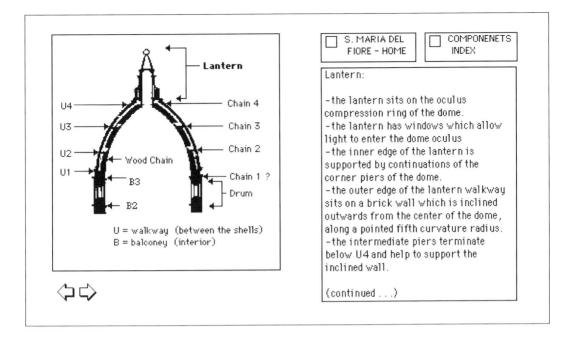

Lantern

U4 — Chain 4

U3 — Chain 3

U2 — Chain 2

U1 — Wood Chain

B3 — Chain 1 ?

B2 — Drum

U = walkway (between the shells)
B = balcony (interior)

S. MARIA DEL FIORE – HOME

COMPONENETS INDEX

Lantern:

-the lantern sits on the oculus compression ring of the dome.
-the lantern has windows which allow light to enter the dome oculus
-the inner edge of the lantern is supported by continuations of the corner piers of the dome.
-the outer edge of the lantern walkway sits on a brick wall which is inclined outwards from the center of the dome, along a pointed fifth curvature radius.
-the intermediate piers terminate below U4 and help to support the inclined wall.

(continued . . .)

14.11
An annotated drawing

same framework by displaying these as selectable points and lines. Thus the user can select a volume to explore a three-dimensional model, a line to take a path through that model, or a point to see an image at a location within that model.

Cyberspace

If a user is placed "inside" a three-dimensional structure through use of a virtual reality interface (as discussed in chapter 13), data navigation is experienced as movement through cyberspace. (This idea was introduced by the science fiction writer William Gibson in his 1984 novel *Neuromancer*, and it has captured the imaginations of many computer enthusiasts.) Files might be arranged as three-dimensional "books" on a "shelf" (rather than as icons on a two-dimensional desktop), for example, so that you could select and open them as you select and open a book.

However, cyberspace provides much greater freedom of movement and shift in frame of reference than physical space. You might, for example, point at a location on a plan to transport yourself instantly into a simulated room. Or you might point at another person inhabiting cyberspace to be shifted immediately into that person's frame of reference—to see and hear what that person sees and hears.

Practical realization of this compelling idea depends on availability of enough computing power to provide real-time animation of realistic images of complex three-dimensional environments (which is not likely to be a stumbling block in the long run) and on availability of adequate, inexpensive, head-mounted stereo display systems—a very difficult technological problem. (Gibson sidestepped the issue of display technology by imagining direct neural implants.)

Implementation Tools

Hypermedia systems typically deal with large quantities of data, so they make considerable demands on memory resources. And they often handle data in multiple forms—text, audio, image, and motion video—so they also demand versatility in input/output capability. As personal computers have developed in power and versatility, they have become increasingly effective hypermedia systems, and a market for hypermedia software and productions has been able to develop as a result.

It is possible to implement access structures and navigation tools with standard procedural programming languages like Pascal and C, but specialized hypermedia software often provides a better starting point. The Apple Hypercard system gained wide acceptance in this role in the late 1980s and did much to popularize the idea of hypermedia.

Hypercard organizes information as collections of structures known as "cards," which are displayed one at a time on the screen (figure 14.12). A card can include text, audio sequences that play when the card is accessed, bitmapped images, and windows for motion video. Nodes can be located on a card and displayed in various ways—typically as small graphic icons. These nodes point to other cards so that, when a node is clicked with the mouse, a new card is retrieved and displayed. Hypermedia productions thus take the form of card "stacks." Libraries of standard details and sequences of perspective views of buildings (figure 14.13) have, for example, been implemented as Hypercard stacks.

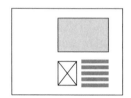

Card (corresponds to a screen)

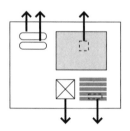

Buttons (designated areas of card) point to other cards, and may also start programs

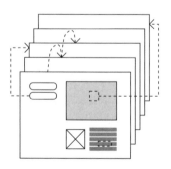

User follows links through a stack of cards

14.12
Hypercard

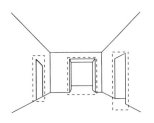

14.13
Areas of a perspective designated as buttons to point to other perspectives

A system such as Hypercard is not just a knowledge-representation scheme but also an interface strategy: a hypermedia network may link tools as well as data. Much as a designer may browse materials in reference systems, so he or she may apply the particular tools of an integrated software tool kit (to which we turn in the following chapter) according to chains of association.

Benefits and Costs of Access Structures

The utility of an access structure must be balanced against the cost of its construction and maintenance. In the design of this book, for example, we decided that a table of contents, an index, figure references, and short lists of suggested readings would suffice as access structures to and from the text. These structures will be used extensively by most readers, they are quick and easy to construct and maintain as the text is developed (particularly if computer tools are used to help with the task), and they do not add significantly to the production cost of the book. On the other hand, we decided that footnotes to the vast related technical literature would not be worthwhile. They would undoubtedly be useful to some readers, but they would take a disproportionate amount of time and effort to develop, and they would encumber the text. Furthermore, since the technical literature evolves very rapidly, they would rapidly become outdated.

Hypermedia authoring tools are designed to reduce the cost and effort of developing and maintaining access structures—particularly large and sophisticated ones. And hypermedia user software is designed to exploit access structures by providing quick, efficient traversal of them through collections of text, graphic, audio, and video material. This shifts the ratio of benefits to costs. So hypermedia technology can be used effectively to provide efficient access to larger collections of material than would otherwise be feasible, to provide richer associations and cross-linkages between items, and to support entirely new modes of investigation such as associative browsing through a hypertext or exploration of a town through a movie map.

Suggested Readings

Ambron, Sueann, and Kristina Hooper (eds). 1990 [1988]. *Interactive Multimedia.* Redmond, WA: Microsoft Press.

Arnheim, Rudolf. 1957. "A New Laocoon: Artistic Composites and the Talking Film." In *Film as Art.* Berkeley: University of California Press.

Barrett, Edward (ed). 1992. *Sociomedia: Multimedia, Hypermedia, and the Social Construction of Knowledge.* Cambridge: The MIT Press.

Barrett, Edward (ed). 1988. *The Society of Text.* Cambridge: The MIT Press.

Conklin, Jeff. 1987. "Hypertext: An Introduction and Survey." *IEEE Computer* 20 (9): 17–41.

Gibson, William. 1984. *Neuromancer.* New York: Ace Books.

Lippman, Andrew. 1980. "Movie Maps: An Application of the Optical Video Disc to Computer Graphics." *SIGGRAPH '80 Proceedings.* New York: Association for Computing Machinery.

Nelson, Theodor. 1981. *Literary Machines.* Swarthmore, Penn.: T. H. Nelson.

Panofsky, Erwin. 1976 (© 1957). *Gothic Architecture and Scholasticism.* New York: New American Library.

Vanier, Dana J. 1990. "Hypertext: A Computer Tool to Assist Building Design." In Malcolm McCullough, William J. Mitchell, and Patrick Purcell (eds.), *The Electronic Design Studio.* Cambridge: The MIT Press.

Yates, Frances A. 1966. *The Art of Memory.* London: Routledge and Kegan Paul.

15

INTEGRATED DESIGN ENVIRONMENTS

15.1
An early conception of an integrated CAD system

An integrated computer-aided design environment is one in which data files pertinent to a project, software tools, and physical devices can efficiently be put to many different uses—possibly by different members of a design team, working in different places, at different stages in a design process—and exploited to the maximum (figure 15.1). Integration is achieved by carefully maintaining the currency, integrity, and security of data files and by organizing computer resources so that these files and appropriate tools for manipulating them are always accessible when and where they are needed by design team members or for use in automatic processes.

Some computer-aided design environments are horizontally integrated, with commonly accessible data supporting the activities of different design team members, representing different design disciplines (architecture, landscape architecture, urban design, structural engineering, mechanical engineering, interior design, and so on), using different tools, at a particular stage of the design process (figure 15.2). Others are vertically integrated, with the development and flow of data systematically organized to support work at successive stages—sketch design, design development, documentation, construction management, and in-use facility management. In general, integration involves maintaining data over time, distributing it spatially, and coordinating work on it.

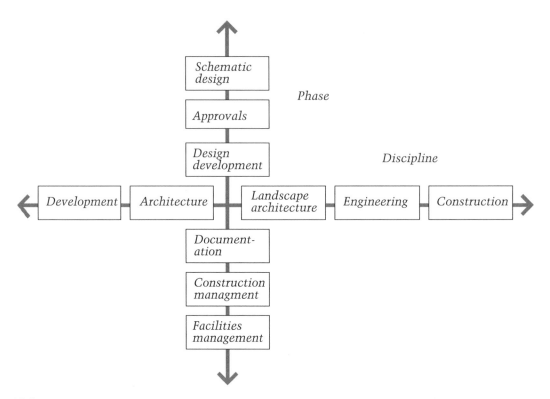

15.2
Horizontal and vertical
integration

The motivation for systematic data development, maintenance, and distribution within a computer-aided design environment is essentially an economic one: data entry processes are slow, costly, and error-prone, so it makes sense to minimize them by keeping data for future reuse and by moving data around. Even more importantly, design team members can become more productive, and their work can be coordinated more effectively, when they have convenient access to relevant, correct, up-to-date information.

Different levels of integration are potentially achievable. The most basic is hardware integration: devices are connected in some way so that they can communicate with each other. Within a given hardware environment, the next level of integration can be achieved by providing for transfer of data files between application programs. (These programs may all be running on the same machine, or they may be running on different machines within a network.) Next, files with related contents may be grouped and linked into databases. Extensive collections of software tools may be designed to operate on the same database, presented within the framework of consistent interface conventions, and grouped into coordinated software tool kits. Finally, sophisticated computer-aided design systems may incorporate controller programs that automatically sequence and coordinate application of software tools to the database to accomplish design work. Each of these levels is built upon the previous one. We shall consider them in turn.

Hardware Integration

Computer hardware is organized in modular fashion, with standards governing the interfaces between modules, so that systems can be configured in many different ways to provide different mixes of functions and different levels of performance, at different costs, as appropriate to particular contexts. For a start, a personal computer or a workstation is organized around an internal high-speed communications bus into which are plugged the processor (or processors), memory boards, specialized boards for controlling input and output devices, and so on (figure 15.3). Components that meet the standards of the bus can then be integrated in a variety of configurations.

On the outside of a piece of computer equipment you will usually find ports into which cables can be plugged. Standards govern these, too. (Most personal computers, for example, have ports adhering to the RS232 or SCSI standards for serial connection of peripheral devices.) Plug-compatible devices are those which, by virtue of adherence to a common standard, can simply be plugged together. Personal computers are often configured with several plug-compatible storage and input/output devices, and larger systems may also be assembled from plug-compatible subsystems.

Personal computers and workstations usually have, as well, drives for portable storage media—floppy disks, removable hard disks, CD/ROM disks, or magnetic tapes. These provide a slow but flexible and reliable means of communication between computers: a disk or tape that has been produced by one computer is simply carried to the other computer and inserted in the drive. The two

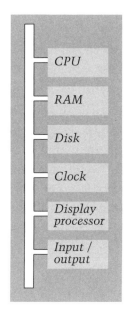

15.3
Internal communication bus

drives must, of course, adhere to a common format standard. If they do not, the format must be converted before the data can be read. When you have access to a personal computer or network equipped with different types of drives, you can do this simply by reading a file on one type of drive and writing it on the other. Sometimes special software simplifies this task by allowing drives to read disks or tapes in "foreign" formats.

An increasingly popular variant of this idea is to employ a portable hard disk (or even a complete laptop computer) that plugs into a serial port. Current files can be loaded from a desktop machine into a laptop computer at the beginning of a trip, worked on during the trip, then loaded back into the desktop machine on return.

Finally, a workstation (and often, today, a personal computer) will have some kind of connection to a communications network. This might be a local area computer network (LAN), a geographically distributed computer network, or the public telephone network. Networks themselves are usually subnetworks of still larger networks.

At the hardware level (figure 15.4), a local area network consists of computational devices (called nodes) connected by data transmission channels (called links). The interface between a node and a link is made by means of a bus-to-phone-line adaptor or a special communications board, which may be built in (if the device is designed specifically for network use) or purchased as an add-on. The links may be twisted pair, coaxial, or fiber optic cables. In a typical network, most of the nodes are personal computers or single-user workstations. Usually, as well, there are servers—additional computers that provide specialized services: these may include file servers (with large disks) for maintaining data in a central location, print servers that control printers, and compute servers that have fast processors for performing large computations. The complement of hardware is usually completed by necessary repeaters, switching devices, and the like. A small local area network may connect a few workstations on a single floor of a building, a larger one may connect workstations at every desk in an entire building, and a still

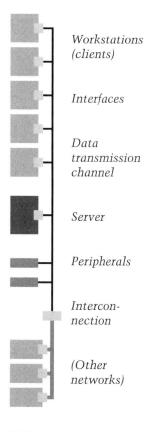

Workstations
(clients)

Interfaces

Data
transmission
channel

Server

Peripherals

Interconnection

(Other
networks)

15.4
Local area network
hardware

Daisy chain

Star

Ring

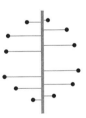

Bus

Hierarchy

15.5
Network configurations

larger one may connect thousands of workstations distributed across a university campus.

Local area networks may be configured in many different ways (figure 15.5). In principle, every node might be connected to every other node, but this quickly becomes infeasible as the number of nodes increases. At the other extreme, a daisy chain configuration reduces redundancy and cost but correspondingly increases vulnerability: all downstream nodes fail if an upstream node fails, and service is lost while nodes are being added. A star configuration is robust and easy to expand, but it makes the central node into a point of vulnerability and a potential bottleneck. In practice, most networks have hybrid configurations that represent attempts to achieve the best combinations of efficient performance, reliability, and expandability under practical constraints on locations of distribution points and cables.

To accomplish device-to-device communication over the physical links, networks rely on communications protocols (figure 15.6). These are complex sets of standards governing the ways that messages are broken down into simple parts, transmitted, and reconstructed. Among the most popular are Ethernet, Token Ring, and Appletalk. They differ significantly in the data transfer speeds that they provide: Ethernet transfers at about ten megabits per second, while Appletalk transfers at about a quarter of a megabit per second.

The user of a personal computer or workstation in a network sees an extended operating system that provides access not only to the resources of the workstation itself, but also to those of the entire network. Thus the user can obtain files from the file server, send files to the print server, run jobs on the compute server, send messages to users of other workstations, and so on. So that the user can accomplish this without detailed knowledge of the location of resources or recourse to arcane commands, network operating systems typically present virtual rather than actual physical resources and leave the details of physical organization to a specialist network administrator.

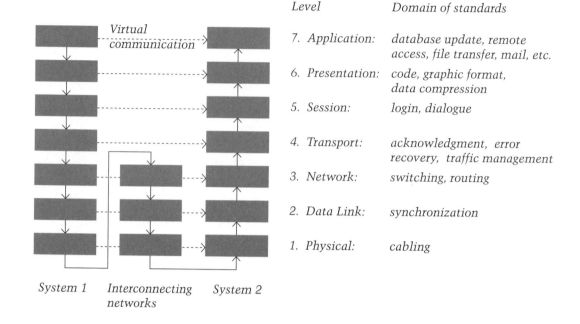

Level	Domain of standards
7. Application:	database update, remote access, file transfer, mail, etc.
6. Presentation:	code, graphic format, data compression
5. Session:	login, dialogue
4. Transport:	acknowledgment, error recovery, traffic management
3. Network:	switching, routing
2. Data Link:	synchronization
1. Physical:	cabling

System 1   Interconnecting   System 2
                 networks

15.6
Network layers, levels of
virtual communication,
and standards

Few local area networks, even if they begin that way, remain isolated systems. Most, today, are connected to other local area networks and to geographically distributed networks. Communications servers called bridges connect networks running the same protocol, and servers called gateways connect networks running different protocols.

Geographically distributed computer networks such as Arpanet, Internet, and Bitnet now encircle the earth (figure 15.7). Typically, a powerful computer serves as a gateway from a local area network to the geographically distributed network. Long-distance, high-capacity links connect the geographically distributed nodes. (It is noteworthy that the latest transatlantic cable has a data transmission capacity about a billion times greater than the original 1866 telegraph cable.) Users can route messages and files to distant workstations; log into servers that provide access to library catalogs, construction products catalogs, and the like; and submit data for processing at supercomputer nodes.

Any telephone connection (even a portable cellular telephone) can also become a network node. Frequently, personal computers (including laptop models) are connected to telephone lines by means of modems (modulator/ de-

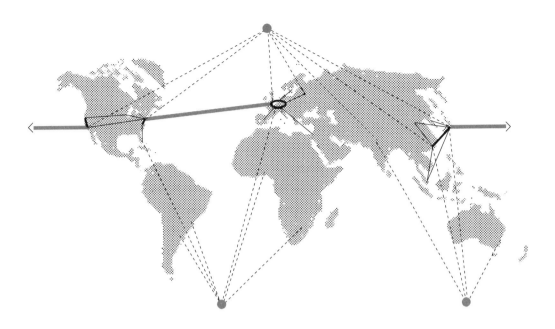

15.7
Global
telecommunications
networks

modulators)—devices that convert digital signals from the computer to analog for transmission and convert incoming analog signals back to digital. (Use of modems becomes unnecessary when telephone systems provide fully digital ISDN service.) Network servers may have dial-in ports, which may in turn function as gateways to local area or geographically distributed networks. Telephone networks are carrying increasing amounts of digital data, and distinctions between telephone and computer networks are fast disappearing.

Eventually, different types of networks will probably blend seamlessly into national and international information infrastructures that are (in the words of Michael L. Dertouzos, a prominent advocate of the idea) "as easy to use and as important as the telephone network, the electric power grid, and the interstate highways." These large-scale utilities will provide information wall sockets wherever they are needed.

In summary, today practical computational work is usually conducted within the framework of a whole hierarchy of electronic communications networks (figure 15.8). At successively higher levels in the hierarchy these networks tend to spread themselves over larger areas and

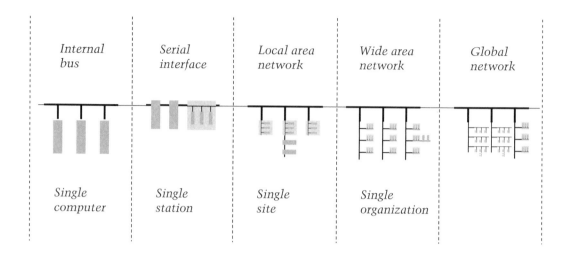

Internal bus   Serial interface   Local area network   Wide area network   Global network

Single computer   Single station   Single site   Single organization

15.8
The digital
communications
hierarchy

to operate at slower rates. At the lowest level are the basic components of your personal computer or workstation connected by a very high speed internal bus—all within a small box. Next, you may have some local input/output and storage devices connected to the serial ports by short cables. Then, in the building where you work, you may have a local area network running on coaxial cable that extends over a few hundred or a few thousand feet. Finally, your local area network may have a gateway to a geographically distributed network that uses satellite links to connect to the other side of the world. You can achieve hardware integration at a particular level in the hierarchy, and between levels, by observing the applicable interface and communications standards.

File Transfer and Translation

Files can be transferred at any of the levels in a communications hierarchy. On a personal computer, for example, a file can be transferred from a floppy disk to the hard disk. Within a local area network a file can be transferred from the disk of the file server to the disk of a workstation (that is, downloaded) or from a workstation to the server (uploaded), or routed to a printer or from one workstation to another. Via a geographically distributed network, a file can be sent rapidly from a workstation in one part of the world to a workstation in another.

In the simplest case, a data file is sent from one place to another so that somebody else can inspect or operate on the data using another copy of the application program that produced it. For example, authors working jointly on a book might transfer text files back and forth between their workstations, or an architect might send some drawing files to a structural consultant who uses the same drafting system. Since word-processing and drawing programs must be able to read back data files that they have produced themselves, and since files produced by different copies of the same program will be in exactly the same format, there is no possibility of problems arising from file format incompatibilities.

A more complex case arises when a data file produced by one application program must be read by a different application program. A page-layout program, for instance, might need to read a text file produced by a word processor and a drawing file produced by a drafting system in order to produce a page file that goes to a laser printer (figure 15.9). To make this possible, the programmers of the page-layout program must know the formats of the word-

15.9
An example of file transfer between applications

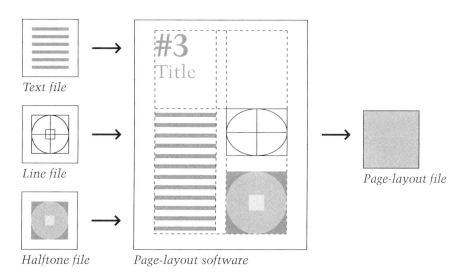

Text file

Line file

Halftone file

Page-layout software

Page-layout file

Source data
format(s)

Target data
format(s)

15.10
The role of a file translator

n² translation paths
between n formats

2n translation paths via
a standard format

15.11
The effect of a standard
format

processor and drafting system files that they wish to import, and they must incorporate in the page-layout software procedures for reading files in these formats and translating them into the formats used internally.

A piece of software for translating data files in some specified source format into some specified target format is known as a file translator (figure 15.10). These translators may be stand-alone applications, or they may be built into word processors, drafting systems, page-layout programs and so on. In any case, file translators provide the logical "glue" needed to integrate specialized application programs into a system with broader capabilities.

There is, however, a fundamental problem with file translators. If there are n different formats to be translated among, then there will be n^2 different translation paths to consider. Thus, if n becomes large, the task of writing file translators soon gets out of hand.

The obvious way to cut this problem down to size is to take one of the available formats as a standard, then write translators from each of the other formats to the standard, and translators back from the standard to each of the other formats (figure 15.11). Only $2n$ translators are needed in this case. The difficulty, of course, lies in defining an appropriate format standard for a class of applications and securing its acceptance among software developers. In practice, there are often competing standards—some official and some de facto. For transfer of files between drafting systems, for example, the IGES and DXF formats have both gained wide acceptance. IGES is an official standard produced by an international working committee, while DXF is a de facto standard simply because drafting systems that use it have a large share of the market. Figure 15.12 lists some other currently popular file-exchange standards.

Unfortunately, file translators do not always do the job perfectly: data may be lost or partially corrupted in the translation process. The fundamental reason for this is that the sets of entities and relationships provided for in the data structures of different programs for performing roughly the same task do not always match exactly (figure 15.13). A source drawing file may contain spline curves,

DXF
—*drawing exchange format*
—*drafted lines and surfaces*

EPS
—*encapsulated postscript*
—*page description*

GIF
—*graphic information format*
—*bitmaps*

IGES
—*international graphics exchange standard*
—*drafted lines and surfaces*

PICT
—*macintosh picture*
—*bitmaps*

RIB
—*renderman*
—*lighting and textures*

TGA
—*image capture format*
—*high resolution bitmaps*

TIFF
—*tagged information file format*
—*bitmaps*

15.12
Some current standards for graphics file exchange

for example, but the target format may not provide for splines. At best, a file translation program can accurately transfer the entities and relationships in the intersection of the sets supported by the source and target formats.

Sometimes file translation is better performed interactively than automatically—either because satisfactory translation procedures have not been developed or because the judgments that must be made are sufficiently important to warrant the user's explicit attention. Consider, for example, the task of translating a scanned image of a sketch into a line drawing—that is, a raster file into a vector file. Procedures for extracting lines from bitmaps do exist, but in most practical contexts they cannot be relied upon to produce a satisfactory result unaided. On the other hand, interactive procedures usually work very well. The simplest approach is to display the bitmapped image as a reference underlay, over which the user then constructs the required line drawing: this allows the user, in light of some understanding of the content and conception of what is really intended, to resolve dimensional and positional ambiguities and to snap lines into definite geometric relationships. A more sophisticated approach is to extract lines automatically, then to adjust dimensions and relationships interactively to achieve consistency with some chosen geometric discipline.

Integration through file transfer, in the ways that have been described, is a venerable technique with a long and distinguished history in computer-aided design. It made its first important appearance in the 1960s, in the widely used ICES Integrated Civil Engineering System. In the 1980s and early 1990s it became particularly important as an immediate way to provide rudimentary integration of the numerous narrowly focused, single-user programs that had proliferated during the personal computer revolution. In the future it is likely to be supplanted, to an increasing extent, by some of the more sophisticated integration techniques described below.

In general, the file-translation capabilities available in a computer-aided design environment will provide a logical

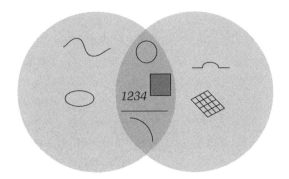

Data format A   Data format A

*Translatable
elements*

15.13
Only elements common
to both formats may be
translated from one to
the other

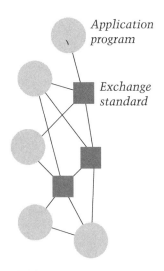

*Application
program*

*Exchange
standard*

15.14
Network of file-
translation paths between
application programs

network of file transfer paths between different application programs, as illustrated in figure 15.14. Translation procedures may be automatic, semiautomatic, or manual and may have differing levels of reliability and efficiency. As a design environment evolves, with the addition of new applications and translators, the transfer network usually grows denser, producing an increasingly highly integrated system. To make maximally effective use of the resources of a computer-aided design environment, a user should know the structure of the current file-transfer network and the characteristics of its links.

Databases

At the most elementary level of consideration, a database is simply a collection of files with related content—text files for the chapters of a book, for example, or drawing files for an architectural project. Even the simplest operating systems provide for grouping and naming such collections in folders or directories and for organizing file hierarchies (figure 15.15). Directories may be grouped into still-larger units called volumes. Administrators of large systems often deal with the mounting of volumes on physical storage devices, and if the operating system's handling of files is sufficiently sophisticated, users may not need to be aware of the details of this (figure 15.16).

Frequently, in the course of most projects, the need arises to shift data from file to file within a database: an

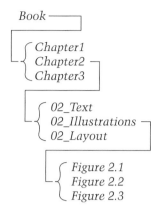

15.15
A file hierarchy

author might want to shift some paragraphs from one chapter to another, or an architect might want to reuse a design motif in a new drawing. Personal computers typically support this by providing cutting, copying to a holding zone, and pasting operations. The Macintosh Clipboard is a well-known implementation of this idea.

In more sophisticated databases there are record-to-record links between files. The door symbols in a plan drawing file might be linked to the records of a door schedule file, for example (figure 15.17). This allows automatic updating: whenever a door is changed in plan, the door schedule can be altered correspondingly. Different operating systems support different strategies for updating linked files. Where multitasking is not available, other work must be suspended whenever updates are being made. In multitasking environments, however, updating can become a task that runs in the background while other work continues.

Where a database can be accessed concurrently by different users and different processes, editing and updating must be coordinated carefully to prevent confusion and conflict (figure 15.18a). Multi-user operating systems thus

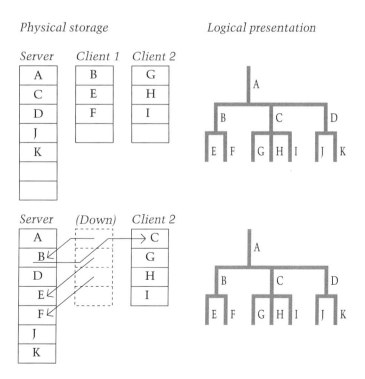

15.16
A virtual file hierarchy is hardware independent

provide for files to be locked, so that two users cannot edit them at the same time (figure 15.18b). Reference may be allowed to locked files, so that multiple users can read but not change them (figure 15.18c). Alternatively, to permit finer-grained control, locking may be implemented at the record level (figure 15.18d).

Combination of shared remote access to a database via a network with file locking and reference yields the possibility of design teleconferencing (figure 15.19). Two or more designers can view the same drawing or geometric model while talking on the telephone and can pass editing control back and forth—much as they might pass a pencil in a conference around a drawing board. Thus desk crits can be given remotely, coordination problems can be resolved without travel to meeting locations, and design reviews can be conducted without assembling jurors.

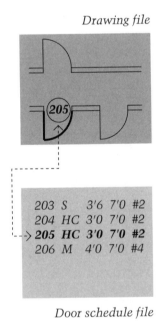

Drawing file

Door schedule file

15.17
A record-to-record link
between files

a. Parallel editing may lead to inconsistencies

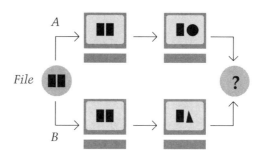

b. File locking prevents parallel editing

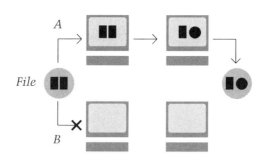

c. File locking with reference

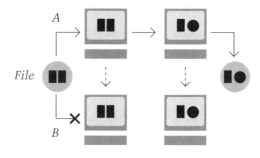

d. Record locking

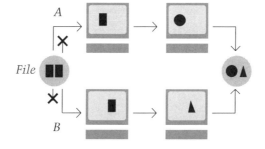

15.18
Coordination of concurrent editing processes

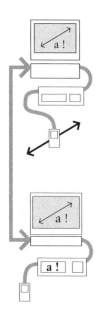

15.19
Teleconferencing using
shared sensors

Coordinated Software Tool Kits

Just as a database is a collection of files with related content, a software tool kit is a collection of programs to perform related tasks. These programs may support different sets of activities, at different stages in the development of a project (figure 15.20). These programs may reside permanently on the disk of a personal computer or workstation, they may be downloaded from a server to workstations as needed, or they may reside on a server that receives input data from workstations and sends back output data. They can be assembled into coordinated systems by presenting them in organized fashion and providing them with uniform interfaces. Usually it makes practical sense to group and coordinate tools that apply to the same types of files or databases—in other words, to create word-processing systems for text files, image-processing systems for image files, drafting systems for drawing files, and so on.

The hierarchical file system of an operating system provides an elementary way to present and organize access to software tools (figure 15.21)—just as you might organize your pencils, pens, erasers, and drafting instruments in a kit box or on a desktop. Depending on the facilities of the operating system, groups of programs may be presented as one-dimensional (character-based) lists, graphic icons on two-dimensional surfaces (a desktop metaphor), or even three-dimensional objects in space.

Within particular programs, collections of tools that the user can select are organized and presented in analogous ways. The basic presentation and selection mechanism is an event loop (figure 15.22). The program presents a selection of tools, the user selects and applies one, the computer does the work and then presents the selection of tools once again, and so on until execution of the program is terminated. Event loops may be nested within event loops, so that interaction with the program is structured in a hierarchy of levels.

Since programs that adhere to familiar conventions and employ familiar metaphors in their presentation of tools are generally easier to learn than programs that do

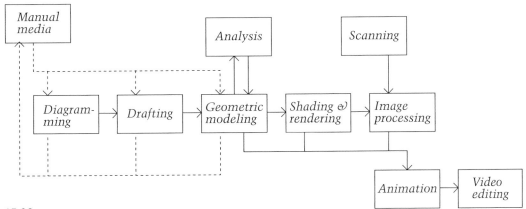

15.20
Possible application
sequence of an integrated
software tool kit

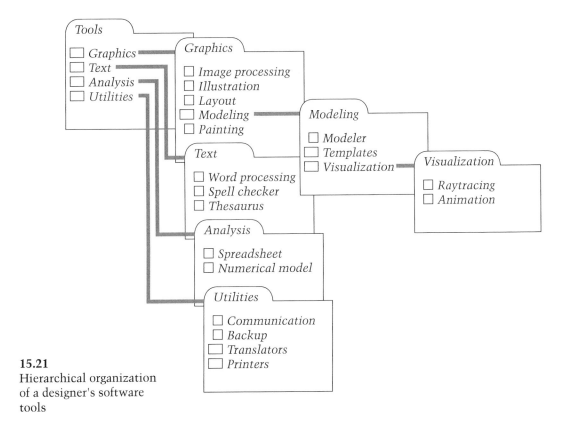

15.21
Hierarchical organization
of a designer's software
tools

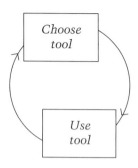

15.22
An event loop

not, there has been a growing tendency to standardize user interfaces (figure 15.23). During the 1980s, for example, Apple was successful at establishing and enforcing a strong user-interface standard for Macintosh software. This commonsense idea is not always straightforward to implement, however, since there may be considerable contention about who sets the standards: hardware vendors have an interest in standardizing the interfaces of programs running on their machines, for example, while software vendors have an interest in standardizing the interfaces of different versions of their products running on different platforms. Nor is it universally beneficial to the user: sometimes the inefficiencies of an outdated or otherwise inappropriate standard interface outweigh the benefits in reduction of learning time.

From a software developer's viewpoint, interface standardization presents itself as an important way to reduce programming and program maintenance costs. The basic idea is to write programs that accept input from standardized virtual devices rather than specific physical devices and that display output on standardized virtual surfaces (figure 15.24). These programs are then run, in particular computing environments, in concert with special driver software that maps from physical input devices to virtual devices and that maps from virtual surfaces to physical output devices. Standardized interactive graphics-interface systems such as X and Windows, and page-description languages such as Postscript and Display Postscript, now commonly provide the standards needed to link virtual and physical devices in this way. This arrangement eliminates costly duplication of programming effort: the same application program can support many different input and output devices, and the same driver software can support many different application programs.

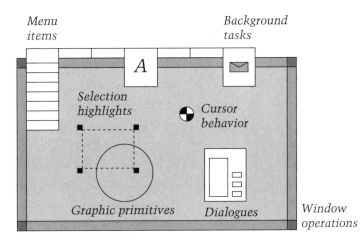

Menu
items

Background
tasks

Selection
highlights

Cursor
behavior

Graphic primitives

Dialogues

Window
operations

Command keys

Mouse
actions

15.23
Elements of an interface
standard

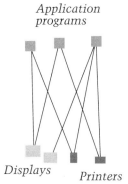

Application
programs

Displays   Printers

Each application
program drives each
output device

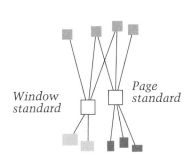

Window
standard

Page
standard

Use of window and
page-description
standards

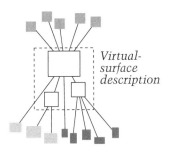

Virtual-
surface
description

Use of a virtual-surface
description standard

15.24
Output integration

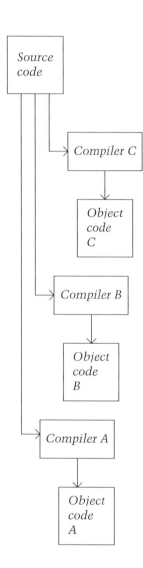

15.25
Compiling a program for
different platforms

Modifying and Customizing the Tool Kit

For similar reasons (and with similar efficiency penalties),
most application programs are now written in high-level
procedural programming languages so that they can be
compiled to run on different machines (figure 15.25). But
compilation can be a source of inflexibility: with many
compilers, the entire program must be recompiled
whenever even the smallest change is made—a very
cumbersome and time-consuming process for large computer-aided design systems that may have thousands of
procedures and millions of lines of code. More sophisticated compilers allow division of a program into parts,
independent compilation, and eventual linkage of compiled
parts. This, however, requires careful organization by the
programmer.

An alternative way to provide for easy modification
and customization of the tool kit is to equip a computer-
aided design system with a macro programming language
that allows standard sequences of operations to be specified, named, and stored for repeated future use. Macro
programming languages are simple to implement and use,
but they are limited by their lack of arithmetic and control
capabilities.

A much more powerful facility for modification and
customization can be provided by a general-purpose programming language that has been extended so that it can
access a computer-aided design system's functions. Versions of Basic, Fortran, Pascal, Lisp, and C have all been
employed in this role. The arithmetic capabilities of these
languages can be used to calculate coordinates, lengths,
areas, and so on that are needed in constructions and
analyses. And the control capabilities can be exploited in
many ways: parameterized procedures can produce instances of standard design elements, loops can produce
repetitive compositions (figure 15.26), conditionals can be
used to match design responses appropriately to contexts,
and recursive procedures can generate fractals. Through
addition of programs written in such languages, a system's
basic repertoire of elements and operators can be extended
indefinitely, and reporting, analysis, and file-translation

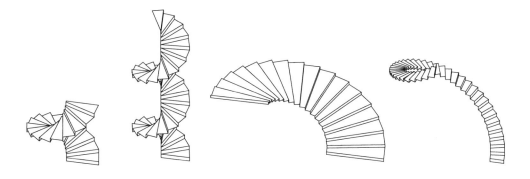

```
(defun SpiralStair ()
```

Interaction

```
;   GET VALUES FOR INDEPENDENT VARIABLES
(setq Height (getdist "Height of Stair:  "))
(setq ORad(getdist "Outer radius:  "))
(setq IRad(getdist "Inner radius:  "))
(setq Riser (getdist "Maximum Riser:  "))
(setq Tread (getdist "Tread at MidRadius:  "))
```

Arithmetic

```
;   CALCULATE DEPENDENT VARIABLES
(setq NumberOfRisers (1+ (fix (/ Height Riser))))
(setq Riser (/ Height NumberOfRisers))
(setq AvgRad (/ (+ IRadOutRad) 2))
(setq Sweep (atan Tread AvgRad))
```

```
;  STAIR LOOP
(setq a 0.0)
(setq elev 0.0)
(setq step 1)
(command "layer" "set" "stair" "")
```

Control Structure

```
(while (<= step NumberOfRisers)
```

```
;   RECALCULATE VARIABLES
 (setq bot elev)
 (setq top (+ bot riser))
```

```
;   DEFINE RISER AND TREAD VERTICES
 (setq in1 (list (* IRad(cos a)) (* IRad(sin a)) bot))
 (setq out1 (list (* ORad(cos a)) (* ORad(sin a)) bot))
 (setq in2 (list (* IRad(cos a)) (* IRad(sin a)) top))
 (setq out2 (list (* ORad(cos a)) (* ORad(sin a)) top))
 (setq a (+ a Sweep))
 (setq in3 (list (* IRad(cos a)) (* IRad(sin a)) top))
 (setq out3 (list (* ORad(cos a)) (* ORad(sin a)) top))
```

CAD system operations

```
;  ADD SURFACES TO MODEL
 (command "3dface" in1 out1 out2 in2 "")
 (command "3dface"out2 in2 in3 out3 "")
```

```
 (setq elev (+ elev riser))
 (setq step (1+ step))
)
;   END LOOP
)
```

15.26
Generation of repetitive
composition by user-
written program

capabilities can be added as required. In the 1980s, for example, numerous extended and customized versions of the popular Autocad drafting and geometric-modeling system were produced by development of programs in an associated version of Lisp.

More recently developed software engineering techniques—particularly that of object-oriented programming—allow independent development of software modules that can easily and rapidly be assembled in "click-together" fashion to produce complete systems. (Apple's Hypercard system was a popular pioneering implementation of an object-oriented development environment.) Thus, where early computer-aided design systems provided fixed repertoires of tools (and so often failed to meet individual needs), future systems increasingly will be freely expandable and customizable.

Task Controllers

In a computer-aided design environment, design tasks are accomplished by applying available software tools to a file or database representing the evolving project, just as designers have traditionally applied drafting instruments to drawings on paper. The various tasks that need to be completed in a design process have preconditions: the required input data must be ready, and the necessary tools and resources must be available. Completion of a task generates new data and frees tools and resources, so that the preconditions for new tasks are satisfied. Typically, at any point in an unfolding design process, the preconditions for many necessary tasks are satisfied. A designer working individually on a project, then, has the problem of choosing which task to take up next, and ultimately of structuring the entire design process as a sequence of tasks (figure 15.27). The manager of a design team has the more complex problem of choosing a subset of tasks for concurrent performance by different team members, and ultimately of organizing the complete design process as a structure of concurrent tasks.

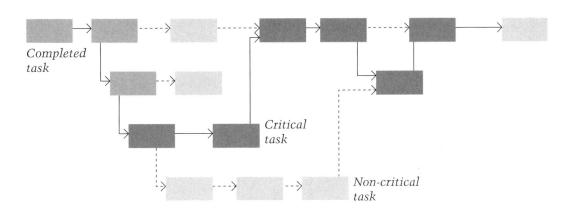

Completed
task

Critical
task

Non-critical
task

15.27
A network of design tasks
and their dependencies

Within a highly integrated computer-aided design system, much of the routine task allocation, scheduling, and initiation work can be automated, with considerable gains in efficiency. The basic idea is to provide a controller program, which maintains a list of tasks that need to be executed and preconditions for their initiation. In a networked system with an integrated database, the preconditions might include successful completion of certain other tasks, availability in the database of certain input data, and availability of a workstation to execute the task. When the preconditions for a task are satisfied, the controller initiates it. Performance might be fully automatic (in the case of well-defined tasks for which procedures have been programmed) or interactive, involving a designer making and recording decisions at a workstation. When the task has been completed successfully, the controller integrates the results into the database, updates its task list, and allocates to some other task the workstation that has been freed.

More sophisticated controllers incorporate backtracking capability, so that they can respond appropriately when tasks fail because of errors in the input or because the design context has become overconstrained. This type of task controller maintains a backtrack target for each task, that is, a predecessor task that should, in the event of failure, be reexecuted to produce new input data.

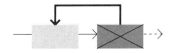

15.28
Failure of a task and
backtracking

All problem-solving programs have control strategies (often incorporating backtracking): project task controllers simply implement the idea at a project-wide scale and in a way that exploits the capacity of a network of processors to execute many tasks concurrently. Use of automated task controllers at this level began to emerge in the late 1980s, as networked computer-aided design environments became increasingly commonplace, and researchers began to explore ways to exploit their less obvious potentials. The Integrated Building Design Environment (IBDE), implemented at Carnegie-Mellon University by a team directed by Steven Fenves, was a pioneering prototype. This integrated under a controller seven independent computer programs running on seven different workstations. Each program consisted of modules to perform particular subtasks in complete design and documentation of an office building. The seven programs dealt, respectively, with basic three-dimensional layout, service core layout, structural system selection, structural system layout and load analysis, structural component design, foundation design, and construction planning. The system was limited in its versatility and architectural sophistication by the limitations of the constituent programs, but it dramatically demonstrated the power of task controllers by automatically producing plausible complete designs in a matter of hours.

In the future sophisticated backtracking task controllers will probably be used to control the division of design tasks between human designers and machines, and thus the way that design intentions are worked out. If you want overall spatial organization to drive a scheme, you would set the task controller to present tasks at that level to you and to work out the details automatically. Conversely, you could set it so that decisions about materials, assemblies, and construction details drive the scheme, and spatial consequences are worked out automatically. Thus the time of the skilled and sensitive human designer (usually the scarcest design resource) is used to best effect.

Future Directions

The basic components of a comprehensive, fully integrated computer-aided design environment are a database, a software tool kit, a facility for extending and customizing the tool kit, and a task controller—all supported by appropriate hardware and operating-system capabilities. As hardware platforms and software engineering techniques have evolved, these components have been provided to different extents and in different ways. In the 1960s and 1970s large-scale, highly integrated, but expensive and inflexible systems were developed around centralized databases maintained on mainframes or minicomputers running sophisticated time-sharing operating systems. Then, as inexpensive personal computers proliferated in the 1980s, smaller-scale systems were developed to run under simple single-user operating systems, and often the only attempt at integration was to provide some fairly primitive file-transfer and file-translation capabilities. The 1990s have seen the emergence of networks of modular, intercommunicating hardware devices, databases, and software tools.

Computer-aided design networks can be organized spatially to deliver capabilities where needed; their modularity enables them to be configured to provide levels of capacity and functionality appropriate to particular tasks and budgets; they are incrementally extensible and adaptable to meet evolving needs; and they can provide frameworks for effective coordination and management of design work. So computer files replace drawing file chests, display screens replace drawing boards, software tools replace parallel bars and triangles, electronic communication links and laser printers replace blackline print machines and mailing tubes, task controllers replace punch lists and bar chart project schedules, and teleconferencing replaces the conference room. These networks are the drawing studios of the twenty-first century.

Suggested Readings

Encarnacao, J., and E. G. Schlechtendahl. 1983. *Computer Aided Design: Fundamentals and System Architectures.* Berlin: Springer-Verlag.

Fenves, Steven J., Ulrich Flemming, Chris Hendrickson, Mary Lou Maher, and Gerhard Schmidt. 1988. "An Integrated Software Environment for Building Design and Construction." *Proceedings of the Fifth Conference on Computing in Civil Engineering.* American Society of Civil Engineers.

Kemper, Alfons, and Mechtild Wallrath. 1987. "An Analysis of Geometric Modeling in Database Systems." *ACM Computing Surveys* 19 (1): 47–91.

Kraemer, Kenneth L., and John Leslie King. 1988. "Computer-Based Systems for Cooperative Work and Group Decision Making." *ACM Computing Surveys* 20 (2): 115–46.

Madron, Thomas W. 1988. *Local Area Networks: The Second Generation.* New York: John Wiley.

Martin, James. 1989. *Local Area Networks.* Englewood Cliffs: Prentice-Hall.

Sherman, Ken. 1990. *Data Communications: A User's Guide.* Englewood Cliffs: Prentice-Hall.

Tanenbaum, Andrew. 1990. *Computer Networks.* Second edition. Englewood Cliffs: Prentice-Hall.

Wix, Jeffrey, and Colin McLelland. 1986. *Data Exchange between Computer Systems in the Construction Industry.* Bracknell, Berkshire, UK: Building Services Research and Information Association.

16

DESIGN DATABASE MANAGEMENT

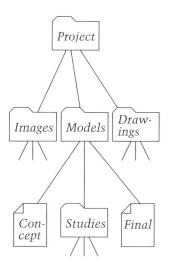

16.1
Project hierarchy

Any serious computer user soon realizes that a collection of data files relating to an ongoing project must be organized clearly and managed carefully. Figure 16.1 illustrates a typical hierarchical organization of drawing files, three-dimensional model files, image files, and text files for an ongoing architectural project. The basic file-management capabilities of an operating system usually suffice for creation and maintenance of this elementary sort of database organization. Use of appropriate standard naming conventions for files and drawing layers provides a way for users to find their way quickly through the hierarchy to data that they need (figure 16.2).

As collections of files grow in size and complexity, however, they become increasingly difficult to manage. Versions of files proliferate and may become confused. Files may be physically scattered around on the disks of different machines. The same information may be represented in different ways in different places, so that updating the database to preserve consistency as design changes are made becomes an increasingly intractable problem. When different members of a design team operate on the database there is a growing danger that the project manager will lose track of changes and lose control of design direction. The processes of backing up and producing hard copy become more and more cumbersome.

AR-Walls	LS-Trees	EL-Lighting
AR-Floor	LS-Shrubs	EL-Power
AR-Ceiling	LS-Cover	EL-Communication
AR-Roof	LS-Pavers	EL-Security
AR-Stairs	LS-Walls	EL-Emergency
AR-Doors	LS-Irrigation	
AR-Windows	LS-Drainage	
AR-Parking		
AR-Fixtures		MP-Piping
AR-Finish	PL-Boundaries	MP-Vents
AR-Notation	PL-Setbacks	MP-Valves
AR-Specs	PL-Easements	MP-Fixtures
	PL-Utilites	MP-Equipment
	PL-Usage	MH-Ducts
		MH-Piping
ST-Columns	FM-OccupantData	MH-Diffusers
ST-Beams	FM-LeaseAttributes	MH-Equipment
ST-Girders	FM-Furniture	MH-Controls
ST-Braces	FM-Equipment	
ST-Plates	FM-Communications	MF-Signals
ST-Decks	FM-Finishes	MF-Sprinklers
ST-Slabs	FM-Plants	MF-Piping
		MF-Equipment

16.2
Part of a typical system of
standard layers

These problems create a need for more powerful and specialized database-management tools than those provided by an operating system. In response, some of the more sophisticated computer-aided design systems (particularly those intended for use on large projects) provide extended facilities for structuring and managing design databases. These facilities build on and customize the basic file-management capabilities of the underlying operating system, so a relatively advanced operating system such as Unix (rather than a simple one such as DOS) provides the best foundation.

Database-management Software

Figure 16.3 illustrates the basic idea of a database-management system. The files constituting the database are permanently stored together and handled as a unit under the centralized control of a database administrator. (They may physically be stored together on the disk of a mainframe or file server, or they may be physically distributed on different machines in a network but logically grouped

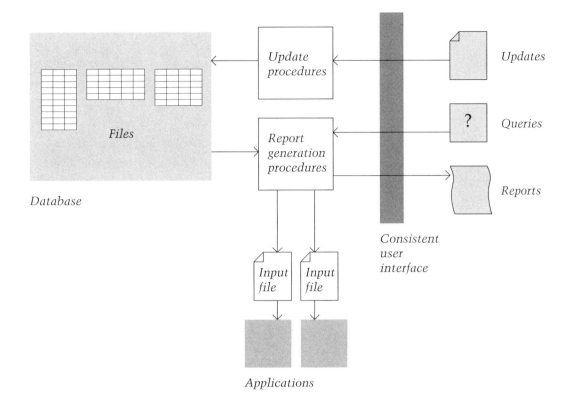

16.3
Basic structure of a
database management
system

in the same directory. This matters to the database administrator, but usually not to the user.) From time to the files are updated by addition, deletion, and alteration of data. Users can query the database to generate text and graphic reports containing the data that they need, structured in whatever fashion is appropriate to the task at hand.

This arrangement has some significant advantages. Details of physical storage and administration of data can be left in the hands of a specialist database administrator, so that designers do not have to worry about them. A centralized database can be designed to eliminate redundancy and inconsistencies in the data, thereby facilitating efficient management and providing better information to users. Access can be controlled with precision, the security of the data can be preserved, and regular, centralized backing up can insure against data loss.

A less obvious, but perhaps even more important, advantage is that application programs can potentially become data independent. In other words, the database maintains all the data that different application programs need for input, and the reporting software of the database-management system generates input files in whatever formats are needed. Conversely, where appropriate, output files from application programs can be used to update the database. Thus the database becomes the receiving and dispatching point for all data, thereby eliminating the need for complicated routing of files through networks, file translators, and the like and greatly facilitating integration of new applications into a system.

The Relational Data Model

Historically, database-management systems have provided for organization of databases as sequences, hierarchies, and networks of records—basic data structures that we have encountered in other contexts. Increasingly, though, systems are now built upon the foundation of the relational data model, a theoretical construct that was introduced in a seminal paper by E. F. Codd in 1970.

From the viewpoint of a user or database programmer, a relational database consists of named tables (which are much like ordinary sequential files), as illustrated in figure 16.4. Rows of these tables are called tuples, and columns are called attributes. Entities are represented by tuples of attribute values. Associated entities have attribute values in common. Tables are always normalized (figure 16.5), so that each entry in a table is a single value, never a set of values. Thus information is represented in a simple, general, and uniform way (by contrast with the specialization, diversity, and complexity of the data structures of application programs), which greatly simplifies the tasks of updating, factoring out redundancy, finding inconsistencies, and generating reports. All operations on a relational database can be carried out with a small set of general procedures. (The database may or may not be physically stored and operated on as a collection of tables: this is a low-level implementation detail that need not concern us.)

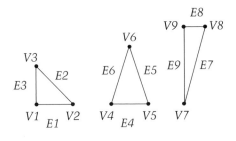

Edges			
Edge	Vertex1	Vertex2	Length
E1	V1	V2	1.00
E2	V2	V3	1.41
E3	V3	V1	1.00
E4	V4	V5	1.00
E5	V5	V6	1.58
E6	V6	V4	1.58
E7	V7	V8	2.06
E8	V8	V9	0.50
E9	V9	V7	2.00

Tuple

Attribute

Attribute value

16.4
A set of lines represented
by a table in a relational
database

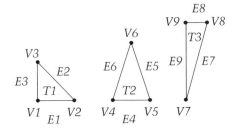

Before normalization

Drawing				
Triangle	Edges			
	Edge	Vertex1	Vertex2	Length
T1	E1	V1	V2	1.00
	E2	V2	V3	1.41
	E3	V3	V1	1.00
T2	E4	V4	V5	1.00
	E5	V5	V6	1.58
	E6	V6	V4	1.58
T3	E7	V7	V8	2.06
	E8	V8	V9	0.50
	E9	V9	V7	2.00

After normalization

Drawing				
Triangle	Edge	Vertex1	Vertex2	Length
T1	E1	V1	V2	1.00
T1	E2	V2	V3	1.41
T1	E3	V3	V1	1.00
T2	E4	V4	V5	1.00
T2	E5	V5	V6	1.58
T2	E6	V6	V4	1.58
T3	E7	V7	V8	2.06
T3	E8	V8	V9	0.50
T3	E9	V9	V7	2.00

16.5
Construction and
normalization of a new
table to represent a set of
triangles

Consider the simple database shown in figure 16.6. A table called *Vertices* represents points by their coordinates. A second table, called *Edges*, represents lines by their bounding vertices and specifies their lengths. And a third table, called *Triangles*, represents polygons by their bounding edges and specifies their areas. This database is updated by execution of procedures that insert and delete tuples, and change attribute values. There might, for example, be update procedures to shift a vertex, to insert a triangle, and to delete a triangle (figure 16.7). The procedure to shift a vertex must change coordinate values in the *Vertices* table as specified, calculate new lengths and areas, and make corresponding changes in the *Edges* and *Triangles* tables. The procedure to insert triangles operates on all tables to insert vertices, edges, and triangles. And the procedure to delete triangles operates on all tables to delete vertices, edges, and triangles. Notice that, if these procedures are correctly written, they will guarantee that the tables always contain consistent data: they will never produce descriptions of shapes that are not triangles, nor will they produce inconsistencies between the recorded vertex coordinates, edge lengths, and areas of the triangles.

Reports are generated by procedures that operate on the tables to extract the required data. Figure 16.7, for example, illustrates procedures for reporting total area and total perimeter. The total area procedure simply sums the entries in the *Area* column of the *Triangles* table. And the total perimeter procedure sums the entries in the *Length* column of the *Edges* table. Other reporting procedures might sort tables in specified ways (figure 16.8), construct new tables to show relations implicit in the existing tables (figure 16.9), or extract tuples with specified combinations of attribute values. Reports may be output as text, or they may be interpreted as graphic displays. A language called SQL (usually pronounced "sequel") is now commonly used for specifying reports from relational databases.

As the examples illustrate, a relational database directly reflects the mathematical definition of a relation on n variables: the Cartesian product of the ranges of those variables is a set of ordered n-tuples, and a relation is a

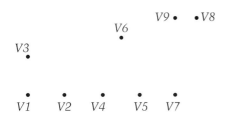

Vertices		
Vertex	X	Y
V1	0.0	0.0
V2	1.0	0.0
V3	0.0	0.1
V4	2.0	0.0
V5	3.0	0.0
V6	2.5	1.5
V7	4.0	0.0
V8	4.5	2.0
V9	4.0	2.0

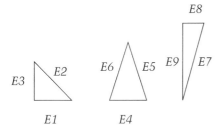

Edges			
Edge	Vertex1	Vertex2	Length
E1	V1	V2	1.00
E2	V2	V3	1.41
E3	V3	V1	1.00
E4	V4	V5	1.00
E5	V5	V6	1.58
E6	V6	V4	1.58
E7	V7	V8	2.06
E8	V8	V9	0.50
E9	V9	V7	2.00

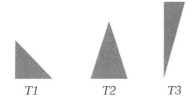

Triangles				
Triangle	Edge1	Edge2	Edge3	Area
T1	E1	E2	E3	0.50
T2	E4	E5	E6	0.75
T3	E7	E8	E9	0.50

16.6
A geometric database
consisting of three tables

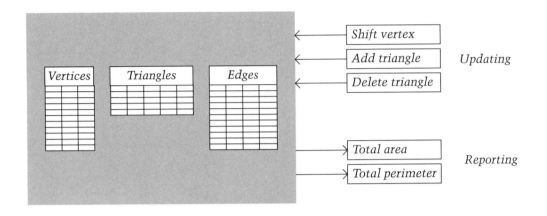

16.7
Updating and reporting
procedures for the example
geometric database

Edges			
Edge	Vertex1	Vertex2	Length
E7	V7	V8	2.06
E9	V9	V7	2.00
E5	V5	V6	1.58
E6	V6	V4	1.58
E2	V2	V3	1.41
E1	V1	V2	1.00
E3	V3	V1	1.00
E4	V4	V5	1.00
E8	V8	V9	0.50

16.8
A sorted table: edges
by length

Incidence		
Vertex	EdgeL	EdgeR
V1	E3	E1
V2	E1	E2
V3	E2	E3
V4	E6	E4
V5	E4	E5
V6	E5	E6
V7	E9	E7
V8	E7	E8
V9	E8	E9

16.9
A new table: edges
incident on specified
vertices

subset of that set. Thus a unary relation such as redness of rooms is a set of room names, a binary relation such as adjacency of rooms is a set of ordered pairs of room names, and so on. Notice that, under this very general definition, things that we usually think of as "entities" and things that we usually think of as "relationships" are treated in exactly the same way, and that both "entities" and "relationships" can have attributes.

The spare mathematical simplicity of the relational data model makes it seem alien to most designers when they first encounter it. But it is, in fact, a very useful conceptual framework for thinking about design, and relational database systems can become extremely powerful design tools. After all, nothing is more fundamental in design than formation and discovery of relationships among parts of a composition.

Linking Graphics and Relational Databases

In principle, a relational database could serve directly as the database for a drafting or geometric-modeling system. In practice, however, high-performance graphics systems usually rely on highly specialized data structures that are organized to maximize efficiency in performance of common editing and display operations; relational databases, which are organized for conceptual simplicity and generality and to facilitate database-management tasks, are just too slow. (This may change as computers become faster and as relational database systems become more efficient, but it has historically been the case.) However, a relational database can be combined with a high-performance graphics system by pairing records for graphics entities in the graphics system data structure with tuples in the relational database (figure 16.10). Thus graphic operations such as insertion and deletion of lines, polygons, or solids can be reflected instantly in the relational database. Conversely, results of reporting operations can be presented graphically.

Consider, for example, a building design represented as an assembly of solids in a solid-modeling system. Each solid represents an architectural element such as a column, beam, door, window, or enclosed room. These solids are

Graphics data structure   *Relational database*

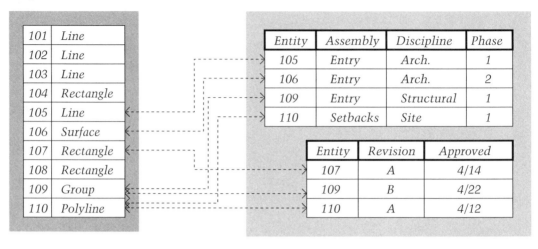

101	Line
102	Line
103	Line
104	Rectangle
105	Line
106	Surface
107	Rectangle
108	Rectangle
109	Group
110	Polyline

Entity	Assembly	Discipline	Phase
105	Entry	Arch.	1
106	Entry	Arch.	2
109	Entry	Structural	1
110	Setbacks	Site	1

Entity	Revision	Approved
107	A	4/14
109	B	4/22
110	A	4/12

16.10
Pairing graphic entities and
rows of tables

paired with tuples in a relational database. The relational
database records nongeometric attributes such as material,
supplier name, catalog number, role in the structural
system, floor on which the element is located, and so on.
Instead of just displaying layers and combinations of
layers, then, the system can display reports based on these
attributes. So an architect might ask to see a plan of all the
partitions on the fourth floor, an axonometric showing all
the structural steelwork in the building, a street-level
perspective showing the exterior cladding elements, a
door schedule sorted by supplier name, a list of all the
nonrectangular solids sorted according to cost, or a schematic plan showing all of the offices larger than 200 square
feet color coded to indicate size. Reports might also be
generated to serve as input files for renderers and anima-
tors, structural-analysis software, cost-analysis software,
and so on. Some of these might be standard types of
reports, selected from a menu or by clicking on an icon.
Others might be highly unusual ones (perhaps responding
to a need to explore some aspect of the design that turns
out to be unexpectedly significant), specified by means of
SQL queries.

In a facilities-management application, room polygons
in a building plan may be paired with tuples recording
attributes such as floor area, type of carpeting, type of wall
finish, yearly rent, types and numbers of power and

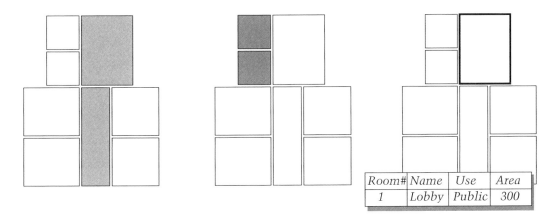

Room#	Name	Use	Area
1	Lobby	Public	300

All public spaces   *All areas under 100 sq. ft.*   *Text report on selected space*

16.11
Reports from a facilities
management database

communications outlets, and the like. Other tables in the facilities database describe the furniture and equipment items housed in the building and the people in the organization. Yet other tables describe relationships among people, furniture and equipment, and rooms: supervisor/ supervisee relations of people (the organization chart), groupings of rooms into floors and zones, assignments of people to rooms, assignments of equipment to people, and so on to whatever level of detail seems important for management purposes. This database is kept current as the condition and usage of the building changes. Text reports about current room occupancy can then be generated by selecting polygons. Conversely, results of SQL queries can be displayed by highlighting polygons in a plan drawing (figure 16.11).

The basic general structure of a computer-aided design system that links interactive graphic-editing capabilities with relational database capabilities is summarized in figure 16.12. Graphic-editing operations are reflected in the database, and the database can also be updated through forms and through text input. Reports from the database are specified through some combination of graphic selection, selection from menus, and SQL commands. These reports are of three kinds: graphic reports (both screen displays and hard copy), text reports, and input files for application programs. Thus the idea of flexible reporting

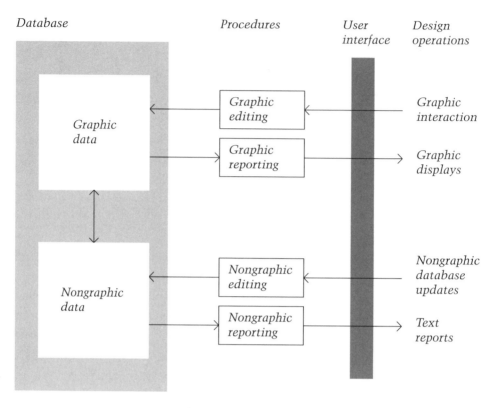

Database   Procedures   User   Design
interface   operations

16.12

Structure of a CAD system
with flexible graphic and
nongraphic reporting
capabilities

replaces the cumbersome and limiting strategy (necessary in less sophisticated computer-aided design environments) of organizing a project in layers and selecting combinations of layers for display.

Project Databases and Horizontal Integration

This type of system can support effective horizontal integration of design processes around project databases— centralized, nonredundant descriptions of designs. All design decisions and changes are recorded in the project database so that it always provides a definitive, up-to-date source of information about the current state of the design. Graphic displays, plotted drawings, textual summaries, and input files are automatically generated (as reports from the database) as needed for particular design purposes. Thus different design team members are provided with views of the project that are appropriate to their needs and roles (figure 16.13): the structural engineer sees structural elements and loads, but is shielded from irrelevant detail about interior finishes and fixtures, while the interior

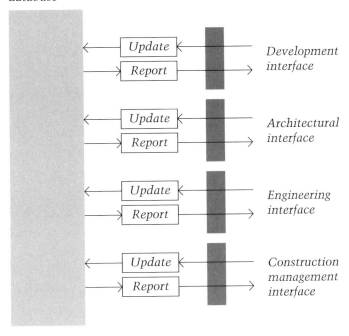

Project
database

Update ← Development interface
Report →

Update ← Architectural interface
Report →

Update ← Engineering interface
Report →

Update ← Construction management interface
Report →

16.13
A system in which different
disciplines are provided
with different views of the
database

designer sees detailed descriptions of interiors but not of the building's footings.

The project description held by such a database must maintain the union of all the data needed by the disciplines and application programs that it integrates. Thus an architectural project database might, for example, link a complete and detailed solid-assembly model with tables of engineering and cost data. This provides the basis for generation of sectional, axonometric, and perspective views and of structural, thermal, lighting, and cost analyses.

Unfortunately, as the scope of such comprehensive databases is expanded to support a widening range of design functions, they become increasingly difficult to design, require management software that is increasingly complex to implement, and make growing demands on a computer system's processing, memory, and communications resources. Thus they have tended to be implemented in limited (and sometimes Procrustean) ways. The limitations show up in the form of restrictions on the shapes and relationships that can be modeled, on the type and amount of nongeometric information that can be included, on the range of applications that can be integrated, on the sequencing and organization of design decision making, and on the size of projects that can be handled.

In the 1970s and 1980s some ambitious, large-scale computer-aided design systems were developed around the idea of a comprehensive, centralized, project database (for example the OXSYS and BDS systems, which were used mostly for hospital design in the United Kingdom, and the SSHA system, which was used for housing design in Scotland). These ran on mainframe and minicomputer time-sharing systems with satellite graphics terminals— an arrangement that made a centralized database natural. The idea fell into disuse during the latter 1980s, as inexpensive personal computers became the environment for most popular computer-aided design systems. In the 1990s, as networked computer-aided design environments have emerged (allowing combination of centralized data with local processing power) and as relational database-management technology has continued to advance, comprehensive project databases have received renewed attention.

Library Databases

Another dimension of integration can be achieved when project databases are used in close conjunction with library databases that contain descriptions of standard components, assembly details, or even complete subsystems. Some of the earliest practical computer-aided architectural design systems, for example, were developed in Europe for use with particular industrialized component building systems and had built-in libraries of component descriptions. These systems provided for selection and assembly of construction components and were able to integrate applications for document production, cost estimation, engineering analysis, and construction management around their project databases. Systems working at a different granularity provided for assembly of standard rooms, or even whole hospital departments, into complete buildings.

The simplest way to relate project and library databases is to provide for selecting components or details from the library and copying them into project databases as required. But this is obviously inefficient. A great deal of data redundancy can be factored out by storing in the project database only location and other parameters that define an instance, together with references back to a library database where type descriptions are held (figure 16.14). The resulting highly compressed project database can be expanded into detailed reports and displays, as required, by procedures that follow the references to the library in order to extract and assemble the needed data.

This factoring of the data reflects the reality that component design and building design have become separate disciplines and allows for library and project databases to be built by different groups of people. The reduction of redundancy resulting from this arrangement also facilitates updating and consistency maintenance, since any change to a standard component description in the library database will automatically and immediately

16.14
Library and project databases

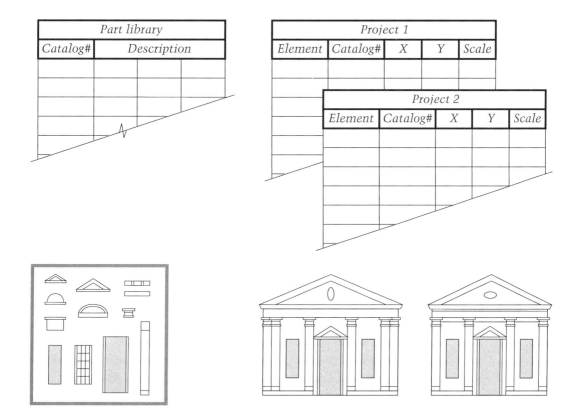

be propagated to all the instances of that component in linked project databases. Global substitution of one standard component type for another (a rounded pediment for a triangular one, say) can be handled with similar ease: it is merely a matter of shifting references (figure 16.15).

Further factoring out of redundancy can be accomplished, in the library database itself, by arranging the standard components or details in type hierarchies, such that subtypes inherit the properties of supertypes (figure 16.16). (Use of object-oriented programming techniques facilitates this.) Changes can then be propagated very efficiently by altering a high-level type, with the result that the alterations are inherited by subtypes and then propagated to instances of these subtypes in projects. Use of this integrated database structure encourages a similarly structured design process based upon a small vocabulary of high-level design elements, definition of type/subtype relations, parametric variation, and spatial instancing.

If references are provided not only from a project database to a library database, but also from the library database to a particular project or version of a project, it becomes very easy to count instances for cost estimation purposes and to automatically generate component schedules, ordering documents, and the like. For obvious reasons, this is an increasingly popular idea with vendors of components that designers might use. Specialized library-based integrated systems have been developed for interior design by furniture, partition, and door and window suppliers, and for small-scale wood construction by lumber suppliers.

Different sorts of library databases are likely to be available in different design contexts, reflecting differences in conditions of production and in the nature of design problems. Where closed industrialized component building systems or proprietary furniture and partition systems are used, the library database describes a stable, well-defined, and carefully coordinated design vocabulary, and project design largely reduces to catalog search (perhaps assisted by search software), component selection, and component positioning and assembly. Similarly, systems for rapid

Part library   *Project*

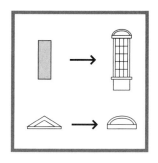

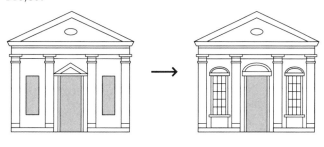

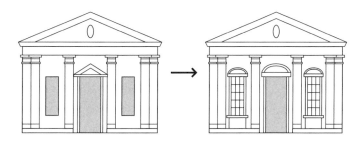

16.15
Global substitutions

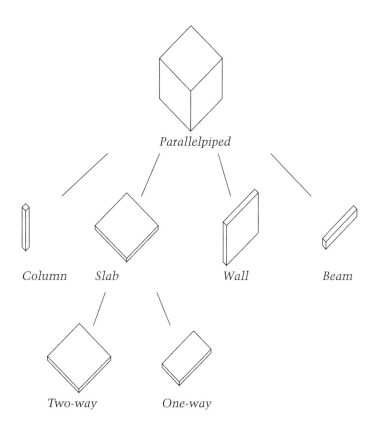

16.16
A simple type hierarchy

production of hotel designs may be built around library databases of standard room types; systems for interior space planning may be built around carefully developed space standards and office configurations; and systems for military base design may radically reduce project design to selecting, adapting, and positioning standard building types. Where a closed system is not used, the library database may contain a large, open-ended collection of available construction products, and keeping the library database up to date becomes a major issue. In landscape design, an open-ended library database can take the place of traditional catalogs of plant material.

Version Control

Project databases evolve through a succession of versions as design decisions are made and recorded. The most fundamental operation involved here is that of saving a version on disk. This can occur at the end of a work session with a computer-aided design system or at some intermediate point. Systems normally provide the options of either saving under the existing name, with the result that a previously saved version is overwritten, or saving under a new name ("saving as") to create a new version. Since design is an uncertain, trial-and-error process, it is usually prudent to save intermediate versions of an evolving project in case you want to go back to them (just as you save your sketches in a more traditional design process). The result, in general, is a tree of project versions—some of which are developed further, and some of which are abandoned—as illustrated in figure 16.17. Eventually, one of the terminal versions is accepted as the final design. Each version is identified, at least, by name and time of creation.

Keeping track of versions and their relationships in the version tree is a fairly straightforward task for a single designer working on a personal computer, but it becomes more complex with a multimember design team working on a multi-user system or in a network. Different team members may create their own versions and work on them in parallel, so that the version tree proliferates rapidly, and

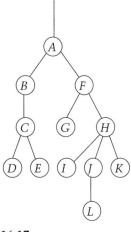

16.17
A version tree

there is need for more precise description of versions and how they relate to each other. A further problem with proliferating version trees is that they rapidly consume available disk storage: this means that they must be pruned regularly, with inactive versions either being deleted or relegated to archival storage (tape or optical disk).

For more compact storage, redundancy may be factored out of version trees by keeping references from versions to their successors and recording only the differences between successive versions. Thus any version can be reconstructed by following a chain of references down the tree. (An analogous facility, but finer grained and usually more limited in scope, is provided by systems that maintain undo buffers so that users can back up through a chain of commands to some previous state of the design.) This structure also facilitates the operation of comparing versions to determine how they differ. Sophisticated computer-aided design systems, then, provide version-management tools for maintaining well-structured, compact version trees.

Sometimes strategies for version control and for geographic distribution and timing of design work can be coordinated to advantage. Part of an international design team might, for example, work in Tokyo, produce an updated version of the project database at the end of each working day, and transmit it to Chicago. A Chicago team might take up this version at the beginning of the working day, develop it further, and transmit the next version to London, where a third team takes it up and then sends its version on to Tokyo, and so on in a twenty-four-hour operation.

Consistency Maintenance

In traditional design processes architects and others must take care to eliminate errors and omissions in sets of drawings and specifications: if they do not, construction problems, building failures, and costly litigation can result. Formalized procedures for recording information in documents and for checking documents are thus used to minimize the possibility of errors slipping through. In a computer-aided design process, application of formalized consistency-maintenance and error-checking procedures to the project database serves the same end and can eliminate a great deal of tedious work and the possibility of human error.

The first principle of consistency maintenance is to maintain a unique, definitive version of the project database that is as free from redundancy as possible. If a rectangular room is described by values for *Length*, *Width*, and *Area*, for example, it is possible for one value to be inconsistent with the other two. But if only two values are recorded in the database and the third is computed from them as required, there is no possibility of inconsistency. Similarly, in a traditional set of architectural drawings it is quite possible (and, unfortunately, not so uncommon), for a plan and a section of a building to be inconsistent with each other, but this sort of inconsistency is impossible if both are generated as reports from a nonredundant three-dimensional geometric database.

The second basic principle is to perform all operations on the database by means of procedures which, by virtue of their formal properties, guarantee production of well-formed, consistent descriptions. As we saw in chapter 11, for example, use of the Euler operators to update a solid model eliminates the possibility of producing non-polyhedral solids, and use of the normalized spatial set operators eliminates the possibility of producing dangling edges and faces. Similarly, in the relational database example discussed earlier in this chapter (figure 16.7), the update procedures guaranteed production of triangles with consistent values for vertex coordinates, edge lengths, and areas.

Where it is impossible to prevent inconsistencies and errors from entering a database, there may at least be ways of finding and correcting them. There is no obvious way to build an operator that will prevent you from entering an incorrectly spelled word into a text file, for example, but you can apply a spelling checker to find words that are not in the lexicon and suggest alternatives that are. You might even go a step further and apply a grammar checker to discover syntactic infelicities. Similarly, where we know

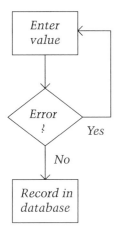

16.18
A simple error correction loop

a design must comply with certain rules, it is often possible and worthwhile to apply checking software. Thus solid assemblies can be checked for spatial clashes, floor plans (if represented in an appropriate way) can be checked for compliance with area, adjacency, and egress requirements, and so on.

Error checking can be a batch process applied to an entire file, resulting in production of an error report, or it can (where logically possible and sufficiently efficient) be an incremental process carried out as a user enters data. A simple error-correction loop that might be built into an input procedure is illustrated in figure 16.18. This might catch wrongly spelled words as they are entered into a text file or spatial clashes as solid elements are instantiated and assembled to produce a three-dimensional model.

A rigorous formal foundation for consistency maintenance can be provided by writing shape grammars for classes of designs (just as syntax checking of computer programs by a compiler is based on a formal specification of the syntax of a programming language). A shape grammar

Starting shape

0

Organization of major subsystems

Refinement of the primary structure

1   →

5   →

2   →

6   →

3   →

7   →

4   →

8   →

16.19
Some of the rules of a shape grammar for simple pavilion structures

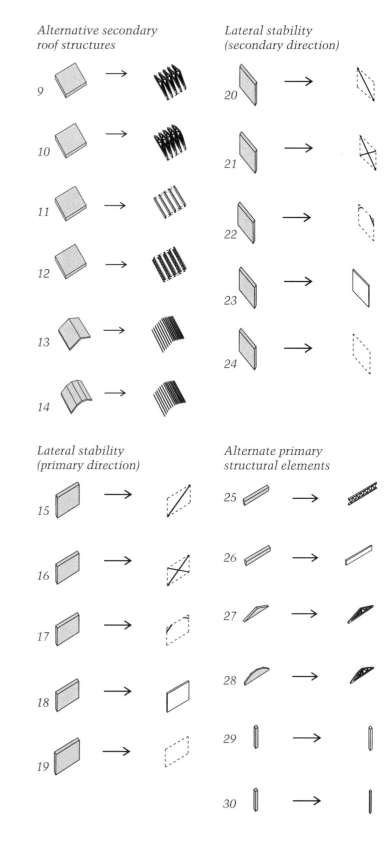

Alternative secondary roof structures

Lateral stability (secondary direction)

Lateral stability (primary direction)

Alternate primary structural elements

16.20
Further rules of a shape grammar (for inserting structural components into schematic pavilion designs)

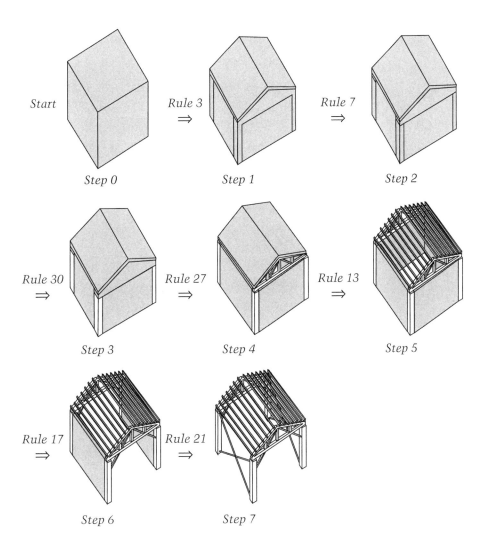

Start

Rule 3
⇒

Rule 7
⇒

Step 0

Step 1

Step 2

Rule 30
⇒

Rule 27
⇒

Rule 13
⇒

Step 3

Step 4

Step 5

Rule 17
⇒

Rule 21
⇒

Step 6

Step 7

16.21
Derivation of a design in
the language specified by
the grammar

specifies a vocabulary of parts and rules for assembling
those parts into complete designs (figure 16.19). The rules,
in effect, specify restrictions on the application of operators. If they are applied generatively to a specified starting
shape, they produce designs guaranteed to be syntactically
correct (figure 16.20). Conversely, if they are applied in
reverse to parse a given configuration, they determine
whether a design is syntactically correct or not. (A configuration is syntactically correct if some sequence of
reductions eventually reduces it to the starting shape of
the grammar.) Formal grammars, syntax checking, and
syntax-directed synthesis have long been commonplace
ideas in computer programming, but their practical application in computer-aided design is still in its infancy.

The Progression of Representations
and Vertical Integration

We have now seen how a centralized database can be used to support a horizontally integrated design process. Unfortunately, effective support of vertical integration through successive stages of a project is a different and more difficult matter: the task of maintaining a project database through these stages is made complex by the need to use very different sorts of representations at different points.

A project might, for example, begin as an unstructured collection of very rough sketches in bitmapped image format, be developed into a few plan and section drawings that precisely fix key ideas, be further elaborated into a three-dimensional wireframe to resolve geometric problems, be developed next into a partial surface model for production or realistic presentation perspectives, and finally become a comprehensive, consistent database with the capacity to support a wide range of engineering and cost analyses. The functions of the database also change. In the early, conceptual stages of a project the design team is likely to be small and closely knit, inconsistencies and ambiguities can be tolerated, quick, rough analyses suffice, and the emphasis is on the use of telling abstractions and rapid, unpredictable production and recording of ideas. At later stages the basic design has been stabilized and the emphasis is on complete and consistent documentation, detailed analysis of cost and performance, and coordination of the work of many specialists.

It makes little sense, then, to attempt organization of a design project around a comprehensive, fully integrated, three-dimensional assembly model from the very beginning—as many of the pioneering integrated computer-aided design systems attempted to do. The demands of this representation tend to force a designer's attention to issues that are irrelevant at a particular stage of consideration and deflect it from issues that are more crucial. A better strategy is to support maintenance of linked representations at varying levels of abstraction and to translate back and forth between them (figure 16.22). As abstract representations are translated into more complete and

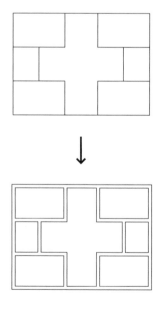

16.22
Translation between representations: single-line plan becomes double-line

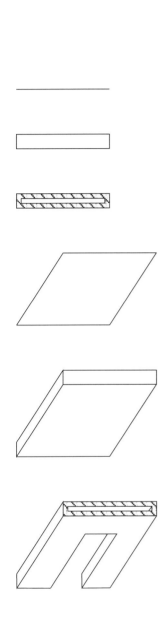

16.23
Some aliases of a wall
element

detailed representations, ambiguities and inconsistencies can be resolved, missing information can be filled in, and increasing attention can appropriately be paid to achieving completeness and consistency of representation.

Where a library database is used, development of a design in this way can be supported by providing library elements with aliases suitable for use at different stages. A wall element, for example, might be shown as a straight line in a highly schematic plan, as a double line in a more developed plan, as a cavity wall in construction plans and sections, and as a rectangular solid in a three-dimensional model (figure 16.23). These aliases provide a basis for translating from one representation to another, in much the same way that a French/English translating dictionary does. Even more importantly, they can be used to maintain linkages between representations at different levels of abstraction so that, for example, deleting a line in a single-line floor plan automatically deletes a corresponding double-line wall from a more developed plan, a cavity wall from construction plans and sections, and a rectangular solid from a solid model.

Default values can be used to allow immediate automatic translation from abstract representations to more detailed ones. To translate from a single-line floor plan to a double-line plan, for example, a default value for wall thickness can be employed. Furthermore, if the data structure allows automatic discrimination between interior and exterior walls, different defaults can be used in those two cases. At a later point the designer can direct attention to the issue of wall thickness, consider whether the default values are, in fact, appropriate, and perhaps change them.

Carried to a logical conclusion, the use of abstraction hierarchies, aliases, and default values removes the traditional distinction between conceptual design and design development and eliminates much of the labor of design development. A fully developed design exists, in unrefined form, as soon as a basic concept has been sketched. Then variations on the theme can be explored, and details can be refined, for as long as time and interest permit.

Document Production by Report Generation

Traditionally, document production has been an expensive and time-consuming aspect of design. But the use of project databases can reduce the expenditure of both money and time. When documents are needed for client presentations, consultant meetings, approvals, bidding, magazine publication, and so on, they can be produced as reports from the current version of the central project database. Standard report formats (both graphic and text) can be predefined, and the production run can often be made overnight—between the end of one working day and the start of the next—and with little or no supervision. This assures that documents always contain the most current information and eliminates the need for temporary suspension of further design work whenever document production efforts must be undertaken.

Access Control and Security

A designer working individually on a project needs access to the entire project database. In a design team, though, different team members may be responsible for different aspects of the design, and it may be desirable from a project-management viewpoint to formalize their areas of responsibility and authority by providing them with access to only those parts of the database that they need to see and manipulate in order to perform their respective tasks. This prevents unauthorized changes to the data, minimizes the possibility of accidental data loss or corruption, and provides a way to control access to any confidential or sensitive information in the database. Generally, team leaders responsible for overall direction and management of the project need broad access to the database, while specialists working on particular aspects may be given much narrower access.

Traditionally, as we have seen, access control has been implemented in ways that are closely determined by the physical organization of data—basically by providing for locking of files, layers, or records. Within the framework of an integrated database-management system, however, access control can be disconnected from physical organization and thus implemented in much more flexible and effective ways. Basically, the idea is to restrict the types of reports that team members can generate from the central database and, conversely, to restrict the types of updates to the database that they can make. For example, a structural engineer might be authorized to generate reports containing information about the structural frame of a building, to download these to a workstation for editing, and to send edited versions back to update relevant portions of the central project database. Other team members might be authorized to generate and download reports on the structural frame, and might even edit their downloaded versions to suggest alternative configurations, but do not have the authority to update its definitive description. In effect, sophisticated, adjustable filters are applied to the input and output channels connecting team members to the central project database.

This sort of access control can be applied not only to horizontal propagation of data among design team members, but also to vertical propagation from stage to stage. As a project progresses, the project manager may formalize decisions by locking finalized parts of the database against further updating. Thus reports from the current database specify the "givens" of the subproblems that remain to be solved. At the inception of a design project, information about site boundaries and fixed site features might be locked in. Later, at the interior space-planning stage, column and core layouts might be locked in. When the project is in construction, updates might be made only within the framework of a highly formalized change-order process.

Backing Up and Archiving

Active versions of project and library databases should be backed up on archival media (usually magnetic tape or optical disk), at regular intervals, as insurance against data loss or corruption due to system malfunctions, human error, or malicious action. As with most kinds of insurance, you can get different levels of protection at different costs: if you invest a relatively large amount of effort in backing up completely, and at frequent intervals, you minimize the risk of losing large amounts of work, but if you invest less effort in backing up less completely, or at longer intervals, you take a correspondingly greater risk.

In a personal computer environment the files maintained on each machine must be backed up from that machine—usually by the user who is responsible for that machine—and there is considerable risk that backing up will be forgotten or carried out with insufficient frequency. But a centralized database facilitates more systematic and reliable backup, since this can be a part of various duties performed by a specialist database administrator (figure 16.24). Elimination of redundancy in the database reduces the time needed for backup (which can be substantial for large databases). It also facilitates efficient incremental backup procedures—backing up only information that has been changed since the last backup.

When a design project is complete, the final backup of the project database becomes an archival record—the equivalent of as-built drawings. Such records are a valuable resource, so they should be preserved in a permanent

16.24
Administrative roles

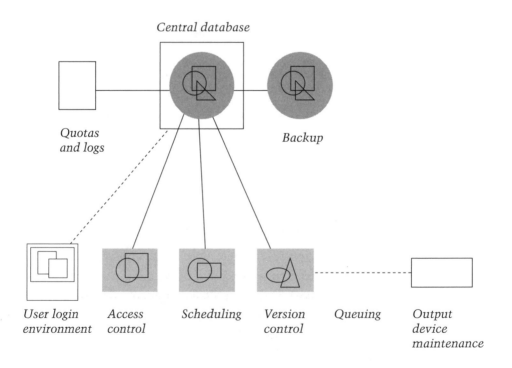

archival database. (Design firms have traditionally maintained archives of rolls or plan chests of drawings, but these consume valuable space, are expensive to keep up, and hold information in relatively inaccessible form.) Electronic archives are compact and accessible and readily allow archived projects to be transferred to facilities-management systems, to serve as the basis for later alteration and addition schemes, to be analyzed statistically to provide cost and scheduling data needed for estimating future projects, and to become quarries from which forms and organizations can be extracted and adapted for reuse in new projects. The advantages of electronic archiving are so great that a small industry concerned with the translation of as-built drawings into digital format has developed.

New Design Products and Roles

For hundreds of years now drawings—intermediate objects between a conception and an executed project—have been the principle tangible products of designers. They have been difficult and expensive to produce, they have served to transmit the culture of design, and designers have often defined and differentiated themselves through their drawing skills. But all this changes when design processes are organized around integrated project databases. The project database becomes the essential, valuable product, and drawings reduce to inexpensive, expendable, automatically generated reports. Increasingly, clients and contractors will demand delivery not just of these reports, but of a copy of the database itself.

As a result of this fundamental reorientation, new divisions of labor and new design roles will gradually emerge. We are likely to see library database specialists who develop elements and details and so build intellectual capital; project specialists (who need knowledge and experience, but little in the way of traditional drawing skills) who make design decisions in particular contexts to generate the content of project databases; analysts who operate on developed project databases to produce engineering and cost analyses; production specialists (with graphic design skills) who format reports and organize document production operations; database managers responsible for physically organizing and preserving the security and integrity of data; and project managers who thoroughly understand issues of systematically building a database, maintaining consistency, and appropriately organizing reporting and updating. This redefinition of skills and roles is likely to be of comparable long-term significance to that which took place in the Italian Renaissance (and was exemplified in the career of Andrea Palladio), when the role of the architect who drew was separated from the role of the craftsman who built.

Suggested Readings

Codd, E. F. 1970. "A Relational Model of Data for Large Shared Data Banks."*Communications of the Association for Computing Machinery* 13 (6).

Codd, E. F. 1990. *The Relational Model for Database Management, Version 2.* Reading, Mass.: Addison-Wesley.

Date, C. J. 1990. *An Introduction to Database Systems.* Fifth edition. Reading, Mass.: Addison-Wesley.

Katz, Randy H. 1990. "Towards a Unified Framework for Version Modeling in Engineering Databases." *ACM Computing Surveys* vol. 22 (4): 375—408.

17

INVESTING IN DESIGN TOOLS

Technical feasibility and intellectual interest do not suffice to make computer methods advantageous. To pay its way in a design office a computer system must do enough design work to cover the interest and wear and tear on the hardware and software, plus the wages (including learning time) of the people who operate it. If the value of this design work is sufficiently great, after these costs are deducted, then an advantage results from use of the computer system. The advantage may follow because the system allows more necessary design work to be done in the same amount of time (a productivity benefit), because it creates opportunities to undertake additional work (a marketing benefit), or because its use adds value to design products or services (a quality benefit).

In practice, different benefits can be achieved through different kinds and levels of investment in computer technology. Furthermore, the balance of costs and benefits changes continually as computer technology advances and different types of computer tools become technically feasible, then available and affordable, then necessary (figure 17.1). (By the beginning of the 1990s, basic word-processing and two-dimensional drafting tools seemed commonplace necessities in most practice contexts; three-dimensional modeling, rendering, and animation tools were widely available and increasingly affordable; and advanced integrated systems built around relational

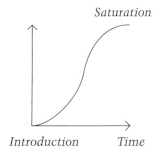

17.1
Diffusion of a technical innovation into practice

databases had reached the threshold of technical feasibility.) So, to practice effectively, designers can no longer rely on acquiring and learning to use established, traditional tools of the trade. They must be alert to the emergence of new computer tools, they must be prepared to invest strategically in these tools at appropriate moments, and they must continually devote some portion of their time to learning the effective use of these tools.

Automating Tasks

The most elementary way to approach investment in computer tools is (in the tradition of Charles Babbage's pioneering analyses of division of labor and automation, and subsequent uses of cost/benefit analysis in manufacturing industry) to break design processes down into discrete tasks, then to consider the availability of computer tools for performing these tasks and the measurable benefits and costs of applying those tools. This type of analysis is illuminating as far as it goes, but it should be used with caution, since it reveals only part of the picture. (Broader consideration may, for example, reveal that some tasks should be eliminated through reorganization of the design process rather than automated.)

Analysis of design tasks typically reveals that staff time and effort are expended at different rates at different stages of a design and construction process, as shown in figure 17.2. The usual pattern for traditional, manual design processes has been for the most intensive expenditure of staff time to occur during the design development and production documents phases (to use standard American Institute of Architects terminology), in which a great deal of detailed decision making is required and large quantities of information must be recorded. This suggests that the productivity benefits of task automation will mostly show up at these later stages, where even a small percentage reduction in expenditure of resources to complete the project is important.

The most obvious way to achieve productivity benefits in design development and documentation is to automate the document-production process—that is, to use computer drafting systems for efficient production of working

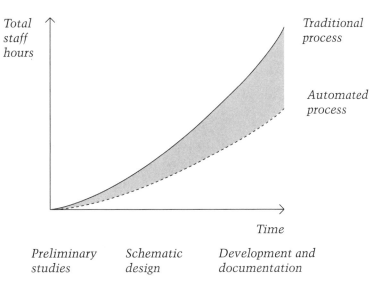

Total staff hours

Traditional process

Automated process

Time

Preliminary studies

Schematic design

Development and documentation

17.2
Productivity benefits become more significant as expenditure of staff resources accelerates

drawings and to use word processors to produce specifications and other text documents. Automated retrieval of construction product data, standard details, building code requirements, and other information needed in design development and document generation may yield further efficiencies. Associated cost and engineering calculations and routine layout tasks (such as layout of parking bays or routing of ducts) may also be automated for still higher productivity.

The reduction in total professional, technical, and clerical staff hours resulting from such automation reduces the cost of completing a project. Depending upon the conditions of practice, these savings might be passed on to a design firm's client in the form of reduced fees, or they might increase the firm's profit margin. Alternatively, they might be converted into added value on design products or services by keeping fee and profit margin constant and putting the resources that are thus freed into additional design exploration and analysis and more complete documentation.

Another way to accrue the productivity benefits of task automation is to increase the throughput of a design firm or department without increasing its size. This potential motivated considerable interest in computer-aided design in China in the 1980s, for example. A massive and urgent building program was being attempted, but there was a critical shortage of trained, experienced architects and engineers, so computer-aided design was seen as an immediate way of increasing the effectiveness of those skilled professionals who were available. Increasing throughput may also allow a design firm to increase its range of services without large staff increases: an architecture firm might, for example, use computerization as a vehicle for expanding into interiors and facilities management or into multimedia presentation services.

A third way to accrue benefits of task automation is in the form of reduced elapsed time to completion of a design. It is often particularly effective to automate a "bottleneck" task in the critical path of a project (figure 17.3) so that the overall schedule can be readjusted advantageously. This sort of indirect effect can be much more significant than the direct time saving resulting from automation of a task.

Reduction of elapsed time can be important in different ways in different contexts. A firm might, for example, want to enhance its capacity to compete for projects with very tight time schedules. Under highly inflationary economic conditions (such as those prevailing in Israel and much of Latin America through the 1970s and 1980s), reduction in elapsed time can produce substantial reductions in eventual construction costs. Where the relative costs of different construction methods (for example steel versus poured-in-place concrete) fluctuate significantly, it is valuable to have the ability to redesign rapidly in response. It is also valuable to have the capacity to respond, by rapid redesign and amendment of documents, to unexpected conditions encountered during construction: this can minimize losses resulting from such emergencies. It is not uncommon, for instance, for construction on a project to proceed ahead of securing necessary building approvals. If an approval is unexpectedly withheld, then on-site work is held up while the necessary redesign takes place, and every additional day of delay can be extremely expensive.

Usually it takes some time for productivity benefits resulting from automation of a task to begin to show up. Typically, there is an initial drop in productivity as designers

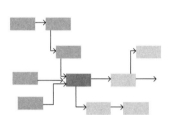

17.3
A bottleneck task

learn to use an unfamiliar new tool, then a steep increase as they find ways to exploit its potential, and finally a stabilization as maximum potential productivity is approached. If (for approximate accounting purposes) the cost of hardware, software, and supplies accrues at a uniform rate, the ratio of benefits to costs will evolve in roughly the fashion illustrated by figure 17.4. After a certain time the cost and benefit curves cross over, and payback on investment in the tool will have been achieved. The investment makes sense (in terms of this sort of analysis) only if payback can be achieved well before the tool becomes obsolete and needs to be replaced—typically in three to five years.

Reducing Communication Overhead

The communication overhead of a design project is the cost of recording information, moving it from place to place, and translating it into different formats as required by participants in the project. It tends to be a larger cost component on major projects than on small ones, since it depends on the number of active communication paths between participants, which increases exponentially rather than linearly with the number of participants (figure 17.5). Large projects sometimes collapse under the weight of communication overhead or must be organized with a strictly hierarchical chain of command that severely restricts cross-communication among participants.

Task automation in itself does little to reduce communication overhead. Indeed it may increase this overhead by requiring additional translation of information into and out of specialized formats: input cost and output plotting time were the downfall of many early attempts to automate the task of producing architectural working drawings. But substantial reduction *can* be achieved by combining task automation with electronic transfer of information. As the microcomputer era of computer-aided design (which largely focused on task automation) has given way to the network era, communication and coordination benefits have become increasingly significant motivations for investment in computer technology.

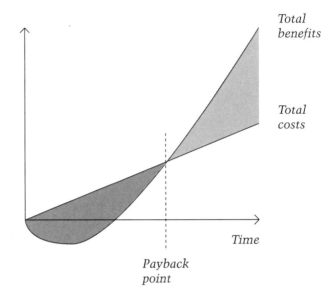

17.4
Evolving ratio of costs
to benefits

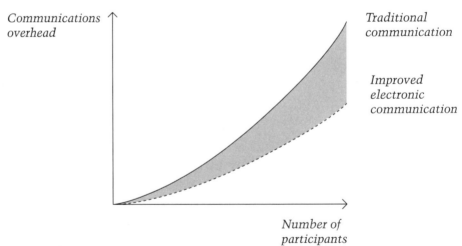

17.5
Benefits of improved
communications become
more significant as the
number of participants in a
design process increases

In many contexts, then, the obvious first step beyond task automation is to invest in some file translators. These are usually inexpensive and eliminate a significant component of communication overhead. An architecture firm and a consulting engineering firm that use different drafting systems might, for example, reduce the costs of doing business together by acquiring IGES or DXF translators to link these systems.

A larger investment, but one that usually pays off very quickly for a design organization, is in the infrastructure of a local area network—cables and connectors, a server, networking software, and staff support. This can eliminate many of the costs that would otherwise result from physical production and circulation of documents within the organization. And better communication usually leads to better coordination of work: a project manager can, for example, keep in closer touch with members of a large design team through electronic access to drawings and use of electronic mail. Use of workgroup support software to automatically check diaries and find meeting times, to support bulletin-board conferencing, and so on can yield even more effective coordination.

Further investment in electronic communications, extending the reach to remote locations, can not only improve coordination, but can also yield locational advantages. In the future many design firms will locate the bulk of their activities in areas where rents and labor costs are low and will communicate electronically with small offices located for more convenient access to clients and sites. When they are on the road, design team members will keep in touch by means of increasingly sophisticated laptop devices.

Highly integrated computer-aided design systems with centralized databases hold the greatest potential for reducing communication overhead. They are also more expensive to develop than less ambitious systems, make greater demands on computer resources, and tend to require greater learning time, so they usually represent much more substantial investments. Furthermore, they are most effective when there is major investment, as well, in

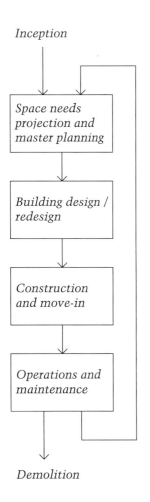

Inception

Space needs
projection and
master planning

Building design /
redesign

Construction
and move-in

Operations and
maintenance

Demolition

17.6
The facilities management
cycle

development of library databases to accompany them. This means that highly integrated systems pay off best where projects are large (so that the advantage of reducing communication overhead is very significant) and levels of workload are high, and are uneconomic for small design organizations with low workloads and mostly small projects. Consequently, attempts to achieve the benefits of broad integration were first made by public-sector organizations responsible for large building programs (such as housing and health authorities in the United Kingdom and the U.S. Army Corps of Engineers). Increasingly, the ability of private-sector design firms to compete for major projects will depend upon their capacity to maintain high enough workloads and high enough levels of ongoing investment in these sorts of systems. Successful major firms will become increasingly capital intensive.

Beyond design and construction, databases describing buildings and site layouts can be transferred to facilities-management systems. This eliminates the time-consuming and expensive step—traditionally necessary for implementation of a facilities-management system in an organization—of carrying out a detailed space and equipment inventory. If an accurate database is available from the start of occupancy, it need only be updated as alterations and additions to the facility and its stock of furniture and equipment are made. Increasingly, large companies, institutions, and government departments are seeking to manage the entire facilities cycle—space and equipment needs projection, project inception, design, construction, move-in, occupancy—in highly integrated fashion through use of an ongoing facilities database (figure 17.6). When they maintain this database internally (as they usually do), they have a very strong incentive to avoid communication overhead either by allocating design work to an internal facilities group with direct access to the database or by using external architects, engineers, and landscape architects with highly compatible computer-aided design systems.

Large design-and-build organizations are in the best position to reap the benefits of close integration between computer-aided design, computer-aided manufacturing, construction robotics, and automated facilities management. As these four technologies continue to mature, and as the linkages between them strengthen, such organizations are likely to become increasingly formidable competitors in the world construction market and to set the standards for the rest of the construction industry.

Eliminating Errors and Omissions

People producing information generate errors, and these errors have costs—both the direct costs of detection and correction and the potentially much larger indirect costs of the practical consequences that can follow from them if they are not detected. Text documents may have typographic errors that need to be removed before the documents can be sent out, numerical input files may have bad values that need to be detected and corrected before an analysis can be run, tabular reports may have spurious entries that need to be identified before the reports can be trusted as a basis for decision making, geometric models may have badly defined polygons that will yield unsatisfactory renderings or animations, and plan drawings may have mislocated elements that will result in costly change orders at the construction stage if they are not caught and corrected. In general, removal of errors adds value to information, while high error contents may make information valueless. So files and databases must (like computer programs) be debugged.

Errors in data may occur (with increasing degrees of insidiousness) at lexical, syntactic, and semantic levels (figure 17.7).

Most lexical errors, such as misspelled words in texts and typographic errors in numerical data, can be detected efficiently by software that checks items against lexicons and range bounds. This sort of software is usually inexpensive, and it eliminates a great deal of tedious and time-consuming proofreading work, so it is an excellent investment. Indeed, it is usually regarded as an essential feature of any well-designed application program.

Syntactic errors usually cannot be detected quite so easily. They enter data when sets of low-level entities do not fit together to produce higher-level entities that are well formed according to some definition: words may not

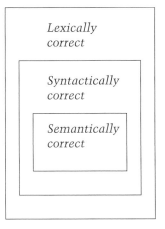

17.7
Levels of correctness

fit together to form grammatical sentences, vertices and edges may not fit together to produce planar polygons, polygons may not fit together to produce well-formed polyhedra, assemblies of solids may be self-intersecting, and so on. In general, they can be detected by procedures that attempt to parse constructions according to pre-defined syntactic rules: if parsing fails, then there are ill-formed objects present. Compilers for programming languages always perform syntax checks in this way. English syntax is more complex and less well defined than Pascal or Lisp syntax, so syntax checkers for English sentences are more difficult to implement satisfactorily. However, English syntax-checking and diagnostic systems for use with word processors now perform well enough to make their regular application worthwhile in many contexts.

In many types of geometric modeling, as we have seen, there are clear criteria of well-formedness. Polygon plans and maps should not have twisted polygons or slivers. Many solid-modeling and rendering programs require the elimination of nonplanar polygonal facets from models. The surface normals of surfaces that are to be shaded by a rendering program must point in the right direction—not, for example, into the interior of a closed solid. We usually require assemblies of solids to be non-self-intersecting: there should be no spatial clashes between beams and ducts, for example. Where these sorts of conditions cannot be rigorously excluded through use of appropriate operators, it is usually highly cost-effective to run checking and diagnostic software on geometric models. This eliminates crashing or unsatisfactory performance of analysis, rendering and animation software due to data errors and the attendant loss of time. It can also detect design errors— particularly spatial clashes—that would otherwise lead to construction problems. Sometimes, as is frequently the case in process plant design or with exceptionally complex architectural geometries, it may even be worthwhile to build a three-dimensional geometric model primarily for the purpose of checking a design's spatial well-formedness.

Higher levels of syntactic checking are feasible in principle and could yield major reductions in wasted effort. Many building code requirements dealing with issues such as access are essentially syntactic, for example, and designs could be automatically checked for compliance if they were represented in an appropriate sort of model. Similarly, plans are well formed with respect to basic programmatic requirements if room areas, proportions, and adjacencies are correct. There is also potential to check for buildability by testing for configurations that are realizable with particular component vocabularies and repertoires of construction machinery or robot actions. In the future designers will probably run proposals through very sophisticated syntax checkers as routinely as computer programmers now do this with program code. Clients will come to expect it, and professional standards of care will demand it.

Even sophisticated syntax checking will not catch all errors, however. It is certainly possible to write a grammatical sentence that makes no sense in a given context or a computer program that runs but produces erroneous results or a well-formed design that is ugly. These are logical or semantic errors—ones having to do with appropriateness of content. Human beings are very good at discovering them, but computer programs (at least as yet) are not: indeed, the famous Turing test for machine intelligence is based on the assumption that if an agent does not make detectable semantic errors in carrying on a free-flowing conversation, then it must have a high level of general intelligence. So it makes practical sense to devote machine cycles to the largely mechanical task of maintaining lexical and syntactic correctness, so freeing human designers to focus on the semantic level.

Reducing Uncertainty

Design requires decision making under uncertainty. One source of this uncertainty is poor data: designers must base decisions on incomplete knowledge of the needs of users and clients, of the performances of the materials and components that they specify, of the conditions that will be encountered in construction, of the actual costs of executing construction work, and of the conditions that will emerge in use. Furthermore, they must contend with random (though perhaps statistically predictable) events such as earthquakes, storms, fires, floods, and nuclear meltdowns. A second source is the imperfection of analysis and prediction techniques: the procedures that are available for predicting costs and performances of design proposals all have some margin of error (no matter how good the input data).

Consequently, performance and cost predictions for a design have some level of uncertainty, and execution carries some risk of dangerous or costly failure. And, where levels of uncertainty are high, it becomes impossible to discriminate between alternative design proposals on performance or cost grounds. Uncertainty and the risk of design failure can never be entirely eliminated, but it is a professional designer's duty to reduce them to acceptable levels. This is done by basing decisions on the best available information and making use of the best available analysis techniques to produce predictions. A design that is well analyzed and carries with it a low level of uncertainty about performance and cost is (other things being equal) a more valuable product than a less analyzed design with higher levels of uncertainty.

Use of computer software to perform the analyses needed to reduce uncertainty about cost and performance consequences of design decisions yields benefits of two kinds. First, and most obviously, it reduces the labor of carrying out the necessary calculations, and so allows the time of skilled engineers and cost analysts to be used to best effect. Second, and often much more importantly, it can reduce uncertainty in ways that would otherwise be infeasible: dynamic seismic analysis of large structural frames to predict behavior and assess the risk of failure during earthquakes, dynamic thermal simulations to predict yearly energy costs for buildings, and precise analyses of acoustic performance of complex auditoria would all be infeasible without sophisticated software and powerful computers to run it. In many cases, use of a computer allows the designer to go beyond simulation and prediction to the more computationally demanding operations of system optimization and sensitivity analysis—thus providing the designer with useful information about how much a proposal can be varied without unacceptable consequences. Sometimes, use of sophisticated computer-based performance and cost-prediction techniques has the major benefit of clearing the way for a project that would otherwise seem to be too much of a gamble.

Providing a better basis for choosing among design alternatives usually has a more beneficial effect at early stages in a design process than at late ones. If you could somehow plot the potential for improvement of performance and cost through better information and analysis, you would probably produce a curve much like that shown in figure 17.8. Major conceptual decisions about siting, orientation, massing, circulation and functional organization, and structural and mechanical systems are usually made at a very early stage and have an enormous impact on eventual cost and performance. Later choices are focused on refinement of detail within increasingly well-determined frameworks, so there is decreasing potential to achieve significant improvements. Thus the most effective way to use analysis and simulation programs is at the earliest possible moment, while it is still possible to respond to the results that they produce, and while there is much to be gained from doing so. These programs work best, in this role, if they present results in compelling graphic format that makes design implications clear.

Unfortunately, however, the schematic project descriptions available at early stages in a traditional design process do not support sophisticated performance and cost analysis: they simply do not contain enough information. One way to partially overcome this difficulty is to apply simplified, approximate analysis procedures that are suited to the available data: these may still yield very worthwhile uncertainty reductions. A second, potentially far more effective way is to use an integrated system that supports design in a hierarchy of abstractions (as discussed in Chapter 16), together with the use of default choices and values. This telescopes the design development process and makes a fully developed (if not final) description of a

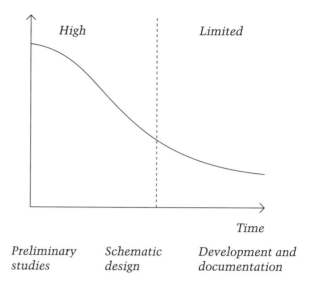

High　　　　　　Limited

Time

Preliminary　　Schematic　　Development and
studies　　　　design　　　　documentation

17.8
Potential for improvement
of performance and cost
through better information
and analysis

proposal available at a very early stage. So you do not have to go through a lengthy and expensive design development process only to discover that some early, fundamental decisions have produced unacceptable performance or cost penalties.

Availability of better performance- and cost-prediction technology leads inevitably to higher standards of care. The designers of the medieval cathedrals were not expected to produce detailed structural analyses of their proposals because the technology for doing so did not exist: there was no choice but to proceed under considerable uncertainty, and failures sometimes resulted. Today, the technology for producing structural analyses is very highly developed, and omission of its use where appropriate is regarded as professionally inexcusable. As new computer-based simulation, analysis, and optimization tools continue to develop, designers will frequently find that they have to obtain access to them if they want to stay in business.

Increasing Client and User Understanding

Technical representations such as plans and sections, while enormously informative to experienced professionals, are often poorly understood by clients and prospective users. Some designers regard this comprehension gap as an advantage—a way of establishing uniqueness and of maintaining a privileged professional position. (It leaves many clients and users with little option but to let the designer make all the decisions.) Other designers, however, want to establish close collaborative relationships with clients and users and will find it worthwhile to invest in computer tools that increase the level of comprehension about what is being considered and proposed. Certainly, clients and users do not like to be mystified and will usually consider more comprehensible presentation a significant value added to design services.

Since the conventions of photographic representation are universally familiar and well understood, realistically shaded perspective images and animation sequences are very effective for communication with clients and users. Instead of (or together with) a plan, a cutaway aerial perspective can be shown. Similarly, sectional perspectives and interior views can replace or supplement traditional sectional drawings (figure 17.9). Combinations of synthesized and scanned images can be used to produce very engaging views out windows or views of buildings or landscape proposals in site contexts. If the rendering process is fast enough (ideally real time), the designer can respond immediately to a client's request to see a proposal from another viewpoint or under different lighting conditions or as it would be experienced by walking along some specified path.

There are some interesting ways to structure presentations and discussions around combinations of physical three-dimensional models with fast perspective rendering and animation. For example, a three-dimensional digitizing wand can be used to indicate perspective viewpoints and directions on a physical model, so that the rendering system can then generate views that place you "inside" the model.

Sometimes—particularly where a proposal is complex or unusual in form or where the conditions of a project demand an unusual number of presentations—it is worthwhile to build three-dimensional surface or solid models solely for the purpose of generating presentations. The more views that are generated from a model, the better the

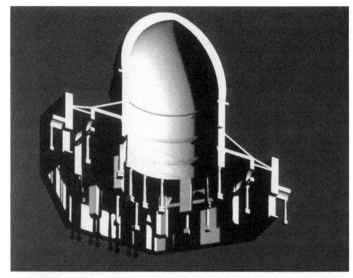

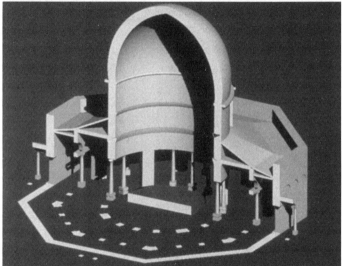

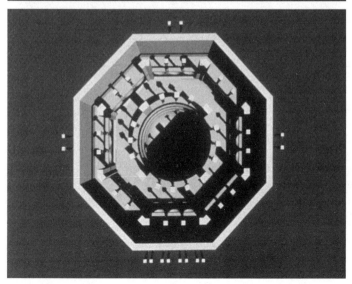

17.9
Unusual cutaway views aid
comprehension of spatial
relationships

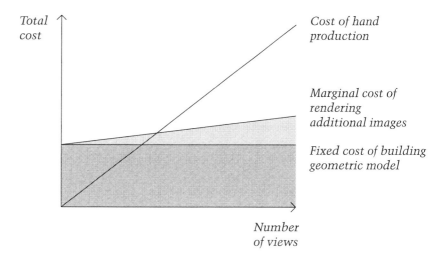

Total cost

Cost of hand production

Marginal cost of rendering additional images

Fixed cost of building geometric model

Number of views

17.10
Payoff from investment in building a model

payoff from the investment of effort in building the model (figure 17.10). If only a few views are needed, then it may be cheaper to produce them by hand, but when many views or animation frames are needed the computer has an overwhelming advantage. Where an integrated system with a three-dimensional database is used, the model exists anyway, and presentations can be generated as an almost free byproduct. (Compare this with the cost of presentation drawings produced by the best professional perspective delineators.)

Increasingly, client presentations are packaged as videotapes, slide sets, and interactive multimedia productions rather than traditional drawings and printed reports. In the future, clients may take home virtual reality presentations to explore at their convenience.

Providing Better Construction Documentation

Another way to add value to design services is to provide better, clearer construction documentation that makes it easier for construction contractors to see exactly what is required, to bid accurately, to plan effectively, and to eliminate errors on the job. (Better does not necessarily mean more detailed. Documents should not show things that are better left to the contractor to work out or that create unneccessary liability—even if the computer makes it easy to show these things.)

One kind of improvement is simply at the reprographic level. Traditional working drawings (particularly if they are produced under time pressure or by insufficiently skilled drafters) often suffer from defects such as poor line quality, sloppy line endings, low contrast, imprecise registration, and illegible lettering. But a plotter or laser printer (if it is maintained in good condition) can consistently produce dense, crisp, uniform lines, uniform hatching and screening, well-formed characters, and precise registration. In general, the use of this output technology is producing expectations of higher graphic quality in the design and construction fields.

Less obviously, perhaps, laser printers and similar devices provide much greater freedom to combine line graphics, halftones, and text than has been possible in the past. The traditional distinction between drawings, specifications, and door and window schedules to document a building largely derives from a distinction between two nineteenth-century technologies: the typewriter for text on small pages, and transparent negatives together with blueprint and blackline machines for line drawings on large pages. Laborious devices such as lettering stencils, rub-on and stick-on lettering, and typing on sticky-back paper have frequently been used when text and graphics needed to be combined. But a large-format laser or electrostatic plotter allows unlimited placement of print-quality text on drawings, and a small-format laser printer allows easy placement of diagrams and halftoned scanned photographs in specifications and the like. Gradually, as the inertia of tradition and institutional constraints is overcome, this will lead to new styles for the presentation of construction documents.

Furthermore, computer techniques inherently provide greater flexibility in the selection and formatting of information to appear on documents. At one level this is provided by the layering capabilities of a two-dimensional drafting system—much as, in the recent past, it was provided by the technique of pin-register photodrafting. At a potentially much higher level it is provided by the reporting capabilities of an integrated computer-aided design system.

The combination of more versatile graphics- and text-production capability with flexible formatting and reporting provides an important opportunity to rethink the entire issue of construction documentation. The content, format, and graphic style of construction documents should be based on rigorous consideration of what contractors and construction workers really need to see, not on the constraints imposed by now-obsolete document-production technology.

Gaining Access to Design Skills and Knowledge

Design skills and knowledge are not always available where they are needed, or the cost of gaining access to them may be prohibitively high. So, in some contexts, another motivation for investment in computer technology is to gain access to otherwise unobtainable skills and knowledge.

If you do not know how to detail a brick cavity wall for a cold climate, or a Roman Corithian capital, or the most efficient layout for a very narrow town house, you will probably want to refer to a standard layout or detail drawing. Designers have always collected, used, and in some cases published standard layouts and details, but practical difficulties of upkeep, dissemination, and retrieval have limited the scale on which this could effectively be done: printed books of details are hard to modify and keep up to date, while details drafted on vellum and stored in a plan chest are cumbersome to handle and have very limited circulation. A computerized storage, updating, and search and retrieval system can very significantly reduce the costs of storing and maintaining a collection of standard layouts and details and can increase its benefits by making the contents more readily accessible to designers. Increasingly, design organizations have the option of either developing their own collections of standard layouts and details or subscribing to commercial services. Such collections are most effective, of course, if they can serve as the library databases of integrated systems.

An alternative approach is to employ a program that, in response to specified requirements, generates rather than retrieves the layout or detail that is needed. Such programs can be written at several different levels of sophistication. They can be simple parametric procedures to provide basic dimensional adaptability, procedures with conditionals that make context-dependent choices, or procedures with sufficiently sophisticated control strategies to accomplish constraint satisfaction or optimization.

Traditionalists may be more comfortable with stored layout and detail collections, since this allows them to feel that they are making contact with sanctioned precedents and working within an established tradition. Modernists, on the other hand, may like the idea that a generative program solves a problem rationally, from first principles. In reality, the distinction just represents a different technical trade-off between storage and computing. If available memory is capacious and inexpensive, and examples of interest are easy to collect and record, then implementation of a storage and retrieval system is attractive. But, if processing power is inexpensive relative to memory capacity, and it is easy to see the general principles underlying a collection of examples, then it may be more attractive to implement a generative system. So you can store a catalog of variant house designs, or you can write a fairly simple generative program to synthesize them as required—the two strategies are functionally equivalent ways of producing what you need (figure 17.11). In practice, the balance is likely to shift gradually from storage and retrieval to generative systems as processing speed increases and as empirical design knowledge gives way to more theoretically structured knowledge.

17.11
Variant Queen Anne house designs produced by a generative program

Replacing and Multiplying Experts

Many design processes depend heavily on the contributions of technical experts. Such experts possess knowledge in specialized domains, such as the detailing of glass curtain walls, the selection of exterior finishes for wood construction, or the configuration of space and equipment for hospital operating theaters. They can provide solutions to problems, give advice, and justify their recommendations by providing reasons and arguments. The completeness of their knowledge and the flexibility of their reasoning capabilities enable them to go far beyond producing stock responses to generic contexts or applying standardized procedures.

Unfortunately, however, such experts are often in short supply. They are not always available when and where they are needed, and accumulated expertise may be lost entirely when an expert leaves an organization. Under these circumstances, there is potential benefit in replacing human experts with expert systems—computer programs that possess similar specialized knowledge and reasoning ability.

The basic structure of a typical rule-based expert system is shown in figure 17.12. At the foundation are a facts base (a collection of assertions about the domain of interest) and a knowledge base (a collection of rules for deriving new facts about that domain). These are operated on by an inference mechanism that can derive conclusions (needed facts) by applying rules from the knowledge base to given facts—some of which may come from the facts base, and some of which may be given in a problem statement. Associated with the inference mechanism is an explanation facility that can trace and display chains of inference in order to explain and justify conclusions. A knowledge-acquisition facility provides tools for capturing relevant rules, encoding them in some suitable fashion, and entering them into the knowledge base. Finally, the interface provides a way for users to pose questions and to receive answers and explanations.

Expert systems can stand alone, as independent applications, but it often makes sense in design to integrate them with geometric-modeling systems. Under this arrangement, facts about a design are automatically extracted from the geometric model to provide a basis for derivation of critical conclusions about it. Furthermore, derived remarks and suggestions about configurations, materials, and dimensions may be presented in the form of annotated or amended versions of the geometric model.

It is possible to build an expert system in a programming language such as C, Lisp, or Prolog. But expert system shells—systems with empty facts bases and knowl-

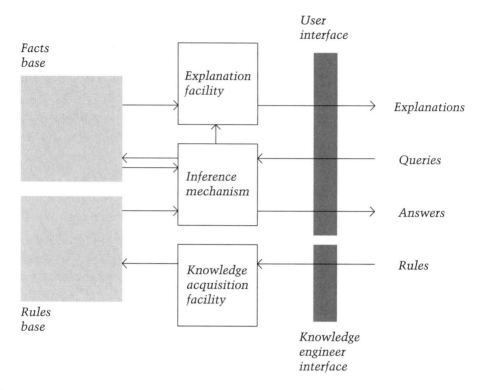

Facts base

Explanation facility

User interface

Explanations

Inference mechanism

Queries

Answers

Knowledge acquisition facility

Rules

Rules base

Knowledge engineer interface

17.12
Structure of a rule-based expert system

edge bases—usually make the task very much easier and quicker. With a shell, development of an expert system becomes a task of collecting, encoding, and entering a sufficient number of facts and rules to provide worthwhile expertise in the domain of interest.

Expert-system shell technology developed rapidly in the 1980s, and this supported development of practical expert systems (with varying degrees of success) in many domains. Examples in specialized design domains include systems for configuring Vax computers at Digital Equipment Corporation, designing paper feeders for photocopying machines, selecting and placing fire alarm equipment in buildings, selecting fasteners for aircraft bodies, configuring racks in space stations, selecting drilling tools and operations for numerically controlled milling machines, generating finite-element meshes from geometric models of parts, laying out traditional Tibetan *thangka* paintings, and answering questions about fire code requirements for buildings.

Not all expert systems deal with such esoteric topics. One of the most interesting architectural systems to date is intended for use on the sales floors of lumberyards and hardware stores and assists in the design of simple timber decks. Using a simple interactive graphic interface, a customer specifies the basic plan geometry and a few other parameters. The system then applies elementary rules of timber construction to "build" the deck in three dimensions, display a rendered perspective view, calculate the amount of lumber required, and apply a current lumber price list to yield the total material cost.

Many designers and traditional design firms rely on accumulated human expertise to give them a competitive edge in specialized types of work. In the future they will face increasingly effective competition from organizations that have invested in development and maintenance of machine-processable knowledge bases.

Expanding Design Boundaries

The domains that designers explore in search of interesting and appropriate proposals for particular contexts are always bounded in some way by the elements and operators of the representations that they use. Furthermore, there are always computational constraints—limits on the amounts of available memory and processing power—that limit the amount of searching possible in the time available to produce a solution. So the final motivation for investing in computer technology to support design, and potentially the most fascinating of all, is to open up new domains for design exploration and to harness machine power to allow more extensive and exhaustive searches than would otherwise be possible.

Traditional drafting instruments, for example, handle only a very restricted formal domain with sufficient efficiency to allow practical design exploration. In other words, the design-exploration processes that they support are tool bound. Constructions of straight lines and small-radius arcs present little difficulty, but complex constructions of large-radius arcs soon become impractical: compasses do not open wide enough, and drawing surfaces do not extend far enough to provide places to plant their points. But even an elementary computer-drafting system has no such limitations and readily supports design within a language of large-radius arcs (figure 17.13).

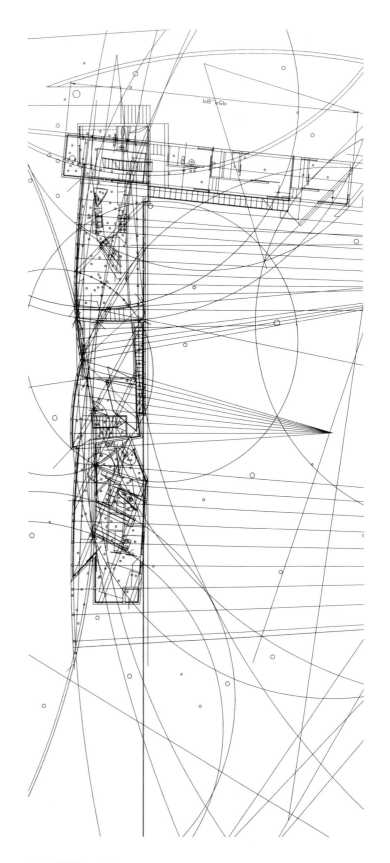

17.13
Computer-generated layout
drawing using large-radius
arcs

Elliptical, parabolic, and spline curves are even more difficult to handle with traditional instruments. There is no easy way to offset these curves to describe walls of constant thickness, for example, or to divide them into segments of equal length. But appropriate computer tools allow a designer to manipulate very complex curves and curved surfaces with almost as much facility as straight lines, plane surfaces, and simple arcs. Douglas Cardinal's Museum of Man in Hull, Quebec was one of the first major buildings to exploit this freedom to explore unconventional architectural geometries.

Even when adequate instruments are available, most practical design processes are compute bound: there is simply not sufficient time to develop and explore a wide enough range of alternatives and refinements, and designers are left at the end with the feeling that they could have done better if they had more time at their disposal. Shrewd designers can now loosen computational constraints on design exploration by harnessing machine power to perform design operations more efficiently, by generating ranges of variants automatically, and by executing automated searches for objects and configurations that satisfy specified requirements.

Other design processes are memory bound: there is not enough space to record ideas. (You can develop an idea only so far on a table napkin or a drink coaster. Fairly soon, you need a large sheet of paper.) Memory bounds must have seemed very close when architects had to draw on scarce materials such as papyrus and parchment. Now paper is cheap, but it is an unwieldly medium for storage and retrieval of large amounts of graphic information. A designer can now substitute high-speed electronic memory for paper, and so gain practical access to larger library and reference databases, store more detailed design descriptions, and record far more sketches and developments of alternatives than even the largest stack of yellow tracing paper can contain.

In general, appropriate use of computer tools removes constraints on the capacities of designers to pursue ideas. This does not guarantee a better result, but, other things being equal, it can allow unskilled and inexperienced designers to produce more adequate work, and it can help ambitious, highly skilled designers to accomplish breakthroughs that would otherwise have eluded them.

Acquiring or Building a System

The simplest, least risky way for an individual designer or small design firm to begin investing in computer tools, and thus gain some of the benefits that we have considered, is to buy a standard personal computer with a laser printer and a modem, plus a small collection of the popular, inexpensive application programs that are distributed by mail-order firms and through computer stores (figure 17.14). A basic program collection might comprise a word processor, a two-dimensional drafting program, a simple three-dimensional modeling and rendering program, a page-layout program, and a spreadsheet. Such programs are usually straightforward to install and are either self-teaching or can be learned from the manual. File-management and data-transfer capabilities in this sort of environment are usually minimal, but this does not matter much when the number of users and the scale of projects are small.

A larger organization might acquire a complete, multiseat computer-aided design system from a turnkey system vendor. Turnkey systems integrate hardware, software, user-training services, and system-support services into a package available from a single source. Compared to personal computers running shrinkwrapped software, these systems typically have greater capacity, wider ranges of functionality, and much more complete integration. This usually comes, of course, at a substantially higher price.

Where a design organization has enough work to justify the investment and can find a turnkey system that matches its needs sufficiently closely, such a system can be an excellent investment. It allows a sensible division of labor—the design firm can concentrate on design issues while the system vendor solves technical computing problems—and is particularly appropriate for organizations that mostly do fairly standardized work, do not have much internal computer expertise, and cannot or do not want to

*Personal
computer
system*

*Turnkey
system*

*Heterogeneous,
custom-
integrated
system*

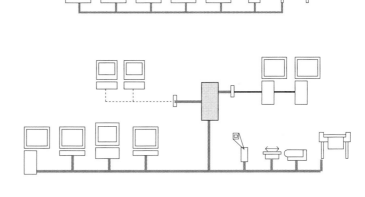

17.14
Basic CAD system
configurations

develop such expertise. There are, however, some risks. Since the turnkey system vendor must attempt to sell to a sufficiently large market in order to recover development costs and make a profit, there is a tendency to over-standardize and thus not match individual user needs closely enough. (This is a particular problem for architects and landscape architects, since many large turnkey computer-aided design systems are designed primarily to serve the needs of manufacturing industry, and do not adapt sufficiently gracefully to architectural and landscape applications.) Furthermore, by acquiring a turnkey system, training staff to use it, and developing a growing body of work on the system (work that is usually difficult to transfer to other systems), the design organization becomes heavily dependent on the system vendor. If that vendor goes out of business, ceases to provide adequate service, or does not invest sufficiently in improving the system, then the design organization faces the possibility of an expensive and disruptive change of system.

Design organizations that do more varied and specialized work are less likely to be well served by turnkey systems. Thus, if they have or can acquire sufficient internal computer expertise, they may find that building their own system from commercially available modules is a more attractive option. Coarse-grained but fairly effective integration can be achieved, without the need for advanced technical expertise or a great deal of development work, by linking a server, workstations or personal computers, and necessary peripheral devices in a network, relying on standard network operating software for file transfer from machine to machine, and building up a kit of file translators for transfer of work from application to application. Such networks can integrate machines from different vendors, support multiple operating systems (Unix, Dos, and Macintosh for example), and can include both sophisticated workstation CAD systems and inexpensive personal computer applications. Thus they can avoid reliance on a single vendor, and they can provide working environments tailored to the different needs of different people in a design organization.

The most ambitious, and certainly by far the most expensive, approach is to begin with an operating system and a programming language and attempt to create a completely new system. Before the computer-aided design software industry developed, design organizations frequently attempted this. It provides the opportunity to tailor a system precisely to an organization's needs, to integrate it thoroughly, and to implement innovative ideas. And it can seem feasible when skilled and enthusiastic programmers produce exciting prototypes fairly quickly. But it rarely succeeds in the face of competition from commercial products that have large installed bases and are supported by organizations with the capacity to sustain high levels of investment in research and development.

Over time, in an effort to combine the strengths of all these approaches, a design organization is likely to evolve a hybrid system. Some aspects of its work will be handled by well-known, standard software running on inexpensive personal computers. Some will be handled by more specialized turnkey systems that form islands of high integration within the general network and with some data transfer paths to and from it. And some will be performed by proprietary programs, customized versions of commercial software, and expert systems that embody some of the organization's unique expertise.

	Personal system	Turnkey system	Heterogeneous network
Level of investment	Low	High	Incremental
Capacity	Low	High	Incremental
Functionality	Low	High	Incremental
Potential for customization	Low	Low	High
Management complexity	Low	Low	High

17.15
Basic CAD system characteristics

Whatever the strategy, the advantages of a highly standardized system must be traded off against those of a more heterogeneous and flexible system that adapts itself to individual designer needs (figure 17.15). Standardization greatly reduces the cost and complexity of system management, but can burden designers with tools and interfaces that are not well adapted to their individual needs. A heterogeneous system usually requires greater management attention and a higher level of management sophistication, but provides better opportunities to take advantage of technical innovations as they emerge, and allows more precise tailoring of computer facilities to roles within the organization.

Costs and Cost Recovery

The basic costs of acquiring and using computer-aided design technology are, obviously enough, those of hardware, software, maintenance and supplies, and staff time (including system management and user training). As the technology has evolved, the relative magnitudes of these costs have altered, so associated accounting and cost-recovery practices have changed as well.

In the early days of computing, hardware costs dominated. This motivated arrangements designed to maximize use of available hardware resources. Typically, large time-sharing mainframes supported numerous remote terminals and processed queued batch jobs. Costs were recovered by charging for computer time (down to fractions of a second) and for disk storage, and service bureaus sold computer time. By the beginning of the 1990s, however, hardware costs had declined greatly and only very large and expensive supercomputers, very specialized peripheral devices such as image setters and laser cutters, and similar anomalies were being handled in this way. Most personal computers, workstations, and related peripheral devices were being acquired for use on an as-needed basis (like automobiles) over a three- to five-year working life. Computer time was increasingly being treated as a virtually free resource: careful accounting of it was no longer thought worthwhile, and direct charging for use of it on design projects was becoming rare.

The cost of developing software has always been very high: a major piece of software can cost as much to develop and bring to market as a large high-rise office building. A software developer can attempt to recover this cost by making a relatively small number of sales at a high price or a larger number of sales at a lower price. Vendors of sophisticated workstation software for specialized applications typically opt for the former strategy, while vendors of more generic personal-computer software products (such as general-purpose word processors or two-dimensional drafting systems) often mass market these as inexpensive products. Design organizations that have very high workflows, or very particular software needs, may find it worthwhile to pay high prices for powerful software that is precisely tailored to meet their requirements—or even to produce proprietary software for their own exclusive use. But smaller design organizations usually must rely on more generic, mass-market software products. Indeed, it was the emergence of a wide range of mass-market software products, as the personal-computer revolution gathered momentum in the 1980s, that finally made computer-aided design feasible for most architects, landscape architects, and urban designers.

Hardware maintenance, software maintenance (fixing bugs, acquiring and installing new releases of software, and so on), and supplies such as paper and disks constitute a significant ongoing cost component in computer operations. In some contexts, randomly occurring system downtime can be tolerated, so hardware repairs and software upgrades need only be made as malfunctions occur. But design organizations that work to tight deadlines cannot afford unexpected work delays due to computer downtime and must guard against them by budgeting for and providing sufficient redundant capacity, performing systematic preventive maintenance, and purchasing rapid-response emergency maintenance services.

In the days when computer-aided design systems were difficult and expensive to use, they often required specially trained operators. The time spent in training these operators, and the wages paid to them for their work on design projects, were substantial additions to the cost of doing design work on a computer. Furthermore, investment in operator training was risky, since operators (with skills in high demand) often chose to leave for other jobs. But as computer skills have become more widespread and as systems have become both less expensive and easier to use, there has been decreasing need for specialized operators, and the associated cost has diminished or been eliminated. Since I am entering this text into a simple word processor as I compose it, for example, I do not have to pay a typist and I do not have to correct the typist's inevitable errors and misunderstandings. (I am not nearly as fast as a professional typist using a more advanced word processor, but elimination of extra work beats speeding it up.) Similarly, when an architect enters design decisions directly into a drafting or geometric-modeling system, there is no need to pay a computer drafting technician to translate pencil sketches into keystrokes or mouse clicks, nor is there need to inspect and correct the technician's work.

While operator costs tend to fall as an organization's use of computer technology matures, the costs of managing the computer system tend to increase: strategic planning for hardware and software acquisition, purchasing and installation, and day-to-day management of extensive computer resources become increasingly critical and time-consuming tasks. This leads to a structure very different from that of a traditional labor-intensive design firm, with its large technical and clerical staff supporting a few senior designers. The mature computer-based design firm is likely to be far more capital intensive, with few technical and clerical staff but a carefully planned and well-managed computer system maximizing the effectiveness of those skilled and experienced designers who have something unique to offer. In this sort of firm, costs are recovered and a profit is made by marketing the skills of its designers at a sufficiently high price—not by charging for large amounts of technical and clerical staff time.

Measurement

It is common practice to measure the benefits and costs of computer technology against a baseline of established practices. In the early days of computer drafting, for example, expected costs of entering and plotting sets of working drawings with a CAD system were frequently compared to the established costs of drafting them by hand. This provided an apparently objective basis for making investment decisions, and for passing on costs and savings.

Such measurement can be very misleading, however, since new technologies and methods may make old baselines irrelevant. (Capture of geometric data during the design phase may reduce or eliminate the need for data entry at the documentation stage, for example, and CAD/CAM and construction robotics may generate demands for information in very different formats from that of traditional working drawings.) Even worse, inappropriate measurement may entrench practices that have outlived their usefulness, and so prevent full realization of the potential benefits of computer technology. In general, clear goals for the future provide a better foundation for strategic investment than baselines from the past.

Conclusion

Production of designs for artifacts and places is an economic activity that usually takes place in a highly competitive environment. Designers and design organizations compete for work on the basis of their ability to deliver designs of high quality, to deliver them at acceptable cost within an acceptable time, and to market their capabilities effectively. As a designer or as a manager of a design organization, you can attempt to compete more effectively by investing in and applying computer technology.

Sometimes a cultural and economic environment demands innovative designs that respond to new needs, exploit new technical or economic opportunities, or fit unique contexts. In this circumstance, strategic investment in computer-aided design technology should emphasize sophisticated instruments that make optimal use of the unique capabilities of exceptionally talented designers—like a Steinway grand in the hands of a great pianist. Ambitious designers who want to position themselves to do innovative work need to make the case that they are worth the necessary investment in computer support.

Sometimes the environment demands commodity designs—useful standard products, generated in quantity like pork bellies or silicon chips, that must be ready at the right time and the right price if you want to profit from producing them. The emphasis in this case is on parametric variation and assembly of standard parts, efficient performance of routine analyses, rapid production of documentation, and close quality control. Strategic investment, then, should emphasize development of appropriate library databases, exploitation of an inventory of previous work, streamlining workflow, and achievement of economies of scale.

And sometimes the environment demands facilitation of do-it-yourself design. Here the need is for inexpensive systems that require little skill to operate but produce acceptable results—like point-and-shoot cameras. Such systems are of limited use to professionals, but they can make it possible for people to design their own decks, kitchens, office layouts, and so on. The role of a professional designer in this context is to specify the vocabulary of components, the assembly rules, and the analysis procedures that form the basis of the system—in effect, to franchise a design style.

Your cultural and economic ambitions will suggest the most appropriate ways for you to invest in computer-aided design technology and to educate yourself to take advantage of it. You may want to be like a performer competitively seeking opportunities to play the best instruments in the best places, like a hog farmer efficiently producing commodities to fill an ongoing need, like George Eastman promising that with his Kodak cameras "You push the button, we do the rest"—or you may create a role that nobody has yet imagined.

Suggested Readings

ASCE Computer Practices Committee. 1976. "Computer Pricing Policy and Methods." *American Society of Civil Engineers Professional Activities Journal* (October 1976): 437–46.

Blau, Judith. 1984. *Architects and Firms.* Cambridge, Mass.: The MIT Press.

Coyne, R. D., M. A. Rosenman, A. D. Radford, M. Balachandran, and J. S. Gero. 1990. *Knowledge-Based Design Systems.* Reading, Mass.: Addison-Wesley.

Gutman, Robert. 1988. *Architectural Practice: A Critical View.* Princeton: Princeton Architectural Press.

International Joint Conference on CAD and Robotics in Architecture and Construction. 1986. *CAD and Robotics in Architecture and Construction: Proceedings of the Joint International Conference at Marseilles, 25–27 June 1986.* New York: Nichols Publishing Company.

Landsdown, John. 1982. *Expert Systems: Their Impact on the Construction Industry.* London: Royal Institute of British Architects.

Landsdown, John, and C. Roast. 1987. "The Possibilities and Problems of Knowledge-Based Systems for Design." *Environment and Planning B: Planning and Design,* vol. 14(3): 255—266.

18

PROTOTYPING

The computer's capacity to reduce design, fabrication, and construction costs by integrating processes around a digital representation need not be limited by the traditional boundaries of the designer's role. In particular, it is now increasingly feasible and economically attractive to drive computer-controlled production machinery directly from CAD models—thus eliminating or greatly reducing production of traditional drawings. Such CAD/CAM (computer-aided design/computer-aided manufacturing) processes have long been common in manufacturing industry, and by the early 1990s they were beginning to penetrate into architecture. The basic CAD/CAM information flow is illustrated in figure 18.1.

One use of CAD/CAM technology is to produce small-scale physical models in materials such as plastic—not the material of the finished artifact; this is known as rapid prototyping. Some rapid prototyping techniques can be used to fabricate components in metal and other materials of finished products. And at a larger scale, CAD/CAM machinery can be used to produce full-size construction components. Finally, the designer's geometric model might be used on the construction site, in conjunction with electronic surveying devices and robotic machinery to position and assemble components.

CAD/CAM can not only cut costs and shorten schedules by reducing communications overhead; it can also

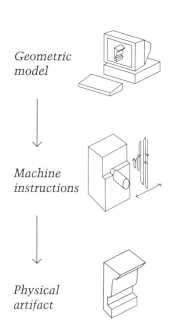

Geometric model

Machine instructions

Physical artifact

18.1
CAD / CAM
information flow

417

reduce a designer's dependence on standardized, mass-produced construction components. It allows fabrication of complex shapes that would be very difficult or impossible to describe and produce in traditional ways. And it links versatile computer-aided design systems directly to flexible production machinery—so eliminating high tooling costs and making short production runs feasible.

Weaving and Embroidering

The story of CAD/CAM technology began, in the nineteenth century, with the Jacquard loom. This device was digitally controlled by means of punch cards (figure 18.2) and could be used to produce arbitrarily complex woven patterns. These patterns could be altered simply by changing the information encoded on the cards. Modern, computer-controlled weaving machines—used, for example, to produce carpets with custom patterns—are direct descendents of the Jacquard loom; the basic difference is that the control information is now encoded electronically, rather than as punched holes.

18.2
Machine instructions in a Jacquard loom

Today, programmable embroidery machines are commonly used to produce arbitrary patterns or text on cloth. Models designed for use in embroidery job-shops are typically driven by personal computers, and reproduce images in standard file formats such as TIFF or Postscript. Thus they link a fabric production technology directly to paint and illustration software.

Printed Patterns

Laser and inkjet printers can also be thought of as descendents of the Jacquard loom. Under computer control, they produce images on paper that can later be transferred to materials such as cloth and metal. Some specialized printers are now capable of transferring images directly to materials other than paper.

In architectural model-making, printers can effectively be used to generate surface patterns and textures. For example, a curtain-wall pattern can be printed out on paper, then the sheets can be mounted on cardboard and used to produce a quick study model of a highrise building (figure 18.3). This technique is particularly useful for evaluating the effects of variation in proportions and colors.

Plotted Templates

Printers and plotters can also be used to produce accurate templates for cutting sheet material. Figure 18.4, for example, illustrates the process of converting a surface or solid model into a collection of separate polygonal shapes, laying out these shapes on a sheet, cutting out corresponding pieces of cardboard, and finally assembling the pieces into a three-dimensional physical model. Using standard CAD system functions, a designer may select and lay out copies of the polygons needed to produce such a model. Alternatively, algorithms for performing these tasks automatically are quite straightforward to implement.

Models of curved surfaces can be produced from flat sheet material by following the procedure illustrated in figure 18.5. First, the surface is triangulated—a process that can be carried out manually by the designer, or by application of a suitable automatic triangulation procedure (see Chapter 10, page 198). Next, the triangulated surface is unfolded into strips, and these are then plotted. Finally, the strips are cut out, scored along the triangulation lines, bent into shape, and fitted together. If the work has been done accurately, the bent strips almost miraculously fit together, and the required shape emerges. Models of complex, multi-faceted polyhedral objects can similarly be produced by unfolding, scoring and cutting sheet material, and finally folding and reassembling as illustrated in figure 18.6.

In general, there are many different ways to unfold a given curved surface or polyhedral object. Usually it is best to minimize cutting and maximize scoring, since this simplifies the subsequent assembly process. Some CAD systems facilitate the process by providing automatic unfolding functions.

Plotted templates are not only useful in construction of scale models from flat sheet materials, but also in production of stick assemblies such as roof truss models; the truss layout is simply plotted to scale, and then used

Print

Mount and cut

Overlay

Assemble

18.3
Printing and cutting a curtain-wall pattern

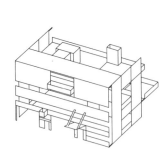

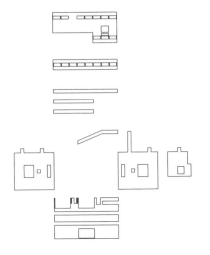

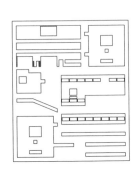

a. Three-dimensional model

b. Primary surfaces unfolded

c. Pieces composed on sheet for cutting

18.4
Converting a model to polygonal shapes and arranging for cutout

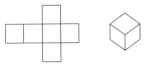

18.5
Folding strips of polygons into regular three-dimensional forms

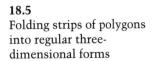 

18.6
Unfolding curved surfaces into strips of polygons

as a base for cutting, positioning, and gluing members. Clothing designers can use computer-plotted templates for fabric cutting. And construction component fabricators may use full-scale plotted templates to control cutting of plywood, sheet metal, and so on.

Computer-Controlled Cutters

An obvious step beyond computer-plotted templates is to make direct use of computer-controlled cutters for sheet material. These devices are closely analogous to the familiar electromechanical plotters that have been around for many years, except that they use some sort of cutting head in place of a pen.

Almost any sort of cutting technology—laser, bandsaw, water jet, flame, hot wire, and so on—can be used in this sort of cutter. And with the right cutting technology, almost any kind of sheet material, from small pieces of paper to large plates of inch-thick steel, can be handled.

The mechanism of a computer-controlled cutter must, in some way, provide two-axis motion of the sheet material relative to the cutting head. One possibility is to keep the sheet stationary and to move the cutting head along x and y axes, as in a flatbed plotter (figure 18.7a). This approach can yield high accuracy, but it limits the size of the sheet to the size of the bed, and some cutting technologies may not be very suitable for use with a moving head. A second, converse possibility is to keep the head stationary and to move the bed in x and y axes (figure 18.7b). And a third possibility is to move the head along one axis while moving the sheet along the other (figure 18.8c); this has the advantage of handling sheets that are limited to the width of the bed in one dimension but are unlimited in the other.

Precise, small-scale laser cutters are increasingly commonly used to cut thin sheets of cardboard, wood, plastic, and metal for architectural models. These devices can also emboss by cutting part-way through. They can render fine detail with great precision, and can be used to produce models of very high accuracy. At a slightly larger scale, computer-controlled cutters are employed to produce cut-plastic characters for signage, architectural ornament, and the like.

a. Moving head

b. Moving bed

c. Combined motion

18.7
XY flatbed motion

18.8
An early demonstration of computer-controlled cutting at architectural scale

One of the first projects to demonstrate the architectural potential of computer-controlled cutting was carried out by Ronald Resch at the University of Utah in the 1970s (figure 18.8). He designed a complex polyhedral monument (on the theme of a Ukranian Easter egg) using a CAD system, then cut the sheet-metal surface elements on a computer-controlled device.

Since cutters are so much like plotters, the information needed to control a cutter is basically just a plot file, and fabricators who provide cutting capabilities typically accept standard CAD-system plot files. Since any line will actually be cut, however, it is necessary to eliminate superfluous lines from drawings and to take some care with the sequence in which lines are cut.

Multi-Axis Milling

Multi-axis milling of three-dimensional solids generalizes the idea of two-dimensional sheet cutting. Drills and circular saws are one-axis devices that can remove material along a line to a specified depth. As we have seen, computer-controlled cutters are two-axis devices that can remove polygons of material. So, three-axis milling devices can be produced essentially by using drill-bits (that can be raised and lowered) as the cutting heads in computer-controlled cutters (figure 18.9). These three-axis devices can thus remove specified volumes of material from solids.

A typical three-axis milling machine has a rotating head into which various different bits can be inserted. Large bits are used for rapid, coarse removal of material, while smaller bits are used for rendering fine detail. With the right sort of cutting head and sufficient cutting power, shapes can successfully be milled from wax, plastic, metal, stone, and many other materials.

The starting point for a three-axis milling process is a surface or solid model that specifies the shape to be produced. This must be converted into a path that the cutting head will follow in order to produce the piece, and that path must be expressed as a sequence of coded motion instructions that the machine can execute (figure 18.10). In simple cases, the cutting path may be computed auto-

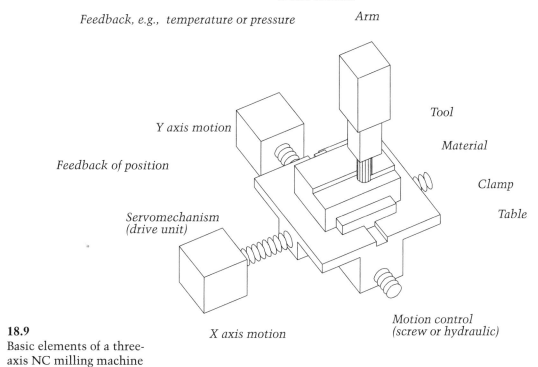

Z axis motion

Feedback, e.g., temperature or pressure

Arm

Tool

Y axis motion

Material

Feedback of position

Clamp

Table

Servomechanism (drive unit)

X axis motion

Motion control (screw or hydraulic)

18.9
Basic elements of a three-axis NC milling machine

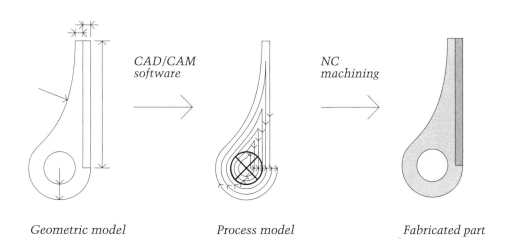

CAD/CAM software

NC machining

Geometric model

Process model

Fabricated part

18.10
Machine toolpath instructions

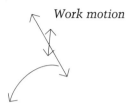

Work motion

Machine motion

18.11
The three axes of a lathe

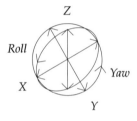

18.12
Five degrees of freedom

matically from the CAD model, but the task of determining appropriate cutting paths can be a far from trivial one, so paths must often be programmed explicitly by skilled operators. Finally, the instructions are carried out—a process that can take many minutes or even hours for complex pieces in materials that require slow cutting.

The range of shapes that can be produced by such a three-axis machine is obviously limited, so variants and elaborations of the three-axis machine have developed to produce classes of shapes not in this range. Lathes, for example, are machines that have two axes of translational motion for the cutting head and one axis of rotational motion for the piece (figure 18.11). Thus they can be used to convert digitally-modeled profiles into solids of rotation.

A four-axis milling machine adds an axis of rotation to the capabilities of a three-axis machine, and a five-axis machine provides two rotation axes (figure 18.12). This can be accomplished by rotating the cutting head, or the bed that holds the piece, or both. Thus the head can reach parts of the piece that are out of reach to a three-axis machine, and shapes with so-called "under-cuts" can successfully be produced (figure 18.13). Similar results can sometimes be accomplished by manually repositioning a piece on a three-axis machine, but this requires an operator intervention that slows the process, and it risks introducing inaccuracies.

18.13
Undercuts

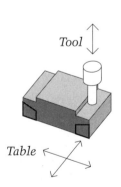

Tool

Table

a. A three-axis machine cannot reach undercuts

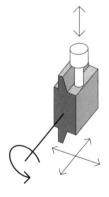

b. An additional degree of freedom solves the problem

Some early experiments with using computer-controlled, multi-axis milling machines to produce architectural simple models from CAD databases were carried out in the 1970s (figure 18.14). Since then, both CAD and milling technology have improved considerably, and it is now possible to produce models of considerable complexity in this way (figure 18.15).

Stone cutting is the most obvious application of automated milling technology to producing full-scale architectural components. This is particularly attractive when the stone shapes are complex and not very repetitive. Some of the stones for New York's Cathedral of Saint John the Divine, and for the columns needed to complete Antoni Gaudi's Sagrada Familia Church in Barcelona, were cut in this way. But the first comprehensive and systematic use of CAD/CAM technology to produce the architectural stonework for a major project was on the Disney Concert Hall, Los Angeles, by Frank Gehry (figure 18.16). Here, the complex, double-curved surfaces of the stone-clad volumes were modeled using an aerospace curved-surface modeling system, then the CAD model was used directly to control the milling machines of an Italian stone supplier. The milled stone pieces were eventually shipped to the Los Angeles construction site where they were positioned and fixed in place on steel frames.

18.14
An early demonstration of computer-controlled milling in plastic foam

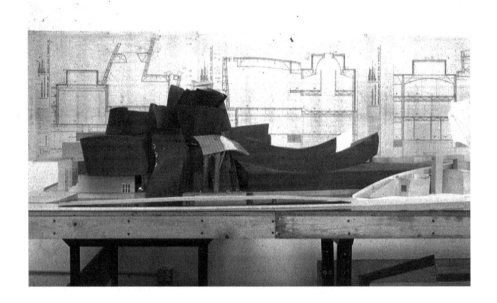

18.15
Architectural model
cut from foam by a
five-axis NC machine

18.16
NC-milled curved
stonework for the
Disney Concert Hall

Incremental Forming

Incremental forming processes are the converse of milling processes; instead of gradually revealing three-dimensional shapes by removing material from a solid, they add material piece-by-piece in order to build up shapes. Whereas milling machines replicate some of the capabilities of a stone-carver's or wood-carver's traditional tools, incremental forming devices are much closer to the process of building up a clay model from small blobs, or to assembling a large sculpture from lots of tiny Lego blocks.

The traditional architect's technique of building up a topographic model, layer-by-layer, from contour-shaped sheets of cardboard is a simple and rather crude example of incremental forming. The process of contour modeling can partially be automated by using plotted templates or a computer-controlled laser cutter to produce the contour layers, which are then positioned manually and glued in place. With sufficient patience, you can build up three-dimensional shapes of arbitrary complexity in this way (figure 18.17).

The rapid-prototyping process of paper lamination more fully automates this layer-by-layer process, as illustrated in figure 18.18. The layers are made from paper board with heat-sensitive adhesive backing, and a computer-controlled laser is used to cut the outline of each layer.

Fused deposition machines use robot arms or similar effectors to trace shapes and deposit liquid wax (figure 18.19). A wax filament is fed to the effector where the wax is heated before placement. Shapes are again built up layer-by-layer, and the deposited wax droplets fuse to previous layers.

Stereolithography machines exploit the properties of photosensitive liquid that solidifies when exposed to laser light (figure 18.20). A computer-controlled laser forms a layer of solid by tracing it in a raster pattern, then the tank filled with the photosensitive liquid is lowered by the thickness of a layer before the next layer is traced. This cycle is repeated until the complete object is formed.

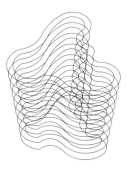

18.17
Incremental forming

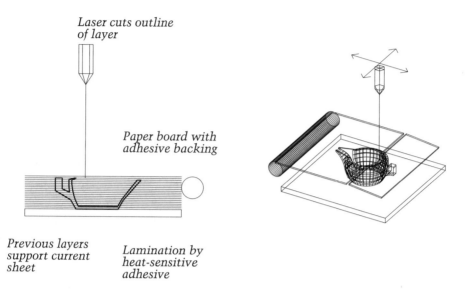

Laser cuts outline
of layer

Paper board with
adhesive backing

Previous layers
support current
sheet

Lamination by
heat-sensitive
adhesive

18.18
Laminated object
manufacturing

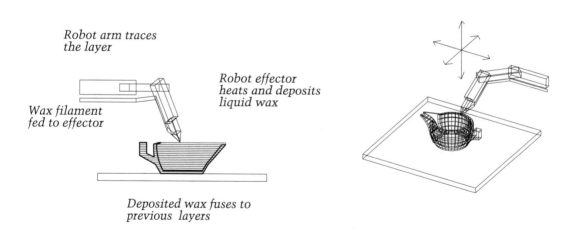

Robot arm traces
the layer

Robot effector
heats and deposits
liquid wax

Wax filament
fed to effector

Deposited wax fuses to
previous layers

18.19
Fused deposition
modeling

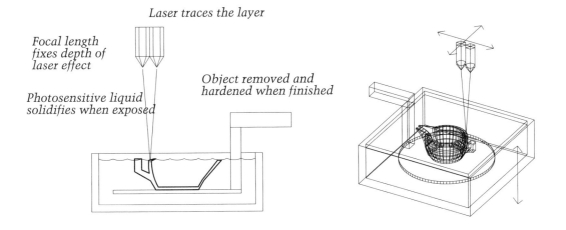

Laser traces the layer

Focal length fixes depth of laser effect

Object removed and hardened when finished

Photosensitive liquid solidifies when exposed

Tank full of liquid lowers after each layer

18.20
Stereolithography

In laser sintering machines, thin layers of photosensitive metal or polymer powder replace the photosensitive liquid of stereolithography. A layer is spread by a roller, the laser scans it to bond the powder in the required locations, and the powder bed then lowers for application of the next layer (figure 18.21). When the shape is complete, the unsintered powder can be removed to reveal the solidified shape.

Three-dimensional printing machines also employ layers of powder (figure 18.22). In this case, though, an inkjet printing mechanism is used to deposit layers of bonding agent. When the shape has been formed, it is cured. This process is particularly effective for producing ceramic moulds to cast metal parts.

By the mid-1990s, these various approaches to incremental forming had emerged as competing technologies, each with characteristic advantages and disadvantages. Figure 18.23, for example, illustrates approximate size ranges for the parts or scale models that can be produced by each one. A designer choosing between these technolo-

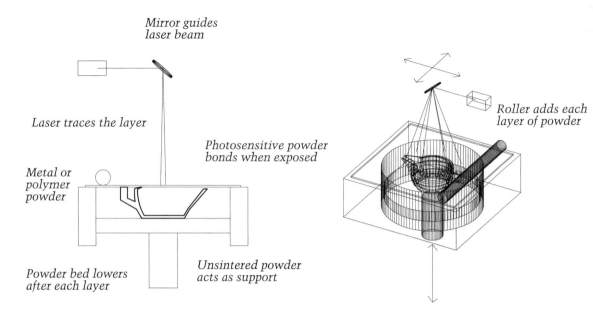

Mirror guides
laser beam

Laser traces the layer

Photosensitive powder
bonds when exposed

Metal or
polymer
powder

Roller adds each
layer of powder

Powder bed lowers
after each layer

Unsintered powder
acts as support

18.21
Laser sintering

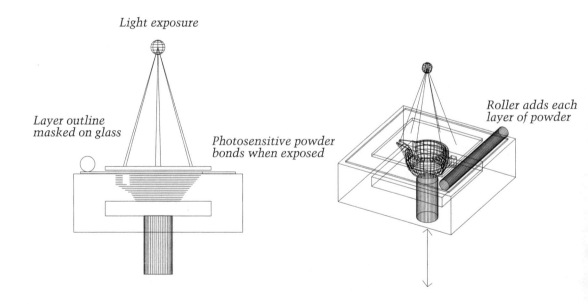

Light exposure

Layer outline
masked on glass

Photosensitive powder
bonds when exposed

Roller adds each
layer of powder

18.22
Three-dimensional printing

Laminated object manufacturing

Fused depostition

Stereolithography
Laser sintering

Three-dimensional printing

18.23
Size ranges for different
protoyping processes

| *<1 in.* | *2 in* | *1/2 ft.* | *1 foot* | *>2 ft.* |

Object size

gies also needs to consider cost (which can be considerable)
and the time needed to produce a finished shape (which
may be many hours).

Because of their fine-grained, incremental character,
these techniques have enormous flexibility, and impose
few limitations on the shapes that can be produced. They
have the unique potential, in some cases, to produce
assemblies with "trapped" elements (figure 18.24). And
there is even potential for one-step production of working
prototypes with moving parts.

At a larger scale, computer-controlled robot arms
equipped with nozzles can potentially be used for layer-by-
layer construction of full-scale architecture. There were
some early experiments with depositing water to construct ice structures, and materials such as sprayed concrete obviously lend themselves to similar treatment.

Reshaping

Not only may materials be cut away to reveal shapes and
incrementally built up to model shapes, they may also be
reshaped through the application of force, heat, steam, and
so on. The blacksmith's traditional craft, for example, is
one of reshaping metal. Shipbuilders have long relied upon
the technique of bending boards around framed supports
in order to produce smoothly lofted hull shapes. And

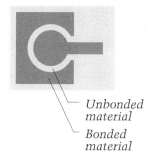

Unbonded
material
Bonded
material

18.24
Forming a trapped element

aircraft and automobile bodies are produced from stamped, bent, and moulded sheets.

Plane curves can be fabricated by bending thin rods, tubes or strips of elastic material, such as steel or wood, around support points as illustrated in figure 18.25a. Extension of the idea to single-curved sheets is straightforward (figure 18.25b). The reshaped material may simply be fastened in place, or it may be deformed permanently by such processes as stressing metal past the elastic limit, heating metal then bending it while it is in a softened state, steam-bending boards, and the like.

Heat-induction bending machines are commonly used to fabricate plane-curved metal components; the metal part is fed through a heating device then subjected to a bending force. These, and other sorts of bending machines, readily lend themselves to numerical control, and so can be employed to fabricate CAD-modeled curved elements.

Similar techniques can be used to bend pipes and rods into space curves, as shown in figure 18.26. Bending machines to accomplish this are, however, correspondingly more complex than those used for plane curves.

Finally, doubly-curved surfaces can be approximated by arrays of height-adjustable, numerically-controlled pins, as illustrated in figure 18.27. This approach is increasingly popular for CAD/CAM production of moulded glass and plastic sheets—automobile windshields, for example—and for curved stamped metal.

Reproducing: Moulds and Dies

Rapid-prototyping machinery can be used not only for direct transformation of CAD models into fabricated objects, but also to produce moulds and dies needed to reproduce those objects in other materials or in multiple copies. For example, three-dimensional printing machines may be used to produce ceramic moulds from which metal parts are then cast. Sometimes there are several reproduction steps in the process of going from a CAD model to a mass-produced artifact; the CAD model might first be transformed into a mould, which is then used to produce a metal die, which finally is used to stamp or otherwise produce the artifact in quantity (figure 18.28).

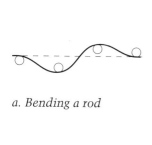

a. Bending a rod

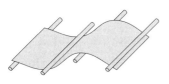

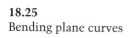

b. Bending a sheet

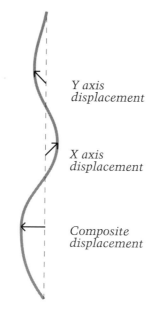

Y axis displacement

X axis displacement

Composite displacement

18.25
Bending plane curves

18.26
Bending a space curve

18.27
Shaping a doubly-curved surface with an array of numerically-controlled pins

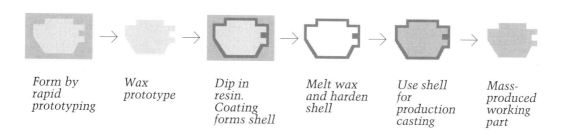

Form by rapid prototyping

Wax prototype

Dip in resin. Coating forms shell

Melt wax and harden shell

Use shell for production casting

Mass-produced working part

18.28
Using a form produced by rapid prototyping to make a production mould

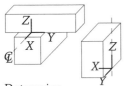
Determine

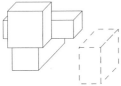
Move

Fix

18.29
Assembly cycle

Assembling

Imagine, now, that you have fabricated all the components for a complex architectural model. To assemble the model, you must first determine the location for each component, then move the component to that location, and finally fix the component in place (figure 18.29). This determine-move-fix cycle is repeated until the model is completely assembled. The logic of full-scale construction is similar, but since components are larger and heavier in this case, the movement operations tend to be much more difficult and expensive.

In general, many different assembly sequences are imaginable for a given model or full-scale building. However, since the assembly must be physically stable in its partially complete states, only some of these turn out to be feasible. Furthermore, some of the feasible sequences may be easier to execute than others—because they allow quick and simple position of new components relative to components already in position, for example. And, especially in full-scale construction, some sequences may be more efficient than others because they require less movement of components, because they make more efficient use of expensive machinery, and so on. Thus determining an appropriate assembly sequence is a very important step in planning a manufacturing or construction process, and designers sometimes have to consider the effects of design decisions on ease or difficulty of assembly (figure 18.30).

Traditionally, builders take dimensions and coordinates from drawings then set work out manually using tape measures, carpenter's rules, plumb-bobs, spirit-levels, and so on. But availability of a CAD model provides many opportunities for automating this task. For example, a study model of a building may be produced by first plotting floor plans, then using these directly to set out walls, columns, and other vertical elements (figure 18.31). Section plots can sometimes be used in a similar way. And, in full-scale construction, CAD models can directly provide coordinate data for input to electronic surveying instruments, laser positioning devices, and other equipment used for establishing positions for components in assemblies.

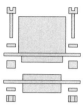

Simplest parts

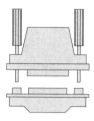

Simplest assembly

18.30
An everyday example of
design for assembly

When robotic devices are used for moving and fixing components, and for related operations, CAD models become potential sources of control information. These robots are not androids in hardhats, but highly specialized devices that are either teleoperated, programmed to perform sequences of operations, or equipped with some (usually primitive) capacity to sense, model, plan, and act to achieve work objectives. Early examples have included the Shimizu Mighty Jack for heavy steel beam positioning, the Kajima Reinforcing Bar Arranging Robot, the Obayashi-Gumi Concrete Placer for pouring concrete into forms, the Takenaka Self-Climbing Inspection Machine, the Taisei Pillar Coating Robot for painting, and the Shimizu Insulation Spray Robot.

The Shimizu Insulation Spray Robot, in particular, illustrates how autonomous robots need geometric models (which may come from CAD systems) of their work environments and of the work that they are to perform. This robot is given a geometric model of the structure that is to be sprayed. The robot computes its position relative to the structure, uses a tactile probe to correct the computed position, executes a spray script, moves to a new position, and so on along the structure.

Complete CAD/CAM Processes

Figure 18.32 illustrates key steps in the design and construction process for one of the first architectural projects to make full use of the CAD/CAM technologies that have now been introduced. The building, designed by Frank Gehry, is a large, fish-shaped pavilion for a site on the Barcelona waterfront.

Early design work on the project resulted in generation of a fairly precise and detailed physical model. The task that next faced the architects was to find an efficient way to develop this design in detail then translate it, quickly and efficiently, into a full-scale construction.

The computer-aided design process began with translation of the complex curved skin of the fish—which had initially been defined by bending wooden ribs—into a digital curved surface model. This was used for visualiza-

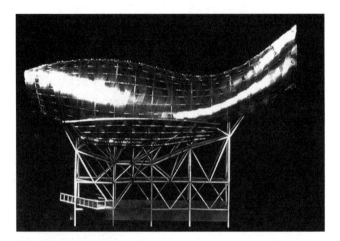

18.31
Steps in an architectural CAD/CAM process. Frank Gehry's Barcelona Fish

a. Physical model

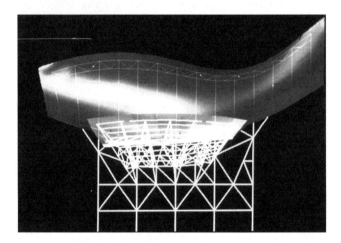

b. Curved-surface model

c. Completed building

Computer model

18.32
Details of the Barcelona Fish

*Corresponding area of
the finished surface*

tion studies and to refine the shape of the skin. A wireframe model of the proposed structural framing was also developed, and this was transferred to the structural engineers to provide a starting point for analysis and structural design.

Next, rapid-prototyping (paper lamination) was used to "build back" a physical model from the digital model. This allowed the architects to check the developed, CAD-modeled design against the original conceptual model.

Finally, the CAD model was used directly to control fabrication and on-site assembly of the curved steel components. Traditional construction drawings were virtually eliminated. Figure 18.31c illustrates the completed building, and figure 18.32 shows details.

For different projects, the Gehry office has explored a number of variants on this process. It has used three-dimensional digitizers to convert physical models into digital models. It has employed other rapid-prototyping techniques, such as five-axis milling of aerospace foam to convert digital surface or solid models into physical models, as shown in figure 18.33

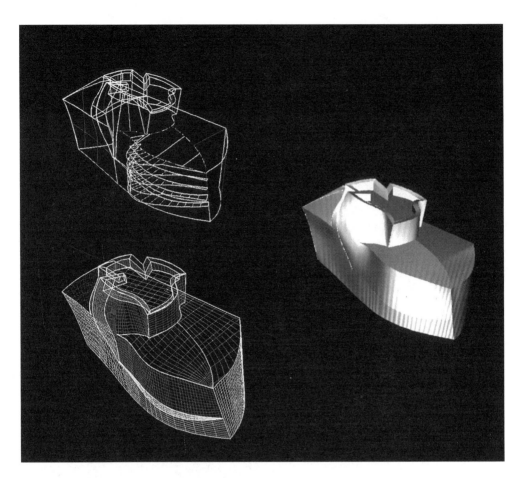

18.33
Three-dimensional CAD model and corresponding NC-milled foam model

Conclusion

In many traditional contexts, designer and fabricator or builder are one, so there is little need to externalize representations of a design. But with modern division of labor between creator and executor of a design came the use of drawings to record and transfer design information. And now, with rapid prototyping and CAD/CAM, drawings are being augmented and sometimes replaced by digital information that controls automated production machinery.

Figure 18.34 illustrates the main potential sources of this control information. Numerically controlled machines can be programmed directly, and some robotic devices can be programmed by manual demonstration. Three-dimensional digitizing devices can be used to create geometric models of existing objects—a process that is useful for producing replacement parts for old machinery, in replacing human bones and joints, and in reverse engineering. And computer-aided design systems can provide geometric models of proposed artifacts. Increasingly, the key task in manufacturing and construction is to convert geometric models (state descriptions of objects) into sequences of machine instructions (process descriptions).

18.34
Alternative information sources for numerically-controlled fabrication

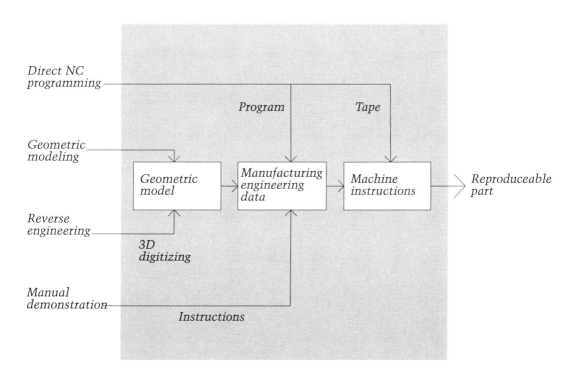

Integrating computer-aided design with computer-aided fabrication and construction in this way not only saves time and money by eliminating the intermediate step of drawing production, it also fundamentally redefines the relationship between designing and producing. It eliminates many geometric constraints imposed by traditional drawing and production processes—making complex curved shapes much easier to handle, for example, and reducing dependence on standard, mass-produced components. Since automated processes tend to be more predictable than many traditional processes, it can allow designers to work with better information about the manufacturability and costs of alternatives. And, since CAD/CAM can significantly shorten the production cycle, it may allow designers to experiment in prototype with forms, materials, and processes before committing to final decisions. In sum, it bridges the gap between designing and producing that opened up when designers began to make drawings.

Suggested Readings

Graham. Glenn. 1988. Encyclopedia of Industrial Automation. New York: Harlow, England, Longman.

Groover, Mikell. 1987. Automation, Production Systems, and Computer-integrated Manufacturing. Englewood Cliffs, NJ: Prentice-Hall.

Jacobs, Paul. 1992. *Rapid Prototyping and Manufacturing.* Dearborn, MI: Society of Manufacturing Engineers.

Kochan, D. (ed.). 1993. *Solid Freeform Manufacturing: Advanced Rapid Prototyping.* Amsterdam: Elsevier

"Rapid Prototyping Shortens Design Cycles". *Engineering Design News.* July 1993.

19

VIRTUAL DESIGN STUDIOS

In principle, an individual designer might initiate a project, develop a design for some artifact, and eventually fabricate the final product—all without the intervention of anyone else. In practice, though, all but the simplest of design and construction tasks are carried out by teams in which there is some division of labor among the members. Thus designers tend to spend large proportions of their time in communicating with each other and in conferring with consultants, regulatory officials, sales representatives, fabricators, construction contractors, and so on.

To minimize communication costs and difficulties (which generally increase with distance), members of design teams have traditionally clustered themselves closely together in offices, studios, and conference rooms to carry out their various tasks. And specialized resources, such as drawing archives, technical reference libraries, and print shops have also been located at these places for easy access. But computer-aided design technology can now be combined with digital telecommunications to reduce or eliminate the need for such co-location (figure 19.1); members of geographically distributed design teams can work together in virtual design studios.

Consider this scenario for the near future. On a construction site for a resort in some remote part of Indonesia, to resolve a problem, an architect boots up her laptop and opens an audio/video window to speak via

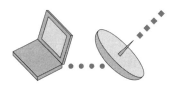

19.1
Computing and telecommunications together

wireless linkage to her structural consultant in Los Angeles. They share concurrent, real-time, interactive access to the CAD three-dimensional model of the project, and they refer to it as they speak. (The definitive copy of the model resides on a server at the home office in Boston.) After some discussion, she decides to bring the client into the conference; he happens to be in a hotel room in Tokyo, as the others can see from the additional audio/video window that now opens. The problem that concerns them is one of site access—a landslide has unexpectedly created difficulties in locating a bridge—so she instructs a software agent to find some relevant satellite images so that the conferees can assess the extent of the damage and consider new locations. As they speak, the agent searches the network, finds a server with the latest satellite data, and soon reports back with what is needed. A course of action agreed upon, the architect sketches the solution on the spot and speaks to an assistant in Boston to give instructions on working out the details. The assistant modifies the geometric model, and a few days later electronically transmits change orders to the contractor's head office in Seoul. A specialized software agent dispatched by the architect preliminarily negotiates a price with its counterpart on the contractor's side, and the agreement is later confirmed by the human principals. This work has been conducted in a virtual design studio.

The Network Infrastructure

Although the telephone, the fax machine, and overnight delivery services initially provided some support for geographically distributed design teams, it was the development of computer networking that really made virtual design studios a serious, practical possibility. During the 1980s, local-area networks (LANs) became commonplace on university campuses, in commercial and industrial organizations, and in design offices. Meanwhile, the Internet international computer network—or, more accurately, network of networks—grew explosively; by 1994 it consisted of more than 8,000 member networks in 45 countries on seven continents. Increasingly, LANs and dial-in commercial networks such as America Online provided gateways to the Internet, so that a huge, world-wide system began to emerge.

Ideally, a design organization's virtual studio environment should be accessible to members of that organization wherever they might happen to find themselves on the face of the earth. The necessary access can be provided through direct connection to high-speed data lines, by dialing in to a host computer via telephone lines, or through wireless connection. During the 1990s the geographic coverage of computer networking became both far more widespread and increasingly dense as more and more buildings were wired for networking, as home and laptop computers were equipped with modems for telephone dial-in, as airline seats were equipped with data jacks, and as portable computing devices were increasingly commonly equipped with wireless modems.

Getting Connected

Almost anyone can connect to the Internet. Technically, all it takes is a line running the Internet protocol—an "IP drop." (The TCP/IP protocol, "transmission control protocol," is the Internet's software standard for encapsulating and delivering its packets of information.) A dedicated IP line is the best connection for anyone running a local area network because it gives each computer on the LAN direct access to the Internet. However, the cost of a direct line is beyond the means of many individuals and small design firms, who normally resort instead to indirect service over ordinary telephone lines. The simplest approach is to use a modem to dial up a commercial service—somebody who has bought an IP line and is now sharing the cost. Where digital telephone service (ISDN) is available, it eliminates the need for a modem. And in some areas, the local cable television system now offers Internet connection. And at a slightly greater cost, you can still use phone lines but connect directly to the Internet itself by means of Internet software, such as SLIP.

The success of a virtual design studio depends very much on having network connections with sufficiently high data transmission rates. Although electronic mail communication can be quite satisfactory at the low data rates (1200 or 2400 baud) typically possible via modem over ordinary telephone lines, virtual design studios make much greater demands on network capacity since large digital images and geometric models must be transmitted without excessive delay, and since realtime audio and video communication capabilities are often needed. So we can expect that virtual design studios will grow in popularity as high-speed network connections become more widely and cheaply available.

These requirements have some fairly obvious spatial implications. For as long as network coverage remains unevenly distributed, the "home base" facilities of design organizations will need to be at locations where excellent, high-speed network connections are available—near to the teleports that have been constructed in some major cities, for example. Installations of specialized and expensive equipment—such as CAD/CAM machines, high-quality output devices, large database servers, and very high speed supercomputers—will also require high-speed network connections so that they can be made as widely and conveniently available as possible. Design team members will carry powerful laptop computers which they can dock into the network on desktops, in hotel rooms, in airplane seats, and so on. When they are on remote construction sites, when they are on the move, and when they are at other places where cables do not reach, they will be able at least to turn to wireless devices.

Clients and Servers

In a computer network, a client is a piece of software that requests a service and a server is another piece of software—usually running on another, perhaps distant machine—that provides it (figure 19.2). More specifically, in a virtual design studio, clients mostly run on the machines that members of the design team carry around or have on their desks, while servers mostly reside at home-base locations and perform the functions of storing and providing remote access to the files that team members need.

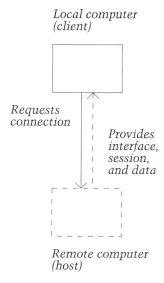

Local computer
(client)

Requests
connection

Provides
interface,
session,
and data

Remote computer
(host)

19.2
Requesting remote service

One simple and widely available sort of client software is called "telnet." It allows users to log into servers from remote locations. You invoke it by typing the command *telnet* followed by the name of the remote computer, and it performs the functions of establishing a connection with the server, accepting and formatting input for transmission to the server, and accepting output from the server and formatting it for display (figure 19.3). The server must, of course, have software that accepts and executes telnet commands. Once you have established a telnet connection to a remote machine, you can use that machine as if it were local. A typical use of telnet is to log into online library catalogs to search for books.

A second common sort of client, called "ftp," allows you to get files from a server and transfer them to your own, local machine, and also to move locally stored files to a remote machine. (The name stands for file transfer protocol.) You invoke it by typing the command *ftp* followed by the name of the remote computer (figure 19.4). It allows you to browse through file directories on the remote machine and select files that you want to transfer.

The simplest way to set up a virtual design studio, then, is to run compatible CAD software on networked machines at the various different locations, and to use telnet and ftp commands to access information and to move CAD files from location to location. For example, an architect might ftp a geometric model to a structural engineer for analysis, or to a CAD/CAM machine shop for fabrication. In addition, electronic mail can be used to communicate comments and instructions.

For this strategy to succeed, consistent file-naming conventions must be followed by all members of the design team, and directories must be organized with care, so that needed information can be located without long and frustrating directory searches. Meticulous version control is also necessary, since it is easy to proliferate slightly differing versions of files, scattered over different physical locations, and to lose track of which version is the definitive one.

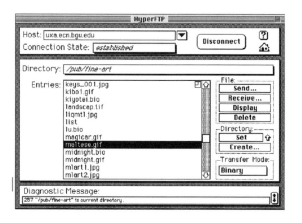

19.3
Telnet: a session with a library catalogue

19.4
Transferring files using ftp

Gophers

The most obvious limitations of "bare bones" virtual design studios based on telnet and ftp are that design team members are forced to use cumbersome typed commands to communicate, and that browsing through potentially large directories to find needed information can be very slow and cumbersome. The Internet Gopher system, which originated at the University of Minnesota, was designed to alleviate these problems by organizing information for more convenient browsing and by providing a much friendlier user interface.

The Gopher system consists of Gopher clients and Gopher servers. The user of a Gopher client first sees a top-level menu of broad information categories. Clicking on one of these yields a menu of sub-categories, and so on to any depth (figure 19.5). At the lowest level are resources such as programs that can be run remotely, files that can be downloaded to the user's machine, and so on.

When a Gopher client is invoked, it connects to its "home server" and requests that server's main menu. The

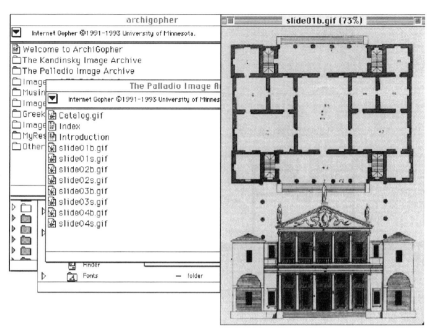

19.5
Gopher: searching and
retrieving elements in a
remote data collection

server is a piece of software that maintains the nested
menu structure and provides access to its resources—
much like a combination of a library subject catalog with
a compliant librarian who goes into the stacks to fetch
requested material. But there is an additional powerful
feature; a menu entry may link to another server, at
another location. Thus Gopher servers can create vast,
interconnected webs providing access to resources that
may be physically located on machines scattered all around
the world. Simply by pointing and clicking—as with a
hypertext document—a user can quickly navigate through
this web. Jumping from server to server is handled automatically as menu items are selected, and the user does
not need to know where resources are physically located.

Thus a design organization can organize and provide
access to its online resources by setting up a Gopher server
on one of its home-base machines. For example, the top-
level menu might identify current projects, then the
menu hierarchy under each project might guide designers
to the CAD files that they need to use.

A particular advantage of the Gopher system is that the resources on each server can be maintained independently of other servers in the network, provided only that the links between servers are kept up. For example, a construction products information system might consist of hundreds of servers—each one maintained by a particular supplier, and providing information about that supplier's products. The home server that ties the whole system together only needs to maintain the top menu levels that will guide users quickly to the server with information about the specific products that are of interest.

The Gopher system can also be used to connect together the units of a virtual design organization. Imagine, for example, that an architecture firm, a consulting engineering firm, a landscape design firm, various component fabricators, and a construction contractor agree to collaborate on some project. Assume that each firm already has its own Gopher server. The communications infrastructure that is needed to support work on the project can quickly be put together by forming appropriate links between the servers.

The World Wide Web and Mosaic

The World Wide Web, or WWW, takes the ideas implicit in the Gopher system one step further. The Web is based on the idea of hypermedia, as discussed in Chapter 14. It was initially developed at CERN—the European Particle Physics Laboratory—but by the early 1990s its use had spread far beyond the physics community.

A WWW server presents a home page—a hypertext document with links to other hypertext pages (figure 19.6). These linked pages might be part of the same document (as in more traditional hypertext systems such as Hypercard), or they might be home pages of servers running on other Internet machines. So the Web, like the Gopher system, has rapidly evolved into an enormous network of cross-linked servers.

WWW browsers are clients that can be used to view home pages, to navigate through the Web by following the hypertext links, and to access resources and retrieve files

19.6
Hypertext distributed over multiple servers

Browsing through cross-referenced images

A home page

19.7
Mosaic: Access to the World Wide Web.

from WWW servers. By far the most popular of these browsers is NCSA Mosaic (figure 19.7). This was developed at the National Center for Supercomputing Applications at the University of Illinois, Urbana-Champaign, and it proliferated explosively throughout the Internet in 1994. The attraction of Mosaic is that it presents consistent, flexible, multimedia, point-and-click interface to the Internet; it can handle text, images, audio, and video. You can also use it to access telnet, ftp, and Gopher servers.

Perhaps the most significant limitation of Mosaic is that it requires a lot of bandwidth to perform effectively; large color images, and audio and video segments, can take a long time to download through the network. Initially, this meant that practical Mosaic use was confined to workstations that had direct, high-speed Internet connections—and even then, operation could sometimes be painfully slow. Telephone dial-up use was generally not feasible. But this limitation will become less important as high-speed Internet connections become more widely available.

A WWW home page accessed through Mosaic can become the online location of a virtual design studio; members of the design organization "go" to that home page much as, in earlier times, they would have gone to the office. The home page graphically presents the resources of the organization—for example as a collection of icons, or as a floor plan with entry points to "departments"—and organization members can follow links from there to find whatever resources they might need.

One department presented by the home page might, for example, be an image library—much like the slide libraries traditionally maintained by design firms and architecture schools. Or there might be a library of three-dimensional CAD models of historically significant buildings. The entire library does not, of course, have to be maintained by one organization on one server; different organizations may maintain specialized collections in areas where they have particular competence or unique resources, and cross-linkages may allow users to explore the whole thing as a unified collection.

Business transactions are also possible through Mosaic. For example, the MIT Press has its catalog of books and journals on a WWW server. Catalog entries present scanned color images of jackets, short descriptions of contents, and author biographies. Users can select books or journals and fill out order forms online; their credit card numbers are charged and the books are delivered by mail.

As with the Gopher system, the World Wide Web provides an opportunity to construct online support facilities "on-the-fly" for ad-hoc design teams that are put together for particular projects. If each constituent organization already has a home page on the web, it is only necessary to set up a new server and home page for the project team, and to provide appropriate links back and forth to the existing home pages.

One difficulty with the hypermedia documents that form the basis of the World Wide Web is that they are far more complex to create and edit than straightforward text documents. It would be nice to have a hypermedia processor that was as easy to use as a word processor, but this has so-far proven to be an elusive goal. WWW pages are created by using a specialized language called HTML (Hypertext Markup Language).

	Different times	*Same time*
Text	*Electronic mail*	*Online forum*
Audio	*Voicemail*	*Telephone*
Image	*Fax*	*Whiteboard*
Video	*Videomail*	*Videoconferencing*

19.8
Communications media

Virtual Conference Rooms

A virtual design studio, like its more traditional counterpart, requires gathering places and conference rooms. In these virtual places, participants satisfy their need to gather around a "table" on which a drawing is spread out or a model is displayed, and to exchange information or conduct negotiations. Typically, participants in a design conference will want to refer continually to the drawing or model as the discussion unfolds, and they may make modifications by sketching or by moving things around.

In general, participation in a discussion may be synchronous (as in an ordinary telephone conversation) or asynchronous (as in an exchange of electronic mail), and the medium of conversation may be text, audio, image, or video. Figure 19.8 shows the eight basic possibilities. Asynchronous communication can be supported electronically by electronic mail systems, voicemail, fax for images, and videomail. Synchronous text communication is supported by the chat-room facilities provided by commercial online services such as Compuserve, by Internet client software such as the Unix talk program, ytalk, or IRC (Internet Relay Chat). The telephone, of course, provides synchronous voice. So-called whiteboard systems, which allow users at separate locations to sketch (using simple paint system tools) in the same graphic

19.9
A computer equipped for videoconferencing. Note the combination of CAD and video windows.

window, provide synchronous image communication. And videoconferencing systems or videophones provide synchronous video. Initially, all of these things developed as separate systems—often with separate communication channels and separate devices (telephones, fax machines, computer terminals, etc.) to access them. Increasingly, though, the separate systems will converge to form integrated, multimodal, digital telecommunications systems.

Since designing is at least as much a social process as it is a technical process, virtual design studios need very high levels of conferencing capability in order to function effectively. Videoconferencing is particularly important for the sorts of negotiations and critical discussions (such as negotiating the details of a construction contract, or giving a desk crit to a student or junior designer) that have traditionally been carried out face-to-face. Augmenting a standard computer workstation with a microphone, miniature video camera, speaker, and video display capability (figure 19.9) makes this possible.

The Internet can carry audio and video over long distances, and performs reasonably satisfactorily for this purpose at times when it is not too heavily loaded. But it was not designed for this sort of use, and it is unlikely to be adequate for long-distance audio/video communication as demand for this capability increases. However, by

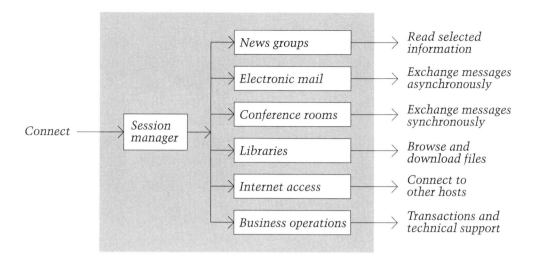

the early 1990s considerable commercial pressure had emerged for development of broadband, switched audio/ video that could deliver services like video-on-demand to homes. As such networks develop, they will potentially be available to support virtual design studios.

When the basic telecommunications capabilities are available, an organization can create virtual conference rooms. These might, for example, be software resources reached from a Mosaic home page. They might be set up to function asynchronously, in "bulletin-board" mode, as places to leave digital models, sketches, site photographs, analysis results, messages, and other data items for convenient pick-up by other team members. (Figure 19.10 shows the usual range of services on a bulletin board). Or they might function synchronously—for example, as entry points to video conferences; when you go there, video windows from other sites open up on your screen (figure 19.11).

Application Sharing

In the videoconference that was shown in figure 19.9, notice that there are not only video windows showing the faces of participants, but that there is also a CAD window showing the proposal that is "on the table" for discussion—much as a cardboard model might be literally on the table in a more

19.11
Video windows

traditional design conference. This is crucial; the video capability would be of only marginal benefit if it were not combined with a capability for all participants to view and manipulate the subject of discussion.

Capacity to put a design "on the table" in a virtual conference room can potentially be provided at several different levels of sophistication. The simplest thing to implement is a software resource that simultaneously displays the same digital image on the workstations of all the participants. This allows a designer to give a visual presentation, much as with color slides or with previously prepared drawings pinned up on the wall. But these images cannot be modified interactively, and this limits participation to watching and verbally commenting.

Integration of a shared whiteboard system (figure 19.12) with videoconferencing software allows participants to point with a cursor at parts of an image, to draw over the top of an image, and to work out ideas by jointly developing sketches. Thus it supports the sort of interaction that has traditionally taken place, using layers of yellow trace, in desk crits—a standard form of interaction in architecture schools and offices.

A still higher level of interaction can be achieved if participants at multiple locations all have access to the same CAD model, and can perform viewing and editing operations on it; this is like getting your hands on the

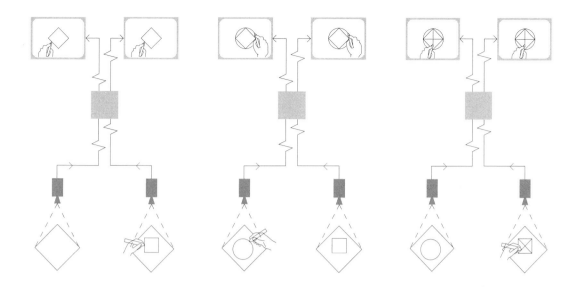

19.12
Overlaid sketching with a
whiteboard system

cardboard model that sits on a real conference table. In different contexts, conference participants might want to share access to other sorts of documents—text files, page layouts, spreadsheets, video segments, and so on. Implementation of such application sharing can present non-trivial conceptual and technical problems, so it is likely to develop fairly slowly. But it is key to the development of sophisticated virtual design studios.

Finally, if all participants have access to immersive virtual reality systems, participants can co-inhabit the same three-dimensional virtual environment; they share the same surroundings, and they see representations of each other. This idea was initially popularized by virtual reality arcade games such as Dactyl Nightmare, but extensions of it to design teleconferencing are fairly obvious. For example, participants might meet "in" an immersive simulation of a proposed building, "walk" through it together, discuss what they see, and make modifications "on the spot."

Efficient Resource Use

Under traditional patterns of design work, specialized facilities such as blueprint shops had limited geographic catchment areas—since work had to be carried physically to them and from them. To have a large enough user base, these facilities had to be located in areas that were sufficiently dense with design organizations. Conversely, small design offices that could not afford their own specialized facilities usually had strong incentives to locate in areas where these facilities were available.

But virtual design studios can change these geographic patterns by supporting fast, electronic submission of work to specialized facilities for processing. For example, a rapid prototyping shop can provide service to a large, geographically distributed group of users by accepting digital geometric models over the network, processing them to produce physical models, then shipping these products to their required destinations via express delivery services.

Computational capacity can also be shared. Imagine, for example, that a virtual design studio has one cluster of workstations in Hong Kong and another cluster in New York. When it is daytime an New York and night in Hong Kong, the New York machines are used interactively for editing and telecommunications while the Hong Kong machines are used to process large rendering and animation jobs. Then, when the work day begins in Hong Kong, the rendering and animation work is shipped back to the now-available New York machines while the Hong Kong machines are taken over for interactive use.

Even more importantly, virtual design studios allow effective sharing of unique human resources. Until now, prominent designers with worldwide practices have had to spend large amounts of their time on airplanes. While virtual design studios do not eliminate the need for on-site inspections and face-to-face meetings, they are likely to reduce the numbers of occasions on which travel is absolutely necessary, they should maintain more effective communication in between occasions for travel, and they will allow uniquely talented and knowledgeable individuals to participate in larger numbers of projects. In design schools, virtual design studios potentially allow visiting design critics to provide criticism of student projects from their home offices or even while they are traveling, and they also open up the possibility of assembling design juries in an entirely new way.

Software Agents

In traditional design organizations, employees frequently act as agents—carrying out tasks that have been delegated to them. Many of these tasks consist of finding, filtering, processing, and reporting information. In a virtual design studio, software agents can potentially perform such tasks automatically. As computer network usage grew rapidly in the late 1980s and early 1990s, software agents became an increasingly active research topic, and by the mid-1990s commercial implementations were beginning to appear.

One sort of agent provides an intelligent interface to the flood of information that arrives over the network—much as a human receptionist deals with mail, telephone calls, and visitors. To control asynchronous communication effectively, for example, an intelligent interface agent residing on a designer's personal machine might automatically prioritize, sort, forward, archive, and delete electronic mail, voicemail, and videomail messages.

Controlling synchronous communication (either face-to-face or in virtual conference rooms) requires a very different sort of agent—one that looks at the online calendars of potential meeting participants, negotiates acceptable meeting times, finds suitable places (either real or virtual) to meet, and eventually notifies participants of meeting times and places. This is likely to become an increasingly complex and important task as we see the development of large virtual design studios involving many, potentially highly mobile participants scattered across the time zones of the world.

Information retrieval agents can be written to traverse the links of the Gopher system, the World Wide Web, or similar resource networks in search of documents on specified topics or answers to given questions. Knowbots, for example, are intelligent agents (largely experimental rather than practical at the time of writing) that are despatched to crawl from server to server looking for answers; when they find relevant material they return with it, else they return empty-handed after completing an exhaustive search. One of the first Knowbot applications, for example, was to find electronic mail addresses corresponding to a specified name. Retrieval agents structured in different ways can also monitor bulletin boards and newsgroups for postings on specified topics, or monitor information streams such as wire service news feeds.

Agents can also be programmed to buy, sell, and automatically perform other such transactions according to specified rules. The increasingly popular Wall Street technique of program trading implements this idea. In an analogous architectural application, a contractor's buying agent might traverse the Web to search out the selling agents of building materials suppliers, then purchase from the one that offered the best price and delivery time.

The first, experimental software agents were mostly programmed using standard software implementation tools. But widespread use of agents is likely to depend on availability of convenient, specialized, agent programming tools and operating system environments that are structured with agents in mind. A pioneering step in this direction was taken in 1994, when the Silicon Valley startup General Magic announced its Telescript agent programming language and related Magic Cap operating system.

Connection to Construction Sites

Historically, design studios have often been found in huts on construction sites or in corners of artisans' shops; connections between the activities of designing, fabricating, and constructing were very close. But in more recent times, design offices have tended to locate themselves away from construction sites (perhaps with satellite offices on site for large projects), and communication difficulties have inevitably resulted—particularly when unexpected conditions are encountered during construction and rapid redesign is needed in response. Since virtual design studios are not location-specific, they provide the possibility of re-creating very close linkages between design team members and the construction site.

The simplest way to accomplish this is to use digital still cameras, video cameras, electronic surveying devices, and so on to collect information that can then be put on a server and thus quickly made available to all members of

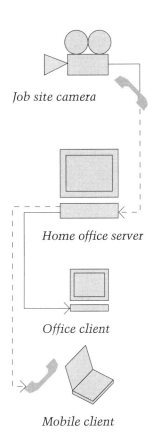

Job site camera

Home office server

Office client

Mobile client

19.13
Uplink from
construction site

the design team—wherever they may happen to be. Or recording instruments might be configured to convey information directly to the server; for example, a digital still camera might incorporate a wireless modem for this purpose (figure 19.13).

Conversely, workstations in site offices can be linked into the network so that the latest design information is immediately available. To bring this information even closer to work locations, construction workers might be equipped with wearable computers that have downloaded files of needed information and wireless linkages into the network. Another, more distant possibility is to equip these wearable computers with headmounted displays and position sensors so that the three-dimensional CAD model of the project can be superimposed, correctly registered, on the actual construction work in progress.

In general, as the technology of wearable computers and personal digital assistants (PDAs) develops, construction is likely to emerge as one of the important applications. These devices will increasingly effectively connect virtual design studios to even the remotest of on-site work locations.

Physical Studio Space

The capabilities of virtual design studios augment rather than replace those of more traditional drawing and modeling techniques, and supplement rather than eliminate face-to-face meeting places. As virtual design studios develop, most practical design processes will involve combinations of traditional and electronic representations, and mixes of electronic and face-to-face communication. Figure 19.14 diagrams the emerging relationship between drawings, physical scale models, digital models, and executed designs in the case of architectural design (similar diagrams can be drawn for other design domains), and illustrates the possible translation paths among the various representations.

This suggests that studio desks should be designed to support all the activities of drawing, physical modeling, and computer work, and to allow easy, casual movement back and forth between these different activities as the

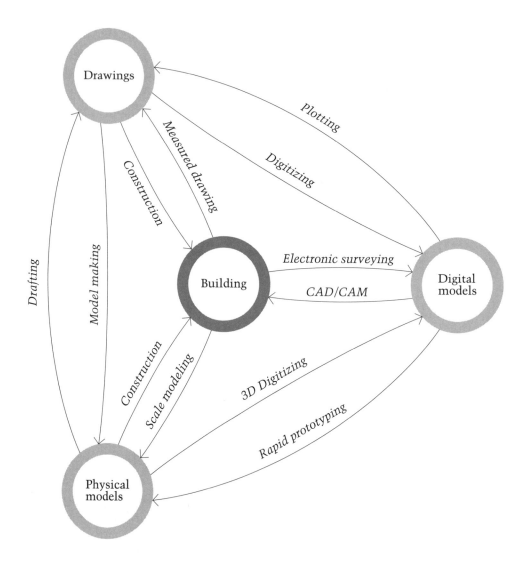

19.14
A design studio fully
integrating traditional
and digital media.

evolution of a project demands. It makes little functional sense to segregate computer workstations away from drawing and modeling in special computer rooms, and the technical imperatives that once necessitated this have largely disappeared as computers have become smaller, cheaper, and more robust.

A second, related requirement is that network access should be easily available anywhere on the studio floor; in particular, it should be possible to dock a laptop computer into the network at any desk, or at any other location where access to virtual design studio resources may be needed. This can be accomplished by means of a suitable cable distribution grid, or perhaps by reliance on wireless communications.

The studio should be equipped with good, convenient facilities for translating back and forth among drawings, scale models, and digital models. Scanners and two-dimensional digitizers translate from drawings and photographs to digital format. Three-dimensional scanners and digitizers are needed to go from physical scale models to digital models. Printers and plotters produce two-dimensional hard copy from digital information. And increasingly, it is feasible to use rapid prototyping devices to generate physical scale models from digital information.

Finally, conference rooms and presentation spaces should incorporate facilities for presenting digital displays as well as drawings and models. At the very least, conference rooms need network connections and large monitors or video projectors. Controls must be organized and positioned for convenient use while presenting. More sophisticated presentation spaces might incorporate powerful workstations for generating realtime walkthrough simulations of design proposals, and even technology for stereo or immersive virtual reality displays.

Conclusion

The rapid development of computer networking and related digital technologies now makes implementation of virtual design studios an increasingly attractive possibility. The idea of a virtual architectural design studio has been developed in some detail here, but similar scenarios could be sketched for virtual graphic design and product design studios, virtual recording studios, and virtual video studios.

Once, designers could set up shop by hanging out their shingles on Main Street. Now they must locate themselves on the Information Superhighway.

Suggested Readings

Buford, John F. Koegel. 1994. *Multimedia Systems*. Reading, Mass.: Addison-Wesley.

Edmonds, Ernest A., Linda Candy, Rachel Jones, and Basil Soufi. 1994. "Support for Collaborative Design: Agents and Emergence." In *Communications of the ACM*, vol. 37, no. 7, pp. 41-47.

Heim, Michael. 1993. *The Metaphysics of Virtual Reality*. New York: Oxford University Press.

Hodges, Matthew, and Russell Sasnett. 1993. *Multimedia Computing—Case Studies from MIT Project Athena*. Reading, Mass.: Addison-Wesley.

Krol, Ed. 1992, 1994. *The Whole Internet*. Sebastopol, CA: O'Reilly Associates.

LaQuey, Tracy. 1993. *The Internet Companion*. Reading, Mass.: Addison Wesley.

Maybury, Mark (ed.) 1993. *Intelligent Multimedia Interfaces*. Cambridge: The AI Press/The MIT Press.

Wojtowicz, Jerzy (ed.) 1994. *Virtual Design Studio*. Hong Kong: Hong Kong University Press.

20

WHAT WAS COMPUTER-AIDED DESIGN?

New tools and new thinking go together. Without the irrigation ditch, the plough, and the wheel we would probably be thinking about running down our next meal. Literature (in the forms that succeeded the oral epic) would be unthinkable without writing and printing.

Drawings and Realizations

We can debate whether the techniques and tools of architectural drawing emerged in response to the growing need of an increasingly complex society to separate design from construction or whether the invention of architectural drawing initiated this separation. Either way, the intellectual activity of exploring and proposing possibilities long ago hived off from the physical activity of creating realities. A first step, perhaps, was to sketch a full-scale layout directly on the ground or a profile on a stone to guide a mason's work. By the time of Alberti drawings had become inexpensive and portable, so the work of the designer could be removed in time and space from the construction site: the project, represented in drawings, became an independent entity. Now designers could make projects not only for execution, but also for imaginary clients and sites. Architecture could comprehend fantasies and utopias.

20.1
Digital design media at
an early stage

Emergence of Digital Design Media

With the computer comes a further disengagement of ideas from matter. Designs break free from the paper plane: the project becomes a collection of symbols in computer memory. The computer can manipulate these symbols automatically, at incomprehensible speed, to help produce ideas that we could not think of by ourselves. The computer display then becomes an electronic cave in which the visible shadows of those ideas flicker and dance at our command.

Digital design media are still in their infancy, and our acquaintance with them is limited compared to our vast experience with traditional media. But the pace of their emergence is accelerating; in the 21st century, digital design media and virtual design studios will be the norm, and use of traditional design tools and media will be increasingly rare and specialized.

As the technology continues to develop, digital models will play increasingly central roles in practical design processes (figure 20.3). They will be handled by sophisticated editing and management software, and they will receive inputs from various combinations of designers, consultants, intelligent software agents, and information extracted from online databases. They will produce input to visualization systems, drawing and report generators, wide ranges of analysis and criticism software, rapid prototyping systems, and CAD/CAM facilities. And, through integration of computer-aided design systems with advanced telecommunications capabilities, they will effectively support the work of geographically distributed virtual design organizations working in virtual design studios.

Rethinking Design

When tools are new (as the computer still is) they often seem strange and are understood in contrast to their predecessors. The automobile was first seen as a horseless carriage, the radio as a wireless telegraph, and the designer's computer as a nonmanual drafting device. But with time,

Computation per dollar: x 10 billion

Data transmission rates: x 1 billion

Number of televisions: x 100 million

Number of computers: x 10 million

1950-1990

20.2
Accelerating pace of technological change

as use becomes commonplace and more mature understanding develops, the old locutions sound increasingly quaint and eventually are discarded. The technology becomes transparent. Today's motorists have long forgotten that they are engaged in horseless travel, and today's architects would smile at the idea of pencil-assisted design. Chroniclers of our era may one day ask, "What was computer-aided design?" To them, it will just be design.

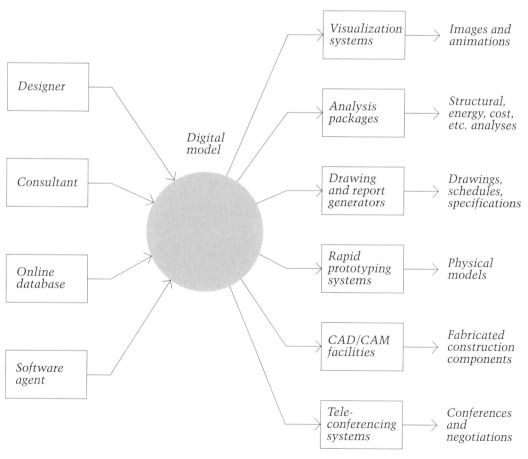

20.3
The integrating role of the
digital model

GLOSSARY

Abstraction hierarchy:
Logical structure for enabling useful work at higher levels not requiring knowledge of what is going on at lower, less abstract level.

Access structure:
Logical framework for locating data, e.g., index.

Agent:
Software program which works unattended to carry out tasks delegated to it.

Algorithm:
A sequence of steps to obtain a reproducible result.

Aliases (abstractions):
Alternative representations of same element (e.g., from library database) with varying degrees of detail displayed.

Aliasing:
Stepped appearance of diagonals. Also called jaggies.

Analog:
Continuous representation having some formal similarity.

Anonymous FTP:
Use of File Transfer Protocol to obtain files from public locations (requiring no login authorization) on remote hosts.

Application program:
Program which accumulates and operates on data to accomplish some useful purpose.

Articulation tree:
Abstract representation of a motion hierarchy in terms of parts, coordinate systems, and degrees of freedom.

ASCII:
Standard for encoding text characters and numerals with binary integers.

Assignment:
The giving of a value to a variable.

Asynchronous:
Occurring at different, or unpredictable times.

Attribute:
Column of a table in a relational data model. Represents a property shared by one or more entities.

Axonometric:
Parallel projection perpendicular to picture plane.

Bandwidth:
Range of frequencies available as a communication channel. Corresponds approximately to data rate.

Bitmap:
An array of pixels. Also called raster. Called bitmap due to analogous allocation of memory locations.

Boundary representation:
The description of enclosed three-dimensional space in terms of several planes and surfaces.

Bridge:
Hardware device which acts as boundary between subnets using like protocols.

Buffer:
A surrounding area within a specific radius of a particular geometric feature (as on a map).

Bus:
Main internal communications channel of a computer.

CAD/CAM :
Computer-Aided Design/Computer-Aided Manufacturing. Using computer-based geometric models as a basis for instructions to numerically controlled machining processes.

Chain:
Sequence of vertices connected to bound a polygon or to form an edge in a polygon mesh. Also called arc or polyline.

Chroma-keying:
The process of mixing two video sequences, e.g., live video with synthetic animation.

Client:
Computer on a network which depends on a server for operation.

Clipboard:
Temporary storage of data last cut or copied and available for pasting.

Clipping:
The reduction of the viewing pyramid for the purpose of removing irrelevant object from view.

Communications overhead:
Cost of recording, transmitting, and translating project information.

Compression:
Reduction in the amount of memory required to store a given body of information. Accomplished by identifying similarities and continuities in the information.

Computer:
Binary logic device (Turing machine) for applying algorithms to data to achieve useful results.

Constrained:
The condition in which the range of possible values for a variable is related to the current values of other variables.

Constraint:
The reduction of the range of allowable values for a variable, based on the current values of related variables.

Constraint solving:
The process of solving a system of variables whose current values, and ranges of possible values, are interrelated.

Construction plane:
Local two-dimensional coordinate system, defined relative to absolute three-dimensional coordinate system, in which geometric objects are created.

Constructive solid geometry:
  The derivation of complex solid modeled objects from simple, well-formed volumetric primitives by means of successive spatial set operations.

Cosine shading:
  See Lambert shading.

Curve:
  An path described by a polynomial equation of degree two or more.

Database:
  A collection of information stored semi-permanently for some particular purpose.

Database-management system:
  System for structuring, streamlining, and managing database in ways not perceptual to users of the data.

Data structure:
  Pattern of references to memory locations useful for organizing information for a particular purpose.

Declaration:
  The reservation of memory space under a specified name.

Depth cue:
  Means of visualizing spatial depth.

Depth sorting:
  The ordering of surfaces in a model from furthest to nearest with respect to a given point.

Design vector:
  Interpolation between different states of a data structure, especially for exploration of intervening states in realtime.

Desktop:
  A metaphor for a two-dimensional work space in which documents and tasks are graphically represented and arranged.

Digital:
  Discrete numerical representation.

Directory:
  Second logical unit of data storage. A collection of files. Also called folder.

Discretized:
  Divided into a finite number of uniform pieces.

Disk:
Random access magnetic memory. Prevalent memory medium at present.

Dithering:
In a color image, the tradeoff of spatial resolution for intensity resolution. Similar to halftoning.

Dolly:
Camera motion along the viewing direction.

DXF:
Drawing eXchange Format. Proprietary name for popular geometric data translation standard.

Dynamic interaction:
Human-computer interaction which provides continuous, realtime feedback amid ongoing operations controlled manually.

Entity:
Basic unit of storage in a geometric database. Usually corresponds to a graphic primitive, transformed, with assigned nongeometric properties.

Environment:
A logical context for a work session. System configuration, software tool kit, data file system, and peripheral device selection presented to a work session.

Ethernet:
Proprietary name for a popular network communications protocol.

Euler operations:
Topological operation specifying relations between vertices, edges, and faces.

Expert system:
Combination of a knowledge base with an inference mechanism and an explanation facility.

Facet:
Planar element in a mesh representing a nonplanar surface.

File:
The principal unit of storage for data and programs.

File locking:
Making a data file in active use by one person unavailable to others.

File server:
Computer designated to serve as central repository of data shared over a network.

File type:
A classification according to the nature and structure of file contents.

Filter:
A means to extract desired data from other data. In image processing, an operation which reassigns the value of each pixel based on some function of the values of its neighbors.

Finite element analysis:
Analysis technique replacing a continuum with a lattice, differential changes to which can be analyzed without concern for distortions to the whole.

Foreground, background:
Images for overlay. For each pixel, foreground value replaces background value unless affected by a mask or a blending or some other such function.

Frame (animation):
A single image in an animation.

Frame (kinematic):
A motionless body to which moving bodies are attached.

Frame of reference:
Scene and viewing variable which remain constant while action variables change.

FTP:
File Transfer Protocol. Client software to permit file transfer from (and sometimes to) a remote host computer.

Fused deposition:
An incremental forming process based on robotically applying a stream of material.

Gateway:
Hardware device which acts as boundary between subnets using different protocols.

Generative grammar:
> Selection of rewriting rules whose repeated and combined applications create designs in a particular world of possibilities.

Geographic Information System (GIS):
> A system for representing spatial entities simultaneously as maps and relational data tables. Using this arrangement, maps may be generated as reports on data queries, and tables may be generated as reports on map queries.

Global illumination:
> Rendering in which the surfaces of the model affect one another and atmospheric effects may be considered.

Gopher:
> Go-for. Menu-based browsing and retrieval software for obtaining files from a web of hierarchically catalogued servers on the Internet, without concern for physical location.

Gouraud shading:
> Lambert or cosine shading plus the representation of specular highlights.

Halftoning:
> In a greyscale image, the tradeoff of spatial resolution for intensity resolution, usually for obtaining multiple intensities from a single color of ink in printing.

Heat-induction bending:
> A reshaping process used especially for curving metal surfaces.

Heterogeneous network:
> Diversified computing resource composed of interconnected programs filling particular niches and incrementally adapted to changing needs.

Hidden-line:
> A view in which edges or portions of edges in a surface model not visible from a given point have been made invisible.

Histogram:
> Graph of distribution of intensity levels showing number of pixels having each level.

Home page:
   Server identity screen for use in a web on the
   Internet. Screen introduces local resources and
   provides links to associated resources and servers.

Hypercard:
   Proprietary name for hypermedia system in which
   nodes are single screens using the metaphor of index
   cards.

Hypermedia:
   Representations employing associative links.

Hypertext:
   Non-linear text in which block of linear text are
   cross-referenced by links.

Hypervoxel:
   Unit of discretized volume in time.

Incremental forming:
   Layer-by-layer addition of material, according to a
   two-dimensional pattern, in order to build up a
   three-dimensional artifact.

Integration:
   Systems working together. "Horizontal"
   integration is the sharing of data among various
   participants at any stage of a project. "Vertical"
   integration is the sharing of data between several
   phases of a project.

Intensity resolution:
   Number of intensity levels available for pixels to
   take on. Measured in bits per pixel.

Interface:
   Human computer interface. Technology and logical
   framework for input and output of work.

Interface integration:
   Sharing of human-computer interaction standards
   between several programs.

Joint constraint:
   Design process which alters the degrees of freedom
   of a joint in mechanism.

Keyframe:
>One of several frames from an animation in which certain properties are altered by the animator and between which the system calculates the intervening frames by interpolation.

Kinematic chain:
>A diagram representing a frameless mechanism, in which all members are jointed on both ends, and for which fixing the relative position of any two of the joints determines the configuration of the entire chain.

Lambert shading:
>The rendering of surfaces in direct relation to their orientation to a light source. Named for Lambert's cosine law expressing the intensity as a function of the angle of orientation.

LAN:
>Local area network. Computers in physical proximity connected and sharing data.

Laser sintering:
>An incremental forming process based on bonding photosensitive powder.

Layers:
>Logical groupings of geometric entities, usually for visibility purposes, in which the member entities remain individually addressable.

Lexical:
>Compared against known lexicons (e.g., for words) or established bounds (for numbers).

Library:
>Database of standard or frequently-used components.

Macro language:
>A language for writing custom ad-hoc programs to run on top of standard programs.

Manifold solid:
>A solid object which obeys Euler's law. Generally lacks dangling edges or faces, or faces which do not bound volumes. A nonmanifold solid model can handle singularities and mix volumetric objects with line and surface objects.

Mechanism:
Framed system of rigid bodies linked in a manner which constrains (but does not prevent) relative motions of those bodies, assembled for the purpose of transmitting an input movement to a controlled output movement.

Modem:
Modulate-demodulate, analog-digital converter used for computer communication over phone lines.

Mosaic:
Browsing software for the Internet. Provides graphical user interface to routine operations such as telnet and gopher. Provides cross-references to other locations.

Motion hierarchy:
Hierarchy of local coordinate systems in which position and degrees of freedom are constrained by higher levels.

Motion path:
Series of changing locations of an object or a camera, relative to coordinate system or to other objects.

Multi-axis milling:
Fabricating by removing specified dimensions of material from a starting volume by means of a cutting head with at least two degrees of freedom.

Multitasking:
The condition of more than one program actively sharing the processor.

Multiuser:
An operating system which accepts simultaneous input from more than one person.

Navigation:
The process of finding one's way through nonhierarchical data.

NTSC:
Video signal standard.

Numerical Control (NC):
Machine control by sequences (programs) of numerical positions and motions descriptions.

Numerical model:
A system of equations which by producing particular outputs as a function of inputs describes or simulates a system or its behavior.

NURBS:
Non-Uniform Rational B-Spline. Spline curve with control points at irregular intervals.

Object snap:
The replacement of pointer input with the position of the nearest existing geometric feature of a designated type, e.g., endpoint or intersection.

Oblique:
Parallel projection, not perpendicular to picture plane, in which one principal plane of the projected geometry remains undistorted.

Operating system:
Software to operate and govern a computer. Performs file management, access control, network operations, and establishes graphical interaction environment.

Paper lamination:
Also called laminated object manufacturing (LOM). An incremental forming process based on bonding cut layers of paper-like material.

Parametric:
Described in terms of a small number of independent (usually dimensional) variables.

Personal system:
Computer and software assembled to support one individual's work.

Perspective:
Non-parallel projection with convergence at viewing point.

Phong shading:
Lambert or cosine shading, plus the smoothing of faceted surfaces by interpolation, plus the representation of specularity.

Picture plane:
Local two-dimensional coordinate system, defined relative to absolute three-dimensional coordinate system, onto which three dimensional objects are projected for viewing.

Pixel:
Picture element. One cell in a discretized image.

Polygon:
A closed two-dimensional path. May be regular or irregular. May include enclosed area.

Polyline:
An entity formed by line segments and curves joined end-to-end.

Postage stamp:
View produced with very small number of pixels for purposes of rapid calculation, used for test images or visual identification of file contents.

Postproduction (video):
Selecting, arranging, and inserting pieces of completed animation or video sequence.

Postscript:
Proprietary name for prevalent page-description language used for laser-printing typography, lines, and tones.

Procedure:
Program module continuing parameterization, internal variable declaration, and an algorithm.

Processor (CPU):
Basic component of a computer. Performs arithmetic and logic operations.

Project database:
Database organized for horizontal integration among several users having different data reporting requirements.

Protocol:
Standard for breakdown and reconstruction of an electronic message.

Quantization:
Rounding of a measurement to the nearest of a finite number of possible values.

Radiosity:
Global illumination model in which the model surfaces are discretized and an energy transfer model is resolved into a solution from which any number of views may be obtained.

RAM:
> Random Access Memory. Semiconductor memory used for temporary storage of active tasks requiring fastest access.

Rapid prototyping:
> Automated production of small-scale physical models as a part of the design process, often by means of incremental forming technologies.

Ray tracing:
> Global illumination model in which for each view the pixel plane is discretized and the effects of lights, surfaces, transparencies, and interreflections are calculated by tracing rays from the viewing point through successive pixels and into and through the model.

Realtime:
> The condition in which results are calculated at least as quickly as they are anticipated, i.e., without perceptible delay.

Relational database:
> Representational structure based on a collection of tables composed of entities sharing particular attributes, each of which is expressed in a single value.

Rendering pipeline:
> Series of two-dimensional representations derived from three-dimensional model and adding successive stages of intelligibility.

Rewriting rule:
> Rule for replacing elements of a composition (not only text) with other, often more differentiated elements.

Ruled surface:
> Object formed by sweeping from one curve to another. Result has no curvature in at least one direction at every point on the surface.

Sampling:
> Digital measurement of analog signal at a regular, discrete interval.

SCSI:
> Serial communication standard, typically used for connecting peripheral devices to a computer.

Sequencer:
Software for arranging events, e.g., sounds or images, in time.

Server:
Central repository of data and administrative information.

Shadow casting:
The calculation and display of shadows cast by a given light or set of lights.

Sharpening:
A filter process which increases the difference between a pixel and its neighbors.

Slow-in/slow-out:
Rate adjustment at the beginning or the end of an animated event for the purpose of eliminating discontinuities.

SMPTE:
Society of Motion Picture and Television Engineers, time code standard, used by sequencing software.

Snap:
The rounding of pointer input to a regular module.

Solid model:
Three-dimensional representation including vertices, edges, faces, and the occupation of enclosed space.

Space curve:
An object having curvature in more than one plane.

Spatial analysis:
In GIS, identification of areas, boundaries, and points (and generation of new maps) implicit in existing data sets.

Spatial resolution:
Number of pixels in a bitmap (measured in two dimensions, e.g., 1024 x 768).

Spatial set operations:
Union, intersection, and subtraction applied to volumetric (solid) objects. Often called boolean operations.

Specularity:
The representation of highlights. The condition in which, for viewing angles approaching equal and opposite the lighting angle, the reflection off a surface is not the color or intensity of the surface but that of the light.

Spline:
    A third- or fourth-order curve defined in terms of
    control points not necessarily coincident on the
    curve.

Spreadsheet:
    A numerical model in which each location in a two-
    dimensional matrix of cells may contain a value, a
    label, or a function, and in which cell locations may
    be given as arguments to functions and in which
    any entry to a cell causes immediate reevaluation of
    any related cells.

SQL:
    Standard query language for filtering data from
    relational databases.

Stereolithography:
    An incremental forming process based on
    solidifying photosensitive liquid.

String:
    Series of characters.

Subshape:
    A subset of all entities stored or displayed.
    Selection set.

Surface model:
    A three-dimensional representation consisting of
    vertices, edges, and faces. Usually represent curved
    surfaces with planar facets.

Surface patch:
    Element within a quadrilateral mesh representing a
    curved surface.

Sweep:
    Projection of a profile along a path, the latter
    usually a line segment or an arc, to form a three-
    dimensional object.

Synchronous:
    Occuring at or sharing one time.

Syntactical:
    Definition of relations by which combinations of
    low-level entities produce well-formed high-level
    entities.

Syntax-directed:
    Constrained to place new entities into particular
    relationships with existing entities.

Task automation:
   The automation of particular activities without any restructuring of the processes they serve.

Task controller:
   Program to execute certain tasks when preconditions are met.

Telnet:
   Client software to support login sessions upon, and remote use of, a remote host computer.

Template:
   In CAD/CAM, a plotted shape or shapes used as a guide for cutting sheet material.

Temporal aliasing:
   The changing stepped appearance of diagonal edges in animation.

Tessellation:
   Cellular mesh which covers an area such that every point is in exactly one polygon.

Text editor:
   Program for creating and revising strings of text characters.

Texture mapping:
   The projection of values from a texture bitmap onto model geometry at time of viewing. Texture map may be sampled (scanned) or synthesized.

Thematic map:
   A selection of features made to map a chosen topic.

Three-dimensional printing:
   An incremental forming process based on bonding inkjet-deposited powder.

TIN:
   Triangulated Irregular Network. Irregular mesh of planar triangular facets usually used to represent terrain surface. Facet density may be varied in correspondence with fineness of detail.

Tone-scale adjustment:
   The remapping of input levels to output levels in order to better match intensity resolution to the dynamic range of an image. Reassigns the value of each pixel based on some function of all values of all pixels in an image.

Tool kit:
   A set of operators which share the same data.

Track:
  Camera motion perpendicular to the viewing direction (usually horizontal).

Transfer (file):
  Moving or copying a file from one computer to another.

Translation (file):
  Moving or copying a file from one data structure to another.

Triangulation:
  The replacement of three-dimensional data, e.g., spot elevations, with a mesh of triangular facets.

Tuple:
  Row of a table in a relational data model. Represents an entity with one or more attribute values.

Turnkey system:
  Uniform, multi-seat system provided along with training and service from a single source.

Turntabling:
  Animation of viewing from regularly changing azimuth.

Variable:
  A name for a designated location in memory into which a value (usually of a declared type) may be assigned.

Virtual camera:
  The condition of manipulating of perspective viewing parameters while viewing the results in real time.

Visible surface calculation:
  The determination, e.g., by depth sorting, of surfaces and portions of a surface model visible from a given point.

Volume:
  Third logical unit of data storage. A collection of files and directories. Normally corresponds to a physical device, e.g., a disk drive.

Voxel:
  Unit of discretized three-dimensional space. Analogous to pixel in two dimensions.

Whiteboard:
Videoconferencing system with capacity to let people in different locations sketch on one shared virtual surface.

Windowing system:
Extension to an operating system to provide a graphical user interface in which windows represent tasks, like papers stacked on a desktop.

Wireframe:
A three-dimensional representation consisting of vertices and edges only.

Word processor:
Program for operating on series of characters recognized as words, lines, and paragraphs.

World Wide Web (WWW):
Hypermedia-based browsing and retrieval software for obtaining files from a web of freely cross-referenced servers on the Internet, without concern for physical location.

INDEX

Investment,
  configuration options,
    408-411
  in a model, 182-183

Irregularity,
  lines, 108
  in plotted output, 129

Jahn, Helmut,
  volumetric design, 250-
    251

Joints,
  descriptions in simula-
    tion, 286
  in motion hierarchy, 283
  types, 284-285

Keyframing,
  between design alterna-
    tives, 299-301
  system, 273-278

Kinematics, 284-286

Knowbot, 457

Knowledge-based systems,
  405-407

Laban, Rudolf,
  notation, 283

Labor,
  allocation, 350
  division of, 5, 381
  replacement of, 2

Lambert, Johann,
  shading, 204-208

LAN (Local area network),
  330-334

Landscape,
  mapping, 94
  modeling, 197-198
  rendering, 225-227

Languages,
  natural, 50

Laser sintering, 429-430

Layer,
  as aid to management,
    353-354
  motion hierarchy instead

of, 281
  sounds, 63-64
  for structuring drawings,
    123-124
  topologies in maps,
    145,147

Le Corbusier,
  see Corbusier

Levels,
  of backup, 379-380
  degrees of freedom, 286
  of errors, 394
  of integration, 328-329
  of numerical abstraction,
    43-44
  of surface detail, 222
  of text entities, 56-57

Lexicon, 49, 394

Library,
  databases, 366-370, 377
  in hypercard, 324
  shape, 116-117
  texture, 223-225

Light,
  ambient, 206
  basic, 205
  diffuse effects, 220
  emitters, 219
  forms in, 185-187
  highlights, 210-213
  in montage, 229
  shadows, 213-218

Limitation,
  of bitmapped images, 96
  of drafting systems, 131-
    133
  of file translation, 336-
    337
  of Lambert shading, 208
  of layer metaphor, 124-
    125
  of project database
    management, 365-366
  of shape selection, 114
  of solid models, 268-269
  of traditional drafting,
    405
  of vertical integration,
    376

Link,
  graphics to relational
    database, 361-364

in hypercard, 324
  physical, 330
  record-to-record, 339
  types, 314-317

Locking, 340-341

Mach, Ernst, 209

Macro programming, 346-
  348

Management,
  access, 378-379
  acquiring a system, 408-
    411
  costs, 412-415
  database, 354-355
  file hierarchy, 353
  productivity, 384-386
  project databases, 364-
    366
  task sequence, 348-350
  turnaround, 386
  uncertainty, 396-399
  version control, 370-371

Map,
  indexing from, 320-32
  generation, 94, 197-198
  GIS, 142-143, 152
  movie, 320-321
  tiled polygons, 143

Mappings,
  color space, 89
  texture, 223-225

Masks, 85

Material properties, 237,
  259

Mathematics, symbolic, 38

Mattes, 83-84

Mechanisms,
  in built environment, 285
  described in kinematic
    chains, 284
  drawing as, 123

Memory,
  hardware types,10
  see also Storage

Milling, multi-axis, 422-425